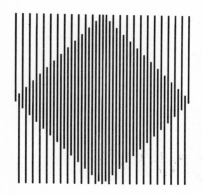

Readings In Personnel Management

Third Edition

HERBERT J. CHRUDEN

Professor of Business Administration
Sacramento State College

ARTHUR W. SHERMAN, Jr.

Professor of Psychology
Sacramento State College

EXAMINATION COPY

Published by

P27 **SOUTH-WESTERN PUBLISHING CO.**

Cincinnati   West Chicago, Ill.   Dallas   New Rochelle, N.Y.
Burlingame, Calif.   Brighton, England

ISBN: 0-538-16270-8

Library of Congress Catalog Card Number: 73-171357

1 2 3 4 5 **H** 6 5 4 3 2

Printed in the United States of America

CHAPTER 4

Organizational Behavior

CHAPTER 5

Union Relations

CHAPTER 6

Remuneration and Security

CHAPTER 1

Personnel Management in Perspective

Personnel management in some form has existed since man first discovered the advantage of group endeavor in working with and through others to accomplish civil or military objectives. As a specialized body of knowledge, however, personnel management has been the subject of study since the turn of the century. The personnel department, furthermore, has come into being only during the past fifty years. In spite of its rapid growth, personnel management is still in a state of development and much more knowledge remains to be acquired about the subject. Further research, for example, is needed in the areas of organizational theory and human behavior. The exact role of the personnel department and the nature of its relationship to the other departments and their personnel, moreover, is currently the subject of considerable study and debate. Many of the tools and processes of personnel management, as will be revealed in this and the chapters that follow, need to be refined still further.

The main purpose of this chapter is to provide the reader with a selected number of articles that provide him with some perspective of the field and with the thinking of current authors concerning it. It is hoped that by reading these articles he will gain a greater appreciation of the progress that has occurred in the field and of some of the issues that are the subject of current debate.

The first article by Eitington discusses a few of the pioneers in personnel management and the contributions that each has made to it. In addition to these pioneers, another well-known leader, who has become known as the "father of scientific management," was Frederick W. Taylor. His work, his views, and his philosophy have been the subject of interpretation as well as misinterpretation and debate by scores of writers for the past fifty years. By now, probably as much has been written about him as was written by him. In order that the reader may analyze for himself Taylor's views relating to the management of people, one of the last articles ever written by him has been included in this chapter.

In the next article Whiting Williams, an early leader in the personnel field, describes his experiences living and working in disguise as a laboring man. These experiences were significant because they represented a pioneer effort to gain insight into worker attitudes and behavior. Williams' research efforts more than a half century ago were quite similar to those that might be used, for example, by a contemporary anthropologist seeking to study the culture of a primitive tribe in the Amazon Basin. It is interesting to note how certain attitudes and values of people today have changed very slightly from those of people in Williams' day.

The rather brief article by Kimmerly indicates how diverse the activities and problems of contemporary personnel management tend to be. Elmer B. Staats, in his analysis of the *Manager of Tomorrow,* discusses some of the major changes that are occurring within our society with particular reference to their implications for managers in government who constitute a significant proportion of the management profession membership. In describing what the personnel functions will be like in tomorrow's company, Frank E. Fischer offers some interesting predictions for the future of personnel management and for the increased skill and responsibility it may demand of its practitioners.

In his article *A New Era in Personnel Relations,* Chris Argyris, a behavioral scientist, challenges certain contemporary personnel practices. Based upon his research, he points out what he considers to be some of the weaknesses of current personnel management and the corrective action required to overcome them.

The Fraying White Collar by Judson Gooding describes one of the most significant changes that is occurring within the nation's work force and its impact on our society and on personnel management. The reader can conclude from this article how important it is for employers to understand and to meet more effectively the needs of the expanding work force of white-collar personnel in order to reduce the mounting frustration of its members.

The final article in this chapter titled *Accounting for Human Resources* by Brummet, Pyle, and Flamholtz represents a new concept in management. While certain welfare economists have long advocated establishing accounting reserves for the depreciation of human assets similar to those for the depreciation of capital equipment, it has been only recently that serious efforts have been made to translate this concept into practice. The use of an accounting system in which human assets are assigned monetary value has been pioneered at the University of Michigan by Rensis Likert and his associates who include the authors of this article. The accounting concepts described in this article very likely will receive more attention in the future.

1—PIONEERS OF MANAGEMENT*

Julius E. Eitington

Personnel management is a multi-faceted discipline to which distinguished individuals from a number of disciplines have made contributions. Therefore, no two observers of the personnel management scene would agree on one or even on several contributors who meet the criterion of "outstanding." This lack of agreement is understandable when one considers that the past fifty years have been a period marked by movements and counter-movements, by diverse philosophies and great innovations.

To a large extent, the problem is complicated further by the definition of personnel management. Does the term involve, for example, solely the traditional functions of a personnel office, such as job evaluation, recruitment, training, employee and union relations, employee services, etc.? Or might it include, too, the advancing concepts contained in terms such as human relations and organizational behavior?

The category of personnel management is also used broadly. Thus in a discussion of the pioneers of or outstanding contributors to personnel management it is just as significant to include the pioneer of the group dynamics movement as it is to identify the most influential authority in the personnel testing field. Further, although personnel management is ordinarily conceived of as a staff function, two line managers whose work and thought have greatly influenced the personnel function seem also worthy of mention.

When assessing "contribution," it is not always easy to assert categorically that an individual was the creator of an idea, the innovator of a technique, or the founder of a movement. Obviously ideas and techniques come from several sources. For example, Dr. Carl Rogers is considered to be the prime developer of the technique of nondirective counseling, but Freud's work in psychoanalysis is certainly basic to that technique. Also, authorities differ as to who was the father of a particular movement. An example is Kurt Lewin versus J. L. Moreno in group dynamics.

---

* From *Advanced Management—Office Executive*, Vol. 2, No. 1 (January, 1963), pp. 16-19. Reprinted with permission.

Be that as it may, here are 12 individuals who, many persons believe, have greatly influenced personnel management during the past 50 years.

In the early part of this period, Dr. Walter Dill Scott (1869-1955), educator and psychologist, was a long-time key figure in personnel management. He is noted for having set up the World War I Army testing program. He was awarded the Distinguished Service Medal for "devising, installing, and supervising the personnel system in the U. S. Army." His work in testing influenced personnel management significantly in industry and government. He was also the joint author of an early textbook, *Personnel Management* (1923).

Dr. Walter Van Dyke Bingham (1880-1952) is considered by many to have been the dean of American personnel psychologists. He worked with Walter Dill Scott and other pioneers in the testing field on the Army testing program in World War I.

In that period Dr. Bingham was Executive Secretary, Committee on Classification of Personnel in the Army (1917-18), and then a Lieutenant Colonel, Personnel Branch, Army General Staff (1918-19). His text, *Aptitudes and Aptitude Testing* (1937), is still a classic in the field. His *How to Interview* (1931), written with B. V. Moore, is a standard text too. He was also joint author of the widely used text, *Procedures in Employment Psychology* (1937). Toward the latter part of his long career, he was Chief Psychologist, Adjutant General's Office, U. S. War Department (1940-47).

Dr. Warner W. Stockberger (1872-1944), a scientist by profession, was the first Personnel Director (1925-38) of the U. S. Department of Agriculture and of the Federal Government. He was also the first President of the Society for Personnel Administration, Washington, D. C. (1937). He was an early pioneer in Federal personnel management, and he had a keen appreciation of the human factor in management.

Dr. Stockberger's work, which included training of many personnel workers who ultimately moved on to other Federal agencies, helped to influence the character of Federal personnel management generally. His efforts were instrumental in changing Federal personnel work from a clerical to a substantive function.

Internationally recognized

Dr. Leonard D. White (1891-1958) was an internationally recognized figure in public personnel administration. He was a teacher at the University of Chicago, a scholar, writer, thinker, idealist, and practitioner. He is credited with many "firsts": he was the author of the first text on public administration (a text which also contained considerable information on personnel management); he was the first to teach public administration in a university classroom; he pioneered in starting the Junior Civil Service Examiner Examination, which attracted liberal arts and social science majors to careers in the Federal Government.

While in Washington with the Civil Service Commission in the 1930's, Dr. White taught a course in Public Personnel Administration at American University. In his class was born an idea which led to the establishment of the Society for Personnel Administration.

More recently, Dr. White served with distinction on the two Hoover Commissions which recommended improvements in Federal personnel management (1948-49, 1953-55). Some of his widely known works include *Introduction to Public Administration* (1926), *The City Manager* (1927), and *Prestige Value of Public Employment* (1929).

Dr. White's work on organization and personnel management was influenced by the scientific management movement. Some of his students, principally Herbert Simon, later challenged Dr. White's adherence to "principles" of organization. The work of the "behavioral scientists" presented many insights about management and organizational behavior, ones which Dr. White and others in his era had not explored.

In retrospect, then, Dr. White's major contributions to personnel management lay in his support to the merit system; his having facilitated the entry of college graduates from *all* disciplines into the Federal service, rather than from the recognized professions only; his having encouraged the building of a personnel "profession"; and his concern with augmenting the prestige of the public service.

The Hawthorne experiments

During the middle period of the past 50 years, the first intensive human relations research study was the Hawthorne experiments. These experiments were conducted at the Hawthorne plant of the Western Electric Co. for twelve years, starting November 1924, by the research staff of Harvard University's Graduate School of Business.

Leader of the world-famous Hawthorne Experiments was Dr. Elton Mayo (1880-1949). Whereas Taylor and his contemporaries viewed management and organization primarily from the standpoint of engineering, Dr. Mayo and his staff applied socio-psychological techniques to managerial problems. From this research, a new theory of human behavior in organizations was created. The research also sparked what has become known as the "human relations" school.

The Hawthorne Experiments led to, among other things, the creation of employee counseling programs in the 1930's, a phase of personnel management which is operative in most organizations today.

The basic account of Dr. Mayo's experiments at the Hawthorne Plant is in *Management and the Worker* (1939) by Fritz J. Roethlisberger and W. J. Dickson. This publication is regarded as a classic, combining research and outstanding social theory and philosophy. As these researchers found it, there is a world of logic of cost and efficiency and a world of logic of sentiment and emotion.

In his *The Human Problem of an Industrial Civilization* (1933) and his *Social Problems of an Industrial Civilization* (1954), Dr. Mayo gave us his scholarly interpretation of the significance of human factors in our industrial culture. His thesis related to the advantages to be derived from involving the worker in the decision-making process. He questioned strongly the "rabble hypothesis"— that materialistic goals are the only motivating force and that authoritarian leadership is essential to get the lazy to work and to keep the grasping in line.

Dr. Mayo, in his *Social Problems of an Industrial Civilization*, said: "For all of us the feeling of security and certainty derives always from assured membership of a group. If this is lost, no monetary gain, no job guarantee can be sufficient compensation."

Another solid contributor to the personnel field is Dr. Ordway Tead (1891-   ). Dr. Tead taught personnel administration, and at Columbia, 1917-18, he was in charge of war emergency employment management courses of the War Department. He continued at Columbia as a lecturer in personnel administration during 1920-50, and from 1951-56 he was Adjunct Professor of Industrial Relations. He was also a faculty member of the Department of Industry at the New York School of Social Work, 1920-29.

Stressed democratic principles

Dr. Tead is widely known as an educator, an editor, a publisher (McGraw Hill Book Co.), an author. His writings, which stressed democratic principles of management, have not been dimmed by more recent research. His better known works are *The Art of Leadership* (1935) and *The Art of Administration* (1951). He also co-authored with Henry C. Metcalf a pioneer personnel textbook, called *Personnel Administration: Its Principles and Practices* (1920).

Dr. Tead's career is a unified one in the sense that in the fields of administrating, editing, and writing, and in teaching of social science and in educational themes he has shown the interrelation of theory and practice in management, higher education, and publishing.

Dr. Chester I. Barnard (1886-1961), an eminent industrialist, is a former president of the New Jersey Bell Telephone Co. and later of the Rockefeller Foundation. In his much-quoted classic, *The Functions of the Executive* (1938), Dr. Barnard analyzed and stressed the sociopsychological and ethical aspects of managerial organization and functions. His book is an early, if not the first, recognition of the import of the informal as well as the formal organizational structure. He viewed organization as a social system.

This view necessitates a high degree of cooperation as opposed to emphasis upon authority and order-giving; the relegation of economic factors as motivators to a secondary role; the individual's identification with the organization based on a strong belief in its codes, as opposed to compliance imposed from without.

Communication responsibilities

Dr. Barnard was also one of the first management authorities to stress the communication responsibilities of executives, to analyze the role of status in organizational endeavor, and to develop systematically an analysis of incentive systems in organizations.

Charles P. McCormick (1896-   ), Chairman of the Board at McCormick and Co.—a Baltimore concern which sells tea, spices, and extracts—is the founder of "Multiple Management" (1932). He conceived the idea of establishing several boards—senior, junior, factory, and sales—as a means of securing participation, and thus ideas, to save the firm from the adverse effects of the Big Depression. Some 500 U. S. organizations now use this means of securing participation, manager development, problem-solving, morale building.

His plan and philosophy are described in *Multiple Management* (1938) and *Power of People* (1949).

To tie together the work and thinking of the early and middle periods, a quotation from John M. Pfiffner and Frank P. Sherwood is appropriate. In their *Administrative Organization* (1960), these men said:

> It seems ironic that during the period when the credos of formal organization were receiving their most literate conceptualization (by Mooney, Urwick, White, Willoughby, and Gulick), the seeds for its decline were being laid by Mayo, Roethlisberger, and Barnard. It was as though a patriarch was being prepared for burial at the time of his birth. However, the point should be made here that the patriarch did not die; he merely metamorphosed (footnote, p. 63).

Tested his ideas about groups

Among the leaders of the more current period, Dr. Kurt Lewin (1890-47) is regarded by many social psychologists as the founder of contemporary group dynamics. Dr. Lewin tested his ideas about groups after he left Germany in 1932 and settled in the United States. His pioneer study on group leadership was carried out at the University of Iowa.

Dr. Lewin found in a classic experiment on 10-year-old boys that democratic leadership was superior to either authoritarian or laissez-faire styles (reported in *Journal of Social Psychology*, 1939). When he moved to the Massachusetts Institute of Technology he conducted research in industry, results of which pointed up the direct relationship between production and participation in the decision-making process.

Also, Dr. Lewin showed during World War II the superiority of group discussion and group decision over lectures in getting Iowa housewives to try less desirable cuts of meat.

Dr. Lewin should be credited, too, with being the father of "sensitivity training." He was probably the first to experiment with discussion groups which were unstructured—that is, they functioned without a leader and without procedures or agenda, all elements of a sensitivity training situation.

In general, Dr. Lewin's ideas and studies on group behavior and social climate have provided industry, education, and government with tremendous insights about groups at work, particularly with reference to authority, decision-making, motivation, and introduction of change.

A disciple of Dr. Lewin, Dr. Leland P. Bradford (1905-), established in 1947 at Bethel, Maine, the first "sensitivity" or human relations laboratory. Since that time his efforts have spawned such training at some thirty-four universities and in a number of regular organizations as well. This has been a uniquely significant contribution to group leadership, and it has a tremendous potential for organizational health. Dr. Bradford is Director, National Training Laboratories, National Education Assn., Washington, D. C. He has served in this post since 1947.

Sensitivity training is a "gut" level experience. It provides the participants with insight into their own behavior. This insight is gained by receiving candid "feedback" from group members as they perceive one's behavior. The method holds great promise for improving interpersonal relations—if conducted on a vertical basis within organizations—for in the leveling process, helpful data are generated on communication difficulties, authority problems, and similar problems. An early summation of the work at Bethel is contained in Bradford's *Explanations in Human Relations Training: An Assessment of Experience*, 1947-53.

Researcher, teacher, consultant

Industrial Psychologist Norman R. F. Maier (1900-), University of Michigan, is a unique and prolific writer, a researcher, teacher, trainer, lecturer, and consultant. His unusually creative work emphasizes the importance of group decisions, employee participation, causation, motivation, and frustration.

As a practical trainer of supervisors, Dr. Maier has stimulated the wide use of "group-in-action" training methods by training specialists. His *Principles of Human Relations* (1952), *Psychology of Industry* (1946), and *Supervisory and Executive Development: A Manual for Role Playing* (1957) have enriched the personnel field immensely.

Dr. Rensis Likert (1903-), who is Director (since 1948) of the Institute of Social Research, University of Michigan, has conducted highly significant human relations research since the 40's. He has pointed up that the old concept of high morale meaning high productivity is much too simple, for, in fact, all kinds of combinations are possible. Dr. Likert's research demonstrates the value to productivity of (1) "supportive" as opposed to threatening supervision and (2) "participative" as opposed to hierarchically-controlled management.

Reports his basic conclusions

In general, supervisory attitudes—that is, those which are "employee centered" as opposed to "production centered"—are basic to productivity. Dr. Likert's findings cast doubt on the long-range success of organizations which use people for short-range goals. His book, *New Patterns of Management* (1961), reports his basic findings and conclusions.

We must also recognize that the contemporary scene can boast a good number of other top-flight thinkers, writers, and researchers. Examples are Carroll Shartle (from Ohio State) who has conducted highly significant studies in leadership; Charles R. Walker and Robert H. Guest (from Yale University) and their work on the human aspects of technology; E. Wight Bakke and Chris Argyris (Yale) and their analysis of the processes by which the individual and the organization adapt to one another's needs.

Still other examples include William Foote Whyte (Cornell) who has analyzed the psychology of groups; Douglas McGregor (M.I.T.) and his ideas on leadership theory, motivation, and goal setting; Melville Dalton (U.C.L.A.) and his sociological analysis of organizations and the men who manage them, including concern with line and staff conflict, power, status, influence maneuvering, and the "implicit and the explicit" organization; Herbert A. Simon (Carnegie) and his analysis of organizational behavior from the standpoint of decision-making, particularly its nonrational character.

All these men are representative of the rapidly expanding field of today's personnel administration.

Questions

1. Why is it difficult to single out a particular group of individuals as having made the most significant contributions to the development of the field of personnel management?
2. What other individuals would you include in your list of contributors who were not mentioned in this article?
3. Who is considered to be the founder of the field of group dynamics? What type of training is an outgrowth of this field?
4. What major contributions did Elton Mayo render to the field of personnel management?

2—THE PRINCIPLES OF SCIENTIFIC MANAGEMENT *

Frederick Winslow Taylor [1]

By far the most important fact which faces the industries of our country, the industries, in fact, of the civilized world, is that not only the average worker, but nineteen out of twenty workmen throughout the civilized world firmly believe that it is for their best interests to go slow instead of to go fast. They firmly believe that it is for their interest to give as little work in return for the money that they get as is practical. The reasons for this belief are two-fold, and I do not believe that the workingmen are to blame for holding these fallacious views.

If you will take any set of workmen in your own town and suggest to those men that it would be a good thing for them in their trade if they were to double their output in the coming year, each man turn out twice as much work and become twice as efficient, they would say, "I do not know anything about other people's trades; what you are saying about increasing efficiency being a good thing may be good for other trades, but I know that the only result if you come to our trade would be that half of us would be out of a job before the year was out." That to the average workingman is an axiom; it is not a matter subject to debate at all. And even among the average business men of this country that opinion is almost universal. They firmly believe that that would be the result of a great increase in efficiency, and yet directly the opposite is true.

The effect of labor-saving devices

Whenever any labor-saving device of any kind has been introduced into any trade—go back into the history of any trade and see it—

* From the *Bulletin of the Taylor Society*, December, 1916, as reproduced in *Advanced Management Journal* (September, 1963), pp. 30-39. Reprinted with permission.
[1] An abstract of an address given by the late Dr. Taylor before the Cleveland Advertising Club, March 3, 1915, two weeks prior to his death. It was repeated the following day at Youngstown, Ohio, and this presentation was Dr. Taylor's last public appearance.

even though that labor-saving device may turn out ten, twenty, thirty times that output that was originally turned out by men in that trade, the result has universally been to make work for more men in that trade, not work for less men.

Let me give you one illustration. Let us take one of the staple businesses, the cotton industry. About 1840 the power loom succeeded the old hand loom in the cotton industry. It was invented many years before, somewhere about 1780 or 1790, but it came in very slowly. About 1840 the weavers of Manchester, England, saw that the power loom was coming, and they knew it would turn out three times the yardage of cloth in a day that the hand loom turned out. And what did they do, these five thousand weavers of Manchester, England, who saw starvation staring them in the face? They broke into the establishments into which those machines were being introduced, they smashed them, they did everything possible to stop the introduction of the power loom. And the same result followed that follows every attempt to interfere with the introduction of any labor-saving device, if it is really a labor-saving device. Instead of stopping the introduction of the power loom, their opposition apparently accelerated it, just as opposition to scientific management all over the country, bitter labor opposition today, is accelerating the introduction of it instead of retarding it. History repeats itself in that respect. The power loom came right straight along.

And let us see the result in Manchester. Just what follows in every industry when any labor-saving device is introduced? Less than a century has gone by since 1840. The population of England in that time has not more than doubled. Each man in the cotton industry in Manchester, England, now turns out, at a restricted estimate ten yards of cloth for every yard of cloth that was turned out in 1840. In 1840 there were 5,000 weavers in Manchester. Now there are 265,000. Has that thrown men out of work? Has the introduction of labor-saving machinery, which has multiplied the output per man by tenfold, thrown men out of work?

What is the real meaning of this? All that you have to do is to bring wealth into this world and the world uses it. That is the real meaning. The meaning is that wherein 1840 cotton goods were a luxury to be worn only by rich people when they were hardly ever seen on the street, now every man, woman and child all over the world wears cotton goods as a daily necessity.

Nineteen-twentieths of the real wealth of this world is used by the poor people, and not the rich, so that the workingman who sets out as a steady principle to restrict output is merely robbing his own kind. That group of manufacturers which adopts as a permanent principle restriction of output, in order to hold up prices, is robbing the world. The one great thing that marks the improvement of this world is measured by the enormous increase in output of the individuals in this world. There is fully twenty times the output per man now that there was three hundred years ago. That marks the increase in the real wealth of the world; that marks the increase of the happiness of the world, that gives us the opportunity for shorter hours, for better education, for amusement, for art, for music, for everything that is worthwhile in this world—goes right straight back to this increase in the output of the individual. The workingmen of today live better than the king did three hundred years ago. From what does the progress the world has made come? Simply from the increase in the output of the individual all over the world.

The development of soldiering

The second reason why the workmen of this country and of Europe deliberately restrict output is a very simple one. They, for this reason, are even less to blame than they are for the other. If, for example, you are manufacturing a pen, let us assume for simplicity that a pen can be made by a single man. Let us say that the workman is turning out ten pens per day, and that he is receiving $2.50 a day for his wages. He has a progressive foreman who is up to date, and that foreman goes to the workman and suggests, "Here, John, you are getting $2.50 a day, and you are turning out ten pens. I would suggest that I pay you 25 cents for making that pen." The man takes the job, and through the help of his foreman, through his own ingenuity, through his increased work, through his interest in his business, through the help of his friends, at the end of the year he finds himself turning out twenty pens instead of ten. He is happy, he is making $5, instead of $2.50 a day. His foreman is happy because, with the same room, with the same men he had before, he has doubled the output of his department, and the manufacturer himself is sometimes happy, but not often. Then someone on the board of directors asks to see the payroll, and he finds that we are paying $5 a day where other similar mechanics are only getting $2.50, and in no uncertain terms he announces that we must stop ruining the labor market. We cannot pay $5 a day when the standard rate of wages is $2.50; how can we hope to compete with surrounding towns? What is the result? Mr. Foreman is sent for, and he is told that he has got to stop ruining the labor market of Cleveland. And the foreman goes back to his workman in sadness, in depression, and tells his workman, "I am sorry, John, but I have got to cut the price down for that pen; I cannot let you earn $5 a day; the board of directors has got on to it, and it is ruining the labor market; you ought to be willing to have the price reduced. You cannot earn more than $3 or $2.75 a day, and I will have to cut your wages so that you will only get $3 a day." John, of necessity accepts the cut, but he sees to it that he never makes enough pens to get another cut.

Characteristics of the union workman

There seem to be two divergent opinions about the workmen of this country. One is that a lot of the trade unions' workmen, particularly in this country, have become brutal, have become dominating, careless of any interests but their own, and are a pretty poor lot. And the other opinion which those same trade unionists hold of themselves is that they are pretty close to little gods. Whichever view you may hold of the workingmen of this country, and my personal view of them is that they are a pretty fine lot of fellows, they are just about the same as you and I. But whether you hold the bad opinion or the good opinion, it makes no difference. Whatever the workingmen of this country are or whatever they are not, they are not fools. And all that is necessary is for a workingman to have but one object lesson, like that I have told you, and he soldiers for the rest of his life.

There are a few exceptional employers who treat their workmen differently, but I am talking about the rule of the country. Soldiering is the absolute rule with all workmen who know their business. I am not saying it is for their interest to soldier. You cannot blame them for it. You cannot expect them to be large enough minded men to look at the proper view of the matter. Nor is the man who cuts the wages necessarily to blame. It is simply a misfortune in industry.

The development of scientific management

There has been, until comparatively recently, no scheme promulgated by which the evils of rate cutting could be properly avoided, so soldiering has been the rule.

Now the first step that was taken toward the development of those methods, of those principles, which rightly or wrongly have come to be known under the name of scientific management—the first step that was taken in an earnest endeavor to remedy the evils of soldiering; an earnest endeavor to make it unnecessary for workmen to be hypocritical in this way, to deceive themselves, to deceive their employers, to live day in and day out a life of deceit, forced upon them by conditions—the very first step that was taken toward the development was to overcome that evil. I want to emphasize that, because I wish to emphasize the one great fact relating to scientific management, the greatest factor: namely, that scientific management is no new set of theories that has been tried on by any one at every step. Scientific management at every step has been an evolution, not a theory. In all cases the practice has preceded the theory, not succeeded it. In every case one measure after another has been tried out, until the proper remedy has been found. That series of proper eliminations, that evolution, is what is called scientific management. Every element of it has had to fight its way against the elements that preceded it, and prove itself better or it would not be there tomorrow.

All the men that I know of who are in any way connected with scientific management are ready to abandon any scheme, any theory in favor of anything else that could be found that is better. There is nothing in scientific management that is fixed. There is no one man, or group of men, who have invented scientific management.

What I want to emphasize is that all of the elements of scientific management are an evolution, not an invention. Scientific management is in use in an immense range and variety of industries. Almost every type of industry in this country has scientific management working successfully. I think I can safely say that on the average in those establishments in which scientific management has been introduced, the average workman is turning out double the output he was before. I think that is a conservative statement.

What scientific management is

What is scientific management? It is no efficiency device, nor is it any group or collection of efficiency devices. Scientific management is no new scheme for paying men, it is no bonus system, no piece-work system, no premium system of payment; it is no new method of figuring costs. It is no one of the various elements by which it is commonly known, by which people refer to it. It is not time study nor man study. It is not the printing of a ton or two of blanks and unloading them on a company and saying, "There is your system, go ahead and use it." Scientific management does not exist and cannot exist until there has been a complete mental revolution on the part of the workmen working under it, as to their duties toward themselves and toward their employers, and a complete mental revolution in the outlook of the employers, toward their duties, toward themselves, and toward their workmen. And until this great mental change takes place, scientific management does not exist. Do you think you can make a great mental revolution in a large group of workmen in a year, or do you think you can make it in a large group of foremen and superintendents in a year? If you do, you are very much mistaken. All of us hold mighty close to our ideas and prin-ciples in life, and we change very slowly toward the new, and very properly too.

Let me give you an idea of what I mean by this change in mental outlook. If you are manufacturing a hammer or a mallet, into the cost of that mallet goes a certain amount of raw materials, a certain amount of wood and metal. If you will take the cost of the raw materials and then add to it that cost which is frequently called by various names—overhead expenses, general expense, indirect expense; that is, the proper share of taxes, insurance, light, heat, salaries of officers and advertising—and you have a sum of money. Subtract that sum from the selling price, and what is left over is called the surplus. It is over this surplus that all of the labor disputes in the past have occurred. The workman naturally wants all he can get. His wages come out of that surplus. The manufacturer wants all he can get in the shape of profits, and it is from the division of this surplus that all the labor disputes have come in the past—the equitable division.

The new outlook that comes under scientific management is this: The workmen, after many object lessons, come to see and the manage-ment come to see that this surplus can be made so great, providing both sides will stop their pulling apart, will stop their fighting and will push as hard as they can to get as cheap an output as possible, that there is no occasion to quarrel. Each side can get more than ever before. The acknowledgment of this fact represents a complete mental revolution.

What scientific management will do

I am going to try to prove to you that the old style of management has not a ghost of a chance in competition with the principles of scientific management. Why? In the first place, under scientific management, the initiative of the workmen, their hard work, their good-will, their best endeavors are obtained with absolute regularity. There are cases all the time where men will soldier, but they become the exception, as a rule, and they give their true initiative under scientific management. That is the least of the two sources of gain. The greatest source of gain under scientific management comes from the new and almost unheard-of duties and burdens which are voluntarily assumed, not by the workmen, but by the men on the management side. These are the things which make scientific management a success. These new duties, these new burdens undertaken by the management have rightly or wrongly been divided into four groups, and have been called the principles of scientific management.

The first of the great principles of scientific management, the first of the new burdens which are voluntarily undertaken by those on the management side is the deliberate gathering together of the great mass of traditional knowledge which, in the past, has been in the heads of the workmen, recording it, tabulating it, reducing it in most cases to rules, laws, and in many cases to mathematical formulae, which, with these new laws, are applied to the co-operation of the management to the work of the workmen. This results in an immense increase in the output, we may say, of the two. The gathering in of this great mass of traditional knowledge, which is done by the means of motion study, time study, can be truly called the science.

Let me make a prediction. I have before me the first book, so far as I know, that has been published on motion study and on time study. That is, the motion study and time study of the cement and concrete trades. It contains everything relating to concrete work. It is of about seven hundred pages and embodies the motions of men, the time and the best way of doing that sort of work. It is the first case in which a trade has been reduced to the same condition that engineering data of all kinds have been reduced, and it is this sort of data that is bound to sweep the world.

I have before me something which has been gathering for about fourteen years, the time or motion study of the machine shop. It will take probably four or five years more before the first book will be ready to publish on that subject. There is a collection of sixty or

seventy thousand elements affecting machine-shop work. After a few
years, say three, four or five years more, some one will be ready to
publish the first book giving the laws of the movements of men in
the machine shop—all the laws, not only a few of them. Let me predict, just as sure as the sun shines, that is going to come in every
trade. Why? Because it pays, for no other reason. That results in
doubling the output in any shop. Any device which results in an
increased output is bound to come in spite of all opposition, whether
we want it or not. It comes automatically.

The selection of the workman

The next of the four principles of scientific management is the
scientific selection of the workman, and then his progressive development. It becomes the duty under scientific management of not one,
but of a group of men on the management side, to deliberately study
the workmen who are under them; study them in the most careful,
thorough and painstaking way; and not just leave it to the poor,
overworked foreman to go out and say, "Come on, what do you want?
If you are cheap enough I will give you a trial."

That is the old way. The new way is to take a great deal of
trouble in selecting the workmen. The selection proceeds year after
year. And it becomes the duty of those engaged in scientific management to know something about the workmen under them. It becomes
their duty to set out deliberately to train the workmen in their
employ to be able to do a better and still better class of work than
ever before, and to then pay them higher wages than ever before.
This deliberate selection of the workmen is the second of the great
duties that devolve on the management under scientific management.

Bringing together the science and the man

The third principle is the bringing together of this science of
which I have spoken and the trained workmen. I say bringing
because they don't come together unless some one brings them.
Select and train your workmen all you may, but unless there is some
one who will make the men and the science come together, they will
stay apart. The "make" involves a great many elements. They are
not all disagreeable elements. The most important and largest way
of "making" is to do something nice for the man whom you wish to

make come together with the science. Offer him a plum, something that is worthwhile. There are many plums offered to those who come under scientific management—better treatment, more kindly treatment, more consideration for their wishes, and an opportunity for them to express their wants freely. That is one side of the "make." An equally important side is, whenever a man will not do what he ought, to either make him do it or stop it. If he will not do it, let him get out. I am not talking of any mollycoddle. Let me disabuse your minds of any opinion that scientific management is a mollycoddle scheme.

I have a great many union friends. I find they look with especial bitterness on this word "make." They have been used to doing the "making" in the past. That is the attiude of the trade unions, and it softens matters greatly when you can tell them the facts, namely, that in our making the science and the men come together, nine-tenths of our trouble comes with the men on the management side in making them do their new duties. I am speaking of those who have been trying to change from the old system to the new. Nine-tenths of our troubles come in trying to make the men on the management side do what they ought to do, to make them do the new duties, and take on these new burdens, and give up their old duties. That softens this word "make."

The principle of the division of work

The fourth principle is the plainest of all. It involves a complete re-division of the work of the establishment. Under the old scheme of management, almost all of the work was done by the workmen. Under the new, the work of the establishment is divided into two large parts. All of that work which formerly was done by the workmen alone is divided into two large sections, and one of those sections is handed over to the management. They do a whole division of the work formerly done by the workmen. It is this real cooperation, this genuine division of the work between the two sides, more than any other element which accounts for the fact that there never will be strikes under scientific management. When the workman realizes that there is hardly a thing he does that does not have to be preceded by some act of preparation on the part of management, and when that workman realizes when the management falls down and does not do its part, that he is not only entitled to a kick, but that he can register that kick in the most forcible possible way, he cannot quarrel with the men over him. It is team work. There are more complaints made every day on the part of the workmen that the men on the management side fail to do their duties than are made by the management that the men fail. Every one of the complaints of the men have to be heeded, just as much as the complaints from the management that the workmen do not do their share. That is characteristic of scientific management. It represents a democracy, co-operation, a genuine division of work which never existed before in this world.

The proof of the theory

I am through now with the theory. I will try to convince you of the value of these four principles by giving you some practical illustrations. I hope that you will look for these four elements in the illustrations. I shall begin by trying to show the power of these four elements when applied to the greatest kind of work I know of that is done by man. The reason I have heretofore chosen pig-iron for an illustration is that it is the lowest form of work that is known.

A pig of iron weighs about ninety-two pounds on an average. A man stoops down and, with no other implement than his hands, picks up a pig of iron, walks a few yards with it, and drops it on a pile. A large part of the community has the impression that scientific management is chiefly handling pig-iron. The reason I first chose pig-iron for an illustration is that, if you can prove to any one the strength, the effect, of those four principles when applied to such rudimentary work as handling pig-iron, the presumption is that it can be applied to something better. The only way to prove it is to start at the bottom and show those four principles all along the line. I am sorry I cannot, because of lack of time, give you the illustration of handling pig-iron. Many of you doubt whether there is much of any science in it. I am going to try to prove later with a high class mechanic that the workman who is fit to work at any type of work is almost universally incapable of understanding the principles without the help of some one else. I will use shoveling because it is a shorter illustration, and I will try to show what I mean by the science of shoveling, and the power which comes to the man who knows the science of shoveling. It is a high art compared with pig-iron handling.

The science of shoveling

When I went to the Bethlehem Steel Works, the first thing I saw was a gang of men unloading rice coal. They were a splendid set of fellows, and they shoveled fast. There was no loafing at all. They shoveled as hard as you could ask any man to work. I looked with the greatest of interest for a long time, and finally they moved off rapidly down into the yard to another part of the yard and went right at handling iron ore. One of the main facts connected with that shoveling was that the work those men were doing was that, in handling the rice coal, they had on their shovels a load of $3\frac{3}{4}$ pounds, and when the same men went to handling ore with the same shovel, they had over 38 pounds on their shovels. Is it asking too much of anyone to inquire whether $3\frac{3}{4}$ pounds is the right load for a shovel, or whether 38 pounds is the right load for a shovel? Surely if one is right the other must be wrong. I think that is a self-evident fact, and yet I am willing to bet that that is what workmen are doing right now in Cleveland.

That is the old way. Suppose we notice that fact. Most of us do not notice it because it is left to the foreman. At the Midvale works, we had to find out these facts. What is the old way of finding them out? The old way was to sit down and write one's friends and ask them the question. They got answers from contractors about what they thought it ought to be, and then they averaged them up, or took the most reliable man, and said, "That is all right; now we have a shovel load of so much." The more common way is to say, "I want a good shovel foreman." They will send for the foreman of the shovelers and put the job up to him to find what is the proper load to put on a shovel. He will tell you right off the bat. I want to show you the difference under scientific management.

Under scientific management you ask no one. Every little trifle,— there is nothing too small,—becomes the subject of experiment. The experiments develop into a law; they save money; they increase the output of the individual and make the thing worthwhile. How is this done? What we did in shoveling experiments was to deliberately select two first class shovelers, the best we knew how to get. We brought them into the office and said, "Jim and Mike, you two fellows are both good shovelers. I have a proposition to make to you. I am going to pay you double wages if you fellows will go out and do what I want you to do. There will be a young chap go along with you with a pencil and a piece of paper, and he will tell you to do a lot of fool things, and you will do them, and he will write down a lot of fool things, and you will think it is a joke, but it is nothing of the kind. Let me tell you one thing: if you fellows think that you can fool that chap you are very much mistaken, you cannot fool him at all. Don't get it through your heads you can fool him. If you take this double wages, you will be straight and do what you are told." They both promised and did exactly what they were told. What we told them was this: "We want you to start in and do whatever shoveling you are told to do, and work at just the pace, all day long, that when it comes night you are going to be good and tired, but not tired out. I do not want you exhausted or anything like that, but properly tired. You know what a good day's work is. In other words, I do not want any loafing business or any overwork business. If you find yourself overworked and getting too tired, slow down." Those men did that and did it in the most splendid kind of way day in and day out. We proved their co-operation because they were in different parts of the yard, and they both got near enough the same results. Our results were duplicated.

I have found that there are a lot of schemes among my working friends, but no more among them than among us. They are good, straight fellows if you only treat them right, and put the matter up squarely to them. We started in at a pile of material, with a very large shovel. We kept innumerable accurate records of all kinds, some of them useless. Thirty or forty different items were carefully observed about the work of those two men. We counted the number of shovelfuls thrown in a day. We found with a weight of between thirty-eight and thirty-nine pounds on the shovel, the man made a pile of material of a certain height. We then cut off the shovel, and he shoveled again and with a thirty-four pound load his pile went up and he shoveled more in a day. We again cut off the shovel to thirty pounds, and the pile went up again. With twenty-six pounds on the shovel, the pile again went up, and at twenty-one and one-half pounds the men could do their best. At twenty pounds the pile went down, at eighteen it went down, and at fourteen it went down, so that they were at the peak at twenty-one and one-half pounds. There is a scientific fact. A first class shoveler ought to take twenty-one and one-half pounds on his shovel in order to work to the best possible advantage. You are not giving that man a chance unless you give him a shovel which will hold twenty-one pounds.

The men in the yard were run by the old fashioned foreman. He simply walked about with them. We at once took their shovels away from them. We built a large labor tool room which held ten to fifteen different kinds of shoveling implements so that for each kind of material that was handled in that yard, all the way from rice coal, ashes, coke, all the way up to ore, we would have a shovel that would just hold twenty-one pounds, or average twenty-one. One time it would hold eighteen, the next twenty-four, but it will average twenty-one.

When you have six hundred men laboring in the yard, as we had there, it becomes a matter of quite considerable difficulty to get, each day, for each one of those six hundred men, engaged in a line one and one-half to two miles long and a half mile wide, just the right shovel for shoveling material. That requires organization to lay out and plan for those men in advance. We had to lay out the work each day. We had to have large maps on which the movements of the men were plotted out a day in advance. When each workman came in the morning, he took out two pieces of paper. One of the blanks gave them a statement of the implements which they had to use, and the part of the yard in which they had to work. That required organization planning in advance.

One of the first principles we adopted was that no man in that labor gang could work on the new way unless he earned sixty per cent higher wages than under the old plan. It is only just to the workman that he shall know right off whether he is doing his work right or not. He must not be told a week or month after, that he fell down. He must know it the next morning. So the next slip that came out of the pigeon hole was either a white or yellow slip. We used the two colors because some of the men could not read. The yellow slip meant that he had not earned his sixty per cent higher wages. He knew that he could not stay in that gang and keep on getting yellow slips.

Teaching the men

I want to show you again the totally different outlook there is under scientific management by illustrating what happened when that man got his yellow slips. Under the old scheme, the foreman could say to him, "You are no good, get out of this; no time for you, you cannot earn sixty per cent higher wages; get out of this! Go!" It was not done politely, but the foreman had no time to palaver. Under the new scheme what happened? A teacher of shoveling went down to see that man. A teacher of shoveling is a man who is handy with a shovel, who has made his mark in life with a shovel, and yet who is a kindly fellow and knows how to show the other fellow what he ought to do. When that teacher went there he said, "See here, Jim, you have a lot of those yellow slips, what is the matter with you? What is up? Have you been drunk? Are you tired? Are you sick? Anything wrong with you? Because if you are tired or sick we will give you a show somewhere else." "Well, no, I am all right." "Then if you are not sick, or there is nothing wrong with you, you have forgotten how to shovel. I showed you how to shovel. You have forgotten something, now go ahead and shovel and I will show you what is the matter with you." Shoveling is a pretty big science, it is not a little thing.

If you are going to use the shovel right you should always shovel off an iron bottom; if not an iron bottom, a wooded bottom; and if not a wooden bottom a hard dirt bottom. Time and again the conditions are such that you have to go right into the pile. When that is the case, with nine out of ten materials it takes more trouble and more time and more effort to get the shovel into the pile than to do all the rest of the shoveling. That is where the effort comes. Those of you again who have taught the art of shoveling will have taught your workmen to do this. There is only one way to do it right. Put your forearm down onto the upper part of your leg, and when you push into the pile, throw your weight against it. That relieves your arm of work. You then have an automatic push, we will say, about eighty pounds, the weight of your body thrown on to it. Time and again we would find men whom we had taught to shovel right were going at it in the old way, and of course they could not do a day's work. The teacher would simply stand over that fellow and say, "There is what is the matter with you, Jim, you have forgotten to shovel into the pile."

You are not interested in shoveling, you are not interested in whether one way or the other is right, but I do hope to interest you in the difference of the mental attitude of the men who are teaching under the new system. Under the new system, if a man falls down, the presumption is that it is our fault at first, that we probably have not taught the man right, have not given him a fair show, have not spent time enough in showing him how to do his work.

Let me tell you another thing that is characteristic of scientific management. In my day, we were smart enough to know when the boss was coming, and when he came up we were apparently really working. Under scientific management, there is none of that pretense. I cannot say that in the old days we were delighted to see the boss coming around. We always expected some kind of roast if he came too close. Under the new, the teacher is welcomed; he is not an enemy, but a friend. He comes there to try to help the man get bigger wages, to show him how to do something. It is the great mental change, the change in the outlook that comes, rather than the details of it.

Does scientific management pay?

It took the time of a number of men for about three years to study the art of shoveling in that yard at the Bethlehem Steel Works alone. They were carefully trained college men, and they were busy all the time. That costs money, the tool room costs money, the clerks we had to keep there all night figuring up how much the men did the day before cost money, the office in which the men laid out and planned the work cost money. The very fair and proper question, the only question to ask is "Does it pay?" because if scientific management does not pay, there is nothing in it; if it does not pay in dollars and cents, it is the rankest kind of nonsense. There is nothing philanthropic about it. It has got to pay, because business which cannot be done on a profitable basis ought not to be done on a philanthropic basis, for it will not last. At the end of three and one-half years we had a very good chance to know whether or not it paid.

Fortunately in the Bethlehem Steel Works they had records of how much it cost to handle the materials under the old system, where the single foreman led a group of men around the works. It costs them between seven and eight cents a ton to handle materials, on an average throughout the year. After paying for all this extra work I have told you about, it cost between three and four cents a ton to handle materials, and there was a profit of between seventy-five and eighty thousand dollars a year in that yard by handling those materials in the new way. What the men got out of it was this: Under the old system there were between four and six hundred men handling the material in that yard, and when we got through there were about one hundred and forty. Each one was earning a great deal more money. We made careful investigation and found they were almost all saving money, living better, happier; they are the most contented set of laborers to be seen anywhere. It is only by this kind of justification, justification of a profit for both sides, an advantage to both sides, that scientific management can exist.

I would like to give you one more illustration. I want to try to prove to you that even the highest class mechanic cannot possibly understand the philosophy of his work, cannot possibly understand the laws under which he has to operate. There is a man who has had a high school education, an ingenious fellow who courts variety in life, to whom it is pleasant to change from one kind of work to another. He is not a cheap man, he is rather a high grade man among the machinists of this country. The case of which I am going to tell you is one in which my friend Barth went to introduce scientific management in the works of an owner, who, at between 65 and 70 years of age, had built up his business from nothing to almost five thousand men. They had a squabble, and after they got through, Mr. Barth made the proposition, "I will take any machine that you use in your shop, and I will show you that I can double the output of that machine." A very fair machine was selected. It was a lathe on which the workman had been working about twelve years. The product of that shop is a patented machine with a good many parts, 350 men working making those parts year in and year out. Each man had ten or a dozen parts a year.

The first thing that was done was in the presence of the foreman, the superintendent and the owner of the establishment. Mr. Barth laid down the way in which all of the parts were to be machined on that machine by the workman. Then Mr. Barth, with one of his small slide rules, proceeded to analyze the machine. With the aid of this analysis, which embodies the laws of cutting metals, Mr. Barth was able to take his turn at the machine; his gain was from two and one-half times to three times the amount of work turned out by the other man. This is what can be done by science as against the old rule of thumb knowledge. That is not exaggeration; the gain is as great as that in many cases.

The effect on the workman

Almost every one says, "Why, yes, that may be a good thing for the manufacturer, but how about the workmen? You are taking all the initiative away from that workman, you are making a machine out of him; what are you doing for him? He becomes merely a part of the machine." That is the almost universal impression. Again let me try to sweep aside the fallacy of that view by an illustration. The modern surgeon without a doubt is the finest mechanic in the world. He combines the greatest manual dexterity with the greatest knowledge of implements and the greatest knowledge of the materials on which he is working. He is a true scientist, and he is a very highly skilled mechanic.

How does the surgeon teach his trade to the young men who come to the medical school? Does he say to them, "Now, young men, we belong to an older generation than you do, but the new generation is going to far outstrip anything that has been done in our generation; therefore, what we want of you is your initiative. We must have your brains, your thought, with your initiative. Of course, you know we old fellows have certain prejudices. For example, if we were going to amputate a leg, when we come down to the bone we are accustomed to take a saw, and we use it in that way and saw the bone off. But, gentlemen, do not let that fact one minute interfere with your originality, with your initiative, if you prefer an axe or a hatchet." Does the surgeon say this? He does not. He says, "You young men are going to outstrip us, but we will show you how. You shall not use a single implement in a single way until you know just which one to use, and we will tell you which one to use, and until you know how to use it, we will tell you how to use that implement, and after you have learned to use that implement our way, if you then see any defects in the implements, any defects in the method, then invent; but, invent so that you can invent upwards. Do not go inventing things which we discarded years ago."

That is just what we say to our young men in the shops. Scientific Management makes no pretense that there is any finality in it. We merely say that the collective work of thirty or forty men in this trade through eight or ten years has gathered together a large amount of data. Every man in the establishment must start that way, must start our way, then if he can show us any better way, I do not care what it is, we will make an experiment to see if it is better. It will be named after him, and he will get a prize for having improved on one of our standards. There is the way we make progress under scientific management. There is your justification for all this. It does not dwarf initiative, it makes true initiative. Most of our progress comes through our workmen, but it comes in a legitimate way.

Questions

1. To what extent, if any, is Taylor's article applicable to conditions in industry today?
2. What did Taylor feel were the factors that encouraged workers to restrict their production?
3. What personnel functions did the author feel should receive special attention in the approach to management that he recommended?
4. Taylor, in his scientific approach to management, has been criticized for having not given adequate recognition to the "human factor." What is your reaction to this criticism after having read this article?
5. How did Taylor feel that the initiative of the worker would be affected by scientific management?

3—WHAT EVERY WORKER WANTS *

Whiting Williams

The first of my rather unusual efforts to understand the worker started when the president of the steel company for whom I was working called me in one day and said that he and his associates didn't think I was doing a good job of bridging the gap between the mind of management and the minds of the workers. Like anyone else under similar circumstances, I went home and proceeded to walk the floor for a few nights. As a result, I went in and asked him if he would give me a leave of absence for six months for the purpose of living the life of our workers.| He gave me permission, but asked the same question that has been asked me ever since by people when they hear of my experiences. Said he: "How will you disguise yourself sufficiently to gain the confidence of the workers?"

I have always had to explain that in the rough labor gangs where I proceeded to live the life of my fellow workmen, all of them accepted me so completely as the ordinary laborer I pretended to be, that it actually hurt my feelings! Only one man pierced my disguise—and he was very intoxicated at the time! He said, "There's something wrong with you, stranger. Either you have been convicted of a serious crime, or you are a victim of some secret sin, or you wouldn't come to work in this God-forsaken town!"

I have to report that what really worried me was the danger of getting too close to the whole situation, especially in various countries abroad. In Russia I was really scared when being interviewed by my fellow coal miners and was suddenly arrested by the secret police who gave me a good work-out before they finally released me.

In 1922, Collier's Weekly asked me to find out the causes of the great railway shopman's strike. That meant I had to go through the picket lines. I will never forget my reception there. We were being taken in under protection of a policeman, and one picket

* From *Connecticut Industry* (May, 1951). An edited version of an address given by Mr. Williams in November, 1950, before the annual convention of the NTDMA. Reprinted with permission.

said, "Hey, has anybody told you about the dynamite that goes off in there? We guys on the outside don't know how many of you dirty scabs get knocked off in there, because the company buries them at night, but it sure does make one hell of a noise!"

During the depression I ran again into unexpected danger. I had been accepted as a bum in Chicago until I made the mistake of drinking out of a milk bottle a harmless looking concoction that looked like milk and water. It goes by the name of "smoke," also by the name of "jungle juice." It was a combination of gasoline and denatured alcohol!

What did I learn that helps explain why it is that today our miracle of production here in America means that we are the sole protection of all the other free nations of the world against Russia? How have we gotten this amazing will to work which now stands us in such good stead? What has made us the protector of the free world?

Fear, Hope and Pride—Important Words

I believe it is our particular idea of what makes us humans tick. I can best give you that idea by telling you of my experience. I took a train in January, 1919, to go to Pittsburgh to get a job in the steel works. I changed my name, put on old clothes, and $25 in my pocket, with the expectation that it was up to me to live the life of a jobless man if my $25 gave out. In four hours I ran onto a very important word. That word is "fear," the fear of the loss of the job. As long as I live, I will never get over the impression made on me of the universality of that particular fear.

Shortly afterward I learned the importance of a second word in the workman's mind. That word is "hope," hope for promotion.

I wish I could claim I pondered why that fear was so intense and that hope so unquenchable. But I thought I knew. All the professors and psychologists said they knew all about it. They said the only value in the worker's mind was money, that that fear was only fear for the loss of income, that that hope was only the hope for a larger income.

I had plenty of time to ponder that question, and the longer I pondered the less adequate that explanation appeared to be. To make a long story short, there is a third word that goes with "fear" and "hope" in the workman's mind. That word is "pride." I believe that pride represents the satisfaction of the two deepest, strongest, most useful of hankerings. Hankering Number One is for our own self-respect—the right to believe that we individually represent certain values in the scheme of things—that we are worth while, important, "somebody." If you think that is an easy satisfaction to enjoy, let me say, on the contrary, the enjoyment of that particular satisfaction represents just about the hardest job that you or I or anyone knows about, for the reason that I have yet to see a human being of any sort who is as sure of his or her right to believe in his or her importance as he or she would like to be.

When I say that, I will gamble that half of you will say "You are right" but half of you will say "You are wrong." But *none* of us are all the time as sure of ourselves as we would like to be. Whether we are drunk or sober, young or old, male or female, sane or insane, all of us are everlastingly trying to fight off the feeling of having to think of ourselves as a human zero of insignificance and unimportance.

That leads to hankering Number Two, the hankering we all have for the confirmation of our right to enjoy our self-respect which comes to us from sources outside ourselves, in the form of recognition, esteem, honor.

I recommend, therefore, as most helpful to understanding the worker's mind, these fundamentals:

First, that today the saving of our physical skin has become infinitely less important as a factor in our human relations than the saving of our social "face." This is so dependent upon our right to think well of ourselves . . ., that our "face" is very easily hurt by some slur, some look of the eye or other small slight.

Secondly, that whereas today at least two-thirds of the human race are bothered by hunger, here in America our hunger for food has become infinitely less important than hunger for attention, recognition, understanding.

As an example of that, I was at a cocktail party not long ago when a friend nudged me and said, "Look at the way that handsome man is annoying that beautiful blonde over there." I looked, and said, "Why, he isn't even looking at her!" My friend said, "Hell, that's what I'm trying to tell you!"

If you want to annoy any human being, beautiful blonde or whatnot, all you have to do is ignore him!

Third, that our hunger finds its chief and surest satisfaction in connection with our jobs, our work. I think I can claim rather varied contacts. To learn about people, I have associated with bums and with workers here and abroad, and I have sat with captains of industry in London, Paris, Berlin, Chicago, and New York. I give you my word, whether they were bums, board chairmen or in betweens, they were all just about equally less sure of themselves than they would *like* to be, all about equally as hungry to maintain "face," to have a word of approval.

But here is the point. Whether they were at the bottom or the top of the ladder, every blessed one of them gave me as final, incontrovertible, proof of certificate: "This is my job; this is the kind of service I give my fellow men; this is the kind of equipment I make useful to my fellow citizens. On the basis of that I demand a certain amount of attention."

The Job—A Measurement of Usefulness

I found, therefore, that the job serves as an amazingly useful scale for measuring the distance we have achieved up from the useless zero. Thus, I finally got a job as a laborer in the cinder-pit of a steel plant. Three weeks later the boss asked me about going into the millwright gang. I supposed only the money would be of interest to the ordinary worker. So when he told me I would get only two cents more an hour I thought it wasn't important. An hour later I had the new tools in my hand, and when I came by old companions I made a sensation. Every blessed one of them greeted me: "Hey, boodie, where you catch-em job? Millwright gang? No more pick and shovel for you! My God, you are one lucky son-of-gun!"

That was the first of a series of experiences that taught me that to every worker his job represents a rung upon a ladder indicating his comparative importance, establishing his position as a man among his fellow citizens outside the job. Every rung represents a distance, partly established by the amount of money but also by the skill and the training required. Thousands of details are involved. A tool designer has a right to consider himself a more important person and citizen than the tool operator, because of his job. Likewise the tool operator considers himself more important than the sweeper-up. Everywhere it's like that.

We have today a serious problem just because the whole trend of these modern times, with which I don't agree, is to lessen the differential between the skilled man and the unskilled by raising the unskilled.

The point is that when we give honor and recognition to the man at the top of the ladder, anyone from the bottom up has the right to consider himself worth while because his job makes him essential to the man at the top.

When I became an assistant repairman in a mine in Wales, I was way down below the lowest level. A thousand feet down there in the darkness, Evan Pugh, the repairman, and I would be hoping for a message to do our stuff. Then one of the miners would come in and say, "Evan, you better come quick before the pit falls in!" Half an hour afterward we would realize that only after we had done that repair job could the whole mine start working again. Then Evan would say to me, "It's very plain to see they can't run their bloody old mine without you and me!"

There is nothing that can compare with a man's job for helping him believe in himself. Everywhere I have gone, I have found the same thing. The reason we have such a grand responsible bunch of locomotive engineers is because they get the kowtowing of all their associates and companions because they have gone from the bottom of the ladder up to the top. What we overlook is that the fireman is likely to say, as one of them once said to me as I rode with him: "You see, the engineer takes himself very serious. I ain't saying nothin', but let me tell you, Mr. Engineer don't get his engine very far unless he gets his power from me!"

Everybody's Job Important to Him

You can't think of anybody whose job doesn't seem to him important. One time I unintentionally insulted the International Secretary of the Hobo Union because I thought he was a tramp. He said, "We 'boes are migratory workers, itinerant laborers; if we don't go to the right part of the country at the right time, millions of dollars worth of crops go to hell. So we *have* to take the train. A tramp only walks for a job. A bum is a guy that neither rides nor walks nor works. He's no good."

But the bum considers himself more worth while than, we will say, the Jungle-Buzzard, because that guy expects to eat mulligan stew without contributing anything to it. But you would hurt the Jungle-Buzzard's feelings if you didn't realize that he is better than a Mission Stiff. The Mission Stiff gets free food and clothes and a clean bed because he fools the keeper of the mission into thinking he has saved another soul. But you would hurt the feelings of the Mission Stiff if you didn't realize that he is better than a Lush Diver, who makes his living robbing drunks. But all these consider themselves superior to the lowest of them all. He is a Scissor Bill:

he will do anything provided he has something in his stomach. If somebody comes along and puts a couple of squares under his belt, he will say, "To hell with the revolution; let's wait a while!"

All these say, "My job is the thing that makes me worth while. It proves that I'm important, that the world needs me!"

Nobody can be sure of the loyalty of his workers unless he understands this absolutely fundamental fact. His job of course puts money in a man's pocket, but most important it also puts self-respect and self-belief in the bottom of his heart. If you miss that, you miss everything!

It is this tie-up of soul and body represented by the job that explains that fear. That fear, in turn, explains many of the peculiarities of workers. It "justifies" unions, limitation of output and so on. It also explains their hope for promotion. Besides an increase in income, this means a larger distance away from that dreadful zero at the bottom.

This tie-up also means that every single one of us would like to take pride in our work. If we can't take pride in our jobs, we can't take pride in ourselves, and then you might as well seek our body at the bottom of the river.

That tie-up also explains why your feelings, my feelings, every worker's feelings, can be hurt more easily during the hours of our job than any other of the twenty-four. Your wives may say you are touchy enough when you come home, but it doesn't compare with your touchiness during the hours of your job. It also explains why big issues come from management's failure to take care of some little annoyance that hurts men's feelings.

Importance of Little Things

In my opinion, many labor leaders understand these fundamentals better than employers, particularly the wish of their members to feel important, if not in their work, then in a strike. They also realize the importance of little things. For instance, while I was working in the mines in Wales I got into a "strike of folded arms." We went to work but we knew if we set hands to tools we would be beaten up by the committee of Reds or Bolshies. They were trying to make us feel important as strikers and they had us sing about the blood red flag of revolution and how it could be pinned to the top of the Houses of Parliament. They did a bang-up job of it.

But they also understood the importance of little things. I said to one of them, "You call yourself a leader. Why don't you have the employers put down gravel so we won't have to walk in mud?" And he said, "When we ask the masters, they tell us 'You are troublemakers; out with you!' If only the masters some years back had seen fit to think of us not so much as troublemakers as trouble-finders, 'twould be a better mine here!"

Those employers made a great mistake in thinking those fellows had gone radical. Because my miner friends explained, "These Bolshies do go too far. We must have law and order. But, after all, these Bolshies do be the mouthpiece of us all for all of us been fair unhappy!" They were made unhappy by all sorts of little annoyances.

Today one reason why the big unions have done as much as they have is because they first send out investigators who bring back all the gripes, big and little. Then they send out their organizers to tell every member of that industry, "If you sign on the dotted line, you will never again be bothered by any of these troubles."

I have found this importance of the job everywhere. But nowhere to the same extent as here in the United States. Here, above every-where else in the world, a man's respectability is based upon his job. The biggest reason, therefore, why we have become the world's protector, is that we, as nowhere else, have made a man's respecta-bility, a man's right to consider himself worthy in the eyes of his companions, dependent on his job.

We have out-produced the rest of the world, for the reason that we have harnessed the performance of useful service to those two hankerings. We have said to our youngsters, "If you would like to grow up into a worthy citizen with the confirmation and esteem of your fellows, all you need to do is climb that ladder of the job!" The biggest difference between Europe and ourselves is this. When you ask, over there, "Who is John Smith?" they assume you mean, "What is the class where he was born? Who is his father? Here we all know, we mean one thing, "What is his *job*? What is the nature of his skill, his equipment, his usefulness as shown by his work?"

Today I am worried because that system of respectability and honor based upon work which has made us great is now under serious threat. That threat gets fairly deep into politics.

You have the greatest of all opportunities to help save our system of making respectability and honor depend upon work. For if I am right about the importance of fear, hope, and pride, then as employers, you have a greater opportunity than anybody else, first, to lessen fear; secondly, to justify hope; and most important and difficult, to build pride in your workers—pride of their skill, pride of their craft, pride of their company, pride of their industry. Pride is the key to their performance.

Value of Personal Contacts

Here are a few of the tools which you can use for building pride. The simplest and one of the most effective tools is making sure that you are utilizing to the full your opportunity for personal contacts. I have been a fan about what can be done by personal contact ever since I got a job in the mines in Germany's Saar Valley. I was told the German miners were going to murder the French engineers who were put over them by the League of Nations. But to my surprise they spoke well of these officers. In explanation, the engineers said, "We are taught in our mining schools always to keep in close touch with our miners. Every day we talk to a few of them face to face till, in a month we contact all of them." Sure enough, I'd be loading coal and along would come the French engineer-manager. He would ask us, "How are you getting along? Have you got good tools? Is the ventilation all right?" Then after talking with us about the cost of living, and so on, he would say, "We will see you again next month."

Most amazed, the Germans would exclaim, "We have been taught to hate every Frenchman, yet they treat us better than we have ever been treated before."

So I say today, American industry is in danger of depending too much on mass arrangements, mass programs. But if you leave out personal contacts, those programs won't work. Our heavy dependence on these big mass plans in industry isn't much more silly than if some husband were to say that he and his wife, in order to avoid divorce, were going to sign a contract that would cover every problem. So if he was blown up by his wife on a Tuesday morning he could point to page so-and-so and say, "See, this clause proves you're wrong!" There is no substitute for personal contact for learning the worker's fears, hopes, prides.

Answering the Why's

The second tool is better communications, fuller explanation of the new machine or new method, why, why, why, all over the place. You can't overdo it. Whether you are a mother in the home or a boss in the factory, when you ask me to do so-and-so "because I tell you" you are destroying my face, my belief in myself. I wish I could put upon the desk of every executive and manager a sign saying, "Explain. If you can't, explain *why* you can't explain."

The next tool I recommend is the freer use of the pat on the back, when deserved. Mind you, I underline the word "deserved" because if you want to lose the respect of a good craftsman, you need only praise as good a job which he as a craftsman knows is lousy. I have had vice-presidents of some of the biggest corporations in America almost weep on my shoulder because they couldn't get from their president one single word to enable them to know where they stood. They would give their right arm to have a report back from the president with two words, "Very good," instead of just two initials.

A manager told me one time in a plant in Cleveland that he called in a foreman and told him that the Vice-President had asked if he could lend him for a couple of weeks to another plant. "I told him I couldn't spare him because he was too useful to me." Result? Big Jim, the foreman, said with tears in his eyes, "I have wondered all these years if you thought I was any damn good. That's the best news ever!"

And there was the mine superintendent who called in a Polish workman one day and said, "Steve, that was a good suggestion you made. Here's a ten-dollar bill." Twenty-four hours later Steve came in and said, "Please, boss, write me a letter; say that you called me good man and gave me ten-dollar bill because I make good suggestion." The boss said, "Steve, I am very busy. Why do you want me to take the trouble to write you a letter? I gave you a ten-dollar bill; what more do you want?" And Steve said, "Because last night I go home and tell my woman you give me ten-dollar bill because I make good suggestion. My woman she say me lousy liar!"

Mrs. Lindbergh tells in her book about how she and Lindy once had a terrible time getting their plane off the water in Africa. Chapter after chapter goes on, and they haven't got the plane up in the air. Finally the time comes, and they take off. Then Mrs. Lindbergh writes a note to her husband, because of the noise in the cockpit. "Was it the gas?" Lindbergh shakes his head. Another note: "Do you think we can make it?" Lindbergh nods his head, "Yes." Then she rather apologizes for the next message. Evidently she felt so pleased and relieved that she wrote him this note: "I think you are wonderful!" and handed it over to him.

Millions of wives today would give their right arms to get that kind of a note from their husbands. The paradox is, though, that most of those wives assume it isn't necessary to write that kind of note to husbands. Why? Because he has a job and they have no such certificate of their worth.

That is a dangerous idea, because when even the best of husbands gets that kind of note from his secretary or from the handsome blonde down the street—"I think you are wonderful"—if the best of husbands gets such a note from anybody who is appreciative, the chances are he will say, "What an intelligent—what a *charming* woman!" This is because you can put it down in the book that nobody, whatever his condition, is as sure of his value as he would *like* to be.

When you give a man a job in your plant you give him something infinitely more important than a chance to make a living. You determine the conditions of his whole life. If he can feel, with your help, the right to consider himself worth while, as playing a worthy part in the protection and maintenance of America, then you have built that man into a happy human being in the way that no other human being of any sort can do as well as you, his employer.

All this has a more important bearing today than ever before, because we are in a war of "isms"—different ideas of human nature and motivation. The best statement I have seen of our American idea was given by Fosdick. He says, "The essence of Americanism and of democracy is to attribute to ordinary human beings extraordinary possibilities."

I believe, after I have observed things in Europe, the reason why Socialism and Communism fail to produce things is just because they attribute extraordinary possibilities only to a few carefully chosen officials. They assume that all of the rest of us are nothing but scissor bills. In other words, all the government has to do is fill our bellies and clothe our backs and then we will be so thankful we will keep them everlastingly in power.

But if there is anything we Americans are not—we are not scissor bills. We don't follow the line of least resistance. We have no respect for a leader who asks so little of us that we can't think better of ourselves than we could before. We hate a leader who takes to himself all the credit and the glory and gives us nothing but the money. But we gladly go through hell for the leader who asks the impossible of us—provided that, when we give it, he shares with us the right to think better of ourselves in the measure of our effort!

All this means, finally, that you can't do your best for yourself, for your workers or for your country, unless you have in mind the limitless possibilities that are placed inside of us by those two hankerings. Rather than fall down and be considered unworthy, we are glad to pay the price of life itself! . . .

Today we are faced in America with what I believe is a tragic paradox. We are being taught that of course nobody works except for money. Nobody should be so silly as to assume that he can get cooperation without paying so much per. At the same time, the fathers, the sons, and the brothers of these workers over in the mountains of Korea are today walking willingly to meet the possibility of death! Why? Because of the money we pay them? No! The only reason they walk willingly to meet death is that as they walk they feel the certainty of your recognition and mine and of all mankind, of the nobility that makes them do it! They would rather die with honor than live without it!

We all know that if we were to withhold that honor, were to take off from their place of honor the names of our honored dead, and were to pay no recognition to our Gold Star mothers, then in time of war, we would stand naked and defenseless before our enemies.

You cannot be a good American unless you understand that. Also in time of peace, what has made us great and what will continue to make us great is our willingness to give honor, recognition to a man in proportion to the usefulness of his service.

Old Evan Pugh used to tell me about an undermanager that he worked for who was very hard-boiled—until he studied human nature as captain of a company on the Western Front during World War I. There he learned about the possibilities of human nature. So when he came back to his old job he put into operation a different way of handling men. One night Old Evan reported: "Yesterday the undermanager down in the pit said to me, 'That do be a first-class job ye've done.' And I do say to him, 'Mr. undermanager, in forty-three years of workin' in this pit—in forty-three years, that do be the first time that any company man do say to me a kindly word about my job.'" Then he continued: "Every man do know that for a kindly word, he'll work his guts out—that no dog behave well for the man with a whip. And every man of sensibility do know that for him, the whip of the tongue and the lash of the lip be worse nor any whip on any dog! Every man must have a chance here on the job to show himself the man!"

My belief, therefore, is that we may come through just because, as I have gone among the other nations, I have found this one thing is true of you and me as Americans—namely, that every one of us would love to have it said of us what the old writer in Ecclesiastes said of the ancient artisans and craftsmen:

> All these have put their trust in their hands,
> And each becometh wise in his own works.
> Yea, though they be not sought for in the council of the people
> Nor be exalted in the assembly;
> And be not found amongst them that utter dark sayings;
> Yet without these shall not a city be inhabited,
> Nor shall men sojourn or walk up and down therein.
> For these maintain the fabric of the world
> And in the handiwork of their craft is their prayer.

As long as you employers help make sure that our prayer remains there in the work of our hands and our hearts and our heads, so long the future of America is safe; but with the utmost seriousness may I say, only so long.

I give you four words as helpful to this understanding of the worker and the gaining of his cooperation. Those four words are: Listen, Explain, Respect, Appreciate!

Questions

1. Mr. Williams reports that the professors and psychologists with whom he talked in 1919 said that the only value in the worker's mind was money and the only fear was for the loss of income. Do you believe that most managers would feel this way? Why?
2. Do you agree with Williams that the trend to lessen the differential between the skilled and the unskilled workers by raising the wages of the unskilled is undesirable? Why?
3. How can the executives of a large company maintain the personal contact with subordinates that Williams feels is important? Are there any dangers in this procedure?
4. This article was written over twenty years ago. Do you believe that Americans exhibit any tendency toward becoming "scissor bills"? What evidence do you have for your belief?
5. Can you think of current industrial personnel problems that might be better understood by having observers "live the life of the workers," as Williams did over 45 years ago? Are there any ethical considerations in such an approach?

4—WHAT IS PERSONNEL? *

Dean Kimmerly

It's screening, interviewing, and hiring.

It's long hours in a smoky hotel room battling out the terms of a contract.

It's analyzing job content.

It's responding to a survey on summer work hours for nonexempt salaried personnel.

It's the Factor Comparison Method of Job Evaluation.

It's the third step of a grievance and the strong prospect of a "Wildcat."

It's Likert, McGregor, Odiorne, Herzberg, Yoder, Peter Drucker, and I. W. Abel.

It's an exit interview at 4 o'clock on a Friday afternoon.

It's a service award program, gripes about cafeteria prices, tears in the office, the suggestion system, and attitude surveys.

It's the "pit of the stomach" feeling when the organizer appears at the plant gate.

It's indecision at 6 a.m. at the height of a raging snowstorm.

It's a Job Analyst, a Wage and Benefits Administrator, a Training Director, a Safety Supervisor.

It's developing an employee appraisal program.

It's recommending a budget for Executive Merit Pay.

It's a Director of Industrial Relations, a Manager of Human Relations, a Supervisor of Employee Relations, a Vice President of Corporate Relations.

It's wage ranges, incentive systems, commissions, and bonuses.

It's a Vice President of Personnel, a Director of College Recruitment, a Manager of Employee Services.

It's manpower planning, executive development, and supervisor training.

* From *The Personnel Administrator*, Vol. 32, No. 5 (September-October, 1969), pp. 46-47. Reprinted with permission.

It's a survey!

It's EEOC forms, frequency and severity charts, location interviewing, a company picnic, unemployment claims, and Workmen Comp. forms.

It's sensitivity training, the management grid, participative management, programmed instruction, and group dynamics.

It's a survey!

It's flower funds, plant tours, seniority systems, hospital visitations, slowdowns, job bidding, employee motivation, a United Fund drive . . .

It's a . . . meeting! A supervisor's meeting, an executive committee meeting, a planning group meeting, a corporate staff meeting—a meeting of the safety group, personnel group, industrial relations group, or the training group—conferences, conventions, seminars, and workshops.

It's arguing a case before the NLRB—and it's serving on an NAB application committee of the River Valley Chamber of Commerce.

It's consulting top management on the feasibility of a revision in the Profit Sharing Plan. It's selling employees on the value of a change in the administration of the recreation fund.

It's long hours. It's headaches, heartaches, stomachaches—and occasionally an ache or pain somewhere else.

It's the small cubicle with the dirty window in the Northeast corner of a congested machine shop.

It's the plush, carpeted corner office on the 40th floor of the new Park Avenue building complex.

It's the one-girl staff—performing her Personnel duties on a time-available basis as she handles the switchboard, brews coffee, and performs her receptionist duties.

It's the staff of 35—excluding support and clerical personnel.

It's $6,700 per year. It's $36,200 per year plus stock options, profit sharing, and the special key executive bonus.

It's the problem of the missing coffee money.

It's the challenge of a 10 percent reduction in force following the phaseout of a $23 million government contract.

It's the foreman—up from the ranks into Personnel.

It's the sharp young MBA from Cornell.

It's reporting to a Plant Superintendent who has been in the game for 35 years and knows all the answers because . . . he's been in the game for 35 years.

It's reporting to the Group Vice President who gives a free hand, judging only on the success or failure of the project . . . with an eye on the budget.

Questions

1. In general, what message is the author seeking to convey in this article?

5—MANAGER OF TOMORROW *

Elmer B. Staats

Your chairman has asked me to outline briefly some of the major factors which will affect the role of the manager in the longer term. Some of you may still be in active governmental roles in the year 2000—just about 30 years from now.

Who is there with the perspective to forecast the problems facing the government manager 30 years from today?

Viewed in retrospect of an equal period of the past, who in or out of government could then have foreseen that:

1. Nearly 400,000 people would be engaged at one time in a program with its primary objective a manned lunar landing?
2. Primary strategic weaponry would be the intercontinental ballistic missle? And the need for an antiballistic missile one of the great debates of the day?
3. Several billion dollars would be planned to provide for a supersonic civilian transport?
4. Social Security and Medicare would have been extended to virtually all of our citizens?
5. Per capita income—influenced heavily by governmental policies and programs—would have increased from $362 to $2,317?

While the 30 years to the year 2000 may or may not bring equally dramatic and unforeseen roles for government, it is imperative that a government manager understand the basic forces which will determine the problems which he will face in the years ahead.

People may differ as to the variables which will determine the role of and the problems facing the government manager in the years ahead, but perhaps could agree on the following:

1. A rapidly growing population, increasingly urban in character.
2. Continued changes in the pattern of family life, with a weakened role of the family unit.
3. Rising expectations which grow from an ever-increasing standard of living where expressed needs will continue to outdistance resources and capabilities to meet them.

* From *Civil Service Journal*, Vol. 10, No. 2 (October-December, 1969), pp. 4-6. From an address by Mr. Staats at the Federal Executive Institute, Charlottesville, Virginia, April 26, 1969. Reprinted with permission.

4. An increase in the reliance on the National Government for financing and leadership of other governmental programs, with accompanying profound effects upon our Federal system of government.
5. A highly intensified struggle to develop and preserve our natural resources and our natural environment which will require additional constraints on exploitation and increased emphasis on scientific research.
6. A further blurring of the lines between what is considered "public" and what is considered "private" in our national economy.
7. And, underlying all of these, the pervasive and unpredictable effect of a rapidly changing industrial technology.

A full discussion of all these factors is beyond the scope of this presentation. But let me discuss three which now appear to be central to the problems of government management in the years ahead.

Growth and urbanization

Toward the close of Thomas Jefferson's life—1825—about 10 percent of our people lived in cities and towns. In 1960 some 70 percent of the population lived in cities and towns—on 1 percent of the land area. The remaining 30 percent lived on 99 percent of the land. By 2000 A.D., 90 percent of the American people will live in urban areas on less than 2 percent of the land, excluding Alaska. One out of 10 Americans will live in 19 States containing half our total land, again excluding Alaska. Much of the nation will still be relatively open area.

During the past 30 years, perhaps the central forces affecting governmental programs have been these dramatic increases and location shifts of our population. The chief effect of these changes has been the necessity to adjust to mass living in large urban areas. In 1935 the population of the United States was approximately 127 million. We are right now a nation of more than 200 million people. In the year 2000—if present trends continue—we may have a population of more than 300 million. The economic and social consequences of our population growth will multiply by geometric progression our responsibilities for providing food and shelter and will complicate daily requirements to maintain law and order.

There will be heavy concentrations of people on the Atlantic and Pacific coasts within 50 to 100 miles of the oceans. The population of the Atlantic seaboard today from Boston through Washington is upwards of 27 million. Bureau of the Census projections show an increase to over 60 million along this 400-mile strip by 1990. An equally massive metropolitan area is foreseen for the 200-mile Pacific coast zone from Santa Barbara to Los Angeles to San Diego and the Mexican border.

Half of the counties of the nation declined in population from 1950 to 1960. But perhaps a more incisive index of metropolitan concentration is the proportion of total national increase that occurred in the metropolitan counties. More than four-fifths of the increase from 1950 to 1960 was in these areas. And the rate of increase for the Negro population in the last three decades has been twice that for the non-Negro population.

Associated with this increase has been the dispersion of population within the central city itself. In the 20 years from 1900 to 1920, the metropolitan population increased 65 percent—a 75 percent increase in the central city, 40 percent outside. In the 20 years from 1940 to 1960, the metropolitan population increased 55 percent—a 27 percent increase inside the central city, 102 percent outside.

For these people the overall projections of expected increases in goods and services, better education, urban renewal, better health, and improved science and technology offer little comfort. Ways must be developed, indeed urgently developed, to provide the substitute for the discipline of the family unit which has played such an important role in our nation's history. In large part, it will come to rest as a problem for the government and the government manager.

Changing federalism

Ten years ago Federal financial assistance to state and local governments amounted to 4 billion dollars a year; 5 years ago it amounted to 8 billion dollars. It is running at about 17 billion dollars a year and is expected to rise to about 60 billion dollars a year by 1975.

It is estimated that Federal aid will constitute approximately 20 percent of the revenue of state and local governments by 1970.

Estimates of the number of Federal-aid programs differ. The figure most frequently cited is 170; another estimate puts the number at 220. These programs are financed through 400 or more separate appropriations, administered by 21 Federal agencies through 150 major Washington bureaus and over 400 field offices.

Programs are carried on in each of the fifty states. Nearly 92,000 units of local government, each with its own taxing, planning, financing, and operating authorities, are eligible for grants-in-aid under one or more Federal programs.

This seemingly endless number and variety of programs have created perplexing problems. For example, funds for job training can be obtained from nine manpower program sources, for adult basic education from 10, for prevocational training and skill training from 10, and for work experience from five. On-the-job training can be financed under five programs; income maintenance is available under nine programs. Eligibility rules, application procedures, allocation formulas, expiration dates, and contracting arrangements vary.

All this creates problems for managers at the local level who frequently have fewer sufficiently skilled staffs than the Federal government has to tackle the maze of differing—sometimes inconsistent—regulations, planning prerequisites, financial matching ratios, reporting requirements, and statistical standards.

This system of seemingly arbitrary organizational patterns and differing legal requirements meshed with local organizations led Lyndon Johnson during his Presidency to send a long message to the Congress on "the quality of American government." He took note of the need to "strengthen the Federal system through greater communication, consolidation, consistency and coordination . . . to improve the quality of government itself—its machinery, its manpower, its methods."

President Richard Nixon, in a statement upon establishing common regional boundaries and locations for five agencies engaged in social and economic services, emphasized his intention to make significant improvement in the quality of government. He said:

> This restructuring expresses my concern that we make much greater progress in our struggle against social problems. The best way to facilitate such progress, I believe, is not by adding massively to the burdens which government already bears but rather by finding better ways to perform the work of the government.
>
> That work is not finished when a law is passed, nor is it accomplished when an agency in Washington is assigned to administer new legislation. These are only preliminary steps; in the end the real work is done by the men who implement the law in the field.

Science and technology

Much of the society we know today is a product of the scientific revolution which is in full tide over much of the world: modern communications, nuclear power, medical care, increased production of food, and a seemingly limitless number of additional achievements.

But this does not tell the whole story.

Without the genius and resources for application, without vigorous and imaginative exploitation of opportunities that scientific insights offered, and without the resolution to apply them to society's purposes, the application of these resources would not have borne fruit.

This is the role of the governmental manager of the future. It is his job to use his imagination to the limit to assure that the benefits of nuclear energy for the civilian economy will not be lost, that the by-products of the space program will be translated into useful application in other areas, and that patents developed in connection with government contracts will be wholly and freely available to the private economy.

The manager of the future will find himself carrying out more and more public policy through contracts, grants, regional compacts, institutes, foundations, and self-contained business-type enterprises which will make management, at one and the same time, both possible and difficult. The line between public administration and private participation will be less clear than ever, while the hybrid will flourish. And it is here the manager will have his work cut out for him—in maintaining the essential responsibility that belongs with government, in understanding the fine difference between supervision and interference, and in judging how well the ends of public policy are being served.

It is doubtful that the government executive of the future can be grown and trained exclusively in the career civil service. He will have to have some first-hand experience with unfamiliar environments: the university environment, the regional environment, the business and research environment. He will have to develop an exchange of persons between government and these allied communities through reciprocal internships and residencies.

In the past the consequences of an average or below-par public service have not been nearly as serious as they are now. As the role of government grows, and as the decisions of public officials at all levels of government have a more and more direct effect both on our daily affairs and on our prospects for the future, the quality of our public service has become a major public concern. In the words of Clarence Randall, known to so many of us:

> Today, as never before, the administration of our government calls for excellence in leadership. We need thoroughly competent executives, acquainted with the most modern techniques in managing large enterprises, from cost accounting to good human relations, from sound staff

work to automatic data processing. We need scientists in our race for preeminence in all fields of research. Above all we need a continuing source of replenishment of this talent.

I take it that is why you are here.

Questions

1. Why are government managers of the future likely to be involved more than formerly in carrying out public policy?
2. On the basis of the predictions made by the author, do you feel that the training required for managers in government will tend to differ to a greater or lesser extent from that required for managers in private enterprise?

6—THE PERSONNEL FUNCTION IN
TOMORROW'S COMPANY *

Frank E. Fischer

In the past 30 years technological changes have helped to double the gross national product, and in the next 30 they will more than double it again. In the field of human knowledge, we are told that four times as much is known today as was known 30 years ago and that scientists will learn as much more in the next 15 years as in all of previous history. As for population, we can expect to grow from a country of 200 million people to 226 million by 1975 and 245 million by 1980.

To those engaged in business management generally and in the personnel function particularly, these prognostications have a special significance, because all these goods, all this knowledge, all these people will be the concern of a shrinking proportion of the population. The group from which our executives and decision makers are drawn—the age group from 35 to 55—will have dropped from 47 percent of the total productive age group to 38 percent by 1980. Roughly this means that three managers will be doing the work that four are doing today.

Tomorrow's manager

To understand what this means for the personnel function, we have to consider first what tomorrow's manager will be like and what kind of work he will be doing. We can be reasonably sure that he will have to know more and learn more than his counterpart today, and that he will be supervising more sophisticated people than he does today. Professor Harold Leavitt of Carnegie Tech predicts that tomorrow's manager will be more of an intellectual, that he will make more of his decisions on the basis of systematic analysis and less by off-the-cuff methods. There is evidence that this is already happening. Not long ago, the American Telephone & Telegraph Co. studied the records of 17,000 college graduates in the

* Reprinted by permission of the publisher from *Personnel*. © January/February 1968 by the American Management Association, Inc.

Bell companies and learned that the single most reliable indicator of their success was class standing on graduating from college; and more recently the Prudential Insurance Co. of America came to the same conclusion.

Tomorrow's manager will also be supervising a different kind of work force. Between 1950 and 1960, the number of professional and technical people employed in business increased 47 percent, and for the first time white-collar workers in industry exceeded the number of blue-collar workers. This trend is expected to continue. The supervision of primarily professional, technical, and other white-collar employees will require a kind of manager different from the one who is now typical in factory management.

At the same time, despite the best possible preparation for his present job, tomorrow's executive may find himself threatened with obsolescence in mid-career. With "knowledge" compounding at such a rapid rate, no manager can be sure that his skills will continue to be needed or even that his job will exist tomorrow. As MIT's Professor Charles Myers has observed, "It is becoming impossible to learn a skill that will continue for a lifetime." In some companies there is even talk about preparing executives for a second career.

Shifts in personnel emphasis

Can personnel specialists meet the needs of tomorrow's manager? Their record in responding to new requirements in the past encourages the belief that they can. The personnel function began as an employment and record-keeping function; later, as workers began to organize, it took on the administration of labor agreements. Increasingly, too, it was charged with carrying out programs largely developed by management.

The personnel department then moved in one or more directions: (1) it became the keeper of the corporate conscience and concerned itself with the morale of the employees; (2) it became "scientific" and introduced systematic techniques for employee selection, salary administration, and other activities connected with personnel; or (3) it began to concoct programs that proved to be more fashionable than useful.

A number of management fads and gimmicks have originated in the personnel department, particularly in the training function. Not long ago, the magic words were "economic education" and "human relations"; later came "brainstorming" and "group dynamics"; and more recently we have been hearing about teaching machines and "human systems development."

The recent record

Aside from busying itself with fads or status-symbol programs, however, the personnel function has shown signs of maturing.

Appraisals are more goal-oriented and tied in with management development as well as compensation. They are regarded less as a personnel "program" and more as a management tool.

Compensation plans and techniques are becoming less complex, top management involvement is more evident, and the plans are better integrated than before. In the past it was not unusual to find responsibility for a company's compensation program fragmented among three or more departments, but now it is recognized that compensation is not a matter of discrete programs and that companies still following that line are probably paying total compensation far beyond what they thought they were paying or need to pay. As a result, it is becoming more common for all elements of the compensation program to report to a single executive.

So-called discretionary bonus plans are giving way to incentive plans based on formulas and distributing funds according to individual performance weighed against planned objectives.

Personnel records and reports are being centralized and put on computers.

Greater attention is being paid to personnel research as an assist in making management decisions.

In divisionalized companies, there is more policy direction by corporate personnel departments but at the same time greater local autonomy in personnel administration.

There is more effort to collaborate with government in personnel matters, such as equal employment opportunity, collective bargaining, wage guidelines, pricing, retraining, and Medicare. For instance, companies are finding that merely pledging to eliminate discrimination or joining the voluntary Equal Employment Opportunity Councils is not enough. Compliance must be positive, and companies are expected to prove good faith by publicizing the fact that appointments are open to minority groups, by recruiting actively from among such groups, and by establishing programs for training them.

The personnel department is beginning to operate internationally, particularly in the areas of compensation and employee benefits.

More attention is being given to the identification of potential managers and to the nurture of talent. As shortages of skills become more acute, recruiting becomes more competitive; and companies worry more about how to retain their college trainees and other "elite" groups.

Training is leaving the classroom and returning to the workplace or a simulation of it. A recent reorientation of the training activity at American Airlines illustrates this trend: Aware of the constant changes in the business environment, the training heads at American Airlines believe that it is not enough to pass on managerial wisdom from one generation to another, that managers have to learn how to relate that experience to tomorrow's requirements. Thus, they act on the principles that the organization should be less a traditional schoolmaster and more a provider of resources and experiences; that training is concerned with improvement in both functional skills (such as budgeting or selling) and social skills (such as communications or counseling); that training should both increase individual competence and improve collaboration within and between groups; and that the best way to teach people management processes like planning, organizing, and controlling is to have them plan, organize, and control.

To implement these principles, the company is making use of problem-solving and simulation techniques, such as business games, in-basket exercises, role playing, and team-task methods.

What's ahead?

In addition to these developments, there are signs of other changes, some of which may have a profound effect on the purpose, staffing, status, and organization of the personnel department in the future. Four related changes of particular significance are: (1) the growing profit-orientation of the personnel function; (2) the shift in personnel work from a mechanistic concept to a creative, innovative one; (3) the interest in furthering an organization, rather than just maintaining or servicing it; and (4) the more direct involvement of top management in the development of the human resources of the business. Just what are the implications of these trends?

1. The personnel function will assume a more important role in the management of the business. It will do more planning and policy-making in the areas of manpower, organization structure, and compensation, among others. It will have more functional authority, especially in large, complex, and growing organizations. In becoming increasingly oriented toward growth and profits, instead of merely administering personnel activities, it will search out profit-improvement opportunities.

This new awareness will mean that personnel people will view their role in a different light. For example: In selecting people, more weight will be placed on what a candidate has accomplished than on the jobs he has held. In management development, more stress will be placed on identifying company and departmental needs and objectives and training people to help attain them. In compensation, it will be important to relate pay to performance and to its motivational impact, as well as to make sure that rates are competitive. In the area of employee benefits, there will be more consideration of the fact that a large part of expenditures are going to people who are not working in the form of retirement benefits, life insurance payments, medical plans, and the like.

In appraising performance, there will be more emphasis on accomplishments against expectations, and appraisal results will be more closely tied to a man's compensation. In organization planning, there will have to be major emphasis on aligning responsibilities and relationships in the individual company to obtain maximum results with the least manpower, instead of seeking symmetrical or conventional organization patterns or uncritically following principles of organization laid down by others.

In summary, the personnel function will no longer be able to justify itself to top management by citing numbers or listing activities—the number of people interviewed or trained or counseled, the number of reports prepared or of records maintained, the number of job descriptions written, or the rate of employee turnover. Rather, personnel will demonstrate its effectiveness by raising the qualification levels of the employees hired; reducing the turnover among key managerial and professional people; recommending or drafting plans, policies, and programs that are adopted by operating management; and initiating organizational and staffing changes.

2. The personnel function will become more creative, less mechanistic. In the future the disparity between the paper programs and actuality will have to be eliminated. The deficiencies of rigid, packaged "personnel programs" will become increasingly apparent.

Most of us are familiar with companies where "management development programs" have been conducted for years, yet half of their top managers are over 55 years old and there are few successors in sight and the companies go outside to find people for many higher-level jobs; where management positions are invariably staffed without consulting the head of the personnel department; and where although the companies have performance appraisal programs, half the executives don't even bother to complete the required forms.

In such corporations most of the top management group have had experience in only one function of the business; there are no inventories of management resources, no plans for management succession, and only a dim notion of future management requirements or how to meet them; participation by top executives in outside management development programs is almost nonexistent; a high proportion of the more promising men recruited on college campuses leave the company within two years; and numerous corporate departments are involved with compensation and employee benefit plans, but no department is responsible for overall policy or coordination in these areas and, for that matter, the compensation plan does not apply to a sizable group of executives in the top levels.

There will be less me-tooism, less concern with imitating industry practice or matching industry averages, and more attention to what's actually required to help the company meet its goals. There will be more concern with ends rather than means, with substance rather than forms, with accomplishments rather than activities. There will be increasing emphasis on what the operating people find workable instead of what is theoretically best or easiest for the personnel department to administer. We already see this trend in the adoption of less complicated job-evaluation plans and in the movement away from automatic merit increases and appraisals based on an employee's activities or traits and toward appraisals based on performance measured against company goals or standards.

3. *The personnel function will be responsible for furthering the organization, not just maintaining it.* Personnel people will devote more time to proposing and promoting changes than to protecting the status quo. Instead of a miscellany of diverse specialties or activities, the personnel department will be regarded as an integrated general management function, responsible for the effective deployment of the

firm's human resources, and, as it becomes more oriented to the requirements of the organization, it will view the needs of individuals in the light of their compatibility with those of the organization.

The personnel managers will recognize and encourage sound management practices, fostering concepts like management-by-objectives and team problem-solving approaches. They will seek new ways to awaken the talents that lie dormant in every organization by searching out opportunities and providing training experiences that are challenging and meaningful, rejecting a commitment to human relations as an end in itself.

In planning and developing his company's human resources, the personnel man will have to raise his sights to plan the form of the future organization and of the firm's manpower requirements; to structure and integrate the work; to identify and select management talent; to appraise and reward performance; to provide learning experiences to ensure growth of both the individual and the organization; and to rotate, transfer, and promote people into appropriate positions.

To handle this responsibility, the personnel man will have to be an individual of singular breadth and influence, sensitive equally to the needs and capabilities of people and to the requirements of the business. How many personnel departments or personnel people today perform this role or qualify for it? Apparently, not many. Some companies establish a separate unit within the personnel department to carry out this creative policy-making and program-planning function. In others, a small, high-level staff, responsible for organization planning and development, is created to work directly with the chief executive officer and his key subordinates, while personnel services for supervisory and employee groups are provided by the regular personnel department.

If this trend continues, there is a real possibility that the personnel department will become, in effect, an employee services organization, catering to the needs of lower-level groups and administering the traditional, routine personnel functions. This threat will be averted only if professional personnel people turn their energies to making the organization more effective instead of making it more comfortable or safe—if they start thinking more about making work productive and meaningful than about making it easy.

4. Top management will become more directly involved in the deployment and development of human resources. The chief executives of a growing number of companies are spending a good deal

of time thinking about the people in the organizations, reviewing
management manpower needs and resources, assessing the performance and potential of their executives, and planning their future
experiences. Michael Haider, Chairman of Standard Oil of New
Jersey, recently wrote:

> In the life of a corporation, today's success is largely a product of
> three types of executive actions taken yesterday: selecting the right
> people; placing them in the right jobs; and seeing to it that they were
> able to grow to meet both their own needs and those of the organiza-
> tion. This activity is not a program in the usual sense, any more than
> selling or making profits are programs. It has no fixed dimensions, no
> timetable, no cutoff point.

How seriously he regards this activity, Mr. Haider points out, is
indicated by the fact that he assumes the executive development
function as his personal responsibility. He, the president, and four
executive vice presidents of the company, acting as a committee, met
37 times in 1964 to review the company's human resources. This
committee is "involved in a continuing examination of management
throughout the Jersey organization. . . . Once a year the chief executive officer of each of the larger affiliates meets with the committee
and reviews in depth his company's development activities and its
replacement situation and appraises the performance and potential
of all his key management personnel. He goes over his replacement
tables, his plans for job rotation assignments, and the specific steps
being taken to increase the effectiveness of his organization."

A company in which the chief executive regards the development
of its human resources as one of his chief concerns will probably
provide the kind of climate in which people are encouraged to grow
and to innovate. Those engaged in personnel work are in an
excellent position to influence—and to benefit from—that climate.

To exert the proper influence, however, the personnel executive
will have to adapt to management's changing expectations of his
role. Thus, to sum up, the personnel executive in the future will:

1. Assume a larger role in profit management.
2. Concern himself more with ends than with means, with accomplishments rather than activities.
3. Devote his efforts to building the organization instead of just
   maintaining it.
4. Assist top management in the effective deployment and development of the company's human resources.

If the personnel function is going to survive as more than management's maid-of-all-work (to use Professor Paul Pigors' phrase)

and if it is to satisfy management's greater demand upon it, there will have to be fundamental changes in its role.

Questions

1. Which of the predicted changes in the functions to be performed by the personnel department of the future do you believe will change the role of this department most significantly?
2. What barriers, if any, within organizations may prevent those changes predicted by the author from occurring?
3. If the changes predicted by the author do materialize, what effects are they likely to have upon the qualifications, status, and salary of a personnel manager?

7—A NEW ERA IN PERSONNEL RELATIONS *

Chris Argyris

Forty-five years ago the whole idea of personnel administration in American industry was viewed as nonsense by the vast majority of employers. Their attitudes in the years just before World War I have been characterized as "employment by crook of the finger" and "dictatorship and autocratic paternalism."

It was into this atmosphere that the pioneers of personnel administration moved. And they moved in, as Thomas Spates puts it in his book *Human Values Where People Work*, with a determination to eliminate the "brutal disregard for human values at the workplace" and to substitute "a code of civilized treatment of employees."

The second era of personnel administration began just before World War II. This second generation of personnel administrators seemed to be concerned less with new ideas and more with defending the gains of the pioneers and expanding them wherever possible. Services were expanded to make up for, or even to push into the background, those negative working conditions that could not be alleviated. Cafeterias, recreational programs, clubs and parties became hallmarks of "good human relations."

Management kept needling personnel people because their function seemed to be no more than trying to keep people happy. And personnel managers sought to defend themselves by trying to make personnel activities more scientific and thus more respectable.

The end result of the first- and second-era personnel programs has been to satisfy the employees' basic needs for food, shelter, clothing, as well as their needs for security. But now that satisfaction of these needs is, to a degree, guaranteed, the old personnel policies no longer tend to motivate productive behavior.

Now a new, third era in personnel relations is about to begin. And despite the gains of the last 45 years, it will bring an urgently needed change.

---

* Reprinted by special permission from *Dun's Review & Modern Industry*, June 1962. Copyright 1965, Dun & Bradstreet Publications Corp.

Personnel administration, in its new form, seeks to meet needs that have been called "self-realizing." Simply put, these needs motivate human beings to strive to enlarge and express their full potentialities, and this process of striving is in itself rewarding. As self-realization increases, responsibility, commitment, competence and a respect for oneself and others also tend to increase. And these qualities are important sources of productiveness and effective leadership.

Tackling this new job promises to be one of the toughest tasks that personnel administrators have taken on. For there seems to be a basic incongruence between the nature of formal organizations like corporations and managerial controls on the one hand and mature individuals on the other. Corporations require employees, especially at the lower levels, to be dependent upon others and submissive to them. These requirements are antithetical to mature human beings who aspire to be relatively independent, self-responsible .and self-controlled.

Formal organization and managerial controls by their very nature assume that human beings, out of a sense of loyalty, will act rationally, and that they will accept, for a fair set of rewards, a world in which they are required to be dependent and subordinate. But research suggests that such an assumption runs counter to the nature of mature individuals. In an attempt to live within the organization and produce what is expected of them, they either tend to fight the organization or to accept it by becoming apathetic and noninvolved.

Management can readily recognize the "fight" reaction. But it has a lot more difficulty discerning acceptance of the organization by the employee when it is based on apathy and noninvolvement. Yet it often happens that after years of apathy and indifference, the individual's capacity for productive, creative work decreases. He no longer even looks for challenging work.

This, of course, often leads management heads to believe that an employee is lazy and not highly responsible. But the fact is that management may well create many of the conditions that cause these problems.

Personnel men are supposed to make top management aware of the causes of these problems and to help solve the problems. But what have the personnel men contributed? The fair answer is: not very much.

Fields of failure

Their present communications programs may tend to increase employee mistrust of management and increase executive isolation. Their human relations programs, emphasizing the equality of everyone, may help some management men to use the authority they have to hide their incompetence. Their programs of employee participation may, in fact, frustrate employees. Their programs designed to increase the employee's identification with his job and with his company may actually decrease his sense of identification.

Programs that attempt to teach basic economics and the importance of cost-cutting and profit making may discourage, frustrate and indeed insult some employees. Leadership training (of the traditional classroom variety) tends to increase the foreman's internal tension, his feeling of hostility toward management and his sense of separateness from the organization. Many management performance reviews, at best, tend to create dependence of the subordinate upon the superior; at worst they breed an incipient conformity. Coaching, as typically carried out by many top managements, tends to block self-development and increase "image development." Executive-development programs can intensify the illness of a corporation by providing a rationalization for the organization not to face its own problems.

In short, many personnel programs simply reinforce the causes of a company's personnel problems and increase an employee's feelings of dependence and conformity. At best, personnel programs protect employees from the tensions of self-realization and responsibility while hopefully "making him happy."

The painstaking statistical research conducted by many personnel men may merely prolong the ineffectiveness of these programs. For one consequence of this research is to eliminate the bias of the human element.

One company's personnel researcher, for instance, not long ago sought to improve his company's rating system by evading the fact that different supervisors used different "internal scales" to measure people. The personnel man suggested a quartile system by which the supervisor had to place 25% of his group in each quartile. Statistically, this makes sense, for it minimizes the differences among supervisors. But it also protects the supervisor from having to come to grip with their biases.

Wage and salary programs tend to reward the average, penalize the outstanding (by not rewarding him adequately) and support the less competent. Selection programs may tend to select accurately for the first job but are not designed to say much about an employee's long-range potential for commitment, responsibility and contribution to organization growth. Top-management training of the classroom variety tends to skirt these human problems and protect the executives from having to face them. All these conditions build up the internal forces that have made personnel administration a defensive operation. Programs are continually developed that are safe and do not rock the boat.

Indeed, some personnel programs that have been cited as examples of "the finest" by such organizations as the American Management Association and the National Industrial Conference Board have this defensiveness built into them. Not long ago the top executives of one large corporation whose personnel program had received just such accolades made a thorough examination of their program, and reached a disturbing conclusion. They knew that the major characteristics of their organization's future were change and growth. Yet they found that their personnel policies were geared to maintaining the status quo. They began to realize that their personnel policies had done precious little to prepare the employees to participate fully in the organization's growth. Nor were their first- and middle-line management any better prepared. The corporation clearly was likely to explode with personnel problems.

Unprepared for change

Another of America's industrial giants recently found that its employees "walked" in the direction of an extremely militant union, while at the same time the very same employees reported that they were receiving excellent wages and benefits. An analysis suggested one of the major problems was the company's personnel philosophy of "taking care of the workers" and protecting them from stresses, strains and pressures.

Finally, it became apparent that the company could not survive unless it made some dramatic changes, including deep cuts in costs. Neither employees nor management were prepared for such actions, and both groups found it difficult to adapt to the new stress. Management defended itself by being unexpectedly severe and harsh.

The employees responded similarly. Again, it makes clear that protective and defensive personnel policies are not enough, for they will not support growth and development.

And that is why a new era in personnel administration is beginning. We are learning that man is free when he is responsible. Making people "happy" or "secure" will no longer be the main philosophy.

Human productivity and growth on the one hand and the idea of pleasure and happiness on the other are not necessarily correlated. To emphasize happiness and pleasure is to overlook the enormous significance of tension for self-realization. And to meet this need I believe that human relations policies will need to be significantly shifted.

The policies of the future will have to emphasize internal commitment, self-responsibility and productiveness. The policy makers must assume that individuals are but one part of the organization and that their importance varies under different conditions. They must also realize that no one can develop anyone else except himself; that if the door to development is locked, it is locked from the inside. Finally, they must assume that the objective of executive development is to help the executive become more aware and accepting of himself and others.

Healthy human beings realize that the objectives for which corporations are created require cooperative effort. They are willing to give of themselves in order to maintain the organization, so as to achieve its (and their) goals.

The over-all objective of the personnel program of the future will be to enhance the "human" effectiveness of the organization so that it can solve any problem over which it has control.

The first step in this process is to diagnose the "human health" of the organization. We are learning that the diagnosis must go beyond the morale survey with its compilation of columns of figures representing how employees feel and what their attitudes are toward various aspects of the organization. The diagnostic methods, if they are to be of help, must capture the complexity of the organization's makeup, indicate the major and the minor factors and at least hypothesize the probable causal connections among them. The diagnostic and research skills involved are complex and difficult, but they can be learned. And they represent one area in which personnel teams will have to be competent.

Another kind of competence that will be needed is the ability to help an organization unfreeze itself and to grow and improve. Implicit in this are the security, confidence and courage to experiment with new ideas.

Flexibility, endurance and a high degree of cohesiveness are necessary if the organization is to cope with the confusion, tension, pressure and pain that usually accompany organizational changes. And by cohesiveness, I do not mean that people must like one another. The deepest and most lasting cohesiveness among individuals is based upon human relationships that permit and encourage each individual to express and realize his potential. Cohesiveness is based more on shared responsibilities than on the compulsion to like and be liked.

Not for outsiders

These factors cannot be manufactured, delegated, ordered, bought or issued to the organization. They must be developed from within. For an outside consultant usually "operates" on a corporation. Through his own skill and techniques he is able to get the company to improve itself without the necessity for top management to understand fully or control the processes of organizational change. And so the company is left increasingly dependent upon the consultant for further change.

Effective organizational development cannot be evaluated or justified by determining whether the desired goal has been reached. The processes by which a change is made must also increase the organization's effectiveness to solve problems through its own internal commitment and administrative competence.

Questions

1. What does the author feel will be the major area of emphasis in the "new era"? How may this emphasis affect personnel policies and practices?
2. What conflict does he feel exists between the requirements of an organization and the behavior of the personnel within it?
3. In what ways does Argyris feel that present day communication programs may tend to increase employee mistrust of management practices? Do you agree or disagree with his position?
4. How does the author feel that cooperative effort and cohesiveness within an organization can best be achieved?
5. To what extent do you agree and/or disagree with this article?

8—THE FRAYING WHITE COLLAR *

Judson Gooding

There are many groups undergoing transitions in America today, but none more rapidly than the country's white-collar workers. The strong mutual loyalty that has traditionally bound white-collar workers and management is rapidly eroding. These workers—clerks, accountants, bookkeepers, secretaries—were once the elite at every plant, the educated people who worked alongside the bosses and were happily convinced that they made all the wheels go around. Now there are platoons of them instead of a privileged few, and instead of talking to the boss they generally communicate with a machine.

The jobs are sometimes broken down into fragmented components, either for the convenience of those machines or so that the poorly educated graduates of big-city high schools can perform them. Despite their air-conditioned, carpeted offices—certainly the most lavish working quarters ever provided employees in mass—the sense of distance and dissociation from management has increased sharply, and the younger white collars are swept by some of the same restlessness and cynicism that afflict their classmates who opted for manual labor (see "Blue-Collar Blues on the Assembly Line," July). All too often, the keypunch operator spends the workday feeling more like an automaton than a human being.

The new masses

The white-collar worker is caught in the middle—and indeed is chief actor—in one of the most basic of the trends now sweeping the country. This is the trend toward a predominantly service economy. Already, the clerk rather than the man on the production line is the typical American worker. Under the broad definition of the white-collar category used by the Bureau of Labor Statistics—covering the whole sweep from professional and managerial through clerical and sales workers—the white collars outnumber blue-collar

* From *Fortune*, Vol. 82, No. 6 (December, 1970), pp. 78-81, 108-109. Reprinted with permission.

workers by 38 million to 28 million. In this article, *Fortune* has excluded supervisors, proprietors, and degree-holding technicians and engineers—workers with authority over other employees or for committing company funds—and even by this narrower definition white-collar workers total about 19 million. Until the economy slowed down last winter, employment in these categories had been increasing by an average of 3 percent a year.

Now that they are needed by the millions, white-collar workers are also expendable. The lifetime sinecure is rapidly disappearing as management experts figure out yet another way to streamline the job, get in another machine, and cut down overhead. William Gomberg, a former union official and now a professor at the Wharton School of Finance, says, "White collars are where administrators look to save money, for places to fire. It's the law of supply and demand. Once you're in big supply, you're a bum." When an unprofitable division is closed or a big contract slips away to a competitor, layoffs are measured in thousands, and the workers usually hit the streets with no more severance benefits than management feels willing and able to provide.

Member firms of the New York Stock Exchange cut payrolls from 101,314 to 86,123 nonsales employees during the first seven months of 1970—a deep slash of 15,191 persons. In just one grim week in October, Sylvania Electric Products, Inc., announced it was discontinuing semiconductor operations and the Celanese Corp. disclosed it was cutting 2,000 employees, most of them white-collar. Steel companies are reducing office staffs by the thousands. The unemployment rate for white-collar workers, "usually somewhat more impervious to a general rise in joblessness," according to the Bureau of Labor Statistics, rose a full percentage point during the first nine months of this year from 2.1 to 3.1 percent.

The pay advantage white-collar workers enjoyed when they were a select group has been eroded along with their job security. Until 1920 white-collar workers got between 50 and 100 percent more pay than blue-collar workers, but by 1952 they had fallen 4 percent behind. The pay gap has grown steadily since then. Raises for clerical workers came to 21.9 percent from 1964 to 1969, while factory workers, already ahead, got raises adding up to 26.2 percent. Production workers made an average of $130 a week last year and clerical workers only $105. A Penn Central station agent with twenty-four years of service complains: "New cleaning men make more than I do, counting overtime, although I'm in charge of running the station and handling the cash." Many white-collar workers feel their status has declined as well. A twenty-nine-year-old secretary in a government agency in Washington says, "We're lower people. Down at our level we're peons, that's what they think of you."

To the labor unions that specialize in white-collar organizing, this is a situation that seems ripe with promise. From 1958 to 1968, the number of white-collar union members increased 46 percent to 3,179,000. With white-collar employment increasing over the long range and factory employment stagnant or declining, union leaders see their white-collar drive as the battle for the future—some would say even for survival.

But the unions are not likely to have it all their own way. There is a countertrend working, too. These white-collar masses are, after all, sharing the same quarters with management; their grievances and problems, more often than not, are on conspicuous display. Precisely because most white-collar jobs have never been frozen by union-shop rules, management has maximum flexibility for imaginative improvements. There is additional opportunity for management in the fact that three-fifths of the lower-level white-collar jobs are held by women. Since women quit to get married or have babies, turnover runs to 30 percent or more in big white-collar operations such as insurance companies and banks. While the turnover is a major headache, it also provides natural opportunities for rapid promotion. Enlightened managers are able to move employees out of those dull, entry-level jobs quite rapidly.

The company in loco parentis

"Those companies that have thought in terms of careers, that have counselors available, that practice job posting, that have thought about progression—they seem to be on the right track," says Fred K. Foulkes, an assistant professor and specialist in job improvement at the Harvard Graduate School of Business Administration. And with a little imagination and effort, the content of almost any job can be improved (see "It Pays to Wake Up the Blue-Collar Worker," September). Even now, the techniques of job enrichment are much more often found in white-collar operations than on factory floors. As union organizers continue to make headway among white-collar workers, managers can be expected to intensify these efforts to retain control of their own staffs through improving the jobs. For management, too, the issue is a vital one.

Generalizations about low-level white-collar workers are difficult because there are pronounced differences not only between the older and younger ones but also between those in harsh environments, like New York City or Los Angeles, and gentler settings, like Atlanta and Minneapolis. Both age and geography affect attitudes. Because many of them got their jobs when work was hard to find, the older workers feel more obligated to their employers. The younger ones expect a job as a matter of course and are far more demanding about working conditions. In the smaller cities, younger workers conform more readily, the men tend to have short hair, and girls dress less eccentrically. In a city like Minneapolis where only 4 percent of the population is black, there are fewer tensions arising from demands for equal opportunity. There is less militancy on other subjects as well, and young workers tend to accept management dictates more readily. Because of these generational and regional differences, inconsistencies abound.

But in the transaction between management and worker, two developments are evident. Old-fashioned loyalty is declining. A twenty-eight-year-old secretary in a New York City bank said, "Loyalty? That's kind of archaic. It's really if you like your job, if it's what you need and what you want. The job is not loyal to you." At the same time, the younger workers expect extensive services from their employers. They want the customary advantages like good vacations, health coverage, and a low-priced company cafeteria; but beyond these they want company-paid training given on company time, medical care at the office, even counseling. This is especially true in the big urban centers where many beginning jobs are filled by recruits from the ghettos. To help young men and women who have substandard educations and have never learned office behavior, some major employers even offer lessons in comportment and suggestions on dress and personal habits. The extent to which some employees rely on their companies became clear when liberalization of New York's abortion laws was announced and the medical department of a big company received a telephone call the same day asking if an employee could get an abortion at the office.

Robert Feagles, senior vice president for personnel of the First National City Bank, says that in the 1950's employees resisted and resented any intrusion on their lives by the company that employed them. He explains: "Then, it was 'Stay out of my life.' Now, with the sad state of society, with family, churches, and the schools often disqualified, the job and the employer become central. The employer is almost the last resort now. The company is the only entity that is not disqualified."

The company as schoolmaster

The new employees, while expecting much more, often bring much less in the way of work experience, qualifications, even education. In Minneapolis, C. Marvin Mandery, General Mills corporate personnel manager, says much more company training is required for entry-level clerical employees today because "in addition to teaching them their jobs, there is the whole business of teaching them to work." For many, he says, "this is their first exposure to a work situation, where in the past most kids had worked before graduation and their families had expected them to take more responsibility at home."

The need to train new employees is even more pressing in major urban centers like New York. The First National City Bank finds it necessary to run a school system as large as those of some small towns, with more than 6,000 employees taking courses each year at a new complex in Queens. The center has a staff of sixty-five; and its elaborate equipment, worth $800,000, includes teaching machines, closed-circuit television, and video tape recorders. "The city schools are not preparing young people in New York for the business world, either in the use of business equipment or in attitude," says Norman Willard Jr., First National City's vice president for training. "Some problems of employee performance—error rate, promptness, and the like—we attribute to the deterioration of the school system. The reading level of the new employees is down, and although this should not be a bank problem, we have to run remedial reading courses."

But imaginative companies are making a virtue of necessity and are using their schools to help attract and hold young workers. If the company school, which seems well on the way to becoming a permanent feature of the American corporation, is a reflection on the state of public education, it is also a tribute to management ingenuity. First National City has already moved dozens of its ghetto recruits up the ladder to teller positions and has found them to be loyal and well-motivated employees.

At the Equitable Life Assurance Society in New York, Edward Robie, senior vice president for personnel, says company training was crucial in making a smooth transition to the computer. Electronic data processing represented "a tremendous technical change in our business, comparable in impact to what happened in industry around the turn of the century when assembly lines were started. Now we grow our own programmers." Alma Sykes, a nineteen-year-old receptionist at Equitable who has combined mornings of classes and afternoons of on-the-job training, explains that she came to Equitable because "I wanted to improve myself. I heard about the training program here, and I heard it was a good place to work. It is."

An antidote for frustration

The company school is only one of the tools available for turning on the white-collar worker. Promotion is another, and it is a powerful instrument indeed. Promotion simultaneously improves income, enhances security, and raises status, and promotion is what the younger white-collar workers talk about and dream of more than anything else. Lawrence Porto, nineteen, who started as a check sorter at First National City Bank two years ago, says, "I found there was more to the job than I saw at first, more opportunity, after I was there a while, and talked to people, saw how they progressed. In six months I went up to clearance clerk. There was more money and responsibility. That was when I started liking it and planned to stay."

Conversely, if promotions are not readily forthcoming, frustration develops quickly. Federal office managers and supervisors who were interviewed agreed that promotion policy is the biggest single cause of discontent in federal government jobs. After less than two years with the National Aeronautics and Space Administration in Washington, George Hamilton, twenty-seven, is chafing at the civil-service rules that prevent his moving up. He is a communication-equipment operator, which is considered a clerical job. He believes he deserves a higher classification and more pay, but says, "The civil service does not classify the job as technical. I can't get more money unless the job is reclassified." He likes everything about his job except the feeling of being blocked off from moving up.

"Young people coming in aren't going to sit around and wait for promotions," says Mrs. Doris Wilkins, twenty-eight, a wages-and-hours assistant in the Department of Labor, with eleven years of government service. "They have younger ideas, a different approach. There's a lot of job hopping in the lower grades to get more money.

It's the only way to get a promotion. It causes a tremendous amount of moves back and forth. The supervisors lose a lot of good employees and they keep on having vacancies."

All too often, the supervisors themselves are impediments to promotion. A reservation sales agent at American Airlines in Los Angeles, Mrs. Adele Velasquez, twenty-three, describes the problem. "Supervisors don't push people upward because of a fear of losing the best people. There is a delaying tactic, which is selfish, to protect themselves. If the group looks good, they look good."

Robie at Equitable terms this behavior "feudal parochialism." He suggests that companies should build some kind of reward into the system for promoting good workers. "As it is, the supervisor is penalized by losing good workers. Short-term pressures on management restrict the success of the promotion policy." Equitable has designated promotion specialists who are continually on the lookout for good openings and good people to put into them. The company also tries to keep its managers under pressure to release good workers to other departments for advancement, unless they have suitable opportunities for them. Parochialism is self-defeating, as Cynthia Crotty, twenty, a typist at Equitable, points out. "If the person is not satisfied, he probably won't stay, and the supervisor will lose him anyway. The more good people he can promote, the more it's to his credit—it just shows he has trained people well."

Mobility from both ends of the telescope

Atlanta's Retail Credit Co. has made job advancement the central tenet of its corporate philosophy—perhaps because its president, W. Lee Burge, worked his way up from a beginning job in Retail Credit's mail room starting in 1936. He now directs 13,000 clerical, administrative, and field employees in the largest credit-information business in the country (1969 revenues: $161 million). "Our objective," he says, "is to provide good careers and challenge individual abilities." Jim Slade, a thirty-year-old computer programmer who learned his job during the two years he has worked at Retail Credit, sees things in much the same way, looking at the company from the other end of the telescope. He says he expects to be in management within ten years, likes the emphasis on promotions from within, and believes Retail Credit is an outstanding company because it has "outstanding management people—that's because they train their own."

In attempting to engage the interest of white-collar workers, management has a good deal more flexibility than in factories, where the pace is inexorably set by production lines or quota requirements. Office work can often be done at a more individual pace. Hours can be shortened or lengthened, the four-day week can be introduced, and, as noted, the high turnover provides many openings for promotions.

Equitable used its managerial flexibility to conduct a trial of the four-day work week at one of its New York data processing offices. The experiment produced a drop in error rates of 20.6 percent, with no decrease in production. Employee satisfaction with work hours improved from 53 percent before the trial to 86 percent, and of course the company obtained more efficient use of equipment because of the longer work hours each day.

Any job can be improved

Many of the techniques used to enrich white-collar jobs are similar in principle to those used with blue-collar jobs. The aim is to increase the worker's role in planning the work, increase his responsibility for its execution, and to broaden his job so that he has a complete unit of work rather than a fragment.

American Telephone & Telegraph has perhaps the most extensive experience in the United States in improving white-collar jobs. At the urging of the company's personnel director for manpower utilization, Robert N. Ford, managers all over the country have initiated hundreds of job improvements, all based on concepts of Dr. Frederick Herzberg of Case Western Reserve University, who teaches that the job content, the "work itself," is the most important factor in employee morale. In one exercise, which is still in progress at Pacific Telephone in Los Angeles, commercial-division manager J. M. Suozzo increased the responsibility given to service representatives and their authority to make decisions. He brought turnover down from 62 percent for 1969 to 48 percent for the first half of 1970. This meant better service for customers and a saving of $3,800 in training cost for each service representative who was retained instead of replaced. The saving came to $332,000 for the first eight months of this year. By promoting operators more rapidly to service representative, Pacific Telephone cut turnover among operators in one division by 41 percent.

Service representative Mrs. Marsha Lang, twenty-three, said she liked the Los Angeles office changes because before "you didn't know how well you were doing. I didn't understand the changes at first, but now I know it is a program for developing decision-making abilities. The supervisors are letting out more line and giving more freedom." After all, she said, with a touch of pride, "we are the persons between the customer and the computer."

In St. Louis, American Airlines improved the morale, and the commitment, of twenty of its agents who handle the boarding of flights. In so doing, the airline illustrated that improvements can be made in almost any sort of white-collar job. Two agents had been assigned to each flight, under direction of a supervisor. Now one of the agents is designated "flight coordinator" and is responsible for getting the flight into the air, without need to clear any but the most unusual decisions. One flight coordinator delayed a take-off to accommodate twenty passengers from a competing airline that had canceled its flight, judging that the additional revenues would justify the delay. He got the request five minutes before scheduled take-off, held the flight until the twenty were aboard—and was complimented for his decision. An agent summed up his reaction to the job change by saying, "I have more confidence in myself now that I see the confidence management has in me."

The deterioration in white-collar morale is not just a passing phenomenon born of the economic downturn. Opinion Research Corp. of Princeton, New Jersey, has charted responses to questions on job satisfaction from more than 25,000 white-collar employees in eighty-eight major American companies over the years since 1955. Using attitudes during the 1955-65 period as a base, Opinion Research Vice President Alfred Vogel finds that job satisfaction has declined since 1965 in several crucial areas.

Worker satisfaction with job security has dropped by 17 percent and with pay by 45 percent. There has been a 30 percent decline in the belief that companies deal fairly without playing favorites, and a 39 percent decline in the belief that the company will do something about individual problems and complaints. Some of the sharpest declines in white-collar ratings show up on company communication efforts. Workers feel increasingly cut off. But employees rate their immediate supervisors better by 23 percent than in the earlier period for listening to what employees say. They downgrade supervisors by

19 percent on taking action on worker complaints—action that is often beyond a supervisor's power.

"The most neglected group"

Improvement experiments like those at A. T. & T., Equitable, and American Airlines are still the exceptions in white-collar jobs. The majority of such jobs are standing still, if not deteriorating, in relative pay, in status, and in worker satisfaction. Professor Eric Trist of the Wharton School of Finance, a specialist in the impact of technology on social systems, calls white-collar workers "the most neglected group in the United States." He points out that "the skilled blue-collar worker is a professional and does unprogrammed work. He is getting more and more money and working less and less hours. He's got it made."

Enlightened managers already proclaim that a central concern in any enterprise must be to provide fulfilling, satisfying work for the people who spend so much of their lives inside company walls. More than economic needs must be met. The importance of this concept is reinforced by the fact that the job, dull as it may be, is the most active involvement that many white-collar workers have with the world around them. Few of those interviewed by *Fortune* claimed much interest in reading, in music, in any cultural activity.

There is a terrible, striking contrast between the fun-filled, mobile existence of the young opulents of America as shown on television, and the narrow, constricting, un-fun existence that is the lot of most white-collar workers at the lower job levels. You can't buy much of what television is selling on the salaries these young workers earn; about all you do is stay at home watching those good things go by on the screen. The result is frustration, sometimes bitterness, even anger. Workers in this stratum cannot but notice that the federally defined poverty standard is climbing toward their level from below, while above them the salary needed to enjoy the glittery aspects of American life soars ever higher, further and further out of reach. For many, the office is the real world, not only a livelihood but a focus of existence. They expect it, somehow, to be more than it has yet become.

Questions

1. In what respects have many white-collar workers been affected adversely by the results of technological progress?

2. What are some of the conditions that serve to encourage the unionization of white-collar workers? That discourage it?
3. Do current trends encourage the employer to become involved to a greater or lesser extent in the personal lives of employees?
4. What are some of the barriers encountered by white-collar workers attempting to achieve promotions?
5. In what ways have technological progress made the job of the white-collar worker less desirable?

9—ACCOUNTING FOR HUMAN RESOURCES *

R. Lee Brummet, William C. Pyle, and Eric G. Flamholtz

One of the important current developments in modern organizations is the refinement of measurement techniques and quantitative analyses which contribute to a scientific approach to management. Financial planning and control practices and accounting measurements are recognized as critical for the successful operation of a large organization. Yet accountants continue to ignore one of the most important resources of an organization—its *people*.

A forthright attack on this problem is now underway in an effect to develop concepts and techniques basic to *human resource accounting*. New approaches, new viewpoints, and new understandings are necessary but the potential is great. Personnel, financial, and general managers alike are reacting enthusiastically.

Human resource accounting is *the process of identifying, measuring, and communicating information about human resources to facilitate effective management within an organization*. In a particular organization, it involves measurements of the acquisition cost, replacement cost, and economic value of human resources, and their changes through time.

The Need for Human Resource Accounting

Business managers do not have adequate tools for evaluating changes in the human assets of their organizations, for measuring the effectiveness of human asset investments, or for optimizing in the allocation of human resources. Managers make decisions which have important ramifications with regard to human resources without information and analytical tools relevant to such decisions. Decisions involving recruiting, hiring, training, supervising, evaluating, rewarding, developing, promoting, transferring, replacing, and discharging people are made almost continuously. Persons within an organization often react to perceived changes of management behavior

* From *Michigan Business Review*, Vol. 20, No. 2 (March, 1968), pp. 20-25. Reprinted with permission.

by increasing or diminishing their performance. However, these perceptions and resultant attitudinal patterns are not being measured and communicated to improve managerial effectiveness. The aim of human resource accounting is to satisfy these needs.

In the management of nonhuman resources, it is accepted practice for the firm to estimate the acquisition costs and relative values of alternative investments which might be chosen to achieve the objectives of the enterprise. One machine, for instance, may require an outlay of $120,000 with an estimated return of 25 percent while another may require an investment of $75,000 and return 18 percent. Once a particular investment decision has been made, managers are held responsible for effective utilization and maintenance of the resources placed under their control.

Unfortunately, this level of sophistication has not been extended to the human resource management process. Outlays which are intended as *investments* in human resources are not recognized as such by accountants despite the fact that expenditures in recruiting, hiring, training, developing, and organizing employees into effective work groups provide *long-term* benefits to the organization. The failure to recognize these investments as organizational *assets* represents a serious void in the information to be used in making rational management decisions.

Investments are typically made in training production workers and sending managers to executive development programs without a systematic evaluation of the expected benefits to be derived in relation to costs to be incurred. Similarly, outlays are made for projects that require new investments in nonhuman as well as human resources. A firm may intend, for example, to increase its capacity by 40 percent to meet a rising sales demand. Yet while managers can identify the physical assets which furnish its present capacity and can project what new investments will be required in plant, machinery and equipment, they may not be able to determine what new investments will be required in human resources. Although it may be known that the production force will have to be increased by 20 percent, it may not be known what it will cost to recruit, hire, train, and organize these workers into a viable unit.

Conventional accounting systems fail to provide information to enable management to determine whether investments in human resources are being maintained and effectively utilized. Managers' decisions may range from those which are direct attempts to enhance the value of the firm's human resources to those which systematically liquidate them in order to show greater short-run profits.[1] In any case, these conditions are not revealed in conventional accounting reports. Management has no means of either measuring its investment in human resources or of determining whether their value is increasing, decreasing, or remaining unchanged.

Further, management does not know whether the firm is allocating its human resources in the most profitable way. For example, a decision to utilize the firm's research staff on one of a number of projects should consider the firm's investment in its researchers, and the project should be expected to generate a return on this investment as well as its physical assets. Unfortunately, management has no method for determining the yield or return the firm's human assets are contributing to earnings.

As the magnitude of financial commitments of organizations to acquisition, improvement, and retention of human resources increases, an assessment of this investment increases in importance. A growing number of corporate managers are becoming aware that their present accounting systems are not adequately meeting their need for such information.

Neglect of Human Resource Accounting

There are several reasons why outlays made as investments in human resources have been traditionally treated as "consumption" rather than "capital" expenditures by economists, and as "expenses" rather than "assets" by accountants. Investments in people have seemed more tenuous than investments in physical assets, and accountants have chosen to ignore their investment character. This treatment is also attributable, in part, to the difficulty of distinguishing between the future benefits of the outlays made for recruiting, hiring, training, and developing people and the portion consumed currently. Further, "people" do not fit intuitive notions of the nature of assets. "Assets" are "things of value owned," according to conventional accounting; and our culture has placed constraints on willingness to imply ownership or to place a monetary value on people. People cannot be "bought" and "sold" as is possible with inanimate objects.

It is important to note that investments in human resources have been treated as expenses rather than assets not because they fail to

---

[1] Rensis Likert, *The Human Organization: Its Management and Value* (New York: McGraw-Hill, 1967), pp. 101-115.

meet the criteria for classification as assets, but because of a conventional bias which limits the concept of "assets" to tangible things. With some exceptions, accounting has reflected a hesitancy to treat "intangibles" as assets, and human resources which are subject to only limited control by managers carry a connotation lacking in tangible substance.

Research in Human Resource Accounting

Research in human resource accounting focuses upon three broad objectives:

1. The development of a human resource accounting system;
2. The formulation of a body of generalizations about the ways in which information provided by a human resource accounting system can be used; and
3. The development of a set of generalizations about the behavioral impact of a human resource accounting system on people.

The initial phase of research involves the development of a human resource accounting system itself. This suggests the need for a body of theory or generalizations for identifying and tracing human resource costs, a set of guidelines for accounting for these costs as assets and expenses, a set of accounts for classifying and reclassifying human resource costs, statements for reporting, and tools for the analysis and interpretation of such statements. Development of human resource accounting systems in a number of different firms will provide the means for accomplishing these objectives while providing useful data for each participating company.

Once human resource accounting systems have been designed and installed in a number of organizations, the second stage of the research may be undertaken. This phase will involve monitoring the way in which the system is being used in order to increase knowledge of the application of the system. Although a number of potential uses of the system are currently anticipated, more will be learned about the specific ways in which human resources information may be used in decision-models. Simulations may be conducted to determine to what extent decisions involving people will be modified if information about human resources is added to decision-models. New tools will be developed for use in decisions concerning human resources. Systematic decision-models may be developed to provide a human-capital budgeting system for use in evaluating alternative investment opportunities in human resources.

The third phase of the proposed research will be aimed at developing a body of generalizations about the behavioral impact of a human resource accounting system on people. The basic thrust of this research will be to determine how people react to being viewed as assets or resources of an organization with a monetary figure designated as the firm's investment in them, whether knowledge of the firm's investment in an individual will affect an individual's attitude toward the organization or his motivation and productivity, and the ways in which knowledge of differential investments in people will affect relationships among peers and between superiors and subordinates.

Conceptual Foundations of a Human Resource Accounting System

For various conceptual purposes, it is useful to view human resources in two broad categories—those which are internal to the firm and those which are external. Internal human resources include individual employees and groups of employees. External human resources include the firm's customers, major suppliers and distributors, and stockholders. The firm invests in each of these groups with the expectation of deriving future benefits in return. Investments are made in training employees and organizing effective work groups, in developing product recognition, acceptance and insistence by customers, in building relationships with suppliers or distributors, and in developing and maintaining stockholder loyalty. At present, research efforts are being focused upon the firm's internal human resources. In a particular organization, the foundations of a human resource accounting system rest upon measurement of the acquisition cost, replacement cost, and economic value of human resources, and their changes through time.

The acquisition cost of human resources

Human resource accounting will make it possible for a company to determine the magnitude of its *investment in people*. Since human as well as physical resources are used in generating income, they should be included in the asset base used to calculate rates of return on investment. Knowledge of the investment in human resources will also serve as a basis for evaluating returns from particular investments in human resources. For example, many firms now invest heavily in formal training programs but have no means for evaluating their payoff or return on investment. In addition, the firm's investment in its human organization may exceed that of all its other assets combined, and while efforts are made to maintain the future service potential of physical assets, deterioration of human assets may go unnoticed. Knowledge of the amount of the firm's investment in human resources should encourage managers to protect this investment as they would their tangible physical assets. Losses from turnover will be quantified to indicate costs to the firm.

The replacement cost of human resources

Knowledge of the cost of replacing the firm's existing human organization may also suggest to management the importance of maintaining human resources. In addition, replacement cost of particular human resources may be helpful in making decisions as to resource utilization or planning for replacement of human resources. For example, in planning for replacement of human resources it may be helpful to know what it would cost to recruit, hire, and train managers to their present level of familiarity and proficiency. If standard costs of recruiting, hiring, familiarizing, and training individuals are made available, the personnel function may find this information helpful in planning and budgeting for replacement and development of human resources.

The economic value of human resources

Human resource accounting should also provide information useful in comparing the value of human resources with the cost incurred in acquiring them. It should facilitate the evaluation of alternative strategies in terms of their impacts on the value of human resources and, in turn, upon future earnings.

Estimates of the current value of the firm's human resources might be developed in several ways. The results from one approach can serve as a check on those obtained from others. One method is to undertake periodic measurements of the behavior of managers and supervisors, their level of technical proficiency, the resulting motivations, loyalties, and behavior of subordinates, and the communication, decision-making, and control processes of the divisions or profit-centers included in the study. Statistical analysis of variations in leadership proficiency levels, motivational, attitudinal, behavioral, and performance variables may yield estimates of expected future returns, which can be discounted to determine the present value of human resources. A simplified illustration of these concepts and their interrelationship is shown in Exhibit I. The underlying theory which is the basis for this approach is presented in Likert's *The Human Organization: Its Management and Value.*

EXHIBIT I. DETERMINING THE VALUE OF HUMAN RESOURCES

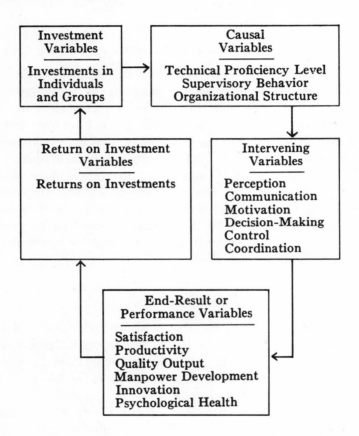

An alternative method of valuing the firm's human resources might involve the discounting of forecasted earnings to determine the present value of the firm, and then the allocation of a portion of this value to human resources according to their relative contribution using the ratio of investment in human resources to total resources. Other possibilities include the use of goodwill valuations from capitalized differential earning power, or capitalized wage and salary payments adjusted for relative efficiency,[2] or by managerial estimates of replacement cost.[3]

Trends in the value of human resources should also be useful as a measure of managerial effectiveness. They should provide an additional measurement to supplement "net income" as an indicator of management performance.

Research in Progress

Since October, 1966, the authors have been engaged, along with executives of the R. G. Barry Corporation,[4] in the development of what is believed to be the first human resource accounting system. This system of accounting for investments in managers was put into operation on January 1, 1968. The Barry Corporation's 1,100 employees manufacture a variety of personal comfort items, including foam-cushioned slippers, chair pads, robes, and other leisure wear, which are marketed in department stores and other retail outlets under brand names such as Angel Treds, Dearfoams, Kush-ons, and Wrap-sak. The corporate headquarters and four production facilities are in Columbus, Ohio. Several other plants, warehouses, and sales offices are located elsewhere. The firm has expanded from a sales volume of about $5½ million in 1962 to approximately $13 million during 1966.

A simplified model of the human resource accounting system developed at the R. G. Barry Corporation is shown in Exhibit II. Its elements can be outlined briefly. First, an attempt has been made to identify human resource acquisition costs and separate them from other costs of the firm. Rules and procedures have been formulated to distinguish between the asset and expense components of human resource costs. Human resource investments are then classified into functional groupings called "functional asset accounts" such as recruiting and acquisition, training, and familiarization, which are, in turn, allocated to personalized accounts for individual employees. Rules and procedures have also been developed for measuring human asset expirations which are recorded as amortization or as losses.

---

[2] R. H. Hermanson, *Accounting for Human Assets* (East Lansing, Michigan: Michigan State University, Bureau of Business and Economic Research, 1964).

[3] Likert, *op. cit.*, p. 103.

[4] The management group from R. G. Barry actively engaged in this research effort include Gordon Zacks, President; Robert L. Woodruff, Jr., Director of Personnel; Edward Stan, Treasurer; Richard Burrell, Controller; and Peter Seldin, Personnel Assistant.

EXHIBIT II. R. G. BARRY CORPORATION HUMAN RESOURCE
ACCOUNTING SYSTEM

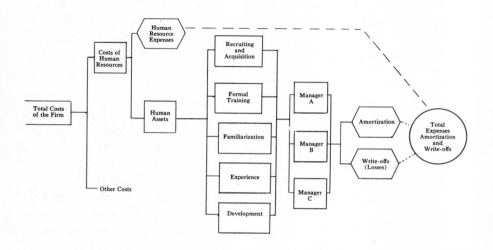

Beginning balances in personalized asset accounts have been established for some 90 members of management on a replacement cost basis. In the future, the system may be enlarged to include other levels in the organization.

The function of human resource accounting is to serve as a managerial tool. It aims to provide management with relevant, timely, quantifiable, and verifiable information about human resources to improve the quality of managerial decisions. Although familiar accounting concepts and terminology are involved, human resource accounting is not designed to be acceptable for use in published financial statements, or to be acceptable for tax purposes. Thus, the research is not constrained by law or accounting conventions. It requires no changes of laws nor any change in conventions of accounting as a reporting function in society. Its use may, as a practical matter, require some rethinking on the part of accountants. However, it can and should be accepted by accountants and financial officers of organizations because of its impressive possibilities.

Although the full development and acceptance of human resource accounting within organizations should not be expected within a few years, the relevance and usefulness of potential results of research in the field cannot be denied. We believe a useful start has been made.

Questions

1. Which of the costs of the personnel program may be regarded more correctly as capital investment?
2. What are some of the possible reasons why the concept of human resources previously has tended to be ignored and is still ignored by the managements of most organizations?
3. What are some of the possible advantages that can accrue from human resources accounting? How may it strengthen the role of the personnel department in the management of an organization?

CHAPTER 2

The Organization and its Human Resources

Since the human resources of an organization constitute one of its most valuable assets, considerable skill and effort should be involved in the recruitment and selection of these resources. In order to acquire the best possible human resources, efforts have been made to improve the various tools used in personnel selection, some of which will be discussed in this chapter. Even the best resources possible, however, cannot function effectively without good organization and management.

The article *Policy—A Vital Force* by Edward Schleh is concerned with a particularly important subject relating to the role of policy in management. It approaches the subject of policy from a practical operating standpoint. Examples relating to the misuse of policy and to the relationship of policy to organizational climate and behavior are cited.

The article titled *The Functional Concept in Organization* by Anderson is concerned with the subject of authority. This article points up some of the difficulties that exist in differentiating functional authority from staff authority within an organization. The difficulty of defining and making the distinction between such types of authority constitutes the basis for one of the major problems encountered by the personnel department in its relations with other departments. *Ground Rules for Using Committees* by Cyril O'Donnell which discusses the role of committees is included because of the important role that committees exercise in the management of personnel. It summarizes most effectively how committees can be used to an advantage within an organization.

In his article *Readying the Unready: Postindustrial Jobs,* Louis E. Davis introduces new concepts relating to job design which recognize the social and psychological considerations as well as those of an economic and technical nature which have been predominant in our industrial society thus far. These concepts, developed as the result of extensive research and experience by the author, seek to provide a solution to a serious problem that currently is confronting our social system and a solution involving a radical departure from those approaches to job structure that have been followed by organizations up to the present time.

The article titled *The Impact of Human Resources on Business* by Henry A. Singer discusses how personnel management can be "humanized" more by giving greater recognition to the nature and importance of the human resources of the organization. He suggests that people be encouraged to be more innovative, to realize their potential, and to identify their personal interests with the objectives of the organization by being given greater opportunity for participation in its operation.

The article *A Hard Look at the Selection Interview* by Vernon R. Taylor is concerned with the role of the selection interview in hiring personnel who are to comprise the human resources of the organization. This author has some very worthwhile criticism to offer concerning the validity of the information gained through the selection interview as it typically is conducted. His article points out why the interview tends to be such an invalid selection tool, and he offers suggestions for the improvement of selection practices.

The relative merits of another selection tool, the psychological test, is discussed in the article by Doppelt and Bennett. This article *Testing Job Applicants from Disadvantaged Groups* discusses the basis for the criticisms of cultural bias raised about tests and how this bias may be reduced. The article, however, attempts to place the role of tests in proper perspective with respect to the entire problem of coping with bias in the selection process. It also recognizes the fact that if an excess of applicants exists the rejection of a portion of them is inevitable.

The last article in this chapter *Red Flags Missed—Wrong Man Hired,* which is authored by Quinn G. McKay, discusses a major pitfall in employee selection, namely that caused by selective perception. This article discusses the causes for selective perception and how they may be avoided.

10—POLICY—A VITAL FORCE *

Edward C. Schleh

"It's policy." Too frequently, this frustrating statement is the prime rationale for ill-considered action. A clerk in a telephone company uses it to explain what appears to be an illogical charge for an extra phone. A department store employee applies it when refusing to give quick cash for a returned garment. A manager finds he is restricted by it in giving an increase to an unusual employee outside of the budgeted increases agreed to at the beginning of the year. A well-publicized decentralization program gets completely nullified by it, by the detailed reports spewed out by the computer to every executive's desk. The trouble is that policy too often is envisaged as control rather than as a vital stimulating force to get something done.

Why should we have policy in the first place? It should give broad direction and encourage employees to work in that direction. It has a two-way function, however. First of all, it should give employees maximum leeway all the way down the line so that they can take creative action to meet their problems. Secondly, policy should be looked at as a form of authority limitation. It really sets parameters on employee action. It therefore limits freedom—the reason why policy is often opposed internally. But some limits are necessary if an executive is to keep his whole company group directed toward the best total company accomplishment.

Policy should be minimal. It should be only that which is absolutely necessary to maintain a broad direction, or uniformity, if you will, in the company. It should encourage judgment rather than prevent it. As a case in point, a sales policy that requires all new dealers be home-office approved may be too tight. The policy may better state the kind of dealer organization to be built and allow some local decisions.

In general, policy should give "intent." This means that policy is ineffectual unless it gives the reasons why. Many policy statements miss this. Executives forget that policy should be aimed at getting

* From *Advanced Management Journal*, Vol. 33, No. 3 (July, 1968), pp. 26-30. Reprinted with permission.

employees to work in a certain direction within certain limitations. It does this best if it gives direction to their thinking and their action.

I recall a financial policy that required that all costs be charged to the department doing the work. It led to poor cooperation between manufacturing plants that had to do work for other plants. In a number of cases, one plant couldn't fully charge another for work requested. The true intent was to get accountability for all cost. If this had been clarified, accounting could have accommodated its charges much better.

Many policies remain after they have outlived their effectiveness. A number of policies should be in for only a period of time or until certain events take place. It is well to consider this period at the time the policy is set up and record it. Otherwise, policies tend to perpetuate themselves and stay in effect long after they should apply. The net effect is an unnecessary restriction on the action of people down the line.

When an executive sets a policy, he should at least set a date on which this policy should be reviewed to be certain that it is still applicable. As a matter of practice, all policies should be reviewed periodically, anyway. It is extraordinary how conditions change so that policies that were once important lose their value. I recall a single product line company that set a policy of functional organization. The company gradually changed so that it was in a dozen different businesses. The functional approach was a major hindrance to vitality in all lines.

Some companies are very proud of the fact that they do not have many written policies. Many policies are, therefore, unexplained. They feel that this gives men more leeway. In most cases they are deluding themselves. How does the man down the line operate without explained policy? He mentally formulates a policy by the action of executives. Since actions of executives vary considerably from day to day and month to month and between individuals, he finds it hard to get a clear-cut picture of policy in practice. In many cases, then, he tends to be super-careful, especially if he gets burned once by taking a direction and being questioned about it.

Unexplained policy usually dampens action. In addition, it may keep a manager from delegating soundly because he isn't sure. Policy is itself a type of authority definition. If it is not clear, it is difficult for a manager to set authority limits realistically for his people. There may always be some unexplained policy that will vitiate it. We have often seen a "wait and see" attitude develop when there is a lack of explained policy.

A form of authority

Policy is, in effect, a form of authority. Authority should normally be set up in light of objectives—what leeway does a man need to get certain accomplishments? An executive should, therefore, first clarify what he wants to achieve where the policy applies and the implications of this achievement. Failure to do this is one of the contributing factors to policy misdirection. Policy must fit the company needs.

For example, a firm may set up a policy of establishing product research or development in many fields. Such a policy must be predicated on an objective of growth in a variety of operations. In addition, the company must be prepared for variable modes of operation; different financial, manufacturing, and sales setups; and other related changes in policy. If it is not, such a policy is futile.

A related problem occurs when a company has different lines of products. Each may need different policies. Broad corporate policies may not apply. This is one of the basic problems of diverse companies or conglomerates. For example, one company had sold shelf items for some years. It then took on a line of products which developed to be a major product division focusing on the construction trade. Inventory policies, sales policies, research policies, all had to be different for this new division or it would be strapped. In a tight cost period, the corporation decided to cut inventories 30 percent. This worked all right with the shelf items. The division serving the construction trade lost 25 percent of its business in one year, however, due to poor service. This loss was greater than all the gains made by inventory reduction in the entire company.

There is always some debate as to who should set policy. There should be little question. It should be the top line man in the operation. However, this does not mean that he should "develop" policy. Policy should normally be developed and proposed as a normal responsibility by every function head and by every manager. After all, these people should know the need. Why do you have a Vice President of Industrial Relations if he is not an expert on industrial relations and can advise on sound policy in this field for the future?

The same applies to the Vice President of Manufacturing or to any other function head. Every expert should take the responsibility for proposing policy in his field and making sure that all policy in his field is vital. He should be made accountable for any crises that occur because of inadequate policy. For example, a Vice President of Sales who is made personally accountable for any crises that occur because of lack of sound sales policy is more inclined to forcefully propose a change in sales policy ahead of time.

How policy is regarded

People at different levels view policy differently. There is a tendency for people down the line to feel that policy is permanent. They look at it as a sort of "sacred cow" with the implication that good loyal employees do not question it—it is a touchy area. Very often executive action above tends to encourage this attitude. Just the suggestion that "You don't see the broad picture" can dry up suggestions. At other times people below get the idea that, if they suggest a change, executives feel that they are simply trying to duck some work or some accountability. This is a sure way to dry up creative proposals for changes in policy.

Since policy often is developed by central staff experts, people below may hesitate to challenge it because they have a high regard for these staff people. The result is a lack of feedup communication for changes in policy, a feedup which an executive desperately needs. The point should be clarified that it is the job of everyone down the line to question policy but live under it as long as it is in force. A Plant Manager in a multi-plant operation ought to be required to scrutinize any policy affecting his plant and make strong suggestions. He, in turn, should encourage his Superintendents to do likewise. The same is true in sales. District Managers who are close to the field problems ought to be encouraged to point up errors in policy that are restricting good sales action in the field.

Broad company policies should be differentiated from sectional, regional, or department policies. Company policies should extend only as far as you absolutely need a certain amount of uniformity throughout the operation. Beyond this, let the individual regions or sections set their own policies to fit their own needs. It is very difficult at best, particularly in a large company, to mastermind all the local requirements in a home office. There are different problems in different locations, or departments.

For example, in a company that was in the mill supply business, one region sold primarily to woodworking plants. Another region sold primarily to steel plants. Another sold to the automobile industry.

Another sold through jobbers entirely. The policies and approaches needed in these different regions were entirely different. Basic sales policy that had been developed in detail could not apply uniformly to all regions. It had to be broad.

Procedure

The difficulty with any policy is that behind each one is a hidden persuader—procedure. Many firms fail to differentiate between policy and procedure. Policy should give the broad intent, the broad parameters within which action should be taken. It should be the purpose of company procedure to merely set up those required procedures that are necessary to carry through the intent of the policy, no more. I should point out that both should be based on the requirements of the bottom level of the organization, whether it be in a plant, a sales department, or a laboratory. They should not unduly restrict action at this level to carry out its work.

Procedure decisions also should be pushed down as far as possible. At an upper level you should ordinarily have only those procedures that are absolutely necessary to maintain reasonable intent of the policy. The difficulty is that central staff people develop the procedure. In the desire to be completely in the clear, they have a strong tendency to develop procedures that are much more restrictive than was the original intent of the policy. A central staff man fears any later deviation which suggests an incomplete procedure.

For example, a central accounts receivable loan expert in a bank chain was unduly concerned about losses and set up tight controls. As a result, profit on the business dropped because the local bank managers were unduly restricted on loans. Central staff must be very carefully restrained from doing this. They should be forced to go down to the first level and prove that their procedures will not unduly restrict that level beyond the intent of the policy and be made accountable for this fact.

The problem is aggravated if a policy is a little vague. The staff man wants to be covered. He, therefore, sets up his procedures even tighter to be absolutely sure that nobody can criticize him afterwards that the procedure wasn't adequate. In a sense both policy and procedure are parameters, but procedure should only be a reflection of policy. It should not be a major addition to it. For example, an airline stated that they wanted to sell maximum seats and vaguely stressed service. Station agents gave little help to passengers on getting the best connections. Customers, therefore, got sour about the company's attitude on service.

If there is a clear policy system and a philosophy of procedure to go with it, people do not feel the need to work around the procedure to get a job done, as they often do. Many companies can be very thankful that conscientious foremen, for example, do constantly violate policies and procedures in order to run their operations. If they followed the book, many plants would come to a standstill. But this is a makeshift form of operation. You get better leadership at all levels if the parameters are clear and broad.

A major contribution that any executive can make to his organization is the sound development of policy. This can be either stimulating or restrictive, depending on the way he approaches it. Ordinarily, he must make sure of his broad objectives first. After that, the policy ought to be stated broadly by intent in light of these objectives. It is important that procedure that follows policy be carefully scrutinized to prevent any negative impact on the bottom level of the organization and possibly a change of policy intent.

A climate should be developed through an accountability system so that a sound feedup of criticism of policy and suggestion is encouraged from the very bottom all the way to the top. There is no top executive who can be so clairvoyant as to understand fully all the needs of the bottom of his organization. He must rely on this kind of communication.

If he approaches it well, policy can be a guiding action force instead of a restrictive control. Which it will be depends on the perception of the executive.

Questions

1. What are some of the requirements of an effective policy?
2. How can the restrictive influences of policies and procedures upon decision making at the lower levels in an organization be minimized?
3. In what respects do policies relate to and affect the exercise of authority?

11—THE FUNCTIONAL CONCEPT
IN ORGANIZATION *

E. H. Anderson

The functional concept in organization has been the subject of much discussion, much difference of opinion, and apparently, much misunderstanding. It is the purpose of this paper to bring the concept into sharper focus in the light of modern conditions and modern usage. In order to do this it is necessary first to re-examine the concept as it was developed originally, second to distinguish it from other concepts in organization, and finally to examine its present application with respect to several situations and types of activity.

The functional concept became the subject of critical study after it was developed into a plan or structure of relationships, usually known as a type of organization, by F. W. Taylor and called by him functional foremanship.[1] This so-called type of organization was adopted generally as an important feature of scientific management by Gilbreth, Gantt and other exponents of the scientific management movement during the early part of the present century. An important exception, however, was Harrington Emerson, who rejected the idea as being unworkable and offered in its stead the line-staff type. From a survey of current management literature, Emerson's plan has won out both in theory and in practice. In so doing, however, the line-staff concept has been so broadened and loosened that it has come to include many features of the functional concept. As a consequence, many writers and practitioners in describing their organization as line-staff fail to recognize the mixture of concepts with the result that their plans of organization are confusing to those who are trying to make them work. As they say, "why do they call this man a staff officer when everybody knows that he makes the decisions and that it is his word that counts? It seems at times that management almost abhors the concept but proceeds nevertheless to make use of it surreptitiously.

---

* From *Advanced Management*, Vol. 25, No. 10 (October, 1960), pp. 16-19. Reprinted with permission.
[1] F. W. Taylor, "Shop Management," *Scientific Management* (New York: Harper & Bros. Publishers, 1957), p. 99 ff.

Functionalization

Organizing according to functions usually leads to the division of a company's total activity into groups of activities having to do with production, sales, accounting, finance and possible others. These functions known usually as major functions may then be further divided into minor functions, such as purchasing, personnel, production control, plant maintenance, advertising, sales promotion, collecting, market analysis, auditing, costing, and so on. This basis of division is distinguished from other bases, such as product, process, equipment, location, shift, and certain characteristics of the personnel, e.g., age, sex, race, nationality, etc.

When these various functions are thus recognized and their activities separated from one another, they are usually organized to constitute departments and sub-departments and placed each under the control of a supervisor or departmental manager. The supervisor or manager is then customarily given full authority over the personnel of his department and held responsible for the accomplishment of the work and the objectives of his function for the benefit of the whole enterprise. This process of dividing the work of the enterprise into functions, sub-functions, and so on, is what is known as functionalization.

Functionalization means, therefore, functional division; it does not necessarily mean or imply the functional type of relationship established for purposes of supervision and control which is characteristic of the so-called functional type of organization. Both of these functional concepts, functional division and functional control, were contained in the plan developed by Taylor and known as functional foremanship. In this plan, the duties of the first or lowest rank of supervisors were differentiated according to what were recognized as the functions of the shop. Taylor applied the principle of functionalization in dividing up and delimiting the duties and responsibilities of his foreman (more appropriately, his assistant foreman). This step, however, is only half of what Taylor did and it is only half of what constitutes the functional type of relationship in organization.

Functional control

The other half of functional foremanship is contained in the peculiar relationship of supervisors or assistant foreman (called

functional foreman) to the workers, and vice versa. This relationship
is one in which each supervisor to whom a certain function is assigned has some authority over all subordinates who may be involved even partially with the execution of his function and, accordingly, one in which all such subordinates may be under the authority
and control of more than one of these supervisors at the same time.
This idea of giving two or more supervisors, each controlling a
different function of the enterprise, concurrent jurisdiction over
the same persons is the peculiar feature that has characterized and
distinguished the functional relationship in organization. The true
functional type of organization is, therefore, one containing both
functionalization, or functional division, and functional control, or
control by special functional supervisors who are given authority
for such a purpose over all subordinates in the organization.

Functional control consisting of supervisory authority limited to
a certain function but not limited to persons and the concomitant
responsibility of persons being made subordinate to two or more
such supervisors at the same time has been hard to comprehend and
often still harder to defend as a practical plan of organization. As
is usually said, it violates the principle of unity of command, it
causes a person to have to serve two masters, and it leads to conflicting loyalties and jurisdictional squabbles. Much of this criticism
is indeed true especially when the plan is not thoroughly understood
by all parties concerned and when it is not adequately implemented
by appropriate procedures, regulations and systems. These conditions, it may be noted, are to some extent true with respect to all
types of organization, but they are an absolute necessity for functional authority and control to operate successfully.[2]

Functional vs. line authority

The application of the functional relationship in supervision and
control throughout all ranks in an organization, as Taylor applied it
to foremanship, has been one of the most perplexing problems in
organizing. The essence of the problem lies in either doing away
with the line supervisors entirely or in somehow integrating functional officers, those with functional authority, with line officers,
those having full authority. It is usually felt that the line officer

---

[2] E. H. Anderson and G. T. Schwenning, *The Science of Production Organization* (New York: John Wiley & Sons, Inc., 1947), pp. 133-137, and 172-181.

with full authority to act in all matters concerning his unit is necessary to cope with personal, local and emergency problems as they arise. Promptness is more to be desired than correctness in some instances, and Gordian Knots do have to be cut sometimes. This being true there is the paradox of reconciling the full authority of one officer with the yet additional authority of another, a functional officer.

The way out of this paradox is much simpler than it may at first appear. This is because there is actually little place in modern industry for "full" authority as the word implies. The authority of the line officer, even the chief executive, is limited by law, by company policy laid down by the board of directors, by resources available, by labor unions, and at all times by custom and accepted standards of conduct. Furthermore, below the level of the chief executive, as soon as the first step is taken toward dividing up the work of the enterprise into operating units, there must be initiated some method of getting the divided parts or units back together again into an integral whole. This is usually best accomplished by establishing policies, procedures, systems and other devices for co-ordinating and controlling certain aspects or elements of activities common to the operations of the various line units. Unless this is done the enterprise is a mere aggregation of distinct operating units, not a single managerial entity.

To the extent that unified control over the various departments or divisions is established by the control of the separate aspects of their activities, the managers or supervisors of such units find accordingly their spheres of activity diminished and their independence curtailed and since the chief executive, due to the limitation of his span of attention and control, cannot personally supervise all the activities necessary for co-ordination and control, his only recourse is to appoint special assistants for the task. In dividing up this work and assigning it to assistants, it is usually most logical to do so on the basis of functions, i.e., activities having each a specific purpose essential to the successful operation and control of the whole enterprise. Such responsibility and authority as may be delegated to these various supervisors of functions must be accordingly withheld or reserved from that delegated to line or operating unit managers because they now have full authority only within limits or with reservations, or, as is said, with strings tied to it. It is thus by a method of reservation, or failure to delegate line officers, that full authority is often restricted and diluted to such an extent that it may not differ greatly from functional authority. In such cases the only distinction may be that the line officer always has residual authority (that not specifically delegated to others) and full authority to act in order to adjust conflicts, eliminate confusion, and meet emergencies. The functional officer, on the other hand, may be said to have only specially delegated authority only over the proper performance of his particular function.[3] As to terminology, therefore, the term "functional organization" is a misnomer; in practice it is always a "line-functional" organization.

The staff concept

The staff officer in an organization is one who, as it is said, wields no authority but merely advises. Actually, however, advising should be the duty of every officer in an organization. No person should be exempt from the responsibility of giving advice as to his particular sphere of responsibility. Whenever there is close and effective cooperation among the officers of the organization the advisory relationships existing—often mutual—are usually too numerous and varied to be classified or represented adequately on an organization chart. They compose what is commonly known as the informal organization. The staff officer is merely one who deals only with information and advice as his major activity. The particular responsibility of the staff officer is to supply authoritative information to all those members who are entitled to receive it; his authority is the authority to get information, within his special field, from all those who may have it. He usually also has the duty of interpreting this information, transcribing it into useful form, and assisting and advising in its use.

In the line-staff organization the members holding line positions ordinarily perform all operations necessary for carrying on the main work of the enterprise and perhaps for short periods of time. The duty of the staff is to assist in such activities as assembling information, planning for the future, improving present procedures, evaluating past performance, and especially in recent years, helping establish and maintain communication with outside agencies. Such activities, though not always needed for usual day-to-day operations,

---

[3] Elmore Peterson and E. G. Plowman, *Business Organization and Management* (4th ed.; Homewood: Richard D. Irwin, Inc., 1958), p. 353.

may be indispensable in enabling the enterprise to operate with efficiency and to reach its stated objectives. In a small organization or simple operation, these activities are usually performed by the chief executive himself, but in a large or complex operation they must be delegated to others, and when so, they should be formally recognized and distinguished in the organization structure.

Functional vs. staff authority

The difference between functional and staff authority is often hard to distinguish, for in some cases it is more nearly a difference in degree than a difference in kind. Functional authority, as often differentiated, is that degree of authority standing somewhere between the so-called full or command authority of the line officer and the advisory or informational authority of the staff officer. It is frequently called "instructional authority" since the relationship between supervisor and subordinate resembles more nearly that between instructor and pupil than that between master and servant.

Functional authority, in practice, is generally exercised and transmitted in the form of instructions, routines and regulations, and pertains more often to methods of procedure than to personal commands or orders for action that may be issued by line officers. The functional officer is neither an impersonal advisor nor a personal boss; he takes motivation and discipline to some extent for granted. In Taylor's plan, it will be remembered, motivation was taken care of by an incentive wage system and discipline was the responsibility of a special foreman.

The several types of officers are perhaps hardest to distinguish when all three are found in the same organization. In general, the functional officer is concerned with activities of a routine nature requiring a high degree of specialized skill, and exercises control over other members of the organization by obtaining their compliance with certain programs and procedures. As is often said, he is a program or procedural supervisor, or a supervisor of procedures, as distinguished from the line officer who is a supervisor of operations and operators, and the staff officer who is a supervisor of knowledge.

It is only when all routine activities and all those requiring a high degree of specialized skill are thus assigned to functional officers that the staff of any organization is left free to perform its true function. The staff was developed as a prop or an aide for the line executive to lean upon and call upon for help; to its officers could be assigned special tasks that relieved the executive of some of his burdens. These officers became known as the eyes, the ears, the brain, and sometimes the tongue of the office of the line executive. The relationship of the staff officer to his superior line executive must be, therefore, intimate and to some extent personal. The staff officer cannot become so engrossed in the performance and perfection of his specialty that he fails to perform as a member of the line team or loses sight of the over-all operation of the line unit. He should not have the specially delegated authority or responsibility for control of only a particular function such as that possessed by the functional officer.

The evolution of organization relationship

The differences in the three types of organization relationships usually come about as stages in the growth of an enterprise and its adaptation to a greater degree of specialization of functions. There should be, in fact, an evolutionary process of organizing, adapting, and re-organizing that leads to the blending of one type into another with expedient mutations and combinations.

The failure to recognize the problems and the processes of a growing and evolving organization structure in a dynamic society is one of the greatest faults of organizers. Furthermore, the tendency to describe new situations and relationships with inadequate concepts and obsolete terminology is one of the greatest obstacles to developing an organization structure that can be understood by its members. In this field, it is hard to say which is the greater obstacle to understanding, using the same words to express different concepts or using different words to mean the same thing.

Functionalism

Finally, it should be noted that functionalism, the application of the concept generally, is one of the major characteristics of modern society. Functionalism is essentially an advanced stage of the division of labor applied to social, industrial and even political organization. Our government, for example, is divided among federal, state, and local authorities; these are again divided among legislative, judicial and executive branches; and the executive branch is again divided among various departments, bureaus, and commissions, each exercising functional control in a particular field. Furthermore, a dominant characteristic of our society is its multiplicity of institutions, associations, and professions each rendering a particular service and each exercising authority within the law over the performance of its respective function. Private industry is also characterized by a vast complex of trade associations, unions, institutes and professional societies each controlling to some extent the performance of its particular function.

The democratic society of America, it may be noted, did not develop according to the principles of line organization, nor of line and staff. Unity of command, the hierarchy, full authority, the subservience of staff, etc., were adapted from military organization. Totalitarianism was anathema to both Thomas Jefferson and Adam Smith.

The concept of the functional officer began with the first Druid, medicine man or priest and it has developed until it has become the professional specialist characteristic of our present-day civilization. These professional specialists began early in our history to associate themselves for the purpose of exchanging experience, increasing their skill, and exercising some degree of control over the practice of their professions. The early guilds, secret orders, and societies formed for such purposes often played a dominant role in the control of social and economic activity. Later, schools and universities were established to train professional practitioners and to certify by appropriate degrees to their competence. More recently associations and institutes have been established to control certain aspects of professional practice, such as entrance requirements, the dissemination of knowledge, standards of performance, codes of ethics, mutual support of members, promotion of the profession, and sometimes scales of charges and remuneration.

These professional associations, through their various programs and agencies, provide modern industry with one of its most essential services. Each association specializing in its particular area or function usually has within its ranks the leaders and the super-experts in each aspect of its field. To them management can go for obtaining competent recruits, advanced technical information, and sometimes specific answers to its problems. They serve industry in the same way to some extent that the various technical corps headquarters serve the combat branches of the Army. General management, therefore, since it cannot hope to have knowledge superior to that of all the functional specialists in its own organization, is provided a source of assistance in supervising, evaluating and controlling its own experts.

By using these associations, general management can delegate authority to its functional experts with some degree of confidence since it now has an agency for evaluating the performance of their various functional responsibilities.

Thus, the functional concept begins with the concept of specialization, it proceeds upward to the lower ranks of management to become functional foremanship, then to the higher ranks as functionalization and functional control, and, finally, to society at large as functionalism. And, last but by no means least, the concept applies not only to the division of activities, but also to both their immediate and their ultimate control.

Questions

1. What criticism does the author raise concerning current use of the term line and staff organization?
2. What is the distinction between the concept of functional division and functional control?
3. What differences are there, if any, between staff authority and functional authority?
4. How does functional authority relate to specialization and to the division of work?
5. What need is there, if any, for functional authority?

12—GROUND RULES FOR USING
COMMITTEES *

Cyril O'Donnell

A camel, someone has said, is a horse designed by a committee—and this is fairly typical of the current attitude toward this form of group activity. The use of committees has been criticized as a way of avoiding individual executive action, as a means of covering up managerial inadequacies, as a form of inefficient corporate "togetherness," and as a device for legitimizing procrastination and indecisiveness. What's more, every one of these accusations is justified, at least in many cases.

What is frequently overlooked, however, is that these are not valid criticisms of committees, but rather of the *misuse* of committees. For a committee that can be charged with any of these faults is not being employed as a committee should be used. Committees do have legitimate functions and, properly used, they constitute an invaluable management tool. The question is, how should they be properly used?

One common error is the confusion of committees with other kinds of joint action. Many people apply the term "committee" to any meeting of two or more people, but this definition is obviously too flexible and imprecise. It would necessarily include such diverse activities as business conferences, staff meetings, meetings of department heads, executive committee meetings, and even luncheon engagements, all of which are designed to serve quite different purposes. Conferences and typical staff meetings are primarily communication devices, utilized for economic purposes; a meeting of department heads may be called to clear up snags or overcome delays in some area that concerns all of them; meetings of an executive committee on which the president sits are held primarily for communication purposes. In none of these instances does a true committee exist.

The true committee

What, then, is a committee? We might define it as *two or more persons appointed by their immediate superior for the purpose of*

* From *Management Review*, Vol. 50, No. 10 (October, 1961), pp. 63-67. Reprinted with permission.

acting or advising their superior about a subject that is not clearly within the competence of any of them.

This implies that the superior does not sit in on the committee meetings; that the membership is confined to two or more of his immediate subordinates; and that the subject matter to be considered is not within the assigned duties of any individual member. Such a committee is properly considered an organizational device because it is performing an activity that, for various reasons, is not otherwise assigned. It may or may not have authority to take action, and it may be either an *ad hoc* group or a permanent committee.

Basic requirements

The proper use of committees is based on two fundamental assumptions. In the first place, it assumes that the structure of the enterprise and the association of activities in this structure conform to the principles of good organization. Experienced business managers recognize that it is not possible, even in a well-organized company, to cover all types of activities or to assign all duties to specific individuals. Even when it is possible to make such assignments, they sometimes prefer not to do so. The important point is that the committee device is not a crutch for poor organization structure—it supplements good structure.

The second basic assumption is that the enterprise has effective managers. Too often the committee device is used to supplement and buttress inefficient men. The use of a committee to support mediocrity in management is an extremely poor and even dangerous device. True, it may sometimes be necessary in the short run. But this situation should be clearly recognized, and vigorous efforts should be made to achieve good organization and employ effective managers as quickly as possible.

The one time when a committee can be legitimately used—and the only circumstance in which its use can be justified—is when it can do a job better than a single manager. This means that the net effect must be superior in the light of such factors as cost, time, decisiveness, justice, and sound judgment.

Pooled experience

There are three situations in which a committee may meet this criterion. To begin with, a committee is a sound organizational device when it is used to obtain the considered views of subordinates about a subject beyond the experience of their superior. If the superior has the breadth and depth of experience represented by the members of a committee, it is obvious that he has no need of group action. Lacking this experience, the superior might conceivably ask for the advice of individual subordinates without organizing a committee. This is quite often done—as, for example, when an executive calls on a department or division manager for his views on a particular subject. Quite often, however, such an informal approach will result in the subordinate's giving views that are narrow in conception and not fully considered. As a member of a committee, the same subordinate would frame his views with an eye to potential questions or criticism of his fellow members, and he would thus be likely to be less extreme and insular in his viewpoint.

A good example of this kind of committee is the typical policy committee, whose purpose is to formulate policy to best fit the needs of the enterprise. For example, the question in the mind of the president may be, "Do we need a policy on pricing, and, if so, how should it be framed?" If he has come up through engineering or production, the president may lack the technical knowledge and experience required to decide a matter of this type. Consequently, he would find it advisable to refer the matter to his policy committee. The members of the committee would develop their views, not only with respect to special interests of the division or function they represent, but also from the viewpoint of the welfare of the company as a whole. Their considered views would result in a consensus, which they would report in the form of a recommendation to the president. In this instance, the committee would be acting in a staff capacity, and it would probably be a standing committee.

Too much power

A second appropriate use of a committee as an organizational device is to exercise authority that is too great for any one man. The authority may be considered too great because it requires broader knowledge than any one man can be expected to have, because there is too much risk of bias or prejudice, or because it is difficult to find a person willing to exercise the authority. Good examples of such committees are investment committees, wage-and-salary committees, and boards of directors. It would be unusual to find a treasurer or a chairman of a board of directors who would be willing to take it on himself to decide how the surplus funds of a firm should be invested— and, indeed, it is likely to be too risky for the firm to rely on the judgment of any one man. Similar considerations are involved with respect to the wage-and-salary committee and the board of directors, which is a committee representing the stockholders. Committees of these types are standing committees that are delegated line authority. They make decisions on a majority basis and are true "plural executives."

Spreading responsibility

A third appropriate reason to use a committee as an organizational device is to diffuse responsibility among several executives. Very often it is undesirable to pinpoint responsibility for action on one person. A good example of this type of committee is the bonus committee, which determines the exact distribution of a fund among the qualified members or recipients. Although the total amount of a bonus fund may be expressed in terms of a percentage of profits before taxes, the method of distributing the bonus is not always directly related to the salaries of the potential recipients; distribution is frequently made on the basis of an evaluation of their contributions to the company in the past year. One manager might well find the assignment of making this evaluation very uncomfortable, and he would be the target of complaints and accusations from those who felt that they were unfairly treated. When a committee is used for this purpose, responsibility is spread among the members, and disappointed recipients are less disposed to complain; they are more likely to be satisfied that no bias or prejudice was involved in the decision of a group.

A committee of this type is likely to be an *ad hoc* group, and it normally has a staff position with respect to the chief executive officer. However, at the option of their superior, the committee may be delegated line authority to act in the situation.

Committee operation

Three important elements are necessary to make committees truly and effectively operational. First, the purpose for which the committee is being established must be distinctly defined. A written statement will help to achieve clarity, and it will eliminate the need for committee members to spend time deciding exactly what they are supposed to be doing.

Second, the authority of the committee must be clearly specified. This is an easy matter, but it should be given careful attention. The committee may perform a staff function, having authority only to investigate and recommend to their superior, or it may be given authority to make decisions. Which is the case must be clearly determined and communicated.

Finally, the chairman of a committee should at all times be appointed on the basis of his ability to conduct an efficient meeting. Efficiency requires that the chairman prepare an agenda in advance so the members will have time to study the subject and consider their views. It means that the chairman must insure that all members are heard from, encouraging the reticent and keeping the loquacious in check. When all the contributions of the members are in, he should state the consensus of the meeting to be sure that he has properly understood it, and he should see that minutes of the meeting are distributed in rough form for correction and review prior to their final distribution.

If these points are given adequate consideration, management can be sure that its committees will operate effectively.

An annual checkup

It is an efficient practice for a company to make an annual audit of its committees, evaluating each one to determine whether it can be justified as an organizational device. If any existing group fails to meet one of the three basic purposes of committees, there is a serious question of its legitimacy.

As this audit is conducted from year to year, managers will gain a thorough understanding of the appropriate use of committees. They will shy away from using committees as crutches for inadequacies, as excuses for delay, or as devices to shift decision-making responsibility, and they will learn to use them to do the jobs for which they are uniquely suited.

When this has been accomplished, the committee will have attained its proper and respected place in the organization structure of the enterprise.

Questions

1. What is a *true* committee and how does it differ from a group of individuals in an organization who may meet at intervals to discuss problems of mutual interest?
2. Under what conditions may a committee perform a task more effectively than an individual manager? less effectively?
3. Is it ever desirable to use a committee for the purpose of dividing the responsibility for making a decision among several individuals rather than to have this responsibility exercised by only one individual?
4. Can you think of any other uses of a committee in addition to those mentioned in this article?
5. How may the use of committees contribute to the more effective management of personnel?

13—READING THE UNREADY: POSTINDUSTRIAL JOBS *

Louis E. Davis

United States' attempts to bring some significant population segments into the economic and social mainstream have so far failed, partly because they were based on a succession of short-lived, inappropriate manpower models. Two factors affecting the texture of societal environment were overlooked: the technology our society uses to provide products and services; and the presence of societal enclaves differing in culture, skills, income, industrial experience, and political status. These factors are related, and manpower policy that ignores them is doomed to fail.

Speeded by changes in social values and developments in technology, the industrial era is showing many signs of coming to a close. The transition into the postindustrial era is discernible in the development of automated technology for goods production, computer technology for provision of services, a tenuous relationship between work and economic production, and the development of new meanings for work and for relationships within and between working organizations.

We should now devote attention to an orderly transition into a postindustrial society. But in the midst of industrial nations there are still preindustrial enclaves of the unemployed, untutored, unskilled, and unsophisticated; and on the international level, there are economically underdeveloped nations among highly industrialized ones.

The objective of much government and private effort is to provide the means of introducing members of these enclaves into productive society. Most of the many transition programs assume that entrance into the economic mainstream leads to entrance into the social mainstream. This is more than a simple equating of economic status with social status. It reflects deeply held beliefs that participation in the economic activities of society serves social and psychological needs and provides the basis for political status.

* © 1971 by The Regents of the University of California. Reprinted from *California Management Review*, Vol. 13, No. 4, pp. 27-36, by permission of The Regents.

Business, industry, and government agencies attempt to induct and train, giving men opportunities to prove themselves on the job. However, government agencies may be overly eager to have the unemployed trained and placed on jobs that may be short-lived. Choosing effective means for merging the unprepared into the economic mainstream presents the problems here discussed.

Many modes of preparing the unskilled for productive activities will be required. The focus here is on those using on-the-job learning and experience (excluding apprenticeship). The on-the-job mode requires that the unprepared be inducted into the work organization in a rapid and orderly fashion, which often means that entry jobs have to be designed *de novo* or by fractionating existing jobs so that they provide progressive learning stages. Job restructuring can provide the means for stepwise learning, but the job segments must be appropriately designed and progression through the segments must be a function of performance rather than of promotion or advancement based on available openings.

A newly developed theoretical framework provides help in understanding the requirements of job restructuring. The concepts were first sketched out nearly twenty years ago in Britain, and Norway has recently employed them as the substructure for a comprehensive program of labor-management relations, but they have yet to come into common practice in the United States. My colleagues and I are employing them as the basis of extensive reorganization of advanced industries. Briefly, one fundamental premise of this school of thought says that in any purposive organization in which men perform the organization's activities, there is a joint system operating—called, in the newly developing language of this theoretical framework, a *sociotechnical* system. When human beings are required actors in the performance of work, the desired output is achieved through the actions of a social system as well as a technological system. Further, these systems so interlock that achievement of the output becomes a function of the appropriate joint operation of both systems. The operative word is "joint," for it is here that the sociotechnical idea departs from more widely held views—those in which the social system is thought to be dependent on the technical system.

The bearing on the question at hand is this: If the needs of the individual (which underlie the functioning of the social system) are not satisfied, then there will be no effective outcome from any program of job restructuring to provide entry and immediate follow-up on jobs.

A second premise supporting the sociotechnical concept is that every system is embedded in an environment and is influenced by a culture and its values, by a set of generally acceptable practices, and by the roles the culture permits for its members. To develop an effective job or organization, one must understand the environmental forces that are operating on it. This emphasis on environmental forces suggests—correctly—that the sociotechnical systems concept falls within the larger body of "open system" theories. These accept that there is a constant interchange between what goes on in a work system or an organization and what goes on in the environment; the boundaries between the environment and the system are permeable. When something occurs in the general society, it will inevitably affect what occurs in organizations. There may be a period of cultural lag, but sooner or later the societal tremor will register on the organizational seismographs.

This, too, bears on the question of job restructuring. It says that programs will fail if they focus on the restructuring of jobs without giving due attention to the societal environment in which the jobs are embedded. Moreover, such programs will fail if they are not addressed to the emergent postindustrial environment whose dimensions are now becoming visible.

Sociotechnical theorists have carried the conceptual development of the discipline beyond these basic premises and are working on a methodology for system analysis that reflects the whole theoretical framework. But the two principles mentioned are sufficient to carry the discussion into the first of the five topics here addressed.

Three meanings of job restructuring

Neither society, the organization, nor the individual is free to ascribe its own meaning to the concept of job restructuring; their differing slants on the concept (like the three sectors themselves) are and must be mutually interdependent. No matter how noble are society's objectives for a program of job restructuring, that program must meet the needs of both an organization and an individual.

Societal goals embedded in the concept of job restructuring are to get unskilled individuals into productive work, to help them acquire skills, and to provide a viable future for them. This listing begins to set some requirements for the outcome of any program of job restructuring.

Society's objectives must also take into account a finding by Clark in his study of the ghetto:

> The roots of the multiple pathology in the dark ghetto are not easy to isolate. They do not lie primarily in unemployment. In fact, if all its residents were employed, it would not materially alter the pathology of the community. More relevant is the status of the jobs held . . . more important than merely having a job, is the kind of job it is.[1]

But the organization is also a partner in restructuring; it has a set of needs that it wants to satisfy, and the meaning of restructuring must address itself to these.

1. Management may see job restructuring as a way of coping with a labor shortage. "Demand" or "structural" explanations aside, it is clear that the economy is currently exhibiting both unemployment and labor shortages. To organizations, job restructuring may mean the ability to fulfill production requirements with available workers.
2. The organization has economic objectives and restructuring must contribute to them. On the basis that today's unskilled and untutored do not contribute adequately to an organization's economic goals, the federal government may partially repay the estimated deficit. This is probably a short-run situation—at least for the American economy.
3. The organization wants its members to adapt and cooperate, learning what is necessary and taking appropriate actions to maintain the productive system in a steady state. The organization will expect this behavior of workers holding restructured jobs. More importantly, it will require that job restructuring for some of the work force not affect adversely the adaptiveness and cooperativeness of other workers whose jobs are not restructured.

Individuals also have requirements and aspirations that affect job restructuring. The first two of these are similar to society's aspirations: entry into gainful occupation and acquisition of skills. Further, the tasks that are performed have to be meaningful to the individual and the role he performs must be meaningful within the organization. Obviously, the term "meaningful" is conceptual shorthand, glossing over the many questions of satisfaction and status that are examined later.

Finally, the restructured jobs must offer some prospects for a desirable future career. The idea of a career at the working level

---

[1] K. B. Clark, "Explosion in the Ghetto," *Psychology Today* (September, 1967).

is novel over most of the industrial world. Accustomed to thinking of jobs as entities in themselves, both managements and unions have lost the sense of the dynamics of working life—the expected progression from stage to stage of development. For many workers there are no dynamics—there is only one job over a lifetime. There is no "career" in the sense of an evolution of the individual matched by an evolution of the work that he does. Job restructuring, particularly if concentrated at the entry level, may be analogous to preparing a man to walk off the edge of a cliff; he is well organized to take the first step, and after that there isn't anything else. The literature—indeed, the whole industrial culture of Western civilization, the United States included—takes the job as a discrete entity, independent of the idea of a career or even of a simple job progression other than promotion.

Trends to static separation

Specialization of work roles is as old as Western history. Western man specialized his work in relation to a particular product, technology, or material, or because he had to acquire certain skills and wanted to grasp them in a certain way.

Although the jobs created by this trend were, for the most part, highly specialized, they were also highly skilled. But, beginning about 1790, the trend toward specialization took a different turn. New power sources required factories where people could be brought together to do their work. The steam engine determined the placement of machines which, in turn, determined the placement of people.

But there was no body of people conveniently ready to be marshalled together for this purpose; there was no industrial work force. The economy of England was essentially agricultural, and its rural population was untutored and unskilled. Two things changed this. The first was the passage of the Corn Laws, which forced large numbers of people off the farms and into the cities, artificially creating a manpower reservoir. The second was a new kind of specialization of labor in which jobs were deliberately broken down so that unskilled people could do them. In fact, almost anything that can be said about the "modern" industrial practice of breaking down jobs can be found in Babbage's book *On the Economy of Machinery and Manufactures*, which was written in 1835 and reflected twenty years of experience.

In the United States, around 1890, Frederick W. Taylor re-
discovered Babbage and created an approach called "scientific management," which is the basis of industrial practice in the United
States today. The environmental field in which Taylor worked was
not unlike that of England a century earlier. The United States
was in a period of rapid industrial expansion, characterized by a
large immigration of unskilled people. Taylor's was the mechanism
by which industry could use these people. He specified the means for
subdividing jobs so that their skill content was reduced to the
minimum. Taylor's approach was widely accepted because American
society held certain values and because the technology of the time
had certain characteristics. For the good of society, or for the good
of an organization, one could use people as "operating units." [2]
Within broad limits, and as long as economic goals were being satisfied, the individual and his needs did not matter.

Scientific management, as developed by Taylor, can be called the
machine theory of organization and is characterized by the following
elements:

1. The man and his job are the essential building blocks of an organization; if the analyst gets these "right" (in some particular but
   unspecified way), then the organization will be correctly defined.
2. Man is an extension of the machine, useful only for doing things
   that the machine cannot.
3. The men and their jobs—the individual building blocks—are to
   be glued together by supervisors who will absorb the uncertainties
   of the work situation. Furthermore, these supervisors need supervisors, and so on, *ad infinitum,* until the enterprise is organized in
   a many-layered hierarchy. In bureaucratic organizations, the latter
   notion ultimately leads to situations in which a man can be called
   a "manager" solely because he supervises a certain number of
   people.
4. The organization is free to use any available social mechanisms to
   enforce compliance and ensure its own stability.
5. Job fractionation is a way of reducing the costs of carrying on
   the work by reducing the skill contribution of the individual who
   performs it. Man is simply an extension of the machine; and the
   more you simplify the machine (whether its living or nonliving
   part), the more you lower costs.

To talk of job restructuring now—at the beginning of the 1970's—
is the evoke this whole dismal history. People have seen this used to

---

[2] R. Boguslaw, *The New Utopians* (New York: Prentice-Hall, 1965), Chapter 5.

get work done cheaply. They have seen it used to control many kinds of workers, and now a number of kinds of professionals. The success of current programs of job restructuring will depend on overcoming or averting the problems that were created by similar movements in history, and this, in turn, will depend on the correctness with which such programs assess the emerging environment, both changes on the social side and in the technology.

Environmental nature and effects

What are some of the forces operating in the social and technological environments? What can be predicted about the short-run future? What effect should these forces have on programs of job restructuring?

Socially, there seems to be a collapse of Western society's basic proposition about the relationship between work and the satisfaction of material needs. The "Protestant ethic" says that man is put into the world to work; to satisfy his basic needs, he has to work hard because the environment is hostile and demands difficult, extended endeavor. This is now being very seriously questioned by American youth, by industrial workers, and (to our great surprise) by the unemployed, although they question it in widely differing ways. People see technology as being capable of providing for material needs without any real effort on anybody's part. Whether this is an accurate or inaccurate perception is, perhaps, irrelevant. It is partly accurate and will grow more accurate over time.

This change implies that the use of individuals to satisfy the economic goals of an organization is no longer a viable social value. People will not let themselves be used. They want other things out of the work situation than the material reward. They want to see some relationship between their own work and the social life that goes on around them and to see some desirable future for themselves in a continuing relationship with the organization.

This change is already explicit in the words of college students about their work expectations. They say, "We want a chance to participate and to control; we want a chance to make a contribution to developing more meaning in what we do." And they carry these words into action, turning down jobs that would put their feet under the corporation board in favor of jobs with the Peace Corps or as members of Nader's Raiders.

That the unemployed may be saying this as well is seen in a study of the Boston area by Doeringer,[3] which indicates that the unemployed seem to be as selective about accepting jobs as the employed are in changing jobs, because there are means—partly provided by society—for the jobless to subsist in the ghetto.

In short, many people in the United States are newly concerned about the quality of working life, about alienation from work, about job satisfaction, about personal freedom and initiative, and about the dignity of the individual in the work place. These questions are now arising because the relationship between work and the satisfaction of material needs is becoming more tenuous.

Another factor is that continuously rising levels of education are changing the attitudes, aspirations, and expectations of many members of our society. Although the focus here is on the United States, I offer an example from Norway because it illustrates so strikingly the connection between education and work expectations.

A few years ago the Norwegian government decided to extend the school-leaving age of children by one year because education was an important requirement for the future society. Very soon, Norway's important maritime industry was seriously threatened by an inability to recruit new workers. Before the school-leaving age was extended, about 80 percent of the boys were willing to go to sea; afterwards, only 15 percent sought seafaring careers. They wanted a different kind of life because the extra schooling had had an impact on them. (A creative solution was found by shifting from a focus on maritime jobs to one on careers.)

Other social forces in the environment might be mentioned. There is the drive toward professionalization; people want to be identified with activities of a professional nature, and we find a movement to provide a dignity for work that is analogous to that exhibited by the professions. The issue of appropriate labor-management relations, as now narrowly defined, has pretty well been settled. Consequently, labor unions are having some difficulty expanding their membership, keeping old members loyal, attracting new members, and so on.

What of the technological side? The most significant aspect of technological development is generally (and somewhat vaguely) called "automation." This means that there are devices in productive work systems that can be programmed to do routine tasks, sense

---

[3] P. B. Doeringer, "Ghetto Labor Markets and Manpower Problems," *Monthly Labor Review* (March, 1969), p. 55.

outcomes, adjust machines if necessary, and continue the work process.

Man once had three roles to play in the production process, two of which have been preempted by machines. Man's first role was as an energy supplier, but since the advent of steam and electricity this role is now practically nonexistent in the United States. Man's second role was as a guider of tools. This is essentially what is meant by the term "skill"—the trained ability to guide tools or manipulate machines or materials—and this role for man is increasingly being programmed into machines. The third contribution remains: man as regulator of a working situation or system, an adjuster of difficulties. Under automation, man's work in the physical sense has disappeared. The notion of skill in the conventional sense has disappeared. What is left are two kinds of skills related to regulation—skills in monitoring and diagnostics, and skills in the adjustment of processes.

This shift in the role of man unites the forces emergent in the social and technological environments in the following way. In conventional work the transformation system can be described as "deterministic." What is to be done, when it is to be done, and how it is to be done are all specifiable. The whole of Taylor's scientific management movement was based on the fundamental idea that the world was deterministic.

In the presence of sophisticated or automated technology, the deterministic world disappears into the machine. Only two kinds of functions are left for man: deterministic tasks for which machines have not yet been devised, and control of stochastic events—variability and exceptions. For example, in modern banks, where third-generation computers are already in use, human functions fall very neatly into these two categories. There are people carrying pieces of paper from one machine to the next (because there is no machine for carrying paper). And there are people handling the indeterminate, randomly occurring situations with which the self-regulating capacities of the computer cannot cope.

In a production system, stochastic events have two characteristics. They are unpredictable as to time and nature. For economic reasons they must be overcome as rapidly as possible. These characteristics impose certain requirements on workers. First, they must have a large repertoire of responses because the specific thing that will happen is not known. Second, they cannot depend on supervision because they must respond immediately to events that occur irregularly and without warning; they must be *committed* to undertaking the necessary tasks on their own initiative.

This makes a very different world in which the organization is far more dependent on the individual (although there may be fewer individuals). Let us trace the chain of causation that determines these differences, starting from the point of view of the organization:

1. If the production process collapses, the economic goals of the organization will not be met.
2. If appropriate responses are not taken to stochastic events, the production process will collapse.
3. If the individual employees are not committed to their functions, the appropriate responses will not be made.
4. Commitment cannot be forced or bought; it can only arise out of the experiences of the individual with the quality of life in his working situation—i.e., with his job.
5. Therefore, highly automated organizations do their best to build into jobs the characteristics that will develop commitment on the part of the individual.

Comparing two industries—one highly automated and one not—will demonstrate these differences very clearly. In the oil refining industry, residual human tasks are almost entirely control and regulation, and the line between supervisor and worker has almost disappeared. In the construction industry, man still retains prominent roles as a source of energy and guidance, and supervision (often at several levels) mediates all system actions.

Management in the oil industry is proud of "advanced and enlightened" personnel practices. They were not adopted for the sake of their enlightenment but because they are a necessary functional response to the demands of process technology.

Here is the point at which both the social and the technological forces can be seen working toward the same end, because "job characteristics that develop commitment" (participation and control, personal freedom, and initiative) are exactly those characteristics beginning to emerge as demands for "meaningfulness" from the social environment.

Most industries are neither all automated nor all conventional. If an industry has some employees whose jobs are designed to meet the requirements of automated technology, then the characteristics of those jobs are visible to, and desired by, all the employees of the industry, and it becomes very difficult to maintain a distinction in job design solely on the basis of a distinction in technological base.

Job design suggestions

A considerable amount of formal and informal experimentation with job and organization design has occurred in the past twenty years in business and industry. Most of the experiments have been done in the United States, Norway, and England. They are usually reported in highly specialized publications, and only occasionally in general, widely read journals. So far, researchers are talking to researchers and rarely to managers or union officials.

The research results point to three categories of job requirements, the first of which concerns the matter of "autonomy"—jobs so designed that those performing them can regulate and control their own work worlds. They can decide when they are doing well or poorly, and they can organize themselves to do what is needed. Management's function is to specify the outcomes desired. Autonomy implies the existence of multiple skills, either within a single person (the French call such a person the "polyvalent craftsman") or within the work group. Autonomy also implies self-regulation and self-organization, a radical notion in the industrial world of the United States. Further, it implies that those working will be managed or evaluated on the basis of outcomes rather than on conformity to rules.

Nevertheless, the research shows that when the attributes of jobs are such that autonomy exists in the working situation, the result is high meaning, high satisfaction, and high outcome performance. This has been demonstrated in such widely different settings as coal mining,[4] chemical refinery maintenance,[5] and aircraft instrument manufacture.[6]

The second category, so far mainly the province of psychologists, concerns "adaptation." The elements of the job have to be such that the individual can learn from what is going on around him, can grow, can develop, can adjust. (This, by the way, is pure biology. It ignores, without meaning to slight, the psychological concept of self-actualization or personal growth.) All living organisms adapt or they cease to exist, and man's every act is adaptive. Too often, jobs created under scientific management principles have overlooked

[4] E. L. Trist, et al., Organizational Choice (London: Tavistock, 1963).

[5] L. E. Davis and R. Werling, "Job Design Factors," Occupational Psychology, 28 (1960), 109.

[6] L. E. Davis and E. S. Valfer, "Studies in Supervisory Job Design," Human Relations, 19:4 (1966), 339.

that people adapt or learn and, in fact, that the organization needs them to adapt. (In automated technology, the very role of the individual depends on *his adaptability and his commitment,* because nobody is around at the specific instant to tell him what to do.) Unintentionally overlooked is that the job is also a setting in which personal psychic and social growth of the individual takes place. Such growth can be facilitated or blocked, leading to distortions having costs for the individual, the organization, and society.

Where the job and technology are designed so that adaptive behavior is facilitated, positive results occur at all levels in the organization, as demonstrated in studies of oil refineries,[7] automated chemical plants,[8] pulp and paper plants,[9] and aircraft instrument plants.[10]

The third research category concerns "variety." If people are to be alert and responsive to their working environments, they need variety in the work situation. Science began to get some notion of this after World War II, when research began on radar watchers. Radar watchers sit in a darkened room, eyeing blips on the radar screen that appear in random patterns. Eventually this blurs into a totally uniform background for the individual; and precisely when the important "foreign" signal appears, the watcher has become incapable of attending to it. Psychologists have also studied this phenomenon in various "deprived environments." Monkeys raised in restricted environmental conditions do not develop into normal adult primates. Adult humans confined to "stimulus-free" environments begin to hallucinate. Workers may respond to the deprived work situation in much the same way.

Specifically, what do the experiments say about the restructuring of jobs? All jobs, even fractionated jobs, should contain categories of activity that are important to the individual's development of self-organization and self-control in the work situation. There are preparatory tasks, transformation tasks, control tasks, and auxiliary tasks in a work process. Preparatory tasks, as the name implies, get the worker ready to do the work required. Transformation tasks

---

[7] *Technical Reports* (London: Tavistock Institute of Human Relations).
[8] E. Thorsrud and F. Emery, *Moten Ny Bedriftsorganisasjon* (Oslo: Tanum Press, 1969), Chapter 6, "Norsk Hydro Plant."
[9] *Ibid.,* Chapter 4, "Hunsfos Paper Plant." Also, E. Engelstad, *The Hunsfos Experiment,* in press.
[10] L. E. Davis, "The Design of Jobs," *Industrial Relations* (October, 1966), 21.

cover the main productive activity. Control tasks give the individual short-loop feedback about how he is doing. (In many cases, this means that people may have to become their own inspectors, to carry out the requirements of providing themselves with feedback.) Auxiliary tasks include getting supplies, disposing of materials, and so on; they may provide relief from other more stressful tasks. If possible, a job ought to contain at least these components in order to incorporate autonomy.

To promote adaptability, the job—given objectives set by the organization—should permit the individual to set his own standards of quantity and quality of performance and to obtain knowledge of results over time (long-loop feedback). Within the context of the conventional industrial culture, this notion is taken to be either heretical or quaint. But research suggests that if overall goals are specified, people will respond appropriately, will determine what is right and wrong, and will work at meeting the goals.

To incorporate variety, the job should contain a sufficiently large number and kind of tasks. Some companies recognize at least one aspect of this need for variety. For instance, in very flat, unvarying situations, such as assembly lines, companies may rotate people through jobs to provide them with variety. This is an artificial mechanism, but it probably does keep workers from falling asleep at the switch.

Another aspect of the need for variety, less well recognized, will become increasingly important in the emergent technological environment. W. R. Ashby [11] described this aspect of variety as a general criterion for intelligent behavior of any kind; adequate adaptation is only possible if an organism already has a stored set of responses of the requisite variety. In the work situation, this means that since unexpected things will happen, the task content and training for a job should match this variance.

A fourth specification for the design of restructured jobs goes beyond autonomy, adaptation, and variety into the study of the total system of work: the tasks within a job should fall into a meaningful pattern reflecting the interdependence between the individual job and the larger production system. In sociotechnical terms, this interdependence is most closely associated with the points at

---

[11] W. R. Ashby, *Design for a Brain* (New York: Wiley, 1960).

which variance is introduced from one production process into another. The variance may arise from human action, from defects in the raw materials, or from malfunction of the equipment. A job must contain tasks and incorporate skills that permit the individual to cope with these variances. If the job does not provide this, the worker cannot control his own sphere of action; worse, he is forced to export variance to other interconnecting systems. In deterministic systems, the layers of supervision, buttressed by various inspectors, utility and repair men, and the like, absorb the variances exported from the workplace.

A related specification is that the tasks within the job ought to build and maintain the interdependence between individuals and the organization. This may occur through communication, through informal groups (if these are appropriate), and through cooperation between individuals. The tasks within the job and the jobs themselves ought to be seen as permitting relationships between individuals, permitting rotation, and encouraging the social support of one individual for another, particularly in stressful work situations. Otherwise, one gets isolation of the individual and conflict in the work situation.

Finally, the job should provide the basis on which an individual can relate his work to the community. Ask many American workers what they do and they will say, "Oh, I work for Company X." This is a good signal that the person either does not know or cannot explain the meaning of his work; it is merely some unspecified and unlocated portion of activity in a featureless landscape called "the company." This perception can have very serious consequences for his performance and for the satisfactions he derives.

The jobholder

The general requirements of job design also suggest some new ways of looking at jobholders. First, the jobholder ought to have some minimal area of decision making that he can call his own. If he is to adapt and to achieve an autonomous working relationship, the content of his tasks ought to be sustained and bounded by recognition of the authority and responsibility required to perform them. However, in tightly interconnected systems and those with high variance, the extension of responsibility and control to encompass the interconnections is a particular requirement of job and organization design.

Second, the content of a job ought to be reasonably demanding of the individual in other than simply physical ways. This is related in part to growth and to learning, to the idea that jobs ought to provide for at least some minimum variety of activity, and to the idea that they should be related to the environment.

One of the problems in modern industrial life is to cope in a meaningful way with individual growth. Promotions are the only mechanism in wide use. Promotion assumes that a man is moved to another and better job. But, in fact, the content of a given job held by a given man may be continually changing. That the same job should be different for people who have been working at it for a long time than it is for a beginner is simply not accepted. The whole standardization movement—represented by standardization of occupations and published job descriptions—is antithetical to this possibility and works against it.

To close this topic, a real example is offered in which some of these job specifications were applied. In 1968, the Director of the Institute for Work Research in Norway asked a colleague and me from the Tavistock Institute of Human Relations, London, to aid in an interesting experiment.[12] A company in Norway was in the process of designing an automated chemical fertilizer plant. They asked if jobs could be designed solely on the basis of the blueprints of the factory before it was built or staffed. In that way, as the physical plant was going up, they could begin to prepare the organization and the jobs and skills of the people who would man the plant when it was finished. The plant has now been in operation for over two years, with remarkable success.

The engineers had designed the plant so that the work to be done (monitoring, diagnosing, and adjusting, there being no physical work done in the plant other than maintenance) would be carried out in three monitoring or control rooms, in front of control panels. The equipment was so sophisticated that it required only one man in a control room. For three work shifts, this would have required nine men. (Other miscellaneous functions brought the total work force to sixteen men, excluding maintenance workers.) Based on the theoretical grounds reviewed above, the research team wished to avoid a situation in which people would work in isolation. But to put two men in a control room would have been economically inefficient.

---

[12] Thorsrud and Emery, *Moten Ny . . .*, Chapter 5.

Therefore, totally new jobs were created by combining the maintenance and control functions. As the completed plant now operates, at least two men are based in each control room, alternately leaving it to perform maintenance tasks. They support each other, and the new job design also brings feedback from the plant by means other than the instruments on the control panels. For the company this meant that maintenance men had to learn chemistry, and chemical operators had to learn maintenance skills. But totally different jobs were developed than had ever existed before. Looking at any of the previous job histories would have revealed none of this. It had to come out of the theory rather than out of past practice. And it has been extremely successful.

To adduce another Norwegian example—an American ocean-going tanker has 57 men; new Norwegian tankers have 15 men. The difference is that between conventional and automated technology. The engineers who designed these Norwegian ships and their automated equipment learned that they could construct almost any kind of arrangement if they knew what kind of social system was wanted on board the ship.

Unexamined questions of policy

All of the foregoing provides a background against which to examine some questions of policy for job restructuring. The first concerns the existing job definitions and job boundaries that are cast in concrete in agreements between unions and managements, in state and federal civil service commissions, in personnel policies, and in a multitude of other ways. What will be required to break these molds? Simply to go to an employer with a proposal for job restructuring is, in many instances, to go to only half of the essential power. The union is the other half. Federal and state governments have contributed to the rigid stance of both halves by institutionalizing jobs and job descriptions. Jobs can be made infinitely better than they are. Jobs can be restructured for entry purposes and for advancement. But the issue must be made a matter of public and private policy, arrived at by open discussion.

The second policy question concerns the commitment to career development (in the sense it has been used throughout this paper) and not specifically to the individual job or to training for the individual job. A career-development approach was employed when the

Norwegian maritime industry, in concert with government and labor, solved its recruitment problem. To get boys to go to sea, the maritime industry built career chains reaching out in both directions beyond the work on shipboard itself. Pretraining equips the boy to work on merchant ships and tankers for a number of years. Then the work and training aboard ship are designed to prepare him for later functions ashore. The man's entire working life is viewed as a continuum; his service at sea is an integral part of this continuum, achieving economic objectives for the maritime industry and preparatory, developmental objectives for the seaman.

American industry has ignored the issue of career development, except for professionals, and its omission is as detrimental to individuals within the mainstream of our productive society as it is to individuals seeking entry to it. Furthermore, planning programs that concentrate on a single entry level do violence to the job-design requirements discussed. The job designer, free to examine an entire logical sequence of activities, might find that some activities in the present entry-level job belonged in a higher stage, and that some in higher stages belonged at the entry level. In short, job restructuring has the potential of improving the whole range of industrial and service jobs [13] but only if commitment to the concept of career progression becomes a matter of public concern.

A third matter of public policy concerns the quality of working life. This matter goes beyond mere satisfaction with working conditions and directly to the essential involvement of individuals in the working world. As noted above, many younger people—who are in the next working generation—quite clearly feel that they need not work to live. But it remains unclear whether this is a response to work itself or to the negative aspects of work as it is organized in American culture.

The following additional questions also require consideration:

1. How flexible must an organization become in permitting individuals to pass through it to some level at which they can stabilize and perform usefully? There is a gain to flexibility, but there is also a cost, and the trade-offs will have to be worked out with the organizations involved.

2. What advantages might be gained from an alteration of on- and off-the-job continued learning? America has only begun to scratch the surface with the manpower programs it has developed so far.

---

[13] W. J. Paul, K. B. Robertson, and F. Herzberg, "Job Enrichment Pays Off," *Harvard Business Review* (March, 1969), 61.

3. What commitment should organizations make to job changes that facilitate the acquisition of knowledge and skills?

Finally, job restructuring should not be reduced to simplification.

Summary

Many planners behave as if one way of putting a job together were as good as any other. It may be possible to cut a skill in two and give half to man A and half to man B. But if that cut destroys any meaning in the work, the job designer had better spare the surgery.

Taking apart a job is very much analogous to disassembling a clock or dissecting an animal: in a clock or an animal, there is an ordered relationship among parts; in jobs, there is an ordered relationship of the individual tasks to the functioning of the whole sociotechnical system. If the needs of individuals for meaningfulness are at issue, then the results of taking apart a job and reconstructing it become very serious indeed. New job structures that are created must be relevant to the social outcomes that are required.

There should also be an ordered set of relationships through which an individual progresses to arrive at a job that is viable and meaningful and that has continuity for him and for the organization. This notion of different jobs as stages in a chain has to be made explicit in any program for job restructuring. The employer must develop a chain of jobs from the entry point into the mainstream of his productive system so that individuals can arrive at some desirable future. Acquiring skills is a transitional act in a person's life. It is unreasonable to expect a person to remain in transition for twenty years, or even two years. He must be able to get to some level, and this level must be specified.

Technology today is so rich in potential variations and arrangements that design decisions can depend almost exclusively on the social side of the situation. Machinery and tools can be organized in a variety of ways that will achieve the same economic objectives. The real question is, what social objectives are to be satisfied? Any program for job restructuring must first define its social objectives with respect to the organization, the individual, and the whole society.

Questions

1. What is a *sociotechnical* system concept discussed by the author, and what is the significance of this concept in structuring jobs?
2. What are some of the major objectives to be achieved through the restructuring of jobs?
3. How does job restructuring relate to training? To career planning?
4. In what ways have changes in attitudes toward work as a means of satisfying human needs forced changes to be made in the structure of jobs?
5. List some of the social outcomes which the restructuring of jobs should seek to achieve.
6. In what respects did the structuring of jobs in the Norwegian fertilizer plant represent a departure from the approach that traditionally has been followed?

14—THE IMPACT OF HUMAN RESOURCES ON BUSINESS *

Henry A. Singer

To cope with escalating demands for goods and services, business institutions increasingly are calling for systems that often have the effect of depersonalizing and dehumanizing personal relationships. Digital identification has become a way of life from telephones to charge accounts and payroll cards to checking accounts; identities are being converted into numbers on computer cards or tapes. As a result, computer hardware has advanced to a point where it is almost beyond the reach of man-machine systems. We must now pause for human relationships to catch up to the state of the hardware.

In an era of mass production and merchandising, it has become apparent that it is a lot easier to mass produce and sell "mod" clothing and psychedelic place mats than to cope with the employees involved in the process. The office buildings, department stores, or manufacturing plants may get larger and larger, the volume of goods may increase horizontally and vertically, but the employee has begun to demand more individual treatment in the face of the overwhelming massiveness of the environment. In many organizations one hears old-timers regret that things are changing, that there is loss of a personal touch, that one never gets to see the boss any more, that the camaraderie of earlier, less pressured times, when businesses were smaller, is missing.

Often employees in the "bull pens" of huge offices—and even department managers—add personal touches, such as flowers and pictures, to their desks to assert their individuality. In the locker rooms (and inside the lockers), there is a tendency to add decoration, to stake out one's individual "territory." The proprietary way in which many employees stake out their work areas is a similar response. Unfortunately, one often hears, "I don't know anything about that item; it's not my department." More often than not the employee knows a great deal about the other department but refuses to risk blurring his identification with his own specialized section. All these

* From *Business Horizons*, Vol. 12, No. 2 (April, 1969), pp. 53-58. Copyright, 1969, by the Foundation for the School of Business, at Indiana University. Reprinted by permission.

are clues to the yearning for more personal identity in the organization. In the efficient and sometimes clinical environment of huge firms, there is an urgent and compelling desire for some feeling of personal value in the overall effort of the enterprise.

Most persons depend on work to fill a need in their lives and to provide the funds to support the "good" and affluent life. At the same time, a great deal of resentment is aroused when it becomes obvious that the organization is indifferent to the individual. Thus the age of personnel administration has arrived—in part, to bring its expertise into recruiting personnel in a tight labor market and, in fact, to keep the personnel reasonably content and motivated on the job. The old slogan of a day's work for a day's pay has yielded to requests for "work breaks" and fringe benefits. Management still complains that people do not turn out the work they used to turn out at less pay; employees complain that with automation the individual turns out more at less cost.

How and why should people put forth their best effort in environments that are impersonal and massive? Some social scientists claim job satisfaction is not necessarily a function of the environment but of individual values. The writer believes both play a factor. The enterprise needs to prove that it does "give a damn" about the individual. For if one learns any principle of pragmatism in business or in life, it is that "no one puts out for anyone else if he feels the other person is not putting out for him." This concept of *quid pro quo* is the notion of reciprocation that Levinson refers to in his discussion of industrial mental health.[1] However, how does the company convey this message? By more and more benefits? Not necessarily, although good benefits are a way of life in all successful companies. Something more must be conveyed. Without communication of a genuine belief in human values, all the benefits will do is train the employee to take all he can get away with doing as little as possible. The message is in management behavior, not in human relations mottos or monthly inspirational booklets but in actual day-to-day behavior by supervisors.

The Human Resources Approach

How can we design and develop a human environment in our business establishments that will foster a sense of personal worth

---

[1] H. Levinson and others, *Men, Management and Mental Health* (Cambridge: Harvard University Press, 1962), p. 141.

and self-esteem? A human resources approach is one that emphasizes the motivation and development of people. It is based on attitudes and practices of key executives; on clear workable standards for operations; developing people; and encouraging innovation.

Sensitivity in the executive suite

For people to believe in the sincerity and genuineness of an improved working climate, the behavior of the key executives of the organization must be consistent with the organization's policies. It does no good to utter fine-sounding platitudes if the executives act in a deprecating, hostile, and negative way in their dealings with people. Those who direct the policy of an organization must be alert to the signs and clues in human relationships that speak more eloquently than their words.

Unfortunately, many executives interpret the human relations point of view as one requiring them to "go easy" on employees or try to make them happy. These are, of course, distortions of the goals of a good human resources program. Firmness and discipline are as important as good humor. Actually, no institution or individual can make a person happy. The best that can be hoped for is a climate in which an individual will gain increased satisfaction in his work activity and will want to reciprocate with better performance. Creation of such a climate begins with the realistic rewards of wage, benefits, and incentives. However, these do not vary much between most successful organizations. The real differences in working climates are found in the attitudes and standards of the businesses.

This approach makes great demands on senior executives because, in addition to the responsibility for planning, directing, and controlling their particular function, they must find time to listen to people, to provide opportunities for people to express themselves, and then to help guide them toward mutually desirable goals. This requires mature executives, men who themselves are sufficiently well organized and emotionally healthy to cope with subordinates who may be less so. In order to help executives develop these qualities, it is desirable to have frequent meetings at which standards of human relationships are explored. These are not necessarily "sensitivity" sessions, since they are more structured than the conventional sensitivity program. They may be designated as committee meetings held to deal with areas of manpower utilization and development. In the process of discussing and exploring ways of coping with human problems within the organization, the executives reflect their own value systems.

A trained specialist who is a member of such a group can contribute significantly by helping to guide such sessions into constructive and positive directions. This means that each session is reviewed and evaluated both in terms of the results of the discussion of the specific subject areas and of the quality and meaning of participant's contributions. This process requires considerable tact and sensitivity on the part of the individual who has this assignment. He will be effective in this area only if he is able to help these talented men in their specialties apply some of their genius to successful development and direction of the company's human resources.

Standards for company operations

Most good organizations have systems and procedures covering many aspects of their operations. Some are voluminous, and almost all are modified in practice. What happens in most business organizations is that emergency solutions are developed for emergency problems. Speaking to the stockholders of Kresge's at their recent annual meeting, H. B. Cunningham, board chairman, noted that, "Change is the only constant in a progressively managed business." The very nature of most business operations requires change and improvisation. High turnover of personnel, new product lines, different layouts, major advertising campaigns, seasonal pressures—these alter the business climate, and it is sometimes difficult to hold to rigid rules and standards.

In the face of such changes, most supervisors act more like fire chiefs than managers; they see their function as putting out fires rather than fire prevention. More energy and effort seem to go into responding to crises than in preventing problems. This tendency is not unique in any one industry. Rules posted in the locker room soon lose all meaning if, in practice, supervisors do not set an example. If the rule is to maintain cleanliness on the floor and the department manager walks past loose boxes, he has set a new standard. If a procedure for unloading merchandise and getting it to the store room is established but the supervisor is busy doing something else and the boxes are left in the receiving room, he too has set a new standard. And sadly, nothing seems to impair profits like delays in the movement of goods.

Establishing workable standards does not mean regimenting the environment. It does mean providing a guide that can be followed and incorporating a failsafe alternative if the first procedure does not work. Most important, both the procedure and the alternate must be realistic and practical. If rules and methods are not consistent with the actual and natural way in which things are done, they will soon become ineffective. One way to prevent this is to have the people who are most successful on the firing line help work out the procedure. It will then not only reflect practical application, but will be more apt to gain acceptance. Of course, management does not yield control if a procedure violates some company policy or objective; after all, management has final approval. However, employees are equally concerned with the overall success of an operation when they help participate in its development.

Developing people

As H. B. Cunningham pointed out in an editorial, "Perhaps the most vital requirement for any institution committed to dynamic growth is motivation. I think we have unusual morale . . . due to the advancement opportunities generated by expansion . . . but more important it is a climate of participation by everybody, a climate of involvement, a climate of job satisfaction." [2] Another executive, Donald P. Jones of Sun Oil Company, noted at a recent conference at the University of Tulsa:

> The development of abilities is in part a dialogue between the individual and his environment. If the employee has it to give, and the environment encourages it sufficiently, the ability will develop. We face this challenge: find the activity in which each employee is best qualified, then encourage him to reach the highest level of achievement of which he is capable. The more successful we are at this, the richer will be the employee's personal fulfillment, and the more significant his contribution to his company's goals.

Each of these leaders is saying that the development of people in an organization is clearly the most important single job of good management. In many organizations today, the environment changes so rapidly that some of the more stable and timeless techniques are difficult to set down, but those organizations that have undertaken the process appear to be among the most successful.

---

[2] H. B. Cunningham, "Management of Change," *Chain Store Age* (July, 1968), p. 16.

Organizational Objectives. A scheme or design must be established of the organization's objectives for the short, medium, and long ranges. This means that upper management must do some hard planning to identify the immediate goals for the next two years; these will be the base for a five-year plan for medium objectives and, finally, the long-range, ten-year projection. A manpower plan can now be designed to identify the kinds of skills and numbers of people needed to cope with the organizational objectives of expansion, product lines, acquisitions, and so on.

Management and Manpower Audit. The second stage requires, first, an appraisal of the organization's resources to help determine what functions are being carried out successfully and to identify those in the organization who are performing effectively. Second, the audit must determine who needs to be trained, upgraded, and coached to bring them up to more efficient performances. When this is done, it will then be possible to determine what additional personnel are needed to strengthen the organization, to fill some key areas, and to augment certain operations.

Job Descriptions and Performance Standards. A common complaint is, "I'm not sure that's my responsibility," or "I never know how I'm doing on my job." Both of these comments reflect a lack of job definitions and appraisals. Every employee should have a clear idea of the dimensions of his job, his responsibilities, and the extent of his authority. Once these are well-defined, there is an objective basis for evaluating his performance. Although the need for clear position outlines seems obvious, many organizations have been reluctant to set them down. What is expected of someone in a marginal supervisory job is often vague. True, some positions do overlap and there are gray areas, but these problems too should be dealt with and not left to chance.

Every supervisor should appraise the performance of his subordinates at least once a year. No one should be considered for a salary increase whose performance has not been appraised, and no one is eligible for appraisal until he has evaluated his own subordinates! In this way we are ensuring that everyone has at least once a year some measurement of his work and some guidance as to his growth needs. In such an environment we are able to establish a management in depth. Every key position will have a backstop, and every man is in training for a better spot. This gives a thrust to an organization's human resources development.

Encouraging innovation

Someone has suggested that maybe the future is a thing of the past. Can we anticipate the future, or can we plan to create the future? Those organizations that have excelled have been those with leadership that had the imagination and courage to create it. Unfortunately, many companies seem to be trend followers rather than trend makers; the gimmicks that succeed in one organization are quickly copied by competitors. What seems even more strange is the tendency on the part of most managers to accept the direction of "second-handers"—people who convey information they have picked up somewhere else without any evaluation or genuine knowledge.

Creativity is not widely distributed in the population, but nowhere is it more needed than in the business world. It is the x factor in profitable operations. An organization can provide a climate that encourages the development of creativity, just as it can the other trends to which we have referred. Research and development divisions are one form of helping to provide technical creativity in the company.

What are some techniques for encouraging creativity throughout the organization? Again we return to the concept of participative management. Regular meetings with teams of key personnel can provide an exchange that sharpens people's awareness and ideas. One becomes aware of a variety of alternatives available even within highly specialized areas. Contests within companies for ideas, art departments that have wide latitude, the encouragement of ideas from everyone, and the rewarding of successful contributions are other ways of encouraging people to think creatively within an organization. A high tolerance for ambiguity and imagination suggests a more dynamic organization. Some of the wildest ideas have turned out to be some of the most exciting and innovative. The whole wave of psychedelic effects, the mod outfits, and the trend toward youthful identification have demonstrated the extent of the influence of novel ideas.

Motivational research has implied that most people live rather narrow lives with little opportunity to express feeling. Since most people are considerably inhibited, the marketplace offers one of the most significant outlets for expression. That is why color, verve, and highly imaginative design in a wide variety of goods and products have such strong influence on impulse buying and on consumer satisfaction. The personal furnishings we possess are often the only things that reflect our feelings.

The creativity within an organization is like a garden, requiring frequent watering and feeding. It cannot be a flash-in-the-pan kind of thing; it must be an ongoing part of the establishment, like concern and awareness of people. The more we communicate to members of an organization that they are important and that their ideas are important the more their self-esteem rises and their willingness and desire to contribute to the organization increases. We must make it possible for people to develop to their fullest potential and to stimulate their creative thinking. In the final analysis, this is the lifeblood of any organization.

The Approach in Action

A human resources approach is one that emphasizes the motivation and development of people. The most powerful tool in this process is the selective reinforcement of successful behavior with immediate rewards. When desired standards are established, members of the organization are rewarded for maintaining them; this becomes the norm for the organization. The second important human resources tool is modeling—behavioral change as it reflects the example of the leadership. The concept that people learn by observing other people and what happens to them is part of everyday knowledge.

In helping to develop people to their fullest potential, the organization should also recognize the role of expectation in shaping behavior. This factor was investigated by Rosenthal and Jacobson in their work with Mexican-American children in south San Francisco; their interest was in the "self-fulfilling" prophecy.[3] The experimental procedure involved nothing more than giving the names of children who had been selected at random from among their classmates to their new teachers at the start of the school year, and describing them to the teachers as children who could be expected to show unusual intellectual gains in the year ahead. Actually, of course, the difference between these children and their classmates, who constituted a comparison group for the purposes of the study, was entirely in the minds of the teachers.

---

[3] Robert Rosenthal and Lenore F. Jacobson, "Teacher Expectations for the Disadvantaged," *Scientific American*, CCXVIII (April, 1968), pp. 19-23.

The objective test procedure demonstrated that the children from whom teachers expected greater intellectual gains made such gains, although, of course, they did not actually differ at the start of the year from the comparison children. The investigators concluded that these results did not occur because the teachers spent more time with the children; the explanation probably lies in the subtle ways in which teachers communicated their expectation, which would induce and reinforce a changed self-image in the child. The communication of expectations is not a gross procedure, but is subtle and frequently indirect. So too, in any organization. If management communicates in obvious or even subtle ways that subordinates are stupid, inept, inefficient, or lazy, they will often respond in those ways. Similarly, they will respond to the attitudes suggested in MacGregor's "Y" theory of management—that most people enjoy work if it is challenging and that people's intellectual and creative potential is greater than we think.

It has been found that it is possible to strengthen achievement behavior through discussion of achievement motivation. For example, management games simulating real-life situations provide tryout situations for developing new ways of thinking and behaving. In effect, a new strategy of behavior comes into play when it can be confirmed and stabilized by rewards in the environment.

Finally, there is clear evidence that participation in any problem-solving or decision-making situation significantly increases the personal satisfaction of the participants. And participation in a decision, when accompanied by public commitment, strengthens the behavior that follows as the classic food habit change studies of Lewin during World War II showed so dramatically. This is a powerful process for generating genuine feelings of personal worth, which support responsible behavior.

In the final analysis, the climate of any organization is the message. If it communicates an interest and respect for its employees, they will reciprocate in kind. If the message is one of deception, when there is a difference between what is said and what is practiced, they too will learn to play this game. If the environment is hostile, irritating, and unstable, the people who remain will develop this response as well. When the climate is healthy, the attitudes of its employees are healthy; the public responds, and the company is successful.

Questions

1. How does the human resources approach discussed by the author differ from the more traditional approach to personnel management?
2. What are some of the common weaknesses in the personnel practices followed by managers and supervisors in their relation with subordinates?
3. What bearing does the performance expectations of a superior toward his subordinates have upon the latter's performance?

15—A HARD LOOK AT THE SELECTION INTERVIEW *

Vernon R. Taylor

The interview is by far the most commonly used selection device. It is also the most expensive generally used. Some ten or fifteen million Americans are interviewed for jobs each year, and the cost is beyond calculation. It includes not only the immediate costs but such intangibles as often negative impact on the employers' public image and the cost of poor hiring decisions resulting from the interviews.

The interview is typically the only means of selection in private industry. We in the public service have prided ourselves that we use a variety of selection methods, usually in combination, and therefore are able to do a better job of selection than private industry. This may have been the case historically, but some of us have been distressed at the recent tendency to rely entirely on interviews when the labor supply gets short, when a list is urgently needed, or when influential groups say they dislike taking written tests. We need to examine the value of this instrument on which we are tending to rely so heavily, and which will so greatly influence the quality of our work force in the future.

The reliance on interviewing and the huge outlay of time and money expended on it suggest that the employment interview must be a proven and critical part of our government and industrial complex. We know that the major cost of most products and services is the cost of labor. We know that on many jobs a good worker will produce five times as much as do some other workers. We know of the millions and billions of dollars that go into the design of such prosaic things as fabrics, highways, and filing systems. Surely we must have proven the value of the interview, which is used to select nearly all of the employees who design and produce these things. This *must* be true at least in public employment, where procedures and expenditures are subject to review by everyone in the community. *This is not the case.*

There has been little research. What research has been conducted suggests that most employment interviews are largely a waste

* From *Public Personnel Review*, Vol. 30, No. 3 (July, 1969), pp. 149-154. Reprinted with permission.

of time. There is very little evidence that any interviewer can do much better than chance in predicting which of several likely applicants would be more successful at a particular job.

For some reason we all seem to feel that we can make accurate predictions of this kind, but the scant evidence says that we cannot. We have only our belief to defend our interviewing.

What are the facts?

Let us look at the facts. They have been summarized by Eugene C. Mayfield in *Personnel Psychology,* Volume 17, No. 3, Autumn, 1964. He reviewed the research reports published on employment interviewing since 1915 to see what generalizations could be made. He made two generalizations that were made by previous investigators:

1. The reliability of interview ratings in general is low. The reliability of the kinds of interviews most commonly conducted is "extremely low." When applicants are interviewed separately by different interviewers, there is very little agreement among their evaluations. This is true even when they obtain the same information.
2. The validity of interviews is usually low, even when the reliability is acceptable. By definition this means that interviews are seldom successful in predicting job performance. He even found that when valid written tests were given prior to the interview and the interviewer knew the results, his predictions were generally no better than those made by the test alone, and frequently worse.

If Mayfield had stopped here, this would have been only another "So what?" report. He did not. After noting that the research was sparse, often taken from a field other than employment, and seldom verified by other researchers, he went on to identify factors that were present when some evidence of validity was found. He found research support for the following:

1. When interviews are *unstructured*: (a) The interviewers do more talking than do the interviewees; (b) The interviewers make their decisions early in the interview, with minimum information; (c) The interviewers get biographical data adequately but fail particularly to understand the applicants' attitude; (d) The reliability is almost never satisfactory.
2. When the interviews are *structured*, these tendencies are reversed: the applicants do more talking, the decisions are made after more information has been obtained, more is learned about attitudes and other nonbiographical factors, and reliability tends to be higher.
3. When panel interviews are used, all interviewers get the same information, they usually get more information, and validity is higher than when single interviewers are used.

4. There are differing techniques of interviewing, some better than others. The technique used affects the outcome of an interview. The techniques can be taught.
5. The interview tends to be a search for unfavorable information, and the final evaluation is more closely related to unfavorable information obtained than to favorable information obtained.

Those of us who have attempted to validate our own interviews have found very little that is inconsistent with Mayfield's findings. The few cases of really significant validity known to the writer have all been in promotional examinations, when the interviewers were furnished with reports from supervisors about the applicants' past job performance. Mayfield did not specifically relate this kind of information to interview validity, but did comment that the interviews in one experiment in which voluminous information was furnished were "quite valid in predicting success."

Another viewpoint is of interest in this connection. Although most government jurisdictions use interviews extensively, the U.S. Civil Service Commission is an exception. The reasons has been explained by Dr. Albert Maslow, Chief, Personnel Measurement Research and Development Center. On the basis of his experience, he regards an interview almost solely as a means of obtaining and recording or verifying information about an applicant (and providing information to him). Once that information has been recorded, he feels that it can be better evaluated through an objective review of the interview record, in relation to other appraisal data, by another person rather than by an interviewer whose judgments will be influenced by his personal feelings and biases. He seems to be saying that factually reported observations and information can lead to valid predictions, but the predictions are most valid when the emotions and attitudes of interviewers are not directly interposed in the interview situation.

The idea that facts make the difference has been stated most clearly by professional recruiters (headhunters) in describing their methods. According to them the important thing in selecting executives is to find men with past records that indicate that they *have done* the kind of thing that the prospective employer wants done. Among these prospects they seek the one whose "chemical reaction" with his prospective employer is good. By "chemical reaction" they mean finding a common background and common views as judged in an interview, so the employer will have confidence in the applicant. The recruiters judge competence on the basis of the record and use an interview to provide for a choice from among equally qualified prospects. The interview provides an opportunity for the employer to learn which prospect most resembles himself in background, ideas, motivation, etc., and will therefore be most pleasing to him.

What should we do about it?

Certain very sound admonitions about interviewing have been repeated time and again in the literature. Their value can hardly be questioned.

1. An interviewer must know the duties of the job he is trying to fill. More important, he must know what specific aptitudes, knowledge, skills, or other attributes are needed to perform these tasks. The best applicant may be one who has the aptitudes and abilities to learn and who is motivated to succeed, rather than one with a year of similar experience. The interviewer must be able to zero in on the critical requirements rather than only make global or mechanical judgments.
2. See that the applicant is made welcome and is treated with dignity by everyone he meets. Interview him in privacy and in comfortable surroundings, without interruptions.
3. Interviewers tend to be concerned with the questions they have in mind and do not give the applicant enough opportunity to talk or to ask questions. Unsolicited remarks by the applicant are sometimes the most valuable information obtained in an interview. They are generally made in response to an open end question such as "Tell me about . . ."
4. If a job offer may be made during the interview or at a later time without further contact with the applicant, the interviewer must *give* information in addition to obtaining information. What is the job *really* like? What are the working conditions, the disadvantages, the further prospects? Why is the job vacant? Without this information the applicant may become only a turnover statistic.
5. An applicant is entitled to fair play over the outcome of the interview. He is entitled to know what his chances are if they have already been determined. It is unfair to let him leave an interview thinking he has been successful if an adverse decision has already been made or is likely to be made. Any serious questions the interviewer has about the applicant's qualifications can be discussed in a constructive and friendly manner.

In addition to these common admonitions, we must add the others which are dictated by research but which have seldom been stated as clearly as by Mayfield:

6. Interviews should be structured. Structuring results in higher reliability and validity by obtaining more information from applicants as well as more uniform information. There are two common types of structure.

The first requires that interviewers ask certain prepared questions of each applicant. This is a common method in personnel systems developed by consulting firms for use in a wide variety of industries or government jurisdictions. An interpretation and method of evaluation is usually given for each kind of answer to each question. This method results in good reliability because uniform information is obtained, and the information is uniformly evaluated. This advantage can be gained by a relatively unskilled interviewer, although the interview tends to be mechanical and stilted. In addition, this produces a tendency to use leading questions—questions to which the desired answers are apparent, with a resulting loss of validity. The same information might often be obtained by questionnaire.

The other common method of structuring requires that the interviewers themselves answer certain questions about each applicant without prescribing how they shall obtain the information. This usually involves use of a factor rating scale on which the interviewers check the degree to which each applicant possesses predetermined abilities and traits. Sometimes a specialized rating scale is developed for a given job or class of jobs. More often a single generalized set of factors is developed. When the latter is done, the interviewers usually need a statement of the factors critical to the job in question to aid in evaluating and weighting the information obtained.

This method results in a more informal and friendly interview, it utilizes open end questions which produce more and better information, and it tends to keep the interviewer quiet and the applicant talking. The additional information obtained results in a more valid evaluation if the interviewer is sufficiently skilled. It obviously requires a higher degree of skill than does a set of prepared questions.

One problem encountered in using a factor rating sheet is the occasional interviewer who does not feel that his interviewing needs the improvement afforded by this kind of structuring. He conducts an unstructured interview and makes a global evaluation. Then he meets the requirements by checking factors so as to justify his rating. His interview was subject to the weaknesses of any other unstructured interview.

7. Interviews should be conducted by a panel whenever possible. Experience indicates that a panel of three interviewers is most effective. When three interviewers work together as a team they assist each other in getting the facts and in following up leads, getting more complete information than would any one of them. Their post-interview discussions of applicant behavior and qualifications result in better clarification of the standards, better interpretation of the information obtained, the intrusion of fewer biases, and more valid evaluation than could be achieved by one of them alone.

8. Interviewers should be trained. It is clear that there are different methods of questioning and of evaluating the resulting information. Some of these methods are better than others, and some of them are appropriate to one situation but not to another. None of these techniques are known and practiced intuitively. If the learning is left to chance, who knows what techniques will be learned? What employer can afford to leave this to chance?

How this training should be conducted cannot be covered here. However, the need for it can be demonstrated easily: record your next few interviews on tape and play the tapes back. Do the same for interviews conducted by others in your own organization. Your own comments as you listen to the playbacks will be the best evidence of the need for training.

9. The interview tends to be a search for negative information, and this is its chief value. Any experienced interviewer will recall the certainty with which many applicants can be eliminated from the competition. On the other hand when several apparently qualified people are identified, it is much more difficult to rank them in order of merit, even in the minds of the interviewers. This is illustrated in panel interviews by the unanimity with which many applicants are rejected and the differences in opinion as to which of the qualified applicants are the best prospects.

The logical application of this principle is that if a comprehensive written or performance test can be used to measure the required traits there is no good reason for combining interview ratings with the test scores. The interview should result only in pass or fail ratings.

This conclusion is a generalization and must be treated as such. It becomes less true as dependable information about applicants' past performance is available to the interviewers, but this is seldom the case in open competitive selection. The generalization may not hold when the only real job requirement is a willingness to work, as is the case in some unskilled jobs. It is often not true when the applicants represent a wide range of education, reading ability, or ethnic groups, and the tests are therefore invalid. In recruiting for a class in such short supply that almost all applicants must be hired, an interview as the entire examination is consistent with this principle, since its effect is then only to pass or fail. These exceptions, however, do not justify many of the practices that are common today.

What else should be done?

The interview is here to stay. It is defended for all the wrong reasons, chiefly because everyone cherishes the belief that, contrary to the general rule, he himself is a peculiarly good judge of character. The real reason we must live with it is that we cannot live without it. It is almost impossible to fill a vacant position without some personal contact with the applicants, and that contact becomes some sort of interview. Instead of fighting it we should join it and make it more effective.

We can do much toward improving our interviews if we apply the knowledge we now have, much of which is summarized above. The most conspicuous and damaging failure at this time is the lack of training. There are few college courses in interviewing, and these are of dubious value. Few governmental or industrial organizations provide in-service training in interviewing. It appears that interviewing has not been recognized as a skill.

Mayfield and others have pointed out the need for a great deal of research. Why do we wait for someone else to do it? We who, by interview, continually make and break careers and make hiring decisions which can make or break major organizations should accept some responsibility. If we cannot carry on simple validation studies of differing techniques, we can at least interest the academic community in doing it for us.

Investigation of the kinds of factors described above is important, but is not the only kind. Whole new vistas might be opened up. One of these is the interpretation of nonverbal communication. Albert Mehrabian, in the September, 1968 issue of *Psychology Today*, points out that nonverbal communication discloses emotions, feelings, and preferences when words do not or when the words are to the contrary. He lists vocal but nonverbal media such as tones, stresses, inflections, and pauses in speech. In addition there are physical acts such as facial expressions, gestures, or bodily rigidity that say more than do the words spoken.

Margaret G. Herman, in a research bulletin issued in draft form by the Educational Testing Service (RB-68-9), has gone much farther. She has summarized the body of research in this field in a manner similar to Mayfield's summary. She finds evidence that people have stable or habitual kinds of behavior patterns which, if interpreted correctly, may tell a great deal about them. In addition, there are transient or changing behaviors that express strong feelings about what is being discussed at the moment and about the person with whom it is being discussed, without ever being put into words. A few of these that have been at least tentatively identified by research are:

1. Talking speed and the rate of eye blinking increase with an increase of stress and anxiety.
2. The voice becomes louder and higher pitched when the speaker is angry or fearful.
3. A lower pitched voice and a lounging bodily attitude indicate an unmobilized body, which is associated with indifference.
4. There is a significant change in voice intensity with a lie response as compared to preceding responses.
5. The verbal content of responses to questions on one subject can be analyzed and compared with typical responses to other subjects. A person who sees only one side of a given problem, or discusses it in conventional terms or platitudes may have a similarly closed mind to most problems. One who typically examines and considers all aspects of a problem may demonstrate that trait in a sample problem posed in an interview.

The interpretation of such behavior, once stated, may seem to be self-evident, almost platitudinous. Recognition and utilization of them may be part of the conscious or unconscious art of all good interviewers, but so far they are little more than observations. How much talking speed is required to yield a measure of anxiety, and how does self-confidence relate to talking speed? What else in addition to a lie is frequently associated with a change in voice intensity? If stereotyped responses are made to familiar problems, would they also be made to new and unique situations?

We do not have good answers to any of these questions. If we could answer them with assurance, consider how much more we could learn about an applicant in an interview of the same length. And note that use of principles such as these (if they are truly principles) could be taught to interviewers.

In summary

The evidence shows that:

1. Most interviews contribute very little to good selection.
2. We have information now that would enable us to do a much better job of interviewing if we would only use it.
3. If interviewing were subjected to the research expended on far less important things, it might take its place with written and performance testing as a reliable and valid selection instrument.

Questions

1. In view of the low validity in the results yielded by selection interviews, why is the interview still utilized so widely?
2. How can the interview be made to serve more effectively as a selection aid?
3. What are some of the suggestions made by the author that may help the interviewer to improve his interviewing techniques?
4. Does the author advocate the use of the structured or the unstructured interview in the selection of applicants?

16—TESTING JOB APPLICANTS FROM DISADVANTAGED GROUPS *

Jerome E. Doppelt and George K. Bennett

Every day people make decisions which affect the lives of other people. When tests play a role in the decision process, considerable feeling may be engendered, not only among those directly concerned but among the "spectators" as well. Those of us who have been seriously concerned with improving the effectiveness of tests have been aware of their limitations and of circumstances which may diminish their usefulness. We have long recognized, for example, that a test of mental ability does not measure native ability but rather it measures the individual's present capability of demonstrating his skills or knowledge. From this demonstration one then makes a decision about the individual's likelihood of success in certain endeavors.

It would be a formidable task to discuss the pros and cons of testing in all the fields in which decisions are, or might be, influenced by tests. We will limit this discussion, therefore, to an area of importance to all of us—the use of tests in the employment of people who are members of "disadvantaged groups."

The term "disadvantaged groups," as used in this discussion, refers to the subgroups in our population who have been victims of educational, cultural, or economic disadvantages. The deprivations suffered by people in such groups are assumed to stem primarily from their membership in the groups. Several observations may be made about the term "disadvantaged groups." First, it seems to be an ethnic or national-origin classification. Negroes and Puerto Ricans are usually included among the disadvantaged; so are Mexican-Americans and Indians. Second, there are subgroups of the white majority who are economically and educationally disadvantaged, but the term is seldom applied to them. Third, the term conveys the impression of a group that is homogeneous with respect to ability and deprivation, in spite of the fact that its members usually show a

* From *Test Service Bulletin* of The Psychological Corporation, No. 57 (May, 1967).

range in abilities and interests. Of course, this range may be restricted when compared with that of the general population.

Employment decisions require the making of predictions, whether the latter are made from mathematical equations or by intuition. We are concerned, therefore, with problems in predicting job success from the test scores of disadvantaged persons. It has been proposed that procedures which are suitable for a majority of applicants are not appropriate for those who may be described as educationally or culturally deprived. This may possibly be so, but one must guard against oversimplified solutions to a complex problem. Naive solutions which are applied equally to all members of a disadvantaged group (or to different groups of disadvantaged) are likely to be ineffective and may even create new problems of undesirable discrimination. Let us consider some of the charges leveled against tests in this context, and evaluate some suggested corrective measures.

Some of the Charges

Anxiety in the Testing Situation. A frequent criticism is that many existing tests do not adequately evaluate the capabilities of members of disadvantaged groups. It is pointed out that the disadvantaged may score poorly because of anxiety about the testing situation and because of low motivation. It is also felt that examiners from the "advantaged" population tend to inhibit the performance of the disadvantaged. This is more likely to be a problem when individual tests rather than group tests are administered and when the examinees are children rather than job applicants, but some feel it is still a problem when testing in employment offices.

Unfairness of Content. It is further maintained that most existing tests, especially verbal measures, emphasize middle-class concepts and information and are therefore unfair to those who have not been exposed to middle-class cultural and educational influences. Consequently, the low test scores which are earned are not indicative of the "true" abilities of the disadvantaged. Predictions of job success made from such scores are therefore held to be inaccurate.

Improper Interpretation of Scores. There is the contention that scores do not have the same meaning for the disadvantaged that they

do for the advantaged. Both the pattern of scores (when a battery
is used) and the level of performance (on even a single test) require
interpretation in the light of the background of the examinee. It is
argued, however, that for interpreting the scores of disadvantaged
persons the usual kinds of background evaluation are not enough.
Test scores of the disadvantaged, it is held, should be compared only
with test scores of others similarly disadvantaged. In this way, a
score which would be considered mediocre, according to norms based
on a national sample, might be considered superior when compared
with the performance of a particular deprived group.

Lack of Relevance. It is charged that test items are often not
related to the work required on the job for which the applicant is
being considered, and that even where relationships can be shown
between test scores and job success, there is no need to eliminate low-
scoring disadvantaged people since they can be taught the necessary
skills and knowledge in a training period after hiring. In addition,
some critics feel that bias against disadvantaged groups frequently
enters into the performance ratings which serve as the criteria for
validating the tests, and this artificially confirms the gloomy predictions made from the scores. Thus, the picture is one of a self-
fulfilling prophecy of doom for the disadvantaged.

Meeting the Criticisms

In response to these charges, reasonable people generally offer
suggestions which they believe will make the tests "fairer" rather
than demand that all testing cease. Eliminating tests entirely would
remove from the hiring process an approach which is potentially
more objective, more color-blind, and more susceptible to verifica-
tion as to effectiveness than most of the other techniques used in
the employment procedure. As John W. Gardner, the present Secretary
of Health, Education, and Welfare, wrote in the book *Excellence* [1] in
reference to testing in schools: "The tests couldn't see whether the
youngster was in rags or in tweeds, and they couldn't hear the accents
of the slum. The tests revealed intellectual gifts at every level of
the population." More is to be gained from the proper use of tests
than from their exclusion; accordingly, some of the corrective measures that have been offered should be carefully scrutinized.

---

[1] New York: Harper & Bros., 1961. Pp. 48-49.

Methods of alleviating anxiety

To allay test anxiety it has been suggested that if an examinee has failed, he be permitted to come back for one or more retests. It is alleged that this procedure would provide the practice in taking tests which is so lacking among the disadvantaged.

Where the test requires demonstration of proficiency, as in type-writing, the test is a sample of the actual skill required for the job, and practice by the applicant between testings would only tend to improve his real skill. The administration of a form that may have been given previously would not result in distorted interpretations of his current typing skill, although it is preferable to have alternate forms available for retesting.

With a general ability test, however, permitting applicants to take it again and again, as a means of reducing anxiety, has serious consequences. Retests are sometimes sought by individuals who hope to become familiar with the nature of the specific test and, consequently, to do better on the retest. If the same form of a test is administered more than once within a short time period, practice between testings is likely to result not in improved general ability that would be pertinent to success on the job but rather in improved scores which may simply be due to practice in remembering answers to specific questions. Furthermore, the examinee may have searched for outside help to provide answers to some items. The validity of scores obtained under such conditions is suspect.

Nevertheless, people who wish to be retested should probably be given the opportunity to take the test or tests again, but any test which is to be given to the same people more than once should have alternate forms. Although the availability of two or three forms of a test is not uncommon, the preparation of a large number of forms is a time-consuming and expensive process. In addition to alternate forms of the *same* test, it would be desirable to have *different* tests, each with several forms, available for testing and retesting. Of course, studies which establish the comparability of scores on the different tests used would be essential.

It is apparent from the discussion above that the successive administration of "real tests" over a short time interval is not always a practical procedure for allaying test anxiety. Rather, it is preferable to provide a practice or demonstration period in which different kinds of tests and answer media are discussed. This kind of activity can alleviate the unfamiliarity and dispel some of the fear of the unknown about the testing situation without compromising any "real tests." In response to this need, The Psychological Corporation has been developing a presentation on tape, accompanied by a practice booklet,[2] to acquaint students and others who might soon be applying for jobs with some of the common types of employment tests. If this approach proves useful, schools and employment offices may find it an economical way to eliminate one source of concern.

As a means of reducing the role of the live examiner in the testing situation, the use of recorded directions to administer actual tests, with both the reading of directions and the timing included on the tape or record, has been suggested. The advantages of such uniform administration are obvious. Moreover, the use of tapes may be more acceptable to those who tend to feel uncomfortable when the examiner is a member of a different group.

Diminishing cultural bias

Either because of their content or style, there are some types of test questions which provoke charges of cultural bias from well-meaning persons even when such charges may have little basis in fact. If it is possible to achieve the purpose of the testing by using measures which do not contain such provocative items, it is manifestly desirable to do so, regardless of the merits of the charges. Many of those who feel that existing tests are too loaded with "middle-class" items to be fair to disadvantaged groups propose "culture-free" or "culture-fair" tests as substitutes. The term "culture-free" is misleading; no instrument which measures behavior can be free of cultural influences. What is sought are "culture-fair" or "cross-cultural" or "culture-common" tests which are measures based on experiences equally familiar or unfamiliar to advantaged and disadvantaged groups. It is often suggested that verbal tests should be replaced by nonverbal measures in order to eliminate cultural bias. However, the preponderant weight of research evidence indicates that nonverbal tests do not measurably benefit disadvantaged groups. In most instances, the disadvantaged score no better on nonverbal or so-called "culture-fair" tests than they do on conventional tests.

Perhaps the answer lies in trying to obtain the "culture-laden" rather than the "culture-free" test. The purpose of employment testing is to select people who ultimately will be successful in one or more jobs. The jobs are inevitably embedded in some cultural matrix,

---

[2] *Test Orientation Procedure (TOP).*

and the criteria of success will undoubtedly be influenced by cultural factors. Thus the abilities to understand oral and perhaps written instructions, to go from one place to another in a reasonable manner, and to cope with simple arithmetic, are activities which are "culture-laden" but which are also likely to be criterion-related. Such behaviors have their parallels in everyday living and can be translated into test questions which are not unfair to disadvantaged applicants.

Prompted by such considerations, a series of tests entitled *Fundamental Achievement Series* is being developed by The Psychological Corporation. The series includes verbal and numerical tests, with many of the items in each test based on "culture-laden" experiences assumed to be quite common in the population.

Investigation of bonuses and separate norms

To compensate the disadvantaged for the effects of deprivation they have experienced, various devices have been proposed to adjust their test scores. One suggestion is that raw score points be given as a bonus, a procedure apparently similar, though not truly comparable, to the awarding of bonus points to veterans taking a civil service examination. Aside from the problems of determining who should be given a bonus and how much bonus, making the award is a discriminatory act which adds nothing to the essential predictive value of the test.

The position that test scores of the disadvantaged should be compared only with the scores of others similarly disadvantaged can become, in some circumstances, a special case of awarding a bonus. Norms based on the disadvantaged provide useful descriptive information and, together with norms for the majority group, the data could be helpful to counselors and psychologists who are advising individuals. But if a separate cutoff score is established for each norms group, in order to yield the same percentage of acceptable cases from the different groups, we have essentially the situation of giving bonus points to the lower-scoring groups.

These approaches to the problem of employing the disadvantaged have little value in selection. Adoption of such procedures would place a burden on the civilian employer which is not undertaken by either the civil service or the military agencies of the United States. It is clearly the obligation of an employer not to discriminate among persons on the grounds of race, religion, or national origin, but it is clearly not the obligation of an employer to hire or to promote the less qualified in an attempt to compensate for some injustice of society in general.

When there is adequate evidence that test scores have different meanings for different groups, an improvement in accuracy of prediction may result from the use of weightings which would be optimum for each group. Experience to date has not revealed frequent occasions for such differential weighting.

Appropriate use of test scores

All of us recognize the importance of the training or apprenticeship period in developing the skills needed for certain kinds of jobs. Some have maintained that during the training period conducted by a company for newly hired people, the disadvantaged can be taught what they need to know, regardless of their scores on the employment tests. Therefore, it is argued, the administration of tests which include questions that have little to do with the job is unjustified. This argument deserves serious examination. Certainly, skills and knowledge can be imparted to motivated people during a training period, and efforts in this direction should be encouraged. Usually such training is more successful for relatively simple jobs which require few skills and operations than for higher level jobs which call for a broader spectrum of previously developed talents. But even in training situations, tests will ordinarily predict the ability to learn *about* the job while on the job, or the ability to complete the necessary training. Many companies would like to hire people who can be promoted to better jobs after they have mastered the entry job. Tests which measure general ability—as reflected in verbal and numerical aptitude—are helpful in identifying applicants who would be suitable for promotion in the future. It is important to remember that tests which seem unrelated to immediate jobs might be useful in identifying those who could advance to higher levels.

Tests, like other predictive instruments, must be evaluated in terms of how well predictions made from them conform with reality as represented by measures of success on the job (criteria). Without an adequate criterion, meaningful and free of bias, it will be difficult for anyone to know what predictors are effective. It is obvious to professional users of tests that criteria must be studied and refined; others may occasionally need a reminder not to forget the criteria while they are busy attacking the predictors.

Summing Up

Companies have been accused of using tests as a means of maintaining unfair discrimination against groups which have already suffered from many forms of discrimination. Such practices are a distortion of the proper function of tests and deserve condemnation. It does not follow, however, that tests themselves merit condemnation. Most users in industry expect the tests to help them identify the people best suited for the jobs to be filled.

From the standpoint of corporate management, the employment function can legitimately be viewed as a type of purchasing operation. It then is the duty of the employment manager to hire those candidates who offer the best promise of contributing to the success of the enterprise. The reason that tests have been used for many years by many employers is that, in management's opinion, the information furnished by tests is valuable in making hiring decisions. If the employer sets his minimum scores too high, he does not fill the available jobs. If he sets his minimum scores too low he hires persons difficult to train, low in productivity, and high in liability to error. Sophisticated personnel officers realize that predictors such as interviews, reference investigations, and tests are part of a total evaluation problem, that of obtaining better workers or of matching workers and jobs more precisely.

Whenever the number of applicants exceeds the number of job openings, some applicants will be rejected. This is one of the hard facts of life. It is not surprising that those who are rejected sometimes attack the selection procedures on the grounds that these are invalid or unfair. Although testing is not free from defect or beyond criticism, appropriately chosen and properly administered ability tests are superior to most available alternatives.

Some of the problems which stem from the testing of disadvantaged groups are of a technical nature and are not related to the issue of discrimination. Reduced reliability is often due to the fact that score distributions obtained from disadvantaged groups are compressed. The same compression (and reduced reliability) is also found when only highly capable individuals are being tested. These problems require technical study and, in some instances, may call for the use of different measures or the development of new and more appropriate tests. The basic issue is not necessarily one of discrimination against a particular subgroup.

Many of the issues in the testing of disadvantaged groups have both psychometric and social aspects. Some of the current testing procedures should be changed to reduce the fear and hostility that may be engendered by materials felt to be biased or unfair. More attention must be devoted to research with actual score and performance data in order to improve the predictive efficiency of tests. Such changes in employment and research procedures will increase the likelihood of employment tests fulfilling their primary mission of helping the employer select the people best able to do the jobs. These approaches are basically psychometric steps.

Discrimination against disadvantaged groups, which is at the root of the concern of many who attack tests, will not be resolved by improved psychometrics alone. Discrimination in the world of work is a social ailment. Although poor showings on tests may be a symptom of the ailment, the use of tests in employee selection is inherently a friendly rather than a hostile act to those who come to the job market from backgrounds of limited opportunity. Society may well have the responsibility of providing effective remedial instruction for those who have been culturally deprived. The rejection of measuring instruments which register the consequence of such deprivation is merely a modern version of killing the messenger who brings bad news.

Questions

1. Specifically, upon what basis are tests criticized for being unfair to the culturally disadvantaged?
2. How may the anxiety of examinees toward tests be reduced?
3. What suggestions does the article offer for the development of test norms for disadvantaged groups?
4. To what extent is it possible through improvements in the construction and use of psychological tests to reduce discrimination in the employment of the disadvantaged? To what extent is it not possible?

17—RED FLAGS MISSED— WRONG MAN HIRED *

Quinn G. McKay

Paul Cheney, president of Space Chemicals, Inc., had just left the Seattle-Tacoma Airport on a jetliner for a business trip to Boston. The purpose of his trip was not to recruit management personnel and yet, as the plane sped eastward, his mind was preoccupied with a staffing problem.

During the past few weeks company officers had concentrated considerable thought and conversation on the critical need for a vice-president to handle production. Space Chemicals, a firm engaged primarily in developing and producing fuels and chemicals for space exploration, had been incorporated for less than a year. Demands from government and private industry had accelerated the company's growth at an unusual rate. Obtaining experienced top managers with the essential technical background was always a critical problem; the industry as a whole had expanded so rapidly that most companies were continually bidding for managers already well established in other firms as well as for those openly seeking new employment.

After changing planes in Chicago, Cheney found himself seated next to a Mr. Rigtrip. Introductions revealed that both were working in the area of space chemicals. During the conversation that followed, Cheney became more and more impressed by Rigtrip's technical knowledge of space fuels and related problems, and by his apparent personal friendship with a great many key men of the industry, both in government and private corporations.

Cheney asked Rigtrip if he would consider an employment offer with another firm. His new acquaintance replied that he was being promoted to the head office in Boston, and, while he much preferred managing the plant in Illinois and did not want to move, he felt that he must accept the promotion.

* From *Business Horizons*, Vol. 6, No. 2 (Summer, 1963), pp. 47-52. Reprinted with permission.

"Wouldn't you at least make a trip to Seattle and look over our setup?" pressed Cheney.

"No," Rigtrip insisted. "I just couldn't consider employment with another firm at this time."

Cheney prevailed on the man until, at the Logan Airport in Boston, Rigtrip reluctantly said, "Well, give me a call in about two weeks when I've had a chance to evaluate my new situation, and we'll discuss it then."

Cheney's call two weeks later resulted in Rigtrip's agreeing to make a trip to Seattle and a three-day visit at Space Chemicals, Inc. During his visit Rigtrip was interviewed privately by each of the top executives. Some of these interviews lasted three hours. He was taken golfing, to dinner, to a cocktail party, and to other activities; during this time, company executives had ample opportunity to observe his actions and reactions in a variety of social and business situations. Finally, Space Chemicals officers agreed unanimously that here was an ideal vice-president for production if only he could be lured from his present employer. Not one negative comment was made about the man's qualifications. In fact, most of the conversation focused on the problem of making an offer that would induce him to come to Seattle.

Finally, just before Rigtrip left to return to Boston, President Cheney made him a salary and stock option offer that was significantly better than his current earnings. Rigtrip said he would consider it, talk it over with his wife, and telephone his answer in the next few days. Four days later the phone rang at Space Chemicals in Seattle, and the president informed the operator that he would accept the charges.

"I've given serious thought to your offer," Rigtrip stated, "and I've called to tell you that I will accept the position of vice-president with your company."

Three weeks later, the new vice-president was on the job in Seattle and, as agreed, was given a comparatively free rein on production matters. The company officers and directors were relieved to have a competent man handling this important aspect of the business. Within a few weeks, however, things began going wrong in production. Finally the situation degenerated to such a state that Rigtrip was asked to resign from the company. As one officer put it, "He turned out to be a complete dud." Shortly after the vice-president's services had been terminated, Cheney found out from the man's former employer that Rigtrip was not really being promoted to the head office in Boston after all. Actually he had made such a mess of things at the plant in Illinois that he was being kicked upstairs to get him out of the way.

In a postmortem of this expensive and disappointing experience, Space Chemicals officers asked themselves, "What went wrong?" Each recalled numerous red flags that had been thrown out during the three-day visit. Certain of Rigtrip's actions and statements, if investigated, would have exposed his deficiencies before he was hired. For example, when asked to describe the responsibilities of his new job in Boston, Rigtrip replied, "I think they'll involve expert advising on critical matters. However, they really haven't been completely outlined yet. That's why I had time to come out here and am now willing to consider this opportunity. I'm an operating man. I must always have a challenge or I'm not satisfied."

When talking about the plant in Illinois, Rigtrip commented, "The plant had shown a good record under my leadership until a little over a year ago when employee turnover started to rise. The real cause of this problem was that the head office insisted on implementing certain policies I knew wouldn't be effective. And they weren't, as evidenced by the way the employees became upset. I was just in the process of getting one of the policies changed to get things straightened out when this promotion came to go to the head office."

Reflecting later on the first statement, Cheney could see that a man who really was the caliber Rigtrip claimed to be would have fully understood his new mission before the transfer occurred. As for the second, it seemed more than a coincidence that a promotion came when performance in the plant was down for a suspect reason.

Why weren't these experienced, mature business executives more astute and objective in their selection process? Why were they oblivious to all of the red flags? These men were and are competent executives, and Space Chemicals has continued as a profitable concern. The problem was not that they were unable to obtain information on the candidate, but that they ignored what was available and at times apparently obvious.

A phenomenon called *selective perception* seems to be a major cause of the difficulty at Space Chemicals and also at many other organizations.

What Is Selective Perception?

Most people find it significantly easier to recall pleasant and satisfying experiences than mildly disturbing or mildly unpleasant experiences. This psychological characteristic, which enables man to ignore or block out certain experiences while recognizing and retaining a consciousness of others, is called selective perception. In human behavior, "monotonous events that seem to bear little *threat* or *promise* are largely ignored."[1] Stated another way, experiences that receive recognition must appear to be either significantly rewarding or significantly dangerous. "Lukewarm" or mildly disturbing experiences go by practically unnoticed and are usually all but forgotten.

Harold J. Leavitt has described selective perception in this way: "People perceive what they think will help satisfy needs; ignore what is disturbing; and again perceive disturbances that persist and increase."[2]

Such human behavior is frequently upsetting to executives who often find that young managers are prone to avoid or even forget unpleasant little tasks such as writing difficult letters or disciplining. On the other hand, this same phenomenon permits a division head to complete a production report even though men and machines are making considerable noise in the background.

A particular aspect of selective perception referred to by the psychologists as hypothesis-theory[3] is of more than casual importance in selecting executives. This natural human characteristic tends to make first impressions unduly important. Most of us at one time or another have used the phrase, "First impressions are the most important." This truism has a psychological basis; humans do not accept all experiences at random.

Managers, like other people, tend to make quick judgments about a person at the first meeting. It is usually an over-all or general evaluation on the order of "I like him" or "I don't like him." After this first evaluation, managers tend to select from subsequent experiences with that man evidence that supports the original judgment and to ignore evidence that suggests the inaccuracy of the judgment.

---

[1] George A. W. Boehm, "That Wonderful Machine, The Brain," *Fortune*, LXVII (February, 1963), 125.

[2] Harold J. Leavitt, *Managerial Psychology* (Chicago: University of Chicago Press, 1960), p. 32.

[3] Theoretical and empirical support for this idea is found in Bruner and Postman's writings. For a review of these works, *see* F. H. Allport, *Theories of Perception and the Concept of Structure* (New York: John Wiley & Sons, Inc., 1955), Chapter 15, particularly pp. 380-83.

In other words, an executive's first impression of a potential employee will usually color reactions to subsequent experiences with that man. For instance, when involved in conversation with a person who has favorably impressed him, or when reading his application forms or letters of recommendation, the manager will tend to pay attention to evidence of high motivation, neatness, alertness, and intelligence while ignoring indications of laziness, unkempt appearance, and/or slowness at learning. Ordinarily, a glaring weakness is required to bring about a change in the original judgment. How obvious the weakness would have to be depends upon the intensity of the first impression, which is, in large measure, determined by the needs of the selector. If a manager's first impression of an applicant is negative, subsequent indications of laziness or ineptitude will tend to make him even more critical of the candidate.

Because this human characteristic may have resulted in the selection of some incompetent personnel and the exclusion of some competent candidates, one must conclude that first impressions are not only important for the applicant but have serious implications for the executive who is doing the selecting.

Implications For Management

At least three closely related areas of the management function are directly affected by selective perception: selecting managers "in" (hiring) or "out" (firing), appraisal interviews, and disciplining. Awareness of the influence of selective perception is more important in selecting managers than in selecting nonmanagement personnel. Interest, aptitude, and personality tests are useful in selecting for lesser jobs. As more and more weight is placed on these test results, the influence of selective perception will be diminished. However, in the case of management positions, objective tests will provide at best only a guide or aid to selection. Most managers are still selected on personal evaluations, judgments, and impressions formed by the executive or executives in charge.

Whenever personal judgment and evaluation are used, selective perception may exercise a significant influence on the final choice. The term "may" must be used because the degree of distortion resulting from selective perception will vary in direct proportion to the intensity of the need or danger for the selector. Cheney and his fellow officers at Space Chemicals had a critical need for a vice-president of production. For some months the intensity of this need had been building up as a result of company growth and of the frustrating results of the search for a qualified man. It is easy to understand how selective perception so completely distorted the personal evaluation of Rigtrip. On hearing Rigtrip use the industry terminology and drop the names of important people, Cheney formed a strong judgment, which he carried to his fellow officers. From each subsequent experience with Rigtrip, Cheney saw and paid attention to evidence which indicated that the candidate would make a good vice-president, because this appeared to satisfy a critical need. In each experience, Cheney literally ignored or blocked out those facts that suggested Rigtrip was less than competent, because to recognize them would be mildly disturbing. Finally, when the situation degenerated to a point of danger, all the officers saw and paid attention to Rigtrip's inadequacies and he was "selected out."

Appraisal interviews are affected much the same way by selective perception. While working with another person, we usually form a total judgment of him on the order of "He is a good worker" or "He is a poor worker." As time passes, this judgment is reinforced through selective perception until sometimes, in extreme instances, it becomes unalterable. This prompts a subordinate to observe honestly that "The boss just can't see anything wrong with that lazy, conniving Joe." If a superior has prejudged a worker to be "good," he literally tends to ignore or is unable to see his weaknesses during the appraisal. When and only when the weakness becomes so glaring as to be dangerous is the threshold reached and a change in judgment forced. An original judgment of a worker as "poor" results in the opposite conclusion.

Appraisal interview forms that require factor-by-factor evaluation are attempts to reduce the distortion of selective perception. These help except where the judgment or set has become so intense as to block out contrary information entirely.

Selective perception can result in unfair disciplinary action. Over the years, President Cheney has had a pleasant, satisfying working relationship with Sterling, the vice-president. Time has created a situation wherein it is difficult for the president to see faulty behavior that warrants disciplinary action. Sterling's misbehavior must reach the point of being dangerous before it will be seen by the president. Other subordinates may feel that Sterling tends to "get away with murder," that Ray, a division manager, on the other hand, has never been fully trusted by the president. Because Ray's misdeeds tend to confirm or satisfy the president's original evaluation, he tends to see all of Ray's missteps and to ignore those acts that suggest Ray is as competent as Sterling. Hence, the urge to discipline Ray is more frequent and more intense than the desire to discipline Sterling, even though their performance may be comparable. Not infrequently a situation of this kind becomes the basis for subordinates' accusations that "The boss is unfair and plays favorites." In such situations, the president may honestly think he is being perfectly objective, because selective perception literally blocks out the good performance of Ray and the bad performance of Sterling.[4] He is probably being objective with the information he sees, but he isn't seeing all the information.

Suggested Action

Few indeed are so naïve as to think the problems connected with selective perception can be completely eradicated. Until we learn more about how the brain gathers and stores experiences, we will have to live with this condition. However, I would urge that steps be taken to minimize the undesirable effects of this human trait in the organizational setting.

Be aware that this influence exists. Most of us readily admit and recognize it in the judgment of others but are prone to deny that it has any bearing on our judgments and our evaluations. Be willing to admit that the phenomenon is at work, whether we can immediately observe it in our own behavior or not. Usually, in a few moments of honest reflection, managers can cite specific incidents of the characteristic at work in their own experience. Be willing to admit that strong personal needs exist and that, in a given situation, it is natural to see those aspects which appear to satisfy the need and to ignore those aspects which mildly suggest this will not satisfy the needs. Recognize that the stronger the need and the more urgent the problem, the stronger and more complete will be the influence of selective perception.

Develop a critical attitude. A totally critical attitude about everything is dangerous, but an appropriately critical attitude may avoid

---

[4] Actually the perceiver must "see" each aspect in order to decide that he wants to reject or ignore. This awareness followed by instant rejection occurs so rapidly that it apparently takes place at the subconscious level.

unpleasantness like that experienced at Space Chemicals. Management should be critical, particularly when a man or a situation appears to have practically no negative aspects. With a man who is "perfect" for the job, it would be wise to say, "No man is perfect. Let me now enumerate all of his drawbacks." Or if a man is "poorly suited," say to yourself, "No man is completely bad. Let me concentrate on his good points." Cultivating the capacity to ask critical questions of one's judgment will help avoid the blind spots created by selective perception.

Closely related to the previous measure is the *development of tough mindedness in answering the questions raised.* When the need to obtain an executive is great and the first judgment of the candidate has been positive, there is a strong tendency to discount the inadequacies of a "good" man even after questioning has revealed them. The greater the necessity to fill a certain management position, the greater will be the desire to dismiss discovered shortcomings as unimportant. Tough mindedness in investigating and evaluating both apparent weaknesses and apparent strengths will minimize the distortion occasioned by selective perception.

When considering a candidate, *ask for an evaluation from another person* who is not likely to be so emotionally involved in the situation as to be preconditioned. A consultant or a fellow businessman outside the company are good sources of objective evaluations. Granted, these outsiders cannot and would not be expected to make a final decision; they would not be adequately acquainted with the needs of the company. But the fact that they are not intimately acquainted with these needs would tend to make them more objective in observing and evaluating strengths and weaknesses overlooked by those in the company.

The judgment of several officers within the company is essential. Their needs, however, may all be identical since they have been conditioned together about the situation. The perception of each would be distorted in the same direction and hence would fail to provide the much needed different perspective. Cheney no doubt discussed Rigtrip with the other company officers when he returned from his trip to Boston. His description of the man was probably a glowing one, which preconditioned the executives who subsequently interviewed him.

When taking a candidate to another person in the company or outside, a more objective evaluation can be obtained if the executive will not bias the evaluator with the introduction. The company president is creating a bias if he walks into the vice-president's office and says, "This is John Downs. I've talked with him and he looks like a very good prospect for the job of division manager. Would you have a talk with him?" Knowing that the boss apparently approves of this man will establish in the vice-president a first impression that will cause him to notice particularly Downs's strengths. If a weakness does appear, the vice-president will tend to ignore it, because recognition of it would mean going against his superior's judgment. Ordinarily the vice-president would need to observe glaring inadequacies before he would be armed with enough confidence to suggest that the boss was wrong. Of course, the relationship between the president and the vice-president is another factor that will either exaggerate or minimize the degree of this influence.

Selective perception is a phenomenon that must be dealt with in executive selection. This human trait biases judgments in selecting as well as evaluating for appraisals and disciplinary actions. The negative effects of selective perception can be minimized if, when selecting executives, a manager will recognize and admit the characteristics, ask critical questions, be tough minded when answering these questions, and, when possible and appropriate, ask an outsider for his evaluation of the candidate.

Questions

1. Would you conclude that Mr. Rigtrip was untruthful in his statements about his employment with the Boston company? Explain.
2. We note that Mr. Cheney reacted favorably to Mr. Rigtrip's use of space chemical terminology and to his familiarity with "big names" in the field. What implication does this have for the interview as a method of assessing qualifications of a prospective employee?
3. Several studies have shown the tendency to rate "old timers" in a company much higher than those individuals who have less service. How does this fact relate to the concept of selective perception?
4. If an executive desires to obtain the frank opinions of his subordinates, how should he proceed?
5. Other than the "red flags" that were missed, what sources of information were available to Mr. Cheney and his fellow officers concerning Mr. Rigtrip's qualifications?

CHAPTER 3

Achieving Performance Effectiveness

While the organization of jobs and the recruitment and selection of personnel to fill them are essential steps in the development of an effective work force, they are only the initial stages in the process. The ability of those who are selected to realize their full potential and to contribute maximally to the accomplishment of the organizational objectives is dependent upon many other factors. Most of these factors are under the purview of leaders who control the destinies of the members of the organization.

In the small organization where the owner is the active manager, the effectiveness of leadership is not likely to receive much attention. In the larger organization, however, where there are many managerial positions to be filled, increasing attention has been given to the development of quality leadership. It is recognized that the productive efficiency, adjustment, and morale of personnel at all levels in the organization are affected by the characteristics of its managers and supervisors. Successful managers are found to be those who establish conditions that will motivate employees toward individual and organizational goals and who learn effective ways of communicating with subordinates about their performance on a continuing basis.

Regardless of the extent of one's knowledge about human motivation and the evaluation of job performance, there is still the gap between knowing what to do and being able to do it, which confronts every manager at one time or another. Fortunately, many management and supervisory training programs provide opportunities for role playing or for trying out new skills in a laboratory environment. After developing some degree of competency and confidence in a training situation, the manager is likely to feel more adequate in the real-life situation.

While managerial personnel have always been responsible for evaluating and developing their subordinates, they have had new demands placed upon them in recent years. Increased emphasis upon providing jobs for disadvantaged persons through government manpower programs and regular employment channels has required that managers and supervisors acquire new attitudes and techniques for developing those individuals who in the past were not usually found in the labor market. Meeting the challenge of developing such individuals requires not only knowledge and understanding but a sincere interest in the employees and their welfare.

A survey of the literature in the journals will reveal a substantial number of articles devoted to the general topic of achieving performance effectiveness. It is believed that the following articles provide representative coverage of the various topics that are considered essential to the attainment of the level of individual and group performance that an organization must have if it is to be successful.

The first article *How To Appraise Executive Performance* by Arch Patton describes in detail the planned performance approach to evaluating executives. The approach described in this article is very similar to what is now referred to as management by objectives. It emphasizes the importance of establishing goals or objectives for the executive and evaluating his performance on the basis of how well he meets them. The planned performance approach is not only designed to cover quantitative targets such as "how much" is achieved but also qualitative targets such as "how well" the executive meets assigned responsibilities.

The next article by Dr. Harry Levinson warns of the danger of executive personnel becoming obsolescent. While many organizations feel an obligation to devoted, long-service executives, they cannot be allowed to block the progress of the organization. How to keep executives from becoming obsolescent is the main focus of the article. Today's executive must not only be able to keep up with the ever-changing conditions on the domestic scene but he should be prepared to meet the demands of an assignment in a foreign country. The article *Developing the International Executive* by H. C. de Bettignies and S. H. Rhinesmith outlines steps to be taken in a training program that will increase sensitivity to themselves and others and provide executives with the communication and human relations skills that they will need for effective performance in other countries.

One of the popular approaches to developing managerial personnel is through the T-group. In the article by John Drotning, T-group or sensitivity training is examined in detail. For those who have not participated in a T-group, Drotning provides an excellent description of what typically happens. He then raises questions as to the applicability of what is to be learned from T-group participation and its relationship to being a manager in the autocratic environment of most business firms. Other questions are raised for the purpose of encouraging the reader to recognize the need for using T-groups judiciously.

The next article by Eitington is also on the subject of T-groups. In this article the author describes the participative process that characterizes the T-group and then he shows how the functions of the T-group can provide understandings about human behavior that have relevance for work groups. Eitington recommends that laboratory training programs be brought into an organization in order to develop more effective, cohesive work groups. In the article *Evaluating and Developing Subordinates* by William M. Fox, the author emphasizes that efforts in developing subordinates can and should be separated from formal evaluations made for the purpose of rewarding or penalizing subordinates. The author suggests having subordinates themselves formulate and monitor specific activity and time targets for improving their present performance and becoming promotable. He cites some useful lessons from nonbusiness organizations that may be used as a basis for facilitating change in individuals.

With the increased attention being given to helping the hard-core unemployed qualify for jobs, the article by Ross Stagner is timely. While he favors the various manpower programs that were created under the Manpower Development and Training Act (MDTA), he observes that many of the current training activities are not achieving their intended purpose because of failure to recognize and be guided by certain psychological principles. How the hard-core perceive institutions and how their motives are satisfied or frustrated are the types of problems that he considers.

The next article by Weatherbee is basically concerned with identifying marginal employees, determining what action to take, and implementing the action. While it is difficult to generalize about how to handle a marginal employee, the author does present some guidelines for identifying and coping with him.

One of the "headaches" that many managers report having is the periodic chore of appraising employee performance and then attempting to tell the employees about it. Robert K. Stolz provides us with some suggestions on how appraisal discussions can be made constructive rather than destructive. One of the most valuable contributions of the article is the statement concerning the laying of a solid foundation for effective appraisal discussions.

The last article in this chapter by Lawrence J. Peter provides a humorous view of how some people are bound to reach their level of incompetence. The Peter Principle as it is now known advises that the individual who is performing well at one level is not necessarily qualified for promotion. It is possible that he can make his best contribution to the organization by being left in his present position where he is performing efficiently.

18—HOW TO APPRAISE
EXECUTIVE PERFORMANCE *

Arch Patton

What makes an executive successful? Why does one man forge his way to the top, while another, equally trained, fails to live up to company expectations? How can we better understand the process by which executives develop?

In hopes of finding answers to these important questions, one of the country's largest corporations made a survey, a few years ago, of the educational, economic, and social backgrounds of more than 100 top-echelon executives. The objective of the study was to discover if the early life experiences of this demonstrably successful group of men had common elements that could be used to improve the corporation's executive selection and development process.

As Diverse as America

The research team carefully studied the early family life of each top-management executive, including his family's financial and social status, the extent of his formal education, subjects studied, marks received, and his early work experience. When the results of the survey were reviewed, it was found that the environment of the company's key executives during their formative years tended to be as diverse as America itself. These highly successful executives came from poor as well as wealthy families, some had Master's degrees while others failed to finish high school, and outstanding and average students were found in equal numbers.

Only one common historic relationship was discovered: *within two years after joining the company, the compensation of each executive topped the average for his age group, and this pay differential above the average widened at an accelerating rate throughout his career.*

The results of this study underscore the dangers inherent in a recruiting process that slavishly follows preconceived ideas of what

---

* From *Harvard Business Review*, Vol. 38, No. 1 (January-February, 1960), pp. 63-70. Reprinted with permission.

it takes to make an outstanding executive. The results indicate, furthermore, that intelligence, courage, aggressiveness, and other qualities making for business success are incubated in virtually every conceivable early environment.

The most significant contribution of the survey may turn out to be a better understanding of the executive development process. For if we cannot prejudge the *capacity* of the individual with any certainty, it follows that we must assign critical importance to the ability to judge on-the-job *performance*. This performance appraisal is a never-ending process, for individuals reach the peak of their ability, or willingness, to accept responsibility at different stages in their careers. As every top executive knows, many apparently well-endowed individuals reach "plateaus" of arrested development early in their careers, while others seem able to draw indefinitely on hidden reserves of strength to take on ever larger responsibilities.

In effect, this means that the soundest basis for judging an individual's ability to handle a higher-level job is how well he is dealing with similar problems in his present job. Or, to put it another way, an executive's past and present performance is the most reliable key to his future performance. This being the case, the ability of management to judge an individual's performance is basic to the continuing success of the enterprise.

Early Appraisal Efforts

The need for sound appraisals of executive performance has been recognized in industry for many years. The first efforts in this direction tended to have psychological overtones and usually consisted of appraisals of traits that were deemed important to a successful executive. Thus, these early approaches did not appraise performance in terms of the results stemming from decisions made or influenced by an individual, but rather in terms of preconceived characteristics that management personnel were presumed to have. Particularly in the years following World War II, performance appraisal was often looked on as an integral part of an executive development program.

Subjective approach

Unfortunately, the executive characteristics appraised in development programs—leadership, initiative, dependability, judgment, getting along with people, ambition, and so on—do not necessarily measure a man's *effectiveness* on the job. Indeed, all too often judgments of performance under such plans reflect what is *thought* of the man rather than what he *does*.

The great weakness in this approach has proved to be the lack of performance criteria that are related to job responsibilities. Such concentration on personality traits ignores the more objective measures of on-the-job performance that are developed from budgets and accounting reports. This highly subjective approach, in turn, has made it difficult for management to communicate its judgment of an executive's performance to the man who has been evaluated. It is the rare individual who will concede that he does not display executive characteristics, and an even rarer boss who can comfortably explain shortcomings of so personal a nature to his subordinate. By contrast, the more objective criteria—rising or falling sales, profit margins, scrap losses, employee turnover, absenteeism, machine down time, and the like—are more readily understood by the subordinate and easier to explain because they are in quantitative terms which are part of the operating language of the business.

Another factor that tends to obsolete trait-oriented appraisals in recent years has been the increasing use of executive incentive plans in industry. More and more companies have found their bonus plans "in trouble" because eligible executives do not believe that incentive payments based on subjective appraisals reflect their individual efforts. This belief apparently results from an instinctive revulsion among executives to having their compensation largely dependent on what senior executives *think* of them. First, they suspect favoritism, and second, they exhibit a subconscious desire to have their performance measured by yardsticks that are based on more tangible, quantitative targets they have learned to understand and trust.

Mathematical approach

Some companies have taken steps to overcome the "popularity contest" aspects of subjective appraisals and to meet the growing need for judging performance in terms of individual targets. Often, however, such procedures have swung to the other extreme in bonus plan administration: setting individual goals for the year in quantitative terms (e.g., increase sales 10% or cut scrap losses 7%) and paying off on "performance" directly keyed to those goals.

This approach has the great advantage of eliminating subjective judgment as the determinant of an individual's bonus. Furthermore, it does measure performance, and in terms that are understandable to the individual.

But the experience of many companies which have adopted this mathematical approach indicates that it, too, has serious shortcomings. The most important weakness revolves around the fact that once the individual targets have been established, mathematics takes over the basic responsibility of management to manage. If the individual goals set at the beginning of the year are consistent between divisions, or between functions within divisions, the mathematically derived payoff at the year's end, undoubtedly, will be unfair. Some executives will be overpaid and others underpaid as a result of forces beyond the control of the individual. An unexpected price war, for instance, may seriously reduce profit margins in one division, while margins in another division benefit from the liquidation of a competitor. With mathematics deciding who gets what bonus, such basic economic shifts go unrecognized.

Then, too, the mathematically derived payoff that results from preset goals merits no adjustment in rewards for the *difficulty* of accomplishment. A manufacturing department, for example, may have surmounted major problems in fulfilling commitments that were easily attained by the sales department, or vice versa. But unless the program permits the *judgment* of management to reflect the difficulty of accomplishment, great incentive values are lost to the inflexibility of mathematics.

Because unfavorable results frequently stem from these relatively extreme approaches to performance appraisal—the wholly subjective and the mathematically determined evaluations—a number of leading companies have blended the best of the two into what appears destined to become a formidable management tool. The remainder of this article will examine in some detail the philosophy underlying the new concept, the administrative problems encountered, and the benefits derived from its use.

Planned Performance

Essentially, this composite approach to appraisal is aimed at providing a sound basis for judging the relative performance of executives, expressed in terms of their individual responsibilities. It establishes annual targets for the individual that are implicit in the job he holds. And it provides for *judging* performance in terms of these targets rather than a purely mathematical measurement. In addition, it relates these individual targets to the short- and long-term goals of the enterprise. This means that each member of the management team is working toward the same agreed-on objectives of the company or division and will be judged by how well he performs these tasks.

Company goals

This approach is called by a variety of names: programed management, management by objective, or planned performance programing. But whatever the title, its users have a common objective: that individual performance be judged in terms of agreed-on tasks reflecting the goals of the business. The first step, therefore, involves the development of long- and short-range company goals. The longer-term objectives are useful in "stretching" executive thinking—in making managers think "bigger"—but are also valuable as a guide to the practicability of the forecast targets:

> Let us assume, for instance, that a single-product manufacturer, after considerable study, sets a five-year goal of doubling his unit volume. As a result, he has decided how much must be added to current sales in the first, second, and later years to attain this goal. The practicability of these estimates, of course, needs to be checked against the ability of the company to manufacture, sell, and finance such increases in volume. It makes no sense, for example, to set goals beyond the company's ability to provide funds at reasonable cost, or to agree to sell more of a product than facilities can be expected to turn out.
>
> Once it is decided that a 15% increase in company volume is a realistic target for the first year, the next step is to determine what must be accomplished by each functional group in order to attain such a goal. To do so necessitates a careful assessment of interfunctional relationships. For instance, perhaps it is possible for the sales department to develop 15% more business by a greater utilization of salesmen's time; but if this is accomplished, new facilities might be needed by manufacturing in order to meet this goal. (These new facilities, in turn, would obviously have to be considered in relation to the forecast needs of future years as well.)
>
> On the other hand, production facilities might be adequate to attain the necessary volume, but the sales department might have to introduce a new line of products in order to reach this figure. If this occurs, of course, other functional areas are likely to be involved. In addition to changes that a new line might necessitate in the sales department, i.e., the introduction of a specialized sales force, the engineering department would be expected to design the new line, credit standards might have to be tightened or loosened, transportation costs or lead times might need alteration, and so on.

Functional tasks

Experience has shown that translating short-term company objectives into 12-month goals for individual functional executives is best done by setting up both quantitative and qualitative tasks to be accomplished during the period. In other words, executive responsibilities include (a) those that can be *measured,* such as sales, behind-schedule production, or credit losses, and (b) those that must be *judged,* made up of the intangibles that arise when an executive develops a new process, establishes a training program, improves the quality of engineering candidates, and the like.

The advantage of separating qualitative and quantitative tasks lies in the very human tendency among executives to "let the numbers decide." It appears to be much easier for a superior to point out shortcomings to a subordinate when he can blame such an unpleasant conclusion on the results of a quantitative evaluation. Explaining weaknesses that must be *judged* impressionistically, while frequently more important to the training process, causes greater discomfort to the superior. The separation of the two induces a deeper awareness of the importance of both elements.

Further, these tasks need to be set up for both line and staff positions—a process that has proved to be a serious stumbling block to performance appraisal programs. Trouble results largely from line-oriented senior executives finding it difficult to visualize the possibility of setting realistic targets for staff jobs. There appears to be an unfortunate tendency among some senior executives to write off the entire approach because of this blind spot where staff is concerned. Thus:

> Dislike of this approach frequently occurs when the responsibilities of staff functions are vague, and their contribution to the management process has not been adequately developed. The senior executive subconsciously questions the value of the staff function, yet has come to believe that "staff is a hallmark of modern management." He remembers the time, a few years ago, when his company had two vice presidents—sales and manufacturing. Today, there may be vice presidents for finance, engineering, personnel, administration, and so on, but the senior executive does not have the same "feel" for these jobs that he has for the line sales or manufacturing jobs with which he grew up.

This problem has been reduced, however, as top management more and more recognizes the need for spending as much *time* in establishing company and functional goals at the outset as it spends in appraising performance at the end of the year. This more thought-ful approach to task setting results in a better understanding of staff activities, as well as a more practical evaluation of the contri-butions that can be made in this area.

A number of techniques have been found helpful in cutting the problem down to size. If the tasks of the line organization are worked out first, for example, the process of thinking through the supporting goals of the staff functions is simplified. Similarly, there appears to be an advantage in setting up quantitative goals first and, subsequently, building the qualitative tasks on this foundation. One company has developed a master list of general goals for each functional area, some quantitative and some qualitative. While indi-vidual tasks will vary, of course, from year to year, these general goals have been found to be worth keeping in mind.

Examples of annual tasks developed as a basis for appraising the performance of a division head, a personnel executive, and a manu-facturing executive are shown in EXHIBITS I, II, and III. The tasks in these examples are obviously fewer than would be the case in real life, but they are adequate to show the kind of tasks that can be used as a basis for appraising the performance of top line and staff executives.

Lower-level tempo

The annual tasks established for the key functions naturally set the tempo for executives below the top functional level. The goals of subordinates are necessarily tied in with the targets set up for the boss. However, some confusion has crept into the picture at this point. There are those who regard goal setting as the job of the subordinate, with the supervisor merely helping the subordinate relate his own tasks "to the realities of the organization," as one commentator put it. The great advantage of this method, in the eyes of its supporters, is psychological. The executive sets his own tasks, hence paces his own development.

My experience indicates that it is unrealistic to expect middle-management executives to be broad-gauged enough to set their own tasks. They do not fully comprehend the goals that have been established for their boss by top management in order to maintain integration between functions. Further, there is little evidence that lower-echelon executives (those without full functional responsibility)

EXHIBIT I. PLANNED PERFORMANCE TARGETS FOR DIVISION MANAGER

Annual target plans

List of major accomplishments needed this year to meet corporation, division, or department goals.

Quantitative targets

Objectives for the year ahead that can be appraised in terms of *how much;* for example, "increase return on investment from 12% to 15%."

1. Increase billings by 17%, maintaining a 50%-30%-20% product mix in Departments A, B, and C.
2. Increase over-all profits (BT) by 35%.
3. Increase asset turnover from 1.3 times a year to 1.5 times.
4. Increase return on total assets from 18% to 21%.
5. Increase inventory turnover from 6.1 to 5.8 months.
6. Expand market share from 21% to 24%.

Qualitative targets

Objectives that can best be appraised in terms of *how well;* for example, "improve technical appraisal program," or "make more effective use of budgetary control."

1. Develop a new line of motors for introduction in 1961. Complete engineering phase, start production engineering.
2. Develop a more effective basis for testing candidates for supervisory positions, with particular reference to individual aptitudes for specific positions.
3. Increase the number of promotable executives by better training methods, including the introduction of job rotation and the establishment of a special assignment program designed to broaden the skills of outstanding men.
4. Start weekly department head meetings as a training and information medium.

are likely to set personal targets that fully "stretch" their capabilities. The political environment in most companies is such that it is very important for executives to "hit the target" they have agreed on. Since "stretched" goals are more difficult to attain, the incentive to play it safe is frequently overwhelming.

This does not mean that lower-level executives should not have an important voice in their job targets. The record indicates they should. But since their tasks are keyed directly to the goals of the functional executive, the latter must determine the targets of a subordinate, virtually in self-protection. Indeed, many of the tasks of the top functional executive are delegated directly to the subordinate:

EXHIBIT II. PLANNED PERFORMANCE TARGETS FOR DIRECTOR OF
PERSONNEL

Annual target plans

List of major accomplishments needed this year to meet corporation,
division, or department goals.

Quantitative targets

Objectives for the year ahead that can be appraised in terms of
how much; for example, "increase return on investment from 12% to
15%."

1. Reduce clerical costs of operating the employment function (recruiting and screening applicants) 60%.
2. Reduce cafeteria operating loss 3%.
3. Increase the typing pool from 25 to 30 employees.
4. Reduce the number of secretaries in headquarters staff by 15.

Qualitative targets

Objectives that can best be appraised in terms of *how well;* for
example, "improve technical appraisal program," or "make more effective
use of budgetary control."

1. Develop a safety training program for the operating divisions.
2. Simplify and reduce the number of clerical salary classifications.
3. Complete the management inventory.
4. Develop an approach to executive performance appraisal that will
   improve bonus plan administration.
5. Speed up new employee indoctrination procedure (estimated target—
   one hour).
6. Develop a program to provide the negotiating group with information
   that anticipates union demands more accurately.
7. Work with the manufacturing function to eliminate "assistants to"
   general foremen and plant superintendents within five years.

● For example, when a chief engineer has responsibility for reducing
the number of motor frames in the product line, he almost certainly
delegates this particular chore to someone on his staff.

● When the top manufacturing executive is charged with cutting 20%
off the lead time in component purchases, this too will be passed along if
he is a good executive.

Thus, the tasks of this lower-level group are much like those of
their superiors. The main difference is in the number of special,
short-term assignments that do not appear in any job description
because they change so rapidly.

Judging performance

With job targets set up for top and middle-management executives, the next step involves determining where each executive's

EXHIBIT III. PLANNED PERFORMANCE TARGETS FOR DIRECTOR OF
MANUFACTURING

Annual target plans

List of major accomplishments needed this year to meet corporation,
division, or department goals.

Quantitative targets

Objectives for the year ahead that can be appraised in terms of
how much; for example, "increase return on investment from 12% to
15%."

1. Cut lead time on component purchases from 120 to 100 days.
2. Reduce WDC to 70% in terms of present prices.
3. Manufacturing's phase of the cost reduction program for the division
   is one third of the $1,500,000 excess saving over last year.
4. Improve delivery schedule performance by 5 percentage points (to
   83%).
5. Reduce spoilage ratio by 2% net from 1959 figure.
6. Improve net allowed hours ratio by 3%.

Qualitative targets

Objectives that can best be appraised in terms of *how well;* for example "improve technical appraisal program," or "make more effective
use of budgetary control."

1. Speed up the recognition and utilization of suggestions developed in
   the suggestion system.
2. Improve production planning on the assembly floor to reduce the
   need for stand-by stocks of subassemblies.
3. Restudy the manufacturing process now used for product "X" to
   reduce the direct labor needs.

---

performance of agreed-on tasks falls in the spectrum from outstanding to poor.

Companies doing the best job of appraising the performance of
their executives appear to have a number of points in common. For
one thing, most of them have incentive bonus plans. The existence
of this constant prod to developing better appraisal techniques seems
to pay off in good results. Perhaps this reflects top management's
willingness to spend more time on something involving a lot of
money.

Another common attribute of such companies is top management's
recognition that the most important aspect of the entire appraisal
process lies in the identification of outstanding and poor performers.
Many appraisal programs bog down because of the time spent trying
to identify minuscule differences in performance among the middle

60% to 70% of the executive group whose performance approximates the average! As a result of the effort spent in this direction, the 30% to 40% of the executives who are either outstanding or poor performers receive inadequate attention. Naturally, this becomes a critically important roadblock to success if the appraisal program includes an unwieldy number of executives.

In this connection, a technique so simple that it hardly seems worth mentioning has proved of considerable value. The outstanding performer and the poorest performer are first identified; then, in pairs, the second most outstanding and the second poorest are determined; and so on in pairs until it becomes difficult to distinguish between the performance of individual executives. Thus, a sense of proportion and reality is built into what otherwise tends to be a swampy morass.

One of the most difficult problems in judging performance lies in the values to be assigned line versus staff contributions. A few companies have developed an approach that appears helpful and sounds practical. While its use seems to be limited to those with incentive plans, there is no apparent need for such a limitation. This approach involves appraising the performance of fully profit-responsible executives (such as division managers) first, line executives (sales and manufacturing) second, and staff executives only after tentative values have been set for the profit-responsible and line executives. In other words, the performance of staff executives is "slotted" around already established relationships among the line executives.

This technique makes sense. The performance of the fully profit-responsible executive can be measured with a good deal of accuracy, by means of share-of-market, return-on-investment comparisons, and the like. Yardsticks for appraising sales and manufacturing executives are also good. However, measures of the staff executive's performance still leave much to be desired, and the evaluation of his performance should benefit from being tied in to the more tangible landmarks used for line executives.

The risk, of course, is that staff executives will be "slotted" on a position-in-the-hierarchy basis, or, in other words, judged by their position on the organization chart rather than by their performance. But a hardheaded judgment of the relative value of the tasks agreed upon, as well as a careful assessment of performance will go a long way toward protecting against this risk.

Action needed

Having determined where individual performance falls in the continuum from outstanding to poor, it is necessary to do something about these findings. One of the recurring problems in appraisal programs is that lower-echelon executives come to believe "nothing happens" as a result of the admittedly time-consuming appraisal effort.

An obvious first step is to see that the individual knows what is thought of his performance, and why. Since management's judgment of his performance is based on results racked up in the attainment of specific tasks, the individual's weaknesses and strengths are clearly delineated, and the supervising executive can discuss reasonably concrete "hits and misses" with the subordinate. This overcomes the natural reluctance among executives to criticize purely personal traits in their subordinates. Further, it focuses attention on specific opportunities for improvement. The planned performance approach, therefore, provides a basis for self-development on the part of the individual, as well as an assessment of "how he is doing."

For performance appraisal to be firmly rooted in a company's way of life it should play a key role in promotions, merit increases, and bonus payments. The outsider reviewing corporate administration practices all too frequently finds top performers, as measured by the appraisal program, doing no better than the average performer where bonuses, merit increases, and promotions are concerned. It may not make sense, but the rationalizations are plentiful. For instance, a top performer will be passed over for a merit increase "because his bonus was boosted this year"; or his bonus will be held unchanged despite outstanding performance "because he recently received a merit increase."

The point is this: if performance appraisal is worthwhile, it should provide the backbone for executive personnel administration.

Early problems

To date at least, only a handful of companies have seriously attempted to set up such a programed approach to performance appraisal. Because most of these pioneering efforts were started in the past few years, it is too early to look for success stories. However, the top executives of companies that have tackled task planning are almost uniformly enthusiastic with results achieved so far. The principal accomplishment, in their view, is the establishment of a task-oriented way of life. Job objectives are more clearly defined and, therefore, better coordinated. Individual executives know what is expected of them and can target their activities more effectively. Last but certainly not least, the annual review of "hits and misses" between superior and subordinate becomes more realistic and more productive of improved future performance.

Needless to say, there have been problems. It is significant, however, that the major problem areas follow a reasonably consistent pattern from company to company. For example:

- The detailed probing of individual job responsibilities essential to this approach takes a great deal of time and necessitates some highly creative thinking. Since executives are human, many of them tend to resist both the effort and the thought processes that are involved. For this reason, it is essential that the chief executive be solidly behind the project. If, for instance, executives come to suspect that their own bonuses may suffer from any neglect of the necessary time and thought requirements, so much the better.

- Another common problem of successful performance programing is the need for a competent and creative "control function." Executives who are to be rewarded or penalized, in part at least, on results developed by the budgeting and accounting function should have great confidence in the control techniques used, as well as the skill and honesty of this group. It is relatively simple to devise yardsticks, but the objectivity and courage of the top control executives must be respected at all levels if these measures are to be effective. Executives need to have faith that tasks set for the various functions are equally difficult, and that figures are not going to be juggled to protect someone's favorite.

The judgment of individual performance in terms of agreed-on tasks (such as those in EXHIBITS I, II, and III) requires maturity of a high order at the top level. One of the great advantages of the approach is the coordination of effort that results from its thoughtful, orderly task-setting process. If top management is overly arbitrary in its judgments, understandable problems develop. The chief executive who looks only to the results, without a careful weighing of the difficulties encountered in the accomplishments, is storing up future trouble.

- The planned performance approach also necessitates a personnel staff of unusual competence. This group necessarily plays a key role in advising top management when an imbalance occurs between functions. Several appraisal programs have suffered because the top personnel executives were unwilling or unable to convince top management of developing problem areas. In one instance, the personnel executive knew that the annual tasks set for one functional group were consistently more difficult to attain than were those of other groups. As a result this group had lost about 25% in bonus income over a four-year period. Top management became aware of the problem only after several promising young executives quit, and a subsequent study disclosed the source of the trouble.

Since this approach to performance appraisal is most effective when confined to executives who importantly influence company profits, many personnel executives find themselves dealing with new and complex problems when an executive appraisal program is adopted. As one personnel vice president put it, "I used to spend 95% of my time on problems dealing directly or indirectly with moves having union overtones. Now, more than half my time is spent on the recruitment, development, organization, and motivation of executives!"

Many personnel executives have found it difficult to effect a change-over. Thus, top management faces a serious handicap, since a strong, capable personnel group is a major ingredient in a successful appraisal program.

- The "cutoff point" of executives to be included in the appraisal program has proved to be another problem area. If too many are included, the programing task becomes monumental. The most effective course appears to involve starting off with a relatively limited group of key executives whose profit impact is unmistakable, and adding levels of executives to the program as its usefulness "proves out." The temptation to include too many, however, is almost overwhelming and needs to be consciously restrained.

Results to date indicate that the programed approach to performance appraisal is not for the laissez-faire management. It is a new way of life—and as difficult as it is rewarding.

Conclusion

The planned performance approach provides several important advantages over earlier attempts at executive appraisal:

1. The long- and short-term objectives of the enterprise become an integral part of the performance appraisal process.
2. The job responsibilities of executives provide the basis for setting individual targets. As a result of the necessity for thinking through the interrelationships between job activities, there is a more effective targeting of individual effort.
3. The outstanding and poor performers receive primary attention, spotlighting those eligible for promotion or merit increases and those requiring training or elimination.
4. Personality plays a less important part in the final evaluation of performance, for the focus is on what a man does rather than what is thought of him. Thus, subjective criteria are replaced by objective ones.
5. Mathematics is put in its proper role, providing guidelines rather than final decisions.

Companies using this appraisal approach believe its greatest contribution stems from the disciplines it imposes on the management process. Planned performance forces a company:

● To think hard about its objectives and review them constantly.

● To study the responsibilities involved in individual positions and determine their relative importance to the business.

● To set practical work tasks for individuals and hold them accountable for their attainment.

● To take whatever action is called for by the information presented to it, in order to build a more effective management team.

In a sense, therefore, such a program involves a down-to-earth executive development program. Since people learn by doing, on-the-job training has great advantages over the more formal executive development programs that bloomed in profusion after the war.

The planned performance approach requires an enormous investment of top management's time in its early years. Since it usually involves a more disciplined way of life in the management process, it needs strong support from the chief executive and those directly under him. Because of the great time demands involved, companies have found it advantageous to limit the number of positions included in the program to those having a clearly recognizable impact on profits.

The approach also requires unusually skilled and resourceful control, market, and economic research functions. Because quantitative yardsticks play a major role in establishing targets and judging performance, they must be demonstrably good or executive belief in the fairness of the process will be undermined. It should be recorded, however, that the performance of executives is subject to constant scrutiny, for decisions bearing on promotions, merit increases, and bonuses are being made by top management almost daily. The question is whether the planned performance approach is worth the time and the effort that are needed to make it effective.

Companies that have worked hardest to develop their skill in this area believe it to be a major improvement over earlier efforts. And the fact that these concerns are pacesetters in industry implies that the competitive pressure exerted by their success with this new management tool will force an ever-widening circle of companies to think in similar terms about executive performance appraisal.

Questions

1. The author states that the programed approach to performance appraisal is not for the laissez-faire type of management. Do you agree? Why?

2. Operative employees have traditionally been evaluated in terms of their productivity or the extent to which they met the specific performance standards of their jobs. How do you account for the delay in using this approach in evaluating executive personnel?
3. What effect would the programed approach to performance appraisal be likely to have on communications among executives?
4. A strong, capable personnel department is said to be a major ingredient in a successful appraisal program. How would you describe a strong, capable personnel department?

19—IS THERE AN OBSOLESCENT EXECUTIVE IN YOUR COMPANY—OR IN YOUR CHAIR? *

Harry Levinson

One of the most painful phenomena of our time is executive obsolescence. And paradoxically, the man who is urged to take specialized training to avoid obsolescence is told at the same time that his new professional knowledge has a half-life of 10 years. That is, half of what he knows will than be obsolete.

The obsolescent executive is not a problem for the future. He is with us *now*. Thousands of executives face the chilling realization that they are no longer effective in their jobs. And their seniors are caught up in the abrasive conflict of having to make a decision about a loyal and previously effective subordinate: what do you do with a man who is no longer able to cope with the increasing complexity or higher operational level of his job?

The problem has reached such alarming proportions that people in several organizations have formed a group to stimulate and coordinate research. Dr. M. Scott Myers, manager of management research and development at Texas Instruments, took the initiative to bring the interested professional parties together for the two meetings they have already had. Stanford Research Institute is helping to formulate and coordinate the research efforts.

Here is how the problem looks in personal terms. Jack Lemond is the purchasing director of a company for which he has worked 20 years. He is intelligent, conscientious in his job, has a pleasing personality and dresses neatly. He is systematic and well organized. He is a good team worker because he wants to be of service to his colleagues; and they like the dependable, cooperative manner in which he responds to their requests. Lemond has done his job well. The company asked no more of him—until a few years ago. Then the winds of change, originating from the realities of the business world, began to push the company toward critical self-evaluation and long-range planning.

Lemond had been so preoccupied with his work that he had given little thought to the broader environment in which today's business

* Reprinted by permission from *Think* Magazine (January-February, 1968), pp. 27-30, published by IBM, Copyright 1968 by Harry Levinson.

operates. He had never before been asked to plan ahead in the detail that was now needed, nor had he been trained to use contemporary technical planning methods. As a result, Lemond lags in organizational planning. He cannot provide, for himself or his superiors, the information about his operation that would enable them to project alternative courses of action. But there is no other position in the company to which he could be transferred without loss of status. Lemond is still 15 years from retirement. The company feels it has an obligation to such devoted, long-service men whose present inadequacies are not alone of their own making. Yet they cannot be allowed to block the progress of the organization.

Three obvious principles

While scientists research the problem, personnel experts debate it, and companies experiment with programs, three principles are obvious to everyone who would pursue a managerial career.

• *Every man should prepare himself for maximum flexibility.*

In my judgment, this means he should become as broadly educated as possible during his college experience. Only then should he specialize. The farther ahead a man must predict for himself and his organization, the more imperative it is that he know the lessons of history. The more complex the issues he must deal with, the more important it is that he understand multiple social forces. The broader a man's education, the more flexibly he can adapt to changing circumstances if his specialty becomes obsolete, or evolve new ways of practicing his specialty.

Once a man has established himself in his career, flexibility means keeping up not only with a specialty but also with the general fields important to most businesses. A personnel executive in an engineering firm, for example, should have, in addition to his own expertise, a rudimentary knowledge of engineering problems and trends as well as a knowledge of marketing, finance, accounting, business law, and economics if he is to share a common perspective with his colleagues. He should keep up with the personnel field by reading, attending conferences, and taking advanced courses. He can keep up in many fields by reviewing the publications which go across so many executive desks unread.

Another way to use business periodicals is to scan them for trends. By this I mean scanning all the copies of one or more general management magazines of a given year, or even a two-year period. The executive can thus note: the subjects most frequently covered, the articles more often mentioned as references, the major focus of research reported, and the most influential writers. He can then look more closely at those focal points. He does not have to become an authority on a given subject, nor does he have to accept uncritically what he reads, but he should know what is going on.

● *Every person who pursues a career, as distinct from a jobholder, should expect to continue his education for the rest of his professional life.*

Some companies already are urging their executives to attend some kind of learning program annually. Many send executives to university refresher courses, and the larger ones have their own in-service or management development programs. Even relatively small organizations pay tuition for advanced courses successfully completed if they somehow relate to the business. Some have established formal programs, open to all executives, leading to advanced degrees. An executive should take advantage of such opportunities, but not limit himself to them. Rather, he should think about what he wants and plan for that goal.

A career man should ask himself what he would do if he were to lose his present job, as the commercial airline flight engineers lost theirs, because of obsolescence. What would he fall back on and what preparation would it take to make his back-up position relatively secure? In effect, every man should have, as he did in college, a major and a minor field. Psychologically speaking, there is no reason why he should not. Most of us can become expert in several fields.

There is a secondary gain to a well-chosen reserve position. A man who has specialized knowledge in two fields can often bridge them to his own advantage and to the advantage of his organization as well. Furthermore, he can also contribute to the development of new fields and more easily become a leader in the new, bridged area.

The third advantage to establishing alternative competence is that it increases a man's sense of independence. He has the equanimity which goes with the knowledge that he does not have to bear a chronically difficult or demeaning situation, with its consequent psychological price in self-respect. In addition, a man who has prepared a reserve position has something to turn to as a major activity when he retires.

An incidental gain from some forms of general education is that a man can share the experience with his wife. In programs such as those at Stanford and the Aspen Institute, provision is made for wives.

Two formidable barriers

• *A man's own feelings are the most powerful agents of obsolescence.*

The two most formidable barriers to flexibility are the factors which usually are the most significant in creating obsolescence: passivity and fear. Every man must fight them to survive; in middle age they can be paralyzing.

The following example illustrates what I mean by passivity. Some years ago I taught at a widely-known university which offered two advanced graduate programs for executives. One group of men was between 30 and 38 years old and the other between 45 and 55. The older group seemed less willing to learn and less able to look at alternative courses of action. They seemed to have more at stake in already fixed positions which they did not want to examine. They behaved as if they had already arrived at a certain level, a defensive position which had to be protected. Compared to the younger group, they had already given up in self-defeat. They would coast along, if they could, in their responsible positions (some were vice presidents). Unfortunately, the vicissitudes of the business world allow little complacency. It did not suprise me, therefore, when several later sought my advice in finding new positions.

Fear manifests itself in other ways. In a company undergoing drastic management changes and rapid expansion under competitive pressure, the president asked the management group to critically review their organization and its needs. To stimulate their thinking, he invited several experts to present contemporary management concepts. The group, numbering nearly one hundred men, was asked to meet in small groups after the presentations with three questions for discussion:

What did this man say that is relevant to our organization?
Of whatever is relevant, what is most important to us?
Who, specifically, in our organization should do something about it?

The management group had no trouble with the first question, some with the second. But none of the groups named a specific person or department in response to the third. They were afraid to respond to the president's invitation, though he was not a punitive man. Furthermore, when the discussion centered on innovation, the management group, in effect, abdicated. They said that the survival of the organization depended on the imagination and drive of younger men who were yet to come. They expressed no confidence in their own ability, despite their record of success, nor did the men in the group seem troubled by abandoning the field to yet unknown rivals.

Executive obsolescence is to a company as rust is to metal. Companies can become like rusting hulls, encumbered by layers of corrosion. Like corrosion, executive obsolescence needs continuous attention.

Brief refresher courses such as those conducted by the American Management Association, the Bureau of Industrial Relations of the University of Michigan, and similar organizations are helpful. Continuing academic education is even more helpful. Management development programs often combine both. Much of the training advantage is lost, however, if a man has no opportunity to talk over with his superiors what he has learned and how he might use it to best advantage in the company.

The most effective device to combat executive obsolescence is responsibility for solving organizational problems. In most companies this is taken to mean, "I tell you what to do and you then have the responsibility for doing it." This is like the parent assigning chores to his adolescent son. Chore assignment is a far cry from the concept: "Here is a problem. Here are the resources available to deal with it. This is how we will backstop you. It's your baby."

No responsibility can be adequately discharged unless the person is prepared to solve the given problem and the organization supports his problem-solving efforts. Preparation usually requires systematic and continuous learning, and organizational support implies consistent interaction with helpful superiors.

Many companies make it a practice to rotate men frequently as part of an effort to combat obsolescence. Much of the time, such rotation is merely movement for movement's sake, assuming that the executive will acquire breadth by moving. Rotation is thus the curse of many organizations. I distinguish between rotation and systematic reassignment. To me, systematic reassignment means a planned change of job with the specific purpose of increasing a man's learning. The goal of systematic reassignment will be clearly stated so both the man and his superiors know exactly what he is to get out of the move. The mode of learning will be specified so that both can know why he is to do his new job by the methods he will follow. And the terminal date of his assignment will be specified so he can have a sense of achievement from his work. Part of systematic re-assignment is teaching. When a man must teach others, he sharpens his own knowledge.

When a man has been promoted out of his depth, his sense of helplessness precipitates passivity and fear, particularly if he is assigned chore responsibilities without adequate resources or support. These days it is not unusual for the job to outgrow the man. This means that closer attention must be given to splitting and redefining jobs and to regrouping human resources to make the most of them.

"Total push"

Finally, the organization must have a "total push" concept. That is, it must maintain continuous pressure on its executives to continue their self-development and thus avoid obsolescence. A decade ago, the total push concept was widespread in public mental hospitals. Patients who are allowed to be inactive tend to withdraw further into themselves and to become dependent on the hospital. The more helpless they become, the less likely they are to leave the hospital. The potential for recovery declines as the length of stay increases. In short, the patients become obsolete as human beings. Chronic patient populations are today a burden on every public mental hospital. Obsolete executives are equally burdensome to every organization.

Many of these suggestions are based on the premise that a man is employed by a company which supports his efforts to better himself. Some companies are too small to offer more than moral support; others may not recognize the need. Without stimulus from a company, a man is more likely to suffer from his own procrastination. Procrastination is the ally of obsolescence. In such cases he will have to carry on his regeneration efforts alone.

If a man is being left behind because he does not have a modern conception of his function, then his task is comparatively easy. He need only refine his specialty. A case in point is an accounting manager who does not know electronic data processing procedures. Enough training is available that he needn't become obsolete, regardless of his age. Without it he will inevitably be displaced.

Men who must shift to a new specialty have it harder. There are always the classic methods: night school and correspondence courses.

In larger cities universities offer extension programs, and some of these lead to degrees. John Carroll University in Cleveland, for example, has a two-year evening program for executives leading to the degree, "Associate in Professional Management." Many communities offer technical training. No man is farther than his mailbox from opportunities. Rather than take a series of unrelated courses, however, he should formulate a continuing program for himself which leads to formal recognized preparation for a specialty, ideally a certificate or degree. Business school catalogs frequently specify the courses required for specialties.

The choice of direction is sometimes difficult. One can learn what skills are in demand by scanning the managerial want ads in larger newspapers like *The Wall Street Journal*, or by talking with personnel placement agencies. College placement officers make it their business to keep up with such trends.

Parkinson's law

Some, of course, will say they cannot afford to develop alternative expertise or build in modes of retaining flexibility. They are too busy building their careers or just doing their jobs. Sometimes they are right: companies do not always allow time for such efforts. But Parkinson's law holds all too often: activity expands to fill the time allocated to it. Some men have had their fill of going to school; they would rather watch TV. They should clearly know the consequences. Some have the illusion that if they just work hard now, the future will take care of itself. It doesn't. Whatever the excuse for inaction, the problem remains: how to build in and maintain adaptive flexibility that will serve a lifetime.

Questions

1. What does Levinson mean by the statement "Every man should prepare himself for maximum flexibility"? What steps should one take to become prepared?
2. One of the complaints of individuals who participate in management development seminars is that they have little or no opportunity to apply what they have learned. What should an organization do to overcome this type of complaint?
3. Is it likely that the problem of executive obsolescence may become more severe in the future? Why?
4. What does the author mean by the "total push" concept?

20—DEVELOPING THE INTERNATIONAL EXECUTIVE *

H. C. de Bettignies and S. H. Rhinesmith

Today's corporate environment is less directed to a domestic market defined by geographic boundaries than ever before. Through concentrations, mergers, and joint ventures, firms are becoming increasingly multinational.

Such an international expansion of corporations presents a *new challenge in finding managerial talents* to staff positions in these ever-expanding foreign operations. The international manager is still a scarce asset, and corporations are finding it increasingly difficult to acquire competent managers for foreign operations who have the special abilities required to perform their jobs in different social, economic, and political environments, as well as under different business and legal conditions.

At the same time, however, recent trends reveal that a majority of international firms do not have any well-defined plans for international executive development. This stands in stark contrast to the sophisticated programs developed during recent years for middle and upper management training in domestic operations. Such a lack of programs for developing international executives is not surprising. Many businesses assume that managers successful at home will be so abroad.

Since management in all countries shares certain functional similarities, many have assumed that these similarities qualify it as a universal profession or science capable of dealing with organizational questions existing in any society. This is not necessarily true, for if management can apply certain principles of organization to any society, these principles or doctrines are still the product of a particular society's way of thinking, its values, its goals, and so on.

Understanding values and points of conflict

Like everyone else, managers are subject to principles of human activity which bear the characteristics of a particular way of life, or

---

* From *European Business* (January, 1970). Reprinted with permission.

culture. The manager is born *into* not *with* a culture. Historically and temporally he is only the latest link in a long chain of influences which partly determine his outlook on life. We define his group's (be it national, social, or professional) way of life as his culture.

He is also part of an environment which influences his motivation and goals. *The first challenge* for an international manager is to become aware of the motivations, values, and goals which condition his behavior. In fact, new training programs have been developed recently as a result of Harvard Psychologist David C. McClelland's studies on motivation, attempting to help international managers in both the developed and developing worlds become more aware of their motivational sources and the effect of these on their management styles.[1] Such training marks the beginning of one serious effort to bring a more integrated managerial style to multinational organizations.

The *second challenge* for the international manager is to become aware of the new culture in which he will work; the manager who works between different cultures or societies works between different, sometimes conflicting, systems. He must understand these points of conflict to gain the perspective necessary for coping with the cultural differences. Recent experiments in universities and the government have revealed methods which business may adopt in helping managers develop these diagnostic skills.[2]

While the ultimate responsibility for adapting to international situations rests with the individual manager, many business organizations can give him support. They do this through experimentation with new multinational structures and the utilization of a variety of leadership and decision-making models. In some organizations an eclectic pattern has developed integrating features from divergent national cultural preferences.

A foreign company operating successfully in Japan, for instance, has to redefine its managers' roles to include responsibilities not usually part of their roles in the home country. The manager is

---

[1] See David C. McClelland, *The Achieving Society* (Princeton: Van Nostrand, 1961) and *Motivating Economic Development* (with David G. Winter) (New York: Free Press, 1969). Also, for the direct application of McClelland's theories to training in the developing world, see "Achievement Motivation Can Be Developed," *Harvard Business Review* (November-December, 1965).

[2] For a report on two of these experimental efforts see Stephen H. Rhinesmith and Donald Nylen, *A Behavioral Approach to International Management Training* (Pittsburgh: Graduate School of Public and International Affairs, University of Pittsburgh, 1969) and Albert Wight, *Handbook on Cross-Cultural Training* (Estes Park, Colorado: Center for Research and Education, 1969).

expected to become personally involved in the life of his employees, and this requirement has to be built into his job definition.

The manager may also be helped by the recent development of a "business culture." [3] This culture incorporates the goals, methods, and conditions of business activities in many societies. The widespread exchange of tools and machines, methods and techniques of organization, ideologies and philosophies is one of the main reasons for its growth.

But even within this international "business culture" that is being created throughout the world, there are mutations which provide managers of different countries with varying outlooks and sets of expectations. What is considered loyalty in Mexico becomes nepotism in the United States; what is participative decision making in Japan becomes weak leadership in Germany, and so on. Because of these differing ways of looking at the same thing, attempts must be made systematically to help managers understand and cope with the specific features within this "business culture."

We contend that managers can operate effectively abroad only when they are: 1) aware of themselves as culturally conditioned individuals, 2) alert to the differences in perception between themselves and others, 3) aware of their own social and emotional needs and attentive to the same needs in others, and 4) willing to work towards meaningful relationships with others through communication and mutual adaptation.

This article suggests *how to prepare the international executive for cross-cultural encounters* by developing in him a sensitivity to the traditions, beliefs, values, and behavior of himself and others. It is based on our experience in the development program entitled "The Managerial Challenge of International Business" offered each summer at INSEAD, in Fontainebleau. It also describes how to analyze new situations so that the manager can reevaluate and adjust his behavior accordingly.

How do we react to foreign environments?

Recently a British businessman told one of the authors how he spent hour upon hour trying to get a simple idea across to his Japanese supplier. He summed up the crux of the communication problem in describing the kind of interpreter needed when dealing

---

[3] For a discussion of one "business culture," see Heinz Hartman, *Amerikanische Firmen in Deutschland* (Kell Wesdeutschen Verlage, 1963).

with Japanese businessmen: someone who can interpret thinking, not just words. One day his interpreter was a man who had lived for many years in the United States and spoke and understood English well. Believing such a qualified interpreter offered him the opportunity to get all his ideas across to a supplier, he spent a number of hours carefully and precisely explaining his whole business philosophy, how he felt business could and should be operated.

When he returned to his hotel he felt satisfied to have finally penetrated the barrier. Shortly afterward he received a telephone call from the interpreter apologizing for not having translated most of the importer's remarks, because they would have offended the supplier.

Effective communication in a foreign environment means more than just understanding the language; it also includes the value system upon which the society is built. In Japan, for instance, advertising surveys have repeatedly proved that "one has to say it in a Japanese way, not simply translate English into Japanese." When distributing products in Japan, one has to take into account the Japanese distributors' system which differs from one's own but without which of course one can't exist—even if one strongly objects to its so-called "irrationality." One must also understand the seniority system—whatever one thinks of it—if one wants to have Japanese employees. All this gives some indication of the problems to be overcome. If unable to cope with his foreign partners' unfamiliar behavior, the manager will be highly frustrated, eventually give up his goals, and certainly fail in his job assignment.

Indeed, an individual coming to live in a foreign environment has difficulty for two reasons. One is *the difference in the norms of behavior between his own country and the host country.* The new international manager can experience frustration and irritation when he finds his "natural" way of behaving to be in constant conflict with the life style of those around him. From this conflict comes the second difficulty, *the anxiety resulting from a sudden loss of familiar surroundings.* Continual uncertainty and ambiguity about how to act and react create discomfort and uneasiness. Many times these feelings influence important decisions on the job and family relations at home.

Four basic reactions

Over the years, four distinctive patterns of human reaction to new and unfamiliar surroundings have been identified: *"flight," "dependency," "fight,"* and *"adjustment."* When a manager responds to a new situation through *flight,* he rejects the people and things around him which cause his discomfort and withdraws from any opportunity to interact with them, placing "blame" either on them or on himself for inadequacy in handling the new situation. He reacts defensively, many times fleeing to fellow nationals in a foreign enclave or manifesting other regressive behavior in order to remove the threatening atmosphere around him and reinstate the security of familiar behavior and beliefs.

Another form of flight is in the opposite direction. In such cases, the manager does not flee from his host culture by joining a foreign enclave but instead flees from his own national identity by joining the host culture. Such behavior, often called "going native," is also a means of reducing tension. Accepting this state of *dependency,* such managers lose much of their ability to operate on their own. They attempt to become part of the local culture and in the process lose the perspective necessary for managing an international business enterprise. While such action may be temporarily satisfying to them personally, in the long run the effects of denying one's own cultural identity are many more times as harmful personally as they are professionally.

Other managers respond to a new culture with *hostility and aggression.* They become irritated with their employees for making them feel ill at ease and become determined to "show the natives how we do it at home." Such individuals *fight* the new environment, trying to change the culture to which they have come, rather than attempting to understand and respond to it. This state of counter-dependence does not provide an avenue for beneficial relationships; many times the manager becomes authoritarian, and communication breaks down between the manager and his employees, something which would not have occurred in his home country.

Fourth, there are managers who begin the slow and painstaking process of cultural and organizational *adaptation and adjustment.* They reject neither themselves nor others, but try rather to adapt to new situations through constant openness and attempts to find mutually acceptable solutions to most problems. This requires an ability and desire to listen for the responses, both verbal and non-verbal, of those around him. At the same time, the manager must gain an awareness of the messages which he is sending out and the possible interpretation which others might have of them. In essence, he must develop the skills of person-to-person communication.

Learning how to learn

We have defined cultural adjustment as a process of continual learning through interpersonal communication and the building of interdependent relationships. There is, however, another dimension to adjustment: developing skills in "learning how to learn."

It is generally accepted that the physical growth of every individual is accompanied by a certain social and emotional growth as well. Although the former is readily observable and easy to measure, the latter's characteristics are not as easy to evaluate. Many times, the only means we have to gauge our social and emotional awareness is through the response of those around us. Our social growth is thus based upon the norms, expectations, values, and beliefs of those with whom we have grown up or spent our lives. In such situations, we seldom need to stop to take stock of the significance of our beliefs or ways of behaving. We, and those around us, accept our behavior as "natural" and correct.

Transplanted to a different culture, however, we are faced with the necessity of a continual reassessment of those values and standards previously taken for granted. The result may be that our outlook and attitudes, or "cultural vision," are highly resistant to change. We may become defensive when we discover that there are certain beliefs which are "frozen" in our way of thinking. We find it difficult to understand or tolerate persons with conflicting beliefs. *The reconsideration of many of these "frozen" values, standards, and ideals is, however, one of the most crucial processes necessary for successful adjustment.* For it is by this process that personal growth and an expanded cultural vision can be realized, resulting in a greater awareness and understanding of the world in which we must operate, and through this to a more effective managerial behavior in a foreign environment.

The learning process described above is a *three-phase cycle of "unfreezing-moving-refreezing."* Of the three phases, the first is usually the most difficult, requiring us to free ourselves from the biases of many years. No matter how much a manager may want to learn, he brings to any new environment a certain ambivalence and resistance to learning and change. Behavior change is threatening; it raises questions of personal inadequacies to meet new challenges and causes anxieties about possible failure and ridicule by others.

Once this fear has been overcome, however, the international manager is ready to learn. *Moving,* the second phase of learning, refers to the period during which he expands his cultural vision in readjusting his attitudes and perceptions. Through this process he becomes aware of alternate perspectives open to him. This is the phase of actual *learning*. The manager accepts or rejects new experiences and re-evaluates his past and present perceptions in order to form new criteria for future decision making in his work and personal life.

In the third phase of the learning cycle, *refreezing*, the manager locks in place his new perceptions and ways of behaving to avoid regressing to a previous mode of behavior. A change—behavioral or attitudinal—has taken place. Its extent, nature, and duration, however, depend very much upon the reinforcements supplied later and the degree to which the manager's new perceptions coincide with those held by his new colleagues and business associates and by the main office.

What can be learned in advance

Preparing international executives to adapt successfully is a growing concern of management specialists throughout the world. Though no two-week or even two-month classroom program can accomplish radical changes in an individual's behavior or attitudes, recent developments in human relations training have shown that *managers can be readied for a change in environment and taught to use new and unanticipated situations* as opportunities for personal growth.

For instance, through simulation of a new and unfamiliar environment, he experiences the feelings caused by cultural conflict and learns to develop an *attitude flexibility*. In a controlled atmosphere the manager—with the help of others—becomes acquainted in advance with the *unfreezing-moving-refreezing* cycle. The basic assumption of the training approach is that *learning flows from doing* and by actual participation the manager acquires a tool for meeting and overcoming the difficulties involved in adjusting to a new environment. Armed with these skills, he should be able to function more successfully abroad.

The training program itself is built on four different elements. The manager is placed in a small group (the basic unit of human relations training programs). If he is willing to expose his behavior and beliefs before others, his *participation*—the first element—allows him to see how his behavior is interpreted by others and to gain insight into himself and his relations with other people. It goes without saying that an adverse reaction, *flight,* manifested by reluctance to participate, will raise the same barriers between members of the training group as it does in a foreign culture.

Learning to risk exposure is important because the same process is necessary to come to understand life in another culture and be understood by the people of that culture. The manager who wants to be successful abroad must be willing to demonstrate to his associates and employees his ideas, feelings, and values so that they may better understand his decision-making criteria.

Feedback

A willingness to act and participate in the training process, however, is not enough. Action must be followed by reaction from other members of the group which constitutes the "new culture" for the participant. These reactions, called *feedback,* enable the manager to become aware of incongruities between his self-image and the image which he projects to others.

This experience, however, is not always easy, and many people, becoming aware of how difficult it is to communicate with one another, discover that communication means not only making themselves understood but *understanding others* as well. Some for the first time realize that a relationship involves *two* people and is a two-way street requiring patience, understanding, and interest.

The development of this sensitivity to others is a prime objective in preparing managers for intercultural experiences. In a foreign environment, the differences in perceptions and interpretations are multiplied a hundredfold, and the challenge of establishing and maintaining relationships becomes even more dependent upon feedback and the communications process.

Atmosphere

The third process is creating the proper *atmosphere.* To reduce defensiveness and encourage members to speak frankly about their feelings, values, and beliefs, an accepting emotional climate is needed. Learning to provide the right supporting atmosphere is beneficial to the other members of the group because they become more sensitive to the fears and hesitations of others and is essential for the individual in order to undergo the difficult process of *unfreezing* without fear of major repercussions.

Unfortunately, this may not be the case outside the training program. In managing abroad, the atmosphere suffers the pressures of performance standards for business and the manager has a difficult time "letting himself go" to experiment with the learning process. His prior experience in the training program, therefore, allows him to build the self-confidence and learning ability necessary to meet the challenge of adjustment in a less friendly or comfortable atmosphere.

The three processes of participation, feedback, and creating the right atmosphere are emotional experiences to which is added the fourth, *intellectual understanding* of what the participant has gone through. He is given a frame of reference in which he can order and structure the relationships between the values and perceptions to which he has been exposed. This "map" of his experiences accompanies the second or "moving" phase of the cycle and enables the manager to compare, sort, evaluate, and accept or reject his newly acquired knowledge.

Such an intellectual map also helps a manager to bridge the gap in relating his training experience to real intercultural encounters. In becoming aware of the methods which he has been using to explain and understand human interaction around him, the participant goes through a training program that blends emotional and social perceptions with intellectual reasoning. By constant analyzing of his own experiences, he can begin to assess the adequacy of his former attitudes and ways of behaving and to prepare for adaptation to a new and unknown environment.

Once abroad, he should be able to transfer what he has learned to any analogous business situation.

Conclusions

To prepare managers for work and life in a foreign environment, the training program must *increase their sensitivity* to themselves and to others and *provide them with the communication and learning skills* that will enable them to *continue the processes after they have left the formal training program*. Through reinforcements built into the manager's experience, he should be able to recognize and cope with the potentially disruptive influences that he will face in a foreign culture.

Growth in *intercultural sensitivity* is fundamentally growth in *interpersonal sensitivity,* and the four conditions necessary for a successful intercultural encounter are also essential for all personal relations. Self-awareness, an awareness of differences between one-self and others, attentiveness to the social and emotional needs of self and others, and a willingness to work toward relationships with others through effective communication—these are the goals of the training program aimed at developing the international executive. As mergers or joint ventures produce more and more multinational companies, executives will increasingly need the specific skills with which to meet the managerial challenge of international business.

Questions

1. What do the authors mean when they say the manager is born *into* not *with* a culture? What implications does this statement have for changing a manager's attitudes and behavior?
2. Why is it unrealistic to talk of a completely international "business culture"? Can you cite any other specific examples of mutations of the type referred to in the article?
3. Define the four distinctive patterns of human reaction that managers have displayed in new and unfamiliar surroundings.
4. Why should a training program to prepare managers for work and life in a foreign environment enable the managers to be more effective in all interpersonal relationships?

21—SENSITIVITY TRAINING DOESN'T WORK MAGIC *

John Drotning

There is an impressive list of business firms using sensitivity training to develop and improve managerial performance. But why? What is a T-group? How does it work?

Laboratory training uses the forces inherent in a small group to increase a person's awareness of his own behavior and its effect on others. Its aim is to break barriers hampering effective communications, to alter power relations, to develop new behavioral norms, and to establish egalitarian relationships.

Sensitivity training doesn't work magic, but it does make some things very clear: primarily, that there is a considerable difference between the knowledge and the skill inherent in a man. A manager's ability to operate effectively in an organization may depend more on personal style than on knowledge (this is especially true in technical fields). The openness of sensitivity training environments can "free up" men so much that they perform better than they would in the "real world."

The following example of a typical T-group illustrates the dynamics of sensitivity training. It describes some of the experiences in which a businessman is supposed to learn or get new and fresh insights about himself and his impact on others.

The first session opens in silence. The businessmen around the round table, usually strangers to one another, look to the leader who introduces himself and says no more. What should we do, what should we say? We feel a bit panicky and perhaps a bit annoyed. What the devil is going on? And the silence gets louder and louder. It is all around us, and it overwhelms and frustrates us. We're tight as bowstrings. The man across from me stares at the ceiling, his neighbor shuffles his feet, another stares at the table. We cast quick glances at one another looking for cues, anything to break the silence.

* From *Management of Personnel Quarterly*, Vol. 7, No. 2 (Summer, 1968), pp. 14-20. Reprinted with permission.

Fingers drum the table, there is a cough while still another member giggles nervously. Won't someone talk?

But the silence and the structurelessness are their own saviors; they force someone to say something. And no matter how simple it is, we grasp and hang on to it to avoid more silence. The ice breaks and relief floods the room. Faces relax, the smiles are more genuine now. Why not introduce ourselves? "A good idea," says my neighbor, and we go around the room like small children at school. But the respite is brief. We know each other's names, but so what. More silence, but not as bad this time. The man at the end of the table (I've forgotten his name already) suggests we order the meeting, elect officers, and set up an agenda. We reluctantly agree.

The sense of discomfort is intriguing and mysterious. Something about the silence, something ambiguous, vague, unexpected, generates tremendous tension in the group—tension so strong it forces us to do something. The stage is set for an exploration of the here and now.

During the remaining sessions we explore the behavior of the group and of each member bit by bit. The emotionality of the conversation increases. Feelings are expressed openly. We begin to talk about ourselves, our fears, our hopes, our desires, and even our sorrows. Repressed or long forgotten events may surface and cathartic displays can tear us apart and leave us in tears. A freely associating man may literally leave the group. I remember one in particular. His face radiated love and he talked, with eyes closed, of an outing with his wife and family. This kindly, balding, benign man left us; he literally was fishing with his family on the banks of the Texas stream.

But unhappy events also take place. We, the group, can be brutal. We focus on the apparent managerial inadequacies of one member. What was his relationship with his former boss, now his subordinate? Why did he let the old guy get away with so much? Why didn't he lay down the law? We exhort our fellow member to listen to us, we make him listen to us! "Go ahead, get mad," we say, "Loosen up, react, do something, but just don't sit there." But he can't let go of himself; he had always kept a tight lid on his emotions, and he won't or can't change now. And rather than healthy anger, we get nothing. Our intense personal criticism creates tremendous internal stress. His hands shake, his lips are dry, he can't get his cigarette lit, he seems near shock. Finally, we quit. I think we are *all* a bit scared.

Ah, but does it work?

There is little doubt that sensitivity training is an emotionally tense experience. It induces anxieties, stimulates interpersonal feedback, introspection, and evaluation.[1] However, several questions arise concerning the benefits and value of this type of training to a business man and his firm. Do the participants learn "how their own motives, feelings, and strategies are seen by others?"[2] In what way is sensitivity training supposed to affect the work life behavior of managers? To what extent are these effects realized in the laboratory? And how much, of whatever is learned, is transferred and used in the home plant three months, six months, and a year after the training? In short, what is the real impact of laboratory training on an organization's effectiveness?[3]

It is surprising that the effect of sensitivity training on executive performance and organization efficiency is still not clear. There are few, if any, definitive studies showing a valid statistically significant relationship between T-group experience and performance in terms of reduced costs, more effective planning and decision making, and higher profits. And reporting that T-group/control group differences just made or failed at a .05 significance level adds insult to injury. After all, if T-groups really affect participant behavior, it ought to contrast with a control group at say the .0001 level. If there is any situation which cries for a less rigid approach to statistical inference, it is in the area of T-group/control group differences. T-group students entertain enough difficulties building operational definitions of before and after behavior without compounding the trouble by using rigid statistical rules.[4]

---

[1] *Business Week,* "Where Executives Tear Off The Masks" (September 3, 1966), pp. 76-83. Also, Robert J. House, "T-Group Education and Leadership Effectiveness: A Review of the Empiric Literature and a Critical Evaluation."

[2] National Training Laboratory pamphlet advertising the 19th Annual Summer Laboratories.

[3] *Business Week* (Sept. 3, 1966), p. 83; Dorothy Stock, "A Survey of Research on T-Groups," in *T-Group Theory and Laboratory Method* edited by L. Bradford, Jack R. Gibb and Kenneth D. Benne, New York, John Wiley & Sons, 1965, pp. 395-442; Martin Lakin & Robert C. Carson, "A Therapeutic Vehicle in Search of a Theory of Therapy," *Journal of Applied Behavioral Science,* Vol. 2, No. 1, p. 35; and John E. Drotning, "Sensitivity Training: Some Critical Comments," *Personnel Journal* (November, 1965).

[4] For example see, C. M. Hampden-Turner, "An Existential 'Learning Theory' and the Integration of T-group Research," *Journal of Applied Behavioral Science,* Vol. 2, No. 4, pp. 367-385.

Moreover, there are some aspects of contemporary sensitivity training which limit its utility to businessmen and their organizations. And these limitations ought to be made explicit. Perhaps the most significant one is that the basic, underlying premise of laboratory training is not compatible with the exigencies of organizational life. Sensitivity training's stress on egalitarianism conflicts with the highly competitive, autocratically administered environment of most business firms.

Can laboratory training—a technique which attempts to change the power relations in organizations by introducing new norms of behavior and egalitarian ideology—affect the hierarchial and authoritarian management in most business firms? [5] An affirmative answer implies that a flat organization structure would replace a vertical one and that superior-subordinate relationships would be minimized. It presumes that democratic management assures maximum organizational efficiency, however defined.

Do we, really, want democracy?

There are degrees of democratic management. All members of an organization may participate equally in decision making as in the case of an Israeli kibbutz. Or in other cases, members may elect leaders to carry out decision making for them. Or leaders may be selected arbitrarily by a small number of people who then make decisions for the majority without the explicit consent of the numbers. And in each there may be various mixtures of authoritarianism and democracy. For example, a kibbutz could be formally democratic and informally authoritarian. And a faculty-governed university is apparently democratic yet it would be a stretch of the imagination to depict such universities as nonauthoritarian institutions. Moreover, many business firms pay only lip service to the principles of democratic management. In subtle and unsubtle ways management can operate in a relatively authoritarian manner. And while the opposite also may be true, an impressionistic view is that it occurs infrequently. And so the question: why are many business organizations relatively autocratic instead of democratic?

It can be argued that a hierarchial structure and a significant degree of authoritarianism are business necessities which foster responsibility, rationality, and coordination.[6] Organizations strive to

---

[5] Abraham Zaleznik, *Human Dilemmas of Leadership* (New York: Harper and Row Publishers, 1965), p. 213.

[6] Herbert A. Simon, *Administrative Behavior* (New York: The Free Press, 1957), pp. 9, 134-145.

achieve specific goals. And to achieve these goals, specific paths are chosen by leaders of the organization. And a member's contribution to progress along this path probably depends on: 1) the style of leadership, 2) peer associations, 3) the task itself, and 4) pay. But individual workers are motivated to produce at unequal rates, and management rewards and punishes these differential performances accordingly. Some succeed, some fail, and some are asked to leave the organization. Excellence is rewarded, failure is not. Certain individuals are singled out for special treatment and an informal heirarchy develops. There is an obvious power inequality which isn't compatible with an egalitarian ideology. Some individuals have more weight than others in the decisions that must be made. "All people are not the same size, and denial of superior talent and leadership are fatal in a highly competitive society." [7] Organizational success requires direction which must emanate from a few rather than many sources. And if some members are able to impose their will on others by means of various sanctions, it would follow that the former cannot interact with the latter as equals. Equalitarianism, by definition, is inconsistent with an unequal division of power within an organization.

Moreover, decisions have differential consequences. Some are well received, some are not. And the response to unpleasant decisions would seem to require the maintenance, not the breakdown, of personal defenses. The utility of completely open, completely frank interaction may be limited in organization life. If a supervisor has to fire or deny a promotion or raise to a subordinate, he may have to disguise the real reasons. A supervisor may defend against possible unpleasant reactions to his actions. At times it may be more mentally healthful to minimize not maximize interpersonal contact in potentially explosive situations. Moreover, certain aspects of managing may require an executive to use secret diplomacy and to manage news to convey different messages to his subordinates and to his superiors in order to obtain consensus from his own group. "The manager, like the good actor, has many 'lines' and many types of 'exists' and 'entrances' and their pacing varies tremendously." [8]

Business executives live in a competitive environment. There isn't room at the top for everyone. Yet this competitive atmosphere appears to exhilarate and stimulate many people. And this drive to compete, to perform well, or to self-actualize when channeled in socially useful

---

[7] Robert Moses, "Confessions of a Reformed Reformer," *Saturday Review* (January 7, 1967), p. 20.

[8] Leonard Sayles, *Managerial Behavior* (New York: McGraw-Hill Book

directions may contribute significantly to economic growth.[9] So given this competitive ethic and the imperatives of the market it seems unlikely that business organizations will nurture and develop totally nonauthoritarian management philosophies. Therefore, to the extent that sensitivity training attempts to substitute egalitarian for relatively authoritarian norms, it is likely to fail in that it will have little or no discernible impact on the participating manager's operating style in the home environment. The argument that power and aggression are more significant aspects of leadership than consideration and sensitivity severely limits the utility of laboratory training to businessmen!

Choice: the essence of leadership

Moreover, sensitivity training may have no impact on a critical aspect of executive behavior—the ability to choose in the face of uncertainty and accept the costs of wrong choices. This significant ability may distinguish successful from less successful executives (where success is defined by rank in the organization). "The essence of leadership is choice, a singularly individualistic act in which a man assumes responsibility for a commitment to direct an organization along a particular path."[10] The importance of decision making becomes even more apparent in the following comment by Douglas McGregor:

> I thought I could avoid being a 'boss.' Unconsciously, I suspect, I hoped to duck the unpleasant necessity of making difficult business decisions, of taking responsibility for one course of action among many uncertain alternatives, of making mistakes and taking the consequences. I thought that maybe I could operate so that everyone would like me—that 'good human relations' would eliminate all discord and disappointment. I could not have been more wrong.[11]

The effective leader acts; he chooses an alternative and accepts the responsibility for its success or failure. Moreover, the ability to tolerate ambiguity, to break rules when necessary, to function without

---

[9] For illustrations of this drive, see the novels of John P. Marquand, John O'Hara, F. Scott Fitzgerald and Sloan Wilson. Also see David C. McClelland, *The Achieving Society.*

[10] Abraham Zaleznik, *Review of "Leadership and Motivation" by Douglas McGregor,* in the *Boston Sunday Herald,* July 10, 1966, p. 22.

[11] A. Zaleznik's comment in *Boston Sunday Herald* as follows: "McGregor captured this idea in what must have been for him a period of intense stress. He wrote Chapter 5 'On Leadership' as he was about to leave the presidency of Antioch College, a position he had held for six years."

support and even in the face of opposition also seems to be necessary ingredients of successful executive behavior.[12] A superior who cannot accept the responsibility for controlling others will generate political activity among his subordinates. And such activity doesn't help the organization achieve its goals. Moreover, the absence of leadership may create anxieties among subordinates who find that they have not developed professionally because of political activity and are wedded to the relatively structureless situation they initially rebelled against.

And even Harvard students

An executive must lead his subordinates, he must be a boss, however unkind the term. He must exercise choice. He must direct subordinates within their area of acceptance. He may even have to be ruthless.[13] How can a T-group's concern with affect and feeling enhance decision making? For example, would former Secretary McNamara's empathy with the feelings of despair, hopelessness, frustration, and futility of the displaced Brooklyn Navy Yard worker have helped his decision? And would the worker's knowledge of McNamara's sympathy have made him less unhappy? McNamara developed alternatives and then selected one according to some decision rule. His uniqueness is his ability to choose—in that case in the face of considerable opposition from the Senate, the military, and even Harvard students.

The personality of individual risk takers and T-group decision makers differs. The former is relatively aggressive, can accept some isolation, and is not unduly concerned about others' criticisms. He may enjoy competition and be a fairly assertive person. In contrast, the desirable T-group decision maker is less ego oriented, more concerned with satisfying social needs, somewhat passive, and oriented toward collective decisions.

While the latter type may seem more appropriate in a democratic society, the former are probably more effective. The relatively authoritarian leader can generate tremendous enthusiasm and cooperation from subordinates. Such a leader who operates without continual reassurance from peers and subordinates commands a good deal of

---

[12] See Melville Dalton, "Managing the Managers," in *Some Theories of Organizations* edited by A. H. Rubenstein & C. Haberstroh (Homewood, Illinois: Richard D. Irwin Inc., 1960), p. 135.

[13] Hanson W. Baldwin, in reviewing *George C. Marshall: Ordeal & Hope 1939-42* by Forrest C. Pogue says, "This quality of ruthlessness—a necessary ingredient of every great general . . ." *New York Times Book Review*, January 1, 1967, p. 1.

respect although not love from others. The ability to choose from alternatives and accept the consequent costs is a scarce commodity, but one that is vital to any organization. Men seem to respect this ability in time of stress. In war the soldier best able to act becomes the leader. And while the business environment obviously is less traumatic than combat, it still contains an element of stress and the ability to choose is respected by superiors, subordinates, and peers.

Thus, if individuality, independence, and assertiveness are the significant elements of successful executive style, sensitivity training would seem to be inappropriate since these characteristics are acquired long before one is likely to participate in a T-group.

Can a man, the sum total of 35-50 years of life, learn enough about himself to alter his style from a week or two in group therapy? Why would a successful executive rely on untested behavioral patterns? There is a tremendous variation in the operating styles of successful managers (success defined in terms of rank in the organization). How believable would an autocratic executive be if he returned home with a different style? The incongruity between his traditional self and his new actions would have a disastrous effect on his ability to manage.

Moreover, this willingness to accept risks is evident in a wide range of styles. For example, remember the contrasts in the informal, personal, charismatic leadership of John F. Kennedy and the formal, military-like bureaucratic style of General Eisenhower. (Or compare the flamboyant enigmatic manner of the equally well-known British politician, George Brown).[14]

In what way should or could sensitivity training alter the styles of successful people to make them more effective? The normative prescriptions implicit in laboratory training may be totally inappropriate for the business environment.

Wanted: one leader with charisma

Furthermore, consider the utility of sensitivity training on leaders in growing organizations as opposed to the kind of leadership necessary in organizations that have arrived. A growing organization needs

---

[14] Mr. Brown upon sitting down to lunch next to the wife of a well-known diplomat said, "You look lovely today, Madame. Shall we have an affair?" When the lady looked a bit surprised he continued, "Surely that has been said to you before." "But not before soup," she murmured. Anthony Lewis, "George Brown Is Too Much," *The New York Times Magazine*, December 25, 1966, p. 6.

decision makers. It may even need charismatic men who can excite and motivate others to accomplish more than they normally would.[15] The group-oriented leader asks for group decisions which of necessity are compromises.[16]

How can an organization grow in size and quality without a single individual as the guiding spirit, one leader who accepts the responsibility and costs of correct and incorrect choices. The costs of wrong decisions in on-going organizations may be much smaller than the costs of incorrect choices in infant organizations where it may be success or failure. But success for growing organizations requires relatively authoritarian, assertive leaders—men who are not easily swayed from their goals. After all, one man built Ford, one man built Eastman Kodak, one man built General Motors, one man built Xerox, one man built the New York Central, and one man built the University of Chicago. Many men have administered and continue to administer these organizations, but it took one driving spirit, one risk taker, one man not too concerned about the personal impact of wrong choices, one man not dominated by the search for personal security, one man able to accept the personal consequences of risk taking, one man strong enough to stand opposition and lethargy, to create the organization and lift it to a point where it could sustain itself. Thus, laboratory training would have little impact on the kinds of behavioral patterns necessary in leaders of developing organizations.

Are there two sides to this argument?

Sensitivity training, indeed, has a limited ability to improve executive performance and organizational effectiveness. First, the equalitarian norms inherent in the T-group clash with the relatively authoritarian behavior patterns characteristic of many business firms. Second, laboratory training does not and cannot direct itself toward another critical aspect of managing, the ability to operate in the face of uncertainty and to make and accept the responsibility for a specific decision. Moreover, this ability is inherent in a wide range of personality styles which may or may not be amenable to sensitivity

---

[15] Abraham Zaleznik, *Human Dilemmas of Leadership,* pp. 147-170 and 221-230. Arch Patton, *What Is An Executive Worth?* (New York: McGraw-Hill Book Company, Inc., 1961), p. 22. Herbert A. Simon, p. 126.

[16] Although this is subject to some doubt. See Donald G. Marquis, "Individual Responsibility and Group Decisions Involving Risk," in *Industrial Management Review* (Spring, 1962), pp. 8-23.

training. A third limitation of laboratory training is simply that, as a change model, it doesn't develop initiative and aggression. And these aspects of executive behavior may be critical to rapidly developing organizations. And finally, that sensitivity training has a positive impact on job behavior after training is not at all clear.

Yet laboratory training *has* value—it is a powerful tool which can be put to good use. The T-group presumably enables one to learn about himself and his impact on others as well as their impact on him. This is a laudable goal. We spend our whole lifetime learning about ourselves; and if sensitivity training can speed up the process, all the better. But most businessmen come to the laboratory for "an educational experience in human relations, not for psychotherapy." [17] The training ought to "objectively" help them identify their personal skill needs by shifting from a therapeutic emphasis to a sociological one.

An important personnel function is to sharpen and hone the human relations skills of executives, and it cannot be neglected. And a sociological T-group may be more compatible and more useful to business than group therapy training. Contemporary T-groups have converted the Basic Skills Training approach into a "safe trip." Present T-groups are designed to improve human behavior by: increasing one's self-awareness, understanding one's desire to control and be controlled, managing anger, understanding loneliness, and expressing one's affection. These goals represent a significant departure from the goals of the founders of sensitivity training who focused on human relations skills development and the translation of laboratory learning to the home environment.[18] The earlier approach seems more suitable to the business environment than the present therapeutic one.

Groups should focus on specific occupational problems of some common interest to all participants. The members' concern with process would become secondary to the effort to solve the problem. The skill needs of the various participants would become obvious to the trainer even though they may be less evident to the members. This latter difficulty could be met by meeting and talking with each participant after his skill lacks are defined. The participant could then alter his behavior as he saw fit. And this sort of an educational T-group may be just as likely (if not more likely) to initiate lasting

---

[17] Kenneth D. Benne, p. 92.
[18] Kenneth D. Benne. While Professor Benne makes no explicit value judgments, it's my impression that he prefers the Basic Skill Training approach to the psychotherapeutic orientation of present day laboratories. Especially see pg. 92.

behavioral changes as a therapeutic one. Moreover, such an approach would facilitate in-house training which might be the most effective way to increase on-going executive interaction.

This approach would minimize the danger of psychological damage as a consequence of training. While bad results may be less frequent than is sometimes implied, it is a potential danger to guard against. But there is a word of caution even with this approach. There is no point in prescribing a remedy for a healthy patient. There ought to be evidence of a reasonably strong need for such training before it is undertaken. If the benefits of sensitivity training are less than the costs, why train? This extremely powerful training technique ought to be used more judiciously than it currently is, especially if the T-group maintains its therapeutic orientation.

Questions

1. Do you agree with the statement that "a hierarchical structure and a significant degree of authoritarianism are business necessities which foster responsibility, rationality, and coordination"? Why?
2. The author states that many organizations such as Eastman Kodak, General Motors, and Xerox were built by one man. What is your opinion?
3. In what ways is today's T-group training different from earlier human relations training programs? What is the author's reaction to the change? Do you agree with him? Why?
4. What does the author mean by psychological damage as a consequence of training?

22—T-GROUP LEARNINGS FOR GROUP EFFECTIVENESS *

Julius E. Eitington

Everyone who is concerned with effective group action, be he line manager, subordinate, trainer, or group dynamicist, is aware, to varying degrees, that group accomplishment depends on a multitude of factors. These include clarity of goals, past history (including success or nonsuccess), cohesion, communication processes, atmosphere, leader and member skills, and the like.[1]

One element in group success, which all too often is overlooked, is that of *participation*. That is to say, to what extent are all members of the group functioning as active rather than passive participants.

Groups in action in the work environment are typically task oriented. This is true whether we are talking about the work group in a planning or problem-solving situation, or in a staff meeting; or about task forces and special study groups; or about committees. In consequence, few groups attempt to assess the nature or extent of participation by group members, despite its potential for augmenting the effectiveness of the group.

Learnings from the T-group

One way to zero in on the problem of member participation in groups is to draw upon the learnings which emerge from experience in the laboratory or sensitivity training situation (the T-group). In the T-group, since there is no formal or assigned task, the concern is solely with analysis of the ongoing behavior of the group. One aspect of this behavior is the issue of participation. Let's examine, then, some of the problems and characteristics of participation in the T-group.

Typically, at the outset, the more verbal or aggressive members of the T-group promptly fill in the vacuum which has been created by the absence of an agenda, procedures, a formal leader, etc. The more

---

* From *Training and Development Journal*, Vol. 23, No. 5 (May, 1969), pp. 44-47. Reprinted with permission.
[1] D. Katz and R. L. Kahn, *The Social Psychology of Organizations* (John Wiley & Sons, Inc., 1966).

reticent members react to the unstructured situation by withdrawal, i.e., by complete silence or limited participation at best.

Trainer role

In time, the trainer may intervene to raise questions about the behavior of the group. The trainer may comment on how (meaning) introductions by the participants were made, how the "agenda" was selected, how decisions, if any, were reached, or about the pattern of participation.[2] In respect to the latter factor he thus may observe: "We've been sitting here and talking for an hour and three members of our group of twelve haven't said anything; I wonder whether anyone feels that this is significant."

This intervention by the trainer may be met by stunned silence or, in short order, by defensive retorts. Some of these responses (by the more verbal ones, obviously) are of this nature:

- "Should everyone participate all the time?"
- "Why can't one participate by listening? The fact that John hasn't said anything doesn't mean that he's not learning from the discussions."
- "Should people participate just for the sake of participation?"
- "We're all big boys here. Why do we have to beg people to participate?"
- "Do you think we ought to embarrass people by calling on them?"

Although rationalizations such as the above are certain to come forth in the early life of the group, they are quite likely to be repeated and rephrased at various intervals thereafter. In fact, the issue of participation, along with other key issues such as the development of trust, the trainer's role, and the role of feedback may bug the group throughout its life. Some groups may grasp the importance of broad participation quite early; some may see its significance at mid-point in the program or thereafter; some may never overcome this barrier to group effectiveness.

Trainer inputs regarding participation

As we have been indicating, the issue of participation is (or becomes) one of vital concern to the T-group. Obviously, each group

---

[2] For an account of a sensitivity training laboratory in action, see Chris Argyris, "T-Groups for Organizational Effectiveness," *Harvard Business Review* (Mar.-Apr., 1964).

will deal with it in different ways. Each trainer will also approach the problem in accordance with his own training style and philosophical base.

In any case, one or more of the following observations are quite likely to be advanced by the trainer and, hopefully, by other group members in support of the trainer in his quest for answers to the question: "Why participate?"

1. To tap the total resources of the group. One of the basic assumptions of group work is that higher quality solutions or decisions are possible through collective rather than unilateral action. Although we may know this in an intellectual sort of way, our behavior in groups all too often evidences that in a more practical sense we ignore this precept. In consequence, potentially valuable contributions by one or more group members are frequently lost.

However, early member rationalization of "participation for the sake of participation" generally loses its validity as the T-group comes to realize that there are positive gains to be had by involving the total group in its activities. The author's experience in the T-group, as well as in back-home work situations, is that it is very difficult for many group members to assume the "gate-keeping" role—e.g., "We haven't heard from John yet. I wonder how he feels about it?" Yet, the group's ability to do this is vital for its growth, cohesiveness, and ultimate effectiveness.

2. To help growth of recessive members. To the extent that we conceive of a group at work *solely* as one which is concerned with its task, we lose the benefits of other values of group work. One allied purpose is to encourage the growth of *all* members of the group, particularly the shyer ones. If the recessive members are not given ample opportunity to test their ideas in the marketplace, to comment on what is going on, we are systematically and selfishly depriving them of opportunities for growth. Participation is something like success, the more we get the more we seek. Similarly, nonparticipation breeds more of the same. The task for an effective group, then, is to break the cycle of nonparticipation (nonsuccess) to one of participation (success).

A successful, hard-hitting group has to learn to make *all* group members feel wanted and to feel adequate. To do otherwise is to function in a self-serving, immature way.

3. To aid growth of the more verbal members. To the extent that the more talkative members can be encouraged to involve others in the discussions, they are learning and growing, too. What are they

learning? They are learning, for one thing, the tough skill of *self-restraint*. That is to say, they are learning to give of themselves, to surrender their (large) share of the available air time to let a less aggressive person into the act. They thus are learning how to establish conditions so that others can grow; in short, *how to give help*. They certainly will learn the value of securing the ideas and contributions of others. They may also be learning how to listen. In general, these opportunities for growth by the total group will be lost to the extent that the aggressive members monopolize the air time to meet their own needs to be heard.

4. To get support for decisions. Although the T-group is not a group which is concerned with the making of "vital" decisions involving program or money as in the back home situation, decision making opportunities do arise; e.g., in regard to choosing or not choosing a leader, agreeing on an agenda, securing consensus on procedures such as breaking for coffee, lunch, or dinner, agreeing to participate in tasks or exercises proposed by the trainer, and the like. What emerges as an important learning, regardless of the nature or complexity of the decision, then, is the importance of *consensus*. For it is consensus that secures commitment from the group to support a decision. Effective T-groups learn in time that wide participation in the making of these decisions, no matter how small, is essential to group effectiveness. For if *all* group members are not heard, how can we be certain we really have consensus?

5. To ventilate and explore feelings. The back-home group at work in its problem-solving role is ordinarily concerned with facts, figures, logic, reason, and knowledge. It typically denies or smothers concern with feelings or emotions. For example, it is quite rare for a member of a back-home work group to say: "This discussion has me completely frustrated. I don't think we're getting anywhere because we've been skillfully dodging issues here." Yet this ventilation of feelings may be precisely what the group needs to get it into gear. Or a participant may be permitted to sit silently throughout the proceedings without anyone inviting him into the discussion. Or a group member may make a suggestion, possibly unpopular or seemingly bizarre, and the rest of the group may not respond at all ("a plop" occurs, as the group dynamics people call it), thus leaving the contributor with a high degree of confusion or resentment concerning the group's silent treatment of his contribution.

In the T-group, by way of contrast, we turn things around and try to explore the *emotional* rather than the intellectual side of group effort. That is to say, we encourage all group members to verbalize their feelings, to comment about behavior—their own and that of others. To the extent that all T-group members do this, we (the group) are better able to understand one another, to strengthen interpersonal relationships, to achieve greater satisfaction, and to progress more rapidly toward group goals.

By way of illustration, one aspect of the exploration of the feeling side of group life is to assure the group that all its members are "with things," that they are not harboring "hidden agendas." Thus, after the group has been going for two or three days, a group member may say, "Hank, you've been silent most of this morning, how come?" Hank, of course, may be sulking, disinterested, fatigued, ill, experimenting, etc. But the group, to be effective, has the need to know *why* Hank is behaving this way. If the group doesn't smoke out Hank's feelings, particularly if they are of a frustrated or resentful sort, it can't do anything about them. Nor can it give Hank a chance to get them out of his system (catharsis).

Participation, then, is a means of liberating rather than bottling up the emotions. As necessary, it becomes a vital form of catharsis. To behave in any other way is to ignore the need that everyone has to express his feelings freely.

6. To build trust. One of the issues which an effective T-group must be able to deal with is that of *trust*. Trust implies a freedom in the group for *all* participants to say what they wish (or need) to say, without fear of any recriminatory or retaliating action. In other words, how open is the group? Is it safe to speak out on a controversial topic? Is it safe to exhibit an emotion such as anger? Is it safe to give feedback to a group member or the trainer? Is it safe to question the validity of the whole T-group concept?

Trust develops as group members become more open, more risk-taking, and more participative. Thus, the group member who sits back and smokes his pipe with a Buddha-like expression on his face not only inhibits his own learning but is likely to inhibit the learning process for the entire group. Thus, a group member may get irritated with this taciturn behavior and say: "How come you're not in the ring with the rest of us? Do you think you're better than we are? How do we know what you're thinking if you just sit there?" If the pipe-smoker recognizes the impact his behavior is making on the group and begins to participate, the group can get on with its business in the full sense of the term. The issue of trust, then, becomes (or is on the way to becoming) resolved.

7. To build intimacy. The T-group also learns in time that the closer group members are to one another, the more meaningful and satisfying the experience becomes. But intimacy, like trust, is dependent upon participation. So if Joe isn't brought out of his shell by the group, i.e., if he is permitted to sit in silence, how can we get adequately close to him? And if we can't get close to him, how can we help his growth in any way? As one trainer put it, "You can't fix the engine if he won't even bring the car into the garage, let alone raise up the hood."

"Getting to know you, getting to feel free and easy" is more than just a line from a popular song. It is basic to success in interpersonal and group relations.

8. To encourage risk-taking. Managers who are familiar with the T-group only through reading or secondhand accounts may have limited insight into its goals and values.

One value which is not commonly recognized is that of *risk-taking*. To the extent that group members can be encouraged to try new ways of behaving, to experiment, to take some risks, they are learning, as persons, to function in more complete and meaningful ways. Participation of a more active sort is one of the risks the quieter group member has to take if he is to learn and to grow. The fear of "making an ass of oneself," of being "clobbered" by a more outspoken member who may disagree, or of "not having anything worthwhile to say" has to be overcome. Overcoming this fear isn't a one-way street, of course. It has to be overcome through support by the entire group. Encouraging the quiet person to take the risk of participation is a challenge to the group; the more effective groups are able to rise to this challenge.

These, then, are eight notions about participation, and are some of the reasons which the trainer or T-group members may advance to encourage the fullest possible group participation. They may (possibly) appear quite "logical" to the reader. Yet, for a T-group in action, the logic takes on meaning only by actually working these problems through. For the barriers to participation are not in the realm of logic, but in the area of feeling or emotion. And emotional learning is a slow, frustrating, painful, and uncertain process.

Applications to the organizational setting

The T-group, as a unique, free-wheeling institution for purposes of individual and group development, obviously is not a model for group action in the plant or office. Yet, it can be a useful source to discover management learnings which have on-the-job applicability. Some of the learnings are:

1. Work groups all too often handicap themselves because they discourage openness, leveling, and full participation of its members. In fact, limited rather than full participation is generally the norm.[3]

2. Most work groups reduce their effectiveness because they deny group members the opportunity to participate freely, if at all, in the area of expression of feelings. Yet feelings may be as vital to the decision-making process as facts.[4]

3. Most work groups are content to live with hidden agendas which serve to support attitudes hostile to full participation.[5] Some of these unstated attitudes are:

> "I want (need) the available air time."
> "I don't really care to listen to other people's ideas and opinions."
> "I don't care about the growth of others."
> "I'm adequately effective by operating this way—don't challenge me on this."

4. Group action, insofar as participation is concerned, is not doomed to the status quo. Bringing laboratory training programs into the organization, in the form of cousin and family training groups, is a road to more effective, cohesive work groups. For in such training endeavors members can learn that there are many "newer" values to be considered in the participation process, values which the work culture ordinarily overlooks.[6]

Questions

1. Why do work groups concern themselves with facts, figures, logic, reasoning, and knowledge to the exclusion of feelings and emotions? What effect does this have on the work group and the organization as a whole?

---

[3] Alfred Vogel, "Why Don't Employees Speak UP?" *Personnel Administration* (May-June 1967).

[4] Douglas McGregor, *The Professional Manager* (McGraw-Hill Boob Co., 1967).

[5] E. L. Shostrom, *Man the Manipulator* (Abingdon Press, 1967).

[6] For the basic works on laboratory training, see:

    a. L. P. Bradford, J. R. Gibb, and K. D. Benne, *T-Group Theory & Laboratory Method—Innovation in Re-Education* (John Wiley & Sons, 1964).

    b. A. J. Marrow, *Behind the Executive Mask* (American Management Assn., 1964).

    c. E. H. Schein and W. G. Bennis, *Personal & Organizational Change Through Group Methods: The Laboratory Approach* (John Wiley & Sons, 1965).

2. What advantages are there in the T-group having no formal or assigned task?
3. What effect does consensus have on the members of a group? What role does participation have on attaining consensus?
4. T-group training is usually provided to managers and supervisors. Would an organization benefit if all employees participated?

23—EVALUATING AND DEVELOPING SUBORDINATES *

William M. Fox

Since World War I much effort and thought has gone into the design of formal merit rating systems as tools for evaluating and developing subordinates. In recent years we have begun to get some good feedback as to the effectiveness of these efforts. Unfortunately, the data are not encouraging.

Evaluation of typical programs indicates three primary trouble areas:[1]

- Lack of motivation on the part of subordinates to *want* to change;
- *Inability* to change—especially in the way they deal with people—even on the part of those who recognize a need to change; and
- *Anxiety* and *resentment* on the part of subordinates—especially on the part of those who are most deficient—toward the program and toward bosses when the approach is implemented conscientiously.

Since these difficulties persist in many programs despite much experimentation and study directed at their solution, the prospects for solving them now by "beefing up" present efforts appear rather dim. A better hope appears to lie in stepping back from them to examine critically the assumptions upon which they are based with the hope of better understanding the factors that facilitate or discourage individual change. New approaches can then be built on firmer ground.

Some useful lessons from nonbusiness organizations

Some worthwhile inputs for improving our "individual change model" can be obtained by analyzing the practices of the service academies, the Marine Corps and other elite military groups, championship teams, certain religious orders, and selected fraternal organizations . . . yes, even some college fraternities, perhaps!

* From *Business & Economic Dimensions* (February, 1969), pp. 17-20. © Copyright IBM Corporation, 1968. Reprinted with permission.
[1] For a sampling of representative survey data, see: Alvin Zander, Editor, *Performance Appraisals—Effects on Employees and their Performance*, Ann Arbor, Michigan: The Foundation for Research on Human Behavior, 1963.

What do these diverse organizations tend to share in common?

Candidates for development are selected on the basis of their suitability for and interest in the organization and its values, not merely on the basis of their interest in and ability to perform the duties of a given position. Candidates must respect and want what the established members of the organization represent, and have reasonable potential for assimilating required skills and values.

Candidates are prepared to accept change. All of these organizations hold out genuine encouragement for an attainable "better self" as they deemphasize or reject parts of the trainee's "old self." A number of means are used to accomplish these goals.

- Typically, trainees are removed from home, friends, and the gang-contacts which support and encourage the maintenance of the "old self" intact.
- Standardized haircuts, uniforms, and neophyte status help to deprive the trainee of a part of his "old self"—aspects of his physical identity.
- Established members of the organization have "been through the mill," and believe in and try to practice the "better self" values being held up to the trainees. Thus, not only do the trainees see that "it can be done," they are more likely to accept values that respected men worked for and hold dear.
- Established members have shown special interest in the trainees by selecting them and devoting time and effort to them. The message is clear—the trainees have the potential for being "better selves," like the established members, or they wouldn't be here! They are "something special," though more in their potentialities than in their "old selves."
- Normally, the trainees are well-motivated volunteers who know something of the organization's values and view "making the team" as a positive achievement. In other words, *the net perception of the trainee at the beginning is that he is being afforded opportunity for growth rather than being demeaned.*

Actual ongoing change is encouraged by

- The presence of "models" with whom the trainees can identify. These models may be present in various forms—dedicated established members of the organization, the living rule in a convent, a veteran hero, a buddy in a buddy system, or a big brother in a fraternity.
- Reward and penalty systems in which the everyday success or failure of established members is judged in part by how well they adhere to "better self" values and help to train others; in other words, training is an important part of every leader's job.
- Living with other trainees—pressure in the group is directed toward change to a "better self." Encouragement and support are provided for movement in the "right" direction, whereas ridicule and rejection face those who do not try to "improve." Trainees want to "belong" and to avoid failure and a return to the "old self."

- Coaching and realistic exercises which encourage the trainees to experiment with and get the feel of new techniques and skills. Though parts of the "old self" must be discarded, each trainee is provided with some personal guidance and choice in picking a "better self" role in the organization to strive toward which best meets his individual needs.

Change, when once realized, is "jelled" and reinforced

- Through refresher courses, maneuvers, and special exercises for established members and through meaningful rewards and penalties to them for their performance as "examples" and trainers.
- Through periodic ceremonies which highlight the traditions, achievements, and future prospects of the organization.
- Through the fact that the majority of established members have accepted the desired values and encourage each other to comply with them.

Typical evaluation and development programs in industry

Too often, the typical approach to merit rating generates criticism of the subordinate's "old self" in the absence of positive definition of a "better self" that he can strive toward and wishes to strive toward.

Criticisms given are often too vague and general. Remember, we aren't talking about training in reading blueprints, mastering a new procedure, or something else that is not really a part of our basic make-up . . . we are talking about changes in a person's motivation and his ways of dealing with people. When you question these things, it's very easy for the subordinate to believe that you're dealing out personal insult and injury. The net effect is that often he feels anxious and threatened. As a result, the evaluation and development interview can readily degenerate into meaningless platitudes, hostile debate, or sullen resentment on the part of deficient subordinates. At best, little is accomplished in the direction of growth or change.

The typical approach forces the supervisor to attempt too much in one sitting with the subordinate and to assume two roles that subordinates often perceive as being contradictory to each other: one minute the boss is sitting in judgment as a powerful spokesman for the company's program, and in the next he is attempting to be a friendly counselor and coach. Few supervisors can perform this type of "instant hat switching" without misgivings, and few can do it with genuine benefit to the subordinate.

Merit rating systems in industry typically employ factors and rating scales that were developed some time ago for a large class of jobs by some central agency with little if any provision for adjustment to changing conditions, unique job requirements, and individual needs. Rarely are they "validated"—that is, checked to see if what the rating scales measure really is important to the success of the organization. Supervisors have their doubts! Subordinates have their doubts! Therefore, often a "stand-off" materializes as far as development goes, with appreciable "gamesmanship" on both sides.

In the traditional approach to development, subordinates often are encouraged to attend classes which teach them concepts of leadership and management that are not even understood by, let alone practiced by, established managers in the organization. Also, established managers often see training activity as an unwarranted appendage to an already over-crowded schedule . . . a relatively unrewarded one that appears to generate few serious penalties for those who are poor at it or ignore it altogether. Little support for special exercises or time-consuming coaching is normally found in final budgets!

Typically, new men are picked to fill specific slots without much regard to their potential for development. Attempts are then made to develop these same men. As a result, it is difficult to form groups of subordinates for development who share a common experience and common aspirations.

Finally, it appears more the exception than the rule when established managers and members of the organization really agree upon, define, and commit themselves to certain "better self" values. Results alone often count for too much in terms of rewards in the short run with little credit going to good form and sound values. There is little guidance and there are too few "models" for the would-be "models!"

So . . . what can I do about it?

Even granting that many of the above indictments are true, I'm not about to climb on a white charger, you may say, and gallop off to reform the organization . . . and get shot down in the process! What can *I* do, in *my* department, with *my* subordinates?

This will depend in part, of course, upon how much freedom you have to experiment within your own jurisdiction . . . but here are some ideas that may prove of value:

- Have each subordinate prepare a written analysis of the important performance factors, responsibilities, and goals of his job as he sees them. Discuss them with him until you can reach some substantial agreement as to what they should be.
- Then have each subordinate write down specific activity and time targets for improving present performance (if the subordinate

wishes to try for merit increases) and for becoming promotable (if the subordinate is interested in this . . . if not, have him prepare a statement to this effect for his file).

- Discuss these proposals with each subordinate until a program evolves that you both feel is definite enough (the goals established and the means for measuring progress toward them must be quite tangible and feasible) and challenging enough, yet achievable.

- Any time that a subordinate wants to discuss his program or whenever significant time targets come up, meet with him to assess progress made and discuss reasons for lack of progress (encouraging the subordinate to assess himself as far as possible), and to establish with him new or refined activity targets or dates, or both, on the basis of past performance and future prospects.

- If other supervisors wish to experiment with this approach, it might be useful to meet with them to compare notes on problems involved in drawing up individual programs and in evaluating the progress of subordinates relative to them.

- In any event, *development* efforts can and should be separated from *evaluations* made for the purpose of awarding pay increases, promotions, and penalties (even though these evaluations will be based upon development data to a large extent). In passing, we should note that other techniques have produced ratings significantly more reliable and valid than those obtained from conventional merit rating scales.[2]

In conclusion

Building on the approach outlined above, the development program should stand a better chance than the typical merit rating system in fitting the motivational level and personality of the subordinate because it is primarily his program, tailored to his needs. At any given time he knows where he stands and has more control over how he will be evaluated. In fact, to a large extent he can evaluate himself through knowledge of his performance relative to his program.

The evaluations you will make for rewarding and penalizing your subordinates will draw upon such data and, therefore, will tend to be merely a formalization of what is anticipated by them—not judgments to be avoided or combated. Hopefully, in this new approach to evaluation and development, you will be regarded more as a coach and helper by your subordinates than as that "so and so in the front office who's trying to play God!"

---

[2] See: Fred McMurry, "How to Use Alternation Ranking: Report on the Reliability of the Alternation Ranking Technique"; Neils Bomholt, "Supervisor's Performance Reports in Scandinavia," *Social Science Research Reports, Volume III, Performance Review and Evaluation*, Standard Oil Company (New Jersey), 1962; Joseph Tiffin, "Six Merit Rating Systems," *Personnel Journal* (January, 1959).

Bibliography

Anderson, Camilla. *Beyond Freud*. New York: Harper and Brothers. 1957.

Fox, William. *The Management Process*. Homewood, Illinois: Richard D. Irwin. 1963. pp. 202-206, 372-373, 380-382.

Houston, George C. *Manager Development: Principles and Perspectives*. Homewood, Illinois: Richard D. Irwin. 1961.

Levinson, Harry, Charlton Price, Kenneth Munden, Harold Mandl, and Charles Solley. *Men, Management, and Mental Health*. Cambridge, Massachusetts: Harvard University Press. 1962.

Rogers, Carl. *On Becoming a Person*. Boston: Houghton Mifflin Company. 1961.

Stein, Morris, Editor. *Contemporary Psychotherapies*. New York: The Free Press of Glencoe. 1961.

Howell, Robert A. "A Fresh Look at Management by Objectives." *Business Horizons*. Fall, 1967. p. 51.

"Increasing Management Effectiveness through Work Planning—A Summary of The Work Planning and Review Program of the General Electric Company's Small Aircraft Engine Department, Lynn, Massachusetts." Flight Propulsion Division of General Electric Small Aircraft Engine Department. 1965.

Levinson, Harry. "A Psychologist Looks at Executive Development." *Harvard Business Review*. September-October, 1962, p. 69.

Meyer, H. H., E. Kay, and J. R. P. French, Jr. "Split Roles in Performance Appraisal." *Harvard Business Review*. January-February, 1965. p. 123.

Questions

1. The author indicates some useful lessons to be learned from nonbusiness organizations. Can you cite any specific examples that would support or refute his hypothesis? Are nonbusiness organizations as different from business organizations as the author indicates?

2. What benefits are likely to result from the author's recommendation that subordinates prepare proposals for improving present performance and establish means for measuring progress toward them?

3. Do you agree with the author's recommendations that efforts to develop employees should be separated from evaluations made for the purpose of awarding pay increases and promotions? Why?

24—A PSYCHOLOGICAL PERSPECTIVE ON MANPOWER PROGRAMS *

Ross Stagner

The Nation's unemployment rate, lower this past fall than at any other time since the Korean conflict, is one of many indications that the country's manpower programs are having some degree of success in combatting unemployment. The more than a million people who have enrolled in Manpower Development and Training Act (MDTA) institutional, on-the-job, and combined training programs, the thousands of job placements through the Job Opportunities in the Business Sector (JOBS) Program, the proliferation of Youth Opportunity Centers, and the thousands who have found work through the Concentrated Employment Programs are evidence that some inroads are being made into helping the hard-core unemployed.

We have initiated some very fine programs in the manpower field. The goals are high, the sentiments impeccable. Yet the Nation's manpower problems are still far from solved. We have not implemented many of our programs as well as would be hoped. Why not? How can we do better? Not surprisingly, I see the deficiencies primarily in applications of psychological knowledge, although other specialists may see quite a different set of adjustments to be made.

Manpower programs in this country traditionally have concentrated on the task of helping people get ahead within our established employment patterns. There is nothing inherently wrong with this, but there is something to be said for questioning whether it is a policy adequate to current needs.

Selection, testing, training, counseling, and job induction programs have in the past sought to qualify people for existing jobs, accepting the employment practice of hiring only people of the highest quality. Only in the last few years has the Federal Government sought to encourage hiring at new standards—standards which would permit employment of those who did not make it over the testing and training hurdles.

---

* From *Manpower*, Vol. 1, No. 2 (February-March, 1969), pp. 19-21.

Another approach (now not much more than a twinkle in the skeptic's eye) is the notion that we may have to foster new institutions—consumer and producer cooperatives organized for inner-city residents, neighborhood organizations, and self-help programs—as opposed to assimilation by existing industry. While this idea will present some psychological problems if it goes into higher gear, psychologists are now most concerned about the inadequacies of the individual-oriented selection and training activities of Federal, State, and local governments and private industry. This, of course, is where we stand today—that is, the preponderance of our energy is going into the individual-oriented programs; hence, they require scrutiny.

In commenting on where we stand with regard to these programs, I must necessarily oversimplify, but I shall try to be fair. Psychologists are concerned with individual human beings. We are interested in how they perceive institutions and practices, how their motives are satisfied or frustrated by situations, what social roles they play, and how these roles affect the deprivations of other human beings. The manpower programs of the Federal Government are also intended to serve the welfare of human beings. Let us examine two or three activities in the light of these statements.

First, let's examine the Employment Service. Three groups of people are directly involved in the functioning of the Employment Service: the staff, employers, and the clients. Staff members perceive ES as an important institution in guiding people to jobs, helping both the worker and the employer. However, not all applicants are equal in their eyes. The neat, brisk, mannerly young man who speaks excellent English will be easy to place; staff members may compete to get him as a client. But the older, illiterate worker with few skills offers a tough problem; the staff may try to avoid him. The person who gets stuck with this client may make half-hearted efforts, convey a feeling of failure and futility to the client, offer some platitudes, and heave a sigh of relief when he departs.

This happens because the ES staff member is also human, and he perceives his social role as a way of getting ahead, of earning money, and winning social approval. The reward system within ES often operates to favor attention to easy cases and to avoid the difficult cases. Rightly or wrongly, staff members believe they are evaluated as doing well when they make many placements. The hard-core case may be complicated and may require many hours of effort, during which the staff man could have placed three or four bright youngsters. Hence, some of the tough cases may be brushed off or handled ineffectively.

This pattern affects the way in which ES is perceived. Certain high school graduates see it as very helpful. Inner-city residents often see it as useless. They quickly learn that ES may not be very helpful in locating jobs for them. Many perceive the bureaucratic routine (more or less correctly) as a runaround calculated to discourage them and get them to leave. A fair percentage of ghetto men see the ES as indifferent or downright hostile.

I do not believe that the addition of electronic data processing will change this aspect of ES. Placement of hard-core cases depends on patient, sympathetic work with individuals. If the reward system were revised to encourage staff to do this kind of job, I am confident they could do it. The Human Resources Employability Development Model, which was issued by the Employment Service in September, is a step in this direction.

Training programs are offered the unskilled in which they may acquire some minimum of marketable skills. High school dropouts are invited to come into vocational training classes. But if these trainees were young men who dropped out of vocational training classes, who found those programs were frustrating and not satisfying, how can they be expected to do other than drop out again?

Many current training efforts seem to a psychologist to be especially deficient with respect to the importance of motivation. Most of the dropouts or hard-core cases have failed repeatedly in various endeavors. When such a person is criticized for poor performance in class, he simply retreats, rejects the training, and refuses to try again. Research in which I have participated on Detroit teenagers in one such program indicated that rather generous praise for very small successes can gradually build confidence and channel energy into efforts to learn. Another experiment showed that such trainees progressed faster and eliminated errors more quickly when given candy or cigarettes for accurate work than when given praise. Other studies suggest that trainees must have very short assignments with immediate reward, attainable in an hour or a day; they cannot maintain effort for several weeks without reward.

Too many training programs fail to make allowance for such factors. They seem to be mere copies of vocational high school courses, with very little use of psychological expertise regarding motivation, reward, scheduling, guidance, and counseling. This is not to say that such training has been useless. Obviously many youngsters have benefited greatly. But the crucial cases have not been handled successfully.

Why do we follow such policies? Government employees learn to act out certain social roles. They find out what they will be rewarded for. If they get penalized for trying innovations, they will learn to stick to tradition. The problem is not with the training personnel but with the pattern to which they must conform.

The result is that MDTA works best for people who need it least. The kind of young person who can adapt to the typical training program adapted fairly well in school. The scared, clumsy migrant boy who doesn't know what he is doing and can't explain this to the instructor receives a scolding or is shunted aside. Soon he becomes discouraged and quits, or he stays to obtain his stipend, but makes no pretense of trying to learn.

Some industrialists have become aware of deficiencies in MDTA programs. They suggest changes to build in a gradually stepped-up work pace, few frustrations at first but more in later weeks, and more exacting standards near the close of training. These ideas make sense to psychologists.

The JOBS Program, a recent innovation in manpower programs, has been an effort to obtain immediate placement of hard-core cases on real jobs. This meets some of the criticisms offered for the MDTA courses but often goes to the other extreme. The worker is expected to adapt suddenly to a totally strange culture. A man who at 35 gets his first regular industrial job has many habits to be broken, others to form. He may be late to work (no alarm clock, staying out late with the boys, can't read bus signs and takes the wrong bus, etc.). He may burst out in irrational rage at a minor criticism from a supervisor. He cannot abandon all his old ways of behavior overnight, anymore than you and I change when we make New Year's resolutions. Thus, carefully planned induction programs are essential to the success of the JOBS placements.

We believe we are getting good results in Detroit by manipulating the group atmosphere within which the ghetto employee functions. This means training supervisors and union stewards in how to deal with the employee, or at least telling them what to expect. It means creating a feeling in the worker that he is not alone, or that he is not surrounded by enemies and critics. We have been using group meetings to ventilate feelings of anger, anxiety, and insecurity, to remove some emotional tensions and then provide explanations of why industry operates as it does. Our successes may be illusory—psychologists sometimes engage in wishful thinking, like everyone else. But it seems that planned manipulation of the social context can facilitate the transition from the ghetto culture to an industrial culture.

Where do we go from here? I can see two courses of action open to us: We can strengthen and improve present programs—and focus them on the most difficult manpower problems—by an infusion of the kind of psychological knowledge I have already mentioned.

We can innovate with new programs which seek to modify the institutional environment, creating new social contexts within which the hard-core unemployed may see fewer obstacles and more opportunities, fewer enemies and more cooperators. We may develop whole industrial enterprises in which the disadvantaged may have a chance to lead and make decisions, rather than being compelled to fit into small, predetermined jobs with few chances for self-expression.

Probably, wise social policy for the next decade calls for experimentation with both kinds of actions. In any event we should never lose sight of the fact that manpower programs aim to help individual human beings, that their motives, fears, and hostilities are crucial factors, and that concern for how the client perceives our efforts is an important element of planning and running the program.

Questions

1. Why do the hard-core cases need immediate reward during training? Why do trainers overlook the importance of immediate reward?
2. What can be done to make Employment Service personnel more responsive to the needs of inner city and ghetto personnel?
3. Can you foresee any employment problems that individuals may have after they are trained and qualify for jobs?

25—STEERING MARGINAL PERFORMERS TO SOLID GROUND *

Harvard Y. Weatherbee

What happens when a manager discovers he has a "marginal" performer among his employees? For that matter, how do you identify a marginal performer—and what do you do about him? In almost every kind of organization—military, educational, government, industrial—there are some individuals who, for want of a better term, are classified as marginal. They may be underqualified or overqualified for the positions they hold; there are all sorts of variations, but the marginal performer is a drag on the efficiency of any operation and on group performance as well.

Typically, operating managers ignore the problem as long as possible, and then resort to one of two standard solutions: They manipulate the work force to transfer the employee out of their own bailiwicks (and in most cases, this maneuver only continues the problem elsewhere) or they get rid of him entirely, by firing him or more gently "letting him go," for instance, when payrolls are being reduced during a recession.

Actually, it is just as difficult to generalize about how to handle a marginal employee as it is to generalize about what a marginal performer is. Each case will be special and should be handled specially, but there are some guidelines both to identifying and to coping with the marginal performer.

Who is he?

A marginal performer might be defined as one who is judged by his manager to be at or close to the lower limit of performance acceptability in his assigned work. Usually, he is not totally unqualified, completely incompetent, or unable or unwilling to achieve minimum acceptable performance. In other words, he is not the absolute failure whose employment should be terminated without question or delay, nor is the marginal performer one whose work has been satisfactory

---

* From *Personnel*, Vol. 46, No. 4 (July-August, 1969), pp. 34-43. Reprinted with permission.

but is no longer required, so that he should be laid off and not replaced. Who, then, *is* the marginal performer? He may be:

- A relatively short-service employee who is not quite making the grade.
- A seasoned employee who has not kept pace with changing requirements.
- A capable employee transferred to a new and different assignment for which he has not developed requisite competence.
- An able employee, thoroughly qualified and competent to handle work previously assigned to him, who has been promoted and placed "at risk" but who has failed to meet the challenge.
- An older, quite probably a long-service, employee who has mentally retired and whose performance is spasmodic or deteriorating seriously.

The list cannot be complete; the marginal employee may be otherwise identified, and he may be found at any level of the organization, but it is important to recognize in any case that the label "marginal" has, or should have, to do with evaluation of an employee's performance in his *assigned* work, not in unusual assignments.

Why is he marginal?

The causes of marginal performance may differ widely with individual and circumstance, and may also overlap. Among them are lack of capacity or ability in terms of education, skills, judgment, et cetera; emotional or behavioral problems, such as alcoholism, drugs, or domestic difficulties; misplaced talent—the square peg in a round hole who is either underqualified or overqualified for his job; lack of interest or other, more absorbing interests; or physical problems that make the work too demanding. In addition, marginal work can sometimes be traced to circumstances, such as organization change or personality conflicts.

Whatever accounts for the unsatisfactory quality of his work, the marginal performer presents us with a decision problem, and there are many external influences affecting the marginal performer that make clean-cut decisions difficult. A manager may be ready to let the marginal employee go except for a crisis—a strike, special patent problem, or a thousand other situations in which the marginal performer has some special and valuable skill or knowledge. Or perhaps the marginal employee was once an excellent performer, or he has a history of solid contributions—a brilliant scientist, for instance, who is fed up with a manager he considers incompetent or incapable of understanding his work or his needs. Again, he may be a fairly new employee who has not had proper orientation, guidance, or supervision (as is often the case with minority-group employees).

Identification techniques

The need to identify and evaluate the marginal performer cannot be evaded, yet it does require an indepth knowledge of the total work environment and the individual's background, as well as of a number of other considerations that will be discussed later. Meanwhile, we might consider some specific identification techniques.

Performance appraisal systems, at least for exempt personnel, are in use in almost all companies, and less formal appraisal systems exist in various forms at the nonexempt and hourly levels. Most systems of this kind measure an employee's actual performance in his assigned work, either against responsibilities and duties as stated in an employee's position guide or against specific, predetermined goals, work plans, and standards mutually agreed upon and understood by the man and his manager.

The existing appraisal system should be utilized in the identification of marginal employees. Arbitrary assignment of percentages or quotas is also used as a means of identifying those whose performance is substandard compared with the performance of others, but quotas tend to oversimplify mechanistically. In any case, the approaches to identification will differ somewhat depending on what level of organization structure is involved—entry-level, early-career positions; middle-management or equivalent individual-contributor positions; and higher-management positions.

Entry-level, early-career positions. It is important that marginal performance be spotted within the first few months and certainly within the first two years of employment, before the person's investment of time hurts his chance for employment in other companies or more suitable lines of work, and before the company's investment becomes too great. (Most probationary periods are established with this in mind.)

Several steps should be followed to keep tabs on performance:

- Clear, specific standards of performance should be developed and reviewed with the new employee. Results to be achieved should be mutually agreed upon, and reviews of progress and causes of success or failure should be held at least quarterly. Skills, abilities, and approaches that contributed to successful performance should be recognized, as well as faults and deficiencies that contributed to poor performance.

- The man and his manager should work to structure the job requirements so that maximum use is made of the employee's strengths, while training and coaching are provided in areas of weakness.
- A summary record of each individual's progress, achievements, and development needs should be regularly updated so that recurring examples of successful and unsuccessful performance clearly emerge.
- Periodic and timely analysis of such performance records will enable the manager to identify those employees who are not achieving minimum acceptable performances on their assigned work. Such analysis might show, for example, that even though an individual's work was consistently well-planned, detailed, and accurate, it was also unimaginative, superficial, and hastily implemented and hence *marginal* in respect to the actual requirements of the particular position.

Middle-management or equivalent individual-contributor positions. The judgments, decisions, and actions of employees in these positions usually have considerable significance to the operations of their particular parts of the organization, and it is expected that the value of their contributions be commensurate with their salary costs. There has been a greater investment in these employees than in those at lower levels; accordingly, the payoff here is higher for promptly identifying and salvaging, if possible, or eliminating the marginal performer.

In identifying him, again several steps should have been taken:

- The man and his manager should agree upon work plans, as called for by the assignment. The results to be achieved, a timetable for accomplishment, and what will constitute acceptable performance should also be mutually understood and agreed upon.
- Periodic reviews of progress should be conducted, during which revisions should be mutually decided on and both successful and unsuccessful aspects of performance discussed. The participants should also specify actions each could take to help the man capitalize on exhibited strengths and improve in areas showing weaknesses.
- The next higher level of management should periodically review the immediate manager's planning with respect to those in his jurisdiction, particularly development actions and assignments and the results of these activities.
- A summary record of each individual's progress, achievements, and development needs should be regularly updated so that recurring examples of successful and unsuccessful performance are brought to light. Recurring negative factors, when isolated, may guide specific action plans for development.
- Normally, a verdict of marginal performance is brought in when measures of performance continue to show unsatisfactory achievement despite the development efforts of both man and manager.

This means that the manager is properly evaluating the man's contributions through assigned work to the success of the business and is not going by personal or irrelevant criteria.

Higher-management positions. The impact on business results of the judgments, decisions, and actions of executives is obvious, and so is the stake that these managers have in their positions. Generally, they have accumulated a strong enough background of experience and have demonstrated sufficiently worthwhile capabilities so that continued utilization of their services in some capacity may be both feasible and profitable, even though a particular manager's accomplishments in his own managerial assignment are less than satisfactory.

The value of these managers' contributions is normally reflected in the business results achieved by the components they manage. If the business results are used as a base, objective measurement of performance may be made through the setting of specific individual goals and performance standards. They may vary with time, place, and business requirements, but they should be mutually agreed upon by each manager and his superior and revised as conditions change. Reviews of business results vis-à-vis individual manager performance will, again, point to marginal output whenever and wherever it occurs.

Top echelon sensitivities

Dealing with these evaluations at any level is a somewhat delicate matter, and it gets stickier as it goes higher. Not all top management people have as clear an understanding of their positions, work goals, and measurements as do those further down the line in the hierarchy. To be sure, communication links at the higher level are more personal and frequent, thus tending to remove some of the unknowns, uncertainties, and surprises; yet it has been observed more than once that executives are poor communicators. Many who espouse formal appraisals for others refuse to go along with such "mechanical measures" for themselves.

Why top executives shun face-to-face appraisals is not altogether a mystery, though. Not only do they see one another more often at higher levels, but generally there are bonus and incentive arrangements that speak strongly in terms of results achieved or not achieved. If business has been good but the bonus is less, the recipient usually gets the message: He hasn't been pulling his weight.

Another reason many top executives stay away from the written appraisal is that they share so much private and sensitive information. In addition, their business relationships become so personal and frequent it is awkward, if not painful, to have to tell a man his performance is marginal.

A parallel is the relationship many executives have with their confidential secretaries. It involves the sharing of company secrets and inevitably has more personal aspects than most, so it's no wonder that many higher-level managers waive formal appraisals for their secretaries. Less charitably, some might call these managers cowards, who sidestep personal confrontation because of possible conflict or difficulty, but more probably they have confused personal relationships with business objectives.

Whatever the reasons, marginal performances at the higher echelons of management are usually adjusted by more subtle means, such as new titles, shifting of assignments, or withheld compensation. Nevertheless, the results can be just as devastating to the individual and to the company.

Alternative solutions

Much more difficult than spotting marginal performance is determining what to do about it, and how and when. In every case, the rule of individual treatment must be observed, but at the same time it is essential to follow company policy if it specifies that any decisions affecting an employee's basic employment relationships require approval at a higher managerial level than that of his own manager.

Essentially, handling the problem of the marginal employee entails *analysis, action determination,* and *implementation.*

Analysis. Not only the individual but his relationship to the needs of the business must first be scrutinized. The employee should be reappraised, with more attention to detail, for strengths and weaknesses. This means a thorough examination of the total man, his record and achievements, his traits and characteristics, his mental capabilities, educational attainments, and general fitness for work, including his physical well-being, his work habits, attitudes, and potentialities.

This exhaustive fact-gathering step in many cases may utilize information already known, uncovered in previous appraisals and discussions and appropriately recorded. On the other hand, it may turn up information that had been overlooked or is so difficult to obtain that the assistance or expert opinions of others, such as physicians or psychologists, are required.

What is being sought are relevant facts that usually are not picked up routinely through the appraisal program. Just as in the case of screening an employee for advancement, it is necessary to go beyond the assessment of present job performance and work accomplishments in order to compare his strengths and weaknesses and to estimate his net worth as a potential contributor to the success of the business. Thus, it is necessary to search out and examine the underlying causes of the employee's shortcomings and the possibilities of correction in terms of his contribution to the company.

Incidentally, this further analysis considering the employee's relationship to company needs often results in a reexamination and updating of stated needs of the business.

Action determination. In dealing with the marginal performer, the courses of action generally open are retention on assignment, transfer, or termination. Preferably, and often feasibly, an economically sound solution is improvement of performance to the point that retention on assignment or transfer is warranted. Termination of employment then becomes a last resort, only after true opportunity and assistance for improving performance have proved to be unsuccessful. It is, in fact, an admission of mutual failure.

Retention on assignment, with coaching and guidance, may involve the setting of a reasonable period of time for the marginal employee to improve his performance against specific plans, standards, and measures. In any event, discussions between the man and his manager are a must. Additional training, education, and guidance may also be in order, depending on needs and circumstance, and sometimes psychological or other counseling may be worth consideration.

Transfer of the employee for a better job-man match, with an appropriate pay adjustment if one is indicated, is frequently found to be a suitable solution from the standpoint both of the business and of the employee. Such a transfer might switch a manager to an individual-contributor assignment, or to a different component or location. Almost always the new position will be at the same or at a lower level, but in rare circumstances it may raise him to a higher level.

A transfer is particularly likely to be the best answer in the case of a marginal performer in an entry-level, early-career position, if his specific training, experience, or abilities are easily seen to be better adapted to a different assignment. However, when factors not specific to the initial job are identified as the cause of subsatisfactory work and corrective steps have failed while the employee was on the initial job, transfer probably won't improve matters.

If the employee is in a middle-management or equivalent individual-contributor position, the alternative of reassignment must be carefully considered and evaluated in the light of the employee's desires and capabilities and the needs of the business, but it is possible that transfer to an entirely different operation might be the solution.

In most cases, the competence of executives whose performance in a particular business situation has been judged marginal should be retained and utilized. Through reassignment to a position more suited to his capabilities—possibly one he formerly filled successfully or a special assignment—the company might expect again to receive worthwhile contributions from the man.

Termination as a course of action may take any of several forms, including "voluntary" quit or optional retirement (at the employee's option) ; forced resignation or optional or early retirement (determined by the company) ; or discharge. When considering termination as a course of action, the manager must give considerable thought to the amount of assistance, if any, the employee should be offered in locating an assignment more suited to his capabilities. It is up to the immediate manager to select and recommend to his manager the course of action appropriate to the individual circumstance, but final determination should be made on the "one-over-one" approval basis.

Implementation. Logically, the decision about a course of action for handling the problem of the marginal employee is followed by the job of planning, scheduling, and implementing the action, but these phases are often considered along with the action to be taken. Now, however, follow-through is called for, progress must be assessed, and necessary changes in schedule, or even in the plan itself, may have to be made.

Procedural requirements include the necessary approvals and the prescribed recording and reporting. As a minimum, each plan of action should include a summary information sheet, a current appraisal, and a specific indication of what action the manager recommends and how and when he expects to take it. It may also be appropriate to submit recommended action plans affecting marginal employees to the general manager or plant manager for his review with the employee relations or personnel manager.

Finally, the action taken should be periodically measured by the manager who recommended it and the employee relations manager. In the case of terminations and their causes, the general manager should be kept posted so that he will be aware of continuing efforts to upgrade the overall work force.

Assessment of results of actions taken to deal with marginal performers will necessarily vary in method, according to the kind of action it is, but basic measures for assessing the results of planned and scheduled action should include not only follow-up on the employee's performance and contribution, but an appraisal of the effect on company-component output and costs, and feedback on employee attitudes.

In addition, each manager at each level of organization should make an annual review of the performance of all employees. He should identify not only the most effective ones, but the least effective (the lowest 10 percent of his work force) and insure that objective evaluations of their performance have been made and that development action is planned and taken.

This is not to say arbitrarily that 10 percent, or any other percentage, should be removed from their positions or otherwise drastically treated; rather, the intent is to make certain that the total career achievements as well as current performances of these people have been carefully, critically, and fairly reviewed, and that proper action has been taken.

The personnel man's role

What role should the personnel or employee relations manager play in resolving the problem of the marginal employee? Adviser? Teacher? Problem solver? Decision maker? Of course, it will depend on the manager's total relationship with management, but there are a few basic operating principles that can serve as guides.

The line manager has the basic responsibility for making decisions about the marginal exempt employee, but the employee relations or personnel manager can be of considerable help to the line manager in analyzing the best course of action to follow in a particular case, so it is to be expected that the line manager will seek this assistance from a staff specialist.

Beyond this, if resources are available, the employee relations manager may also be in a position to provide expert counseling and advice to the manager and the employee by means of psychological testing, depth interviewing, man-manager position matching procedures, and so forth.

In the final analysis, handling marginal performance is a war against failure, which, in today's tight labor market, represents a substantial dollar loss. The personnel manager's job is to reduce this loss and help managers rescue the marginal performer before his abilities and potential contribution are negated by management inaction. The personnel manager should also keep in mind that many problems can be avoided by improving initial selection methods and procedures.

The key is close man-manager relationships in the first two years of employment—with clearly identified goals, managerial coaching, and full opportunity for the individual to perform. These conditions should help to identify the marginal performer before his investment of time damages his opportunity for correction and reversal or chances in other companies or in other kinds of work, and before company investment and managerial association arrive at the point of no—or little—return.

Questions

1. What are the different reasons for considering an employee marginal?
2. How may the personnel appraisal system be used in identifying marginal employees?
3. Why is it important to identify managerial personnel who are performing marginally?
4. What can the personnel department do to minimize the number of marginal employees?

26—CAN APPRAISAL INTERVIEWS BE MADE EFFECTIVE? *

Robert K. Stolz

Why is it that the appraisal interview continues to present a gigantic headache to just about everyone concerned—top management, personnel men, the appraisers, and the appraised? Certainly, the theory behind the interview is clear enough: the line manager, after appraising the performance of a subordinate, should discuss the results with him to help him see his strengths and weaknesses more clearly; this discussion and clarification will motivate the subordinate to build on his strengths and eliminate his weaknesses. It must be conceded that there is nothing wrong with this theory—provided it works.

Many people, in fact, claim that it does—but there is a growing and articulate school of thought that holds that in practice the core of the discussion is the manager's review of his subordinate's weaknesses and that for this reason the interview tends to undermine the subordinate's self-confidence. These skeptics also say that the interview places the superior in the uncomfortable position of being a judge over his subordinate and thus injures the superior-subordinate relationship.

The truth of the matter, it seems to me, lies somewhere between these extremes. Experience tells us that the typical manager does *not* fall apart at the first breath of criticism from his superior and that the appraisal interview, therefore, cannot be so destructive as its opponents maintain. The arguments of the "nonbelievers," then, seem to involve a considerable amount of distortion. At the same time, even the staunchest "believers" have begun to see that appraisal discussions frequently don't bring a fraction of the benefits originally anticipated. And it has become clear that many managers do resist holding appraisal discussions.

* From *Personnel*, Vol. 38, No. 2 (March-April, 1961), pp. 32-37. Reprinted with permission.

Two pertinent observations

In recent years, I have audited a great number of management development programs in various industries and have thus had a chance to interview several hundred managers who had participated in appraisal discussions either as superior or as subordinate. From these interviews on how the appraisal discussions were handled and what, if anything, they accomplished I have drawn two observations relevant here:

1. In companies where people are judged on the basis of the results of their work and where an attempt is made to orient the appraisal discussion to the job, rarely if ever is a healthy relationship between superior and subordinate destroyed. I *have* found one or two cases in which a basically poor relationship was brought to a head by the discussion, but I don't consider this an unhealthy move.

On the other hand, in companies whose rating forms focus on personality traits, appraisal interviews are usually carried out halfheartedly, in an atmosphere of mutual embarrassment, and with little success. But such appraisal programs are probably in the minority today.

2. Every company has some managers—perhaps many, perhaps a few—who are really skillful in communicating appraisal results to their subordinates. The interviews these men hold, I am convinced, do have a positive effect on the subordinates' development. The effect is not usually a dramatic one, but I have run into a few cases in which the interview brought about a pronounced improvement in performance.

Trouble is, of course, that these men represent the exception rather than the rule. Most appraisal discussions are conducted in a perfunctory manner, and therefore prove sterile.

Let me illustrate this point with an anecdote. A senior executive once told me how pleased he was about an appraisal interview he had just held. What made it so worthwhile, he explained, was that it had enabled him to get across an important criticism of the subordinate in question—that he was a poor delegator and, as a result, was constantly creating bottlenecks as well as frustrating his own subordinates.

Later on, I discussed the appraisal interview with the subordinate and was amazed to discover how he had interpreted his boss's words. "The boss told me he hoped there would be more delegation around here in the future," he said. After a moment's reflection, he added, "It's about time the boss started delegating more himself!"

So the message was lost. And it has been lost in many thousands of instances.

These discussions are not destructive, but neither are they constructive. Though the subordinate usually thinks he got something out of his appraisal interview, he isn't quite sure what. And though the manager agrees that it was a worthwhile discussion, he can't offer very much evidence that anything important was accomplished. But then, who knows? It may be, as the believers maintain, that the discussion represented a beginning, the opening of a door, or that it accomplished more than is yet evident on the surface. These are possibilities, of course, and I willingly concede them. But I am still convinced that the majority of appraisal discussions have little or no effect.

Where and why communication breaks down

If this is so, the key question becomes: Why does so little real communication take place in a situation that fairly screams out for an honest and frank exchange of views?

Goodness knows, it isn't because companies haven't tried. They have tried just about everything. First they tried the "personnel sandwich" approach—telling the subordinate his strong points, then slipping in a few remarks about his weaknesses, and finally ending up with a review of his strengths. But this didn't work. Too often, the superior failed to put the meat in the sandwich, or the subordinate resented what he recognized as a technique.

So the "call it by another name" approach was invented. Under this plan, the superior would introduce the appraisal interview by saying to the subordinate, "Now I don't want you to consider this an appraisal interview. This is something different—a self-development planning conference!" Trouble was, what usually followed wasn't "something different," and everyone knew it. So this didn't work too well, either.

Then industry tried the "self-appraisal" approach. Some personnel men seem convinced that this is the answer, but self-appraisal has run into difficulty, too, and, in my experience there is not much lasting enthusiasm for it among line managers. One company calls it the "cat and mouse" approach. Under this method, though it is obvious that the boss has already appraised the subordinate, he refuses to tell him the results. Instead, he sits back and says, "Now suppose you tell me how you appraise your own performance." And the subordinate thinks to himself, "What are you trying to do—play cat and mouse with me? I know you've appraised my performance. If you've got something to say, say it. If not, let's get back to work."

I don't mean to debunk techniques, for we do, of course, need them. It seems to me, however, that we have relied on them too much and have unwittingly allowed insincerity and evasiveness to creep into our approaches.

Needless to say, we cannot explain this simply by accusing management, or individual managers, of being gimmick-happy or prone to hypocrisy and equivocation. There are many reasons why a manager may try to skirt the real issues in an appraisal discussion— with or without the aid of these techniques.

It may be that he has never developed an atmosphere of mutual confidence and trust with his subordinate, and is now finding that without such an atmosphere it's pretty difficult to have a frank exchange of views. Or he may feel that a frank discussion would injure his personal relationship with the subordinate. Or he may lack confidence in his appraisal findings, or in his ability to deal with questions that the subordinate might raise in a more open discussion—questions like: "What's the real reason I didn't get a raise last January?"

So there are a lot of reasons why superior and subordinate don't get down to cases in appraisal discussions.

In view of all this, what can be done to stimulate a franker and more honest discussion? No one knows the complete answer to this, but here are a few suggestions.

Laying a solid foundation

First, companies must recognize more clearly that they can have effective appraisal discussions only if they lay a sound foundation for them long before the interviews are held. Among the elements of a sound foundation are these:

- The superior must have nurtured an atmosphere of understanding and trust. This sounds terribly elementary—but the battle can be won or lost right here.
- The superior must have put enough time and effort into his appraisal to have confidence in it. Only then can he feel comfortable about discussing it.

• The appraisal discussion must fit naturally into the way the business is run and the normal relationship of the superior and the subordinate. This means that everyone must understand that appraisal and the communication of appraisal results are part of the basic management job. To further this understanding, the superior and subordinate should get together some months ahead of appraisal time and agree on the critical requirements of the latter's job. At the same time, they should decide on the elements of performance that should be examined continuously as evidence of how well the requirements are being met. (Managers will recognize this as simply a part of the management job.) The appraisal discussion then becomes something normal and expected.

A job-centered "mutual confession of sin"

Second, most managers need help on the conduct of the interview itself. It should be pointed out to them that when major job problems have to be faced one effective technique is what might be called the "mutual confession of sin." The superior who starts out by saying, "Joe, I've been giving considerable thought to your performance recently and have concluded that you are a poor planner" is not likely to get an honest exchange of views. But he might get at the issue quite effectively by saying, "Joe, one problem that's been bothering us both is that production of your department has been consistently behind schedule for a number of months. I don't really know what the trouble is. Maybe it's my fault. Maybe I haven't given you the support or the budget that you need. But in all honesty I would like to question, too, whether or not you have been planning your production properly. Let's talk about it."

This lays the foundation for effective discussion. It gets at the problem. It assures the subordinate that he isn't being made the fall guy and that he's going to have his day in court. This saves face, but it goes far beyond that and it isn't devious or evasive. What it involves is a realistic acknowledgment that failure to achieve the desired results is rarely attributable to the subordinate alone. This mutual-confession-of-sin approach says to the subordinate: "We've got a problem. We're in this together. Let's discuss it."

Tackling the real issues

My third suggestion on how to stimulate a franker and more honest exchange of views is preceded by a lot of *ifs*. If a manager has developed a climate of respect and trust, and *if* he and his

FUNDAMENTALS OF SUCCESSFUL
APPRAISAL INTERVIEWS

EFFECTIVE COMMUNICATION of appraisals, says the author, is not easy
and can never be guaranteed. But it *is* possible if the following points,
derived from hundreds of interviews with both the appraisers and the
appraised, are constantly borne in mind:

1. Successful communication of appraisal results depends more on
   mutual respect and trust than on technique.
2. The problem of appraisal discussion cannot really be separated
   from the problem of appraisal. A sound appraisal system—one
   that both the superior and the subordinate have confidence in—
   is a foundation-stone of the appraisal discussion.
3. The line manager must be willing to take the time at the outset
   to identify the really critical requirements of the subordinate's
   job so that his performance appraisal can be focused on these
   requirements.
4. The appraisal discussion should center on results achieved on
   the job and not on the subordinate's personality.
5. Subordinates distrust evasive techniques and beating around the
   bush. If a sound foundation for the appraisal discussion has
   been laid, the supervisor should strive for frankness and candor,
   rather than worrying about whether he is being sufficiently
   tactful.

subordinate are agreed on the critical requirements of the subordinate's job, and *if* he has given sufficient time and attention to his
appraisal, then he should be forthright in the appraisal discussion.
In studying the approaches of men known in their companies as
skillful in communicating appraisal results, I have been struck by
one point above all others—their willingness to be direct and to get
at the basic issues. This is done tactfully, of course. No one is arguing for a "get tough" policy.

But many companies have leaned too far in the other direction.
They haven't trusted their managers to have a normal sense of tact—
and have devised endless ways of sugar-coating the pill. This sugar-
coating has simply encouraged the managers to duck the real issues
and avoid discussing what is really on their minds.

The single complaint most common among subordinates, I have
found in interviewing them after appraisal discussions, is not that
the appraisal wasn't fair—an occasional response—or that the superior was callous and undiplomatic—a very rare one. It was that the

boss obviously had something on his mind but wouldn't come out with it honestly and straightforwardly.

It seems clear that the men being appraised do not, for the most part, share their bosses' reluctance to talk about the appraisal results—that they are in fact eager for fuller and freer discussion in the appraisal interview. If the company and its individual managers recognize that the interview is a difficult and demanding situation and try to fulfill its requirements as outlined here, they can, I believe, achieve greater success than they have so far in communicating appraisal results.

Questions

1. How can the appraisal interview contribute to the achievement of efficient employee performance?
2. Stolz believes that managers have relied too much on communication techniques and have unwittingly allowed insincerity and evasiveness to creep into performance interviews. Do you believe that the method which he recommends assures success in communicating performance appraisal to the employee?
3. The article refers mainly to appraisal interviews between executives and their subordinates. Would the suggestions contained in the article be applicable to first-line supervisors in their appraisal of subordinates?
4. The author states that the appraisal discussion should center on results achieved and on the job and not on the subordinate's personality? Do you agree? Why?
5. What is involved in the "mutual confession of sin" approach that is likely to make for success in appraisal situations? Are there other situations, other than the job, where it may be applied to good advantage?

27—WHEN YOU REACH YOUR LEVEL OF INCOMPETENCE *

Lawrence J. Peter

> My observation is that whenever one person is found adequate to the discharge of a duty by close application thereto, it is worse executed by two persons, and scarcely done at all if three or more are employed therein.
>
> —*George Washington*

For any healthy business firm, incompetence is not a major problem. There is, however, a place where incompetence is rampant. It is a never-never land called the hierarchy, an organization whose members are arranged in ranks or grades; each rank except the lowest is filled by promotion from the rank below.

Having made an extensive study of hierarchies, I founded a new science, hierarchiology, and enunciated the first hierarchiological theorem, *The Peter Principle* (naming it, modestly, after myself):

> In a hierarchy, each employee tends to rise to his level of incompetence. Every post tends to be occupied by an employee incompetent to execute its duties.

This explains Washington's observation. As soon as two or more people are employed on a task, they form a hierachy, and sooner or later some of them reach a level of incompetence.

To show how the hierachy fosters incompetence, I will cite a firm named Hierarchy Paper Processors, Inc.[1] HPP occupies a tall building, with most employees of the lowest rank laboring on the ground floor, somewhat fewer of higher rank on the second, fewer still on the third, and so on up to the penthouse, where the founder-president works alone.

A batch of new employees, Messrs. One to Ten, is just starting with the HPP. Each has a diploma, certifying that he has been a competent college student; he is thus qualified for promotion to the world of commerce and eligible for the rank of Deputy-Assistant Junior Paper Processor at HPP. The 10 recruits are shown to their desks and given documents to process.

---

* From *Think*, Vol. 34, No. 2 (March-April, 1968), pp. 8-11. Reprinted with permission.

[1] I often use fictitious names, in order to protect the guilty.

A year passes. It is promotion time. But Messrs. One to Five have proved incompetent. Mr. Five often applies his rubber stamp upside down. Mr. Four forgets to ink his stamp pad and makes illegible impressions. Mr. Three is persistently unpunctual. Mr. Two's handwriting is indecipherable. Mr. One is impertinent to his superiors. These five are not eligible for promotion. They will stay in the positions they are incompetent to fill. They have reached what I call their *level of incompetence.*

Messrs. Six to Ten have worked competently in the lowest rank, so they are eligible for promotion to Assistant Junior Paper Processor.

Two years pass. Messrs. Six, Seven, and Eight have proved incompetent. Mr. Six cannot stand the extra responsibility and has an ulcer. Mr. Seven is mentally unequipped for the more difficult work and is too slow at it. Mr. Eight has developed an egregious facial tic most incommodious to HPP's public image. They will receive no further promotions; they have reached their level of incompetence.

Messrs. Nine and Ten, having shown themselves competent at this time, are promoted to the rank of Junior Paper Processor.

Three years later, under the strain of his heavy work load, Mr. Nine's social drinking has escalated to alcoholism. His frequent absences and slowed mental processes mark him as unfit for promotion. He has reached his level of incompetence. Mr. Ten is promoted to Paper Processor, works competently there and, four years later, rises to Senior Paper Processor. But in that position he suffers two heart attacks; his doctor says, "Take it easy. Slow down. Don't work so hard." Mr. Ten does take it easy; he slows down. Now he cannot get through all his work and so he is disqualified for further promotion.

All ten employees have now reached their levels of incompetence.

This situation is not the result of any particularly inept personnel policy at HPP. The same thing happens in every hierarchy. *It must happen.* It is inevitable.

The perennial problem

Escalation to incompetence levels has always been inevitable. We see it in the Biblical account of the promotion process: ". . . thou hast been faithful over a few things, I will make thee ruler over many things . . . ." (Matthew, 25:21)

Yet, of course, there is no guarantee that the employee who has faithfully done a few things will be competent to do many things. This is the essential weakness of the hierarchy and of the promotion process.

The weakness reveals itself wherever hierarchies exist. Chinese Premier Chou En-lai complained last year that incompetents in the ministries of foreign affairs, defense, finance, and industry had undermined their country's reputation and set back its foreign policy. Chou is helpless before the entrenched incompetence of his own hierarchies.

Some critics call my principle dangerous—it gives subordinates an unfair means of belittling their superiors. That is not so. The principle applies at all levels, even the lowest. Messrs. One to Five, as we saw, reached their level of incompetence in the lowest rank. In all hierarchies you will find people who muddle through their working lives without winning a single promotion.

Other critics say the principle may once have been true, but that scientific hiring and placement techniques now put the round pegs in the round holes and eliminate occupational incompetence.

The techniques may be impressive, but what about the results? I examined the process of vocational aptitude testing as it is commonly used by personnel departments. The applicant takes a battery of tests, each designed to measure an aptitude—general intelligence, computational skill, mechanical dexterity, persuasiveness, and so on. The aim is to place the employee promptly in a job which utilizes his greatest attributes and highest competence.

For example, a young commerce graduate, I. Selwyn, applied for a post with Tackie Wood Products, Inc. His aptitude tests placed him at the following percentiles:

Persuasiveness	87th percentile
Intellectual	78th percentile
Computational	76th percentile
Mechanical	60th percentile
Clerical	45th percentile
Artistic	43rd percentile
Social Service	29th percentile

On the strength of his good showing in persuasiveness and computational skills, Selwyn was hired as a salesman. He turned out to be a successful one. In time he was promoted to district sales manager; in this post his paperwork left something to be desired, but he still spent part of his time selling to major customers, and his total performance was felt to be good.

Next he was promoted to general sales manager, where he had no contact with customers and was simply required to recruit, train, organize, and stimulate the sales staff. Note that Selwyn scores far below average in service to his fellowmen; that is the quality he now uses regularly. His unscrupulous, crafty methods of staff manipulation have reduced morale—and sales—to a low level. In accordance with the Peter Principle, he has achieved final placement at his level of incompetence.

I find that the main effect of aptitude testing—apart from providing a livelihood for test compilers and administrators—is to ensure the competence on initial placement; therefore promotion is hastened, but necessarily to an area of less competence! In the end, the employee arrives at his level of incompetence in less time than he would have done without the testing!

Even machines are subject to the Peter Principle. If a machine does good work at one level, it will be "promoted" to more and more difficult work until eventually it reaches its level of incompetence.

I have discovered a number of signs which, to the discerning observer, suggest that an employee has achieved final placement.

Phonophilia is an abnormal craving for telephones, intercom devices, and voice recorders. The employee rationalizes that, if he can sufficiently improve his communications arsenal, he may be able to get some work done.

Papyromania, the accumulation of needless masses of papers and books, shows, to a moral certainty, that the employee is at his level of incompetence.

A nonphysical sign of final placement is the Auld Lang Syne Complex, persistent complaining about the present, and a romantic idealization of halcyon days when the employee was at his level of competence.

Many such indices of final placement will be described in my forthcoming book on this subject.

Also, I find, certain physical ailments tend to be associated with final placement at the level of incompetence. They include: high blood pressure, constipation, obesity, allergies, insomnia, peptic ulcers, cardiovascular complaints, and alcoholism. The patient commonly suffers two or more of the ailments at once, and thus exhibits the Final Placement Syndrome.

Medication and surgery give only temporary relief, because they do not touch the cause of the condition. Either the original ailment soon recurs, or the patient develops one or more of the other ailments.

Psychotherapy is sometimes employed, but seldom succeeds, because it cannot restore the patient to a condition of vocational competence.

A cure for the FPS

Substitution is a technique that will cure the Final Placement Syndrome or, if tried in time, prevent its occurrence. In Substitution the patient neglects—usually succeeds in forgetting, in fact—the duties of his position, which he is incompetent to carry out, and busies himself instead with something that he *can* do. These substitute duties he carries out to perfection.

Here is a case history. I. Walker had reached his level of incompetence as a prison warden. Instead of vainly struggling to carry out the duties of his post, he devoted himself to organizing the pedestrian traffic about the halls and stairways of the prison. With colored lines and arrows, one-way corridors, and rush-hour monitors recruited from among the better-behaved convicts, he contrived that no prisoner need ever jostle another.

Walker spent little time in his office: he continually prowled the building and grounds, trying to catch someone crossing a line or defying an arrow; he escorted parties of visiting penologists around the prison; he traveled extensively, lecturing on his system. He was always busy, happy, and healthy: he had achieved a perfect Substitution.

But few employees have the initiative or the opportunity to work out such elaborate Substitutions. Life at the level of incompetence is usually a long series of frustrations and illnesses.

A better course is to avoid the ultimate promotion: to rise as fast as you can to a position one rank below your level of incompetence *and stay there.*

I do not recommend refusing the unwanted promotion. In our society such a refusal arouses the suspicion of one's employer and the scorn of one's family and friends. The best way is to arrange *never to be offered* the promotion that would lead to final placement.

In other words, *create the impression that you have already reached your level of incompetence.* Invent an ulcer and keep taking pills for it. Occasionally pause halfway up a flight of stairs, cock your head as if listening and remark to a colleague, "Hear it? The heart pounding like a sledgehammer! I oughtn't to climb stairs, you know, but . . . ," and you smile bravely and plod on.

Or show some nonmedical sign of incompetence: leave desk drawers open at the end of the workday; keep your documents in an apparent muddle; or assume a petty, niggling concern with something that is not your job at all (a Pseudo-Substitution) such as salvaging paper clips and rubber bands from wastepaper baskets.

Creative incompetence

Such techniques for avoiding the unwanted ultimate promotion I classify as Creative Incompetence. My files bulge with hundreds of stratagems that have achieved the desired stability for their practitioners.

Creative Incompetence will give best results if you choose an area of incompetence that does not directly handicap you in doing your present work. Creative Incompetence can keep you productive, preserve your peace of mind, and prolong your life. Surely it offers as great a challenge as the traditional drive for higher rank!

In recent months I have introduced hierarchiology to the world by means of lectures and magazine articles. A textbook, *The Peter Principle* is ready for publication. I confidently expect that before long some philanthropist will endow a Chair of Hierarchiology at a major university. When he does, I shall be ready for promotion to that position having proved myself competent in my present endeavors.

Questions

1. In many organizations most employees are expected to demonstrate their promotability to higher positions. Is this a sound policy according to the Peter Principle?
2. What is your opinion of Peter's advice to rise as fast as you can to a position one rank below your level of incompetence and stay there?
3. Do you know of any other examples of Creative Incompetence that individuals have used to avoid being offered the unwanted ultimate promotion?

CHAPTER 4

Organizational Behavior

In a study of personnel management, consideration must be given not only to the face-to-face relationships between superiors and subordinates but also to the organizational framework in which they carry on their daily activities. Organizations are formally characterized by authority and responsibility that are assigned to job holders who, according to the organizational chart, have a fixed relationship to each other for the performance of their duties. In reality, however, the organization never functions in quite the manner outlined on paper. There are a variety of individual and group forces that will have a modifying effect upon that which has been so neatly arranged by the experts in organizational and manpower planning. This disparity between what is planned and what actually happens is not necessarily the result of poor planning. It is explained better by the fact that an organization is comprised of people; and where there are people, one is likely to find complexities that are not easily understood or explained.

Traditional organizational theory, which is still a governing influence in modern management, is predicated primarily upon what people *should* do rather than upon what they *actually* do. It uses a logical approach to human activities rather than a behavioral science approach. While organizations must have certain objectives and principles to guide their activities if successful results are to be achieved, a greater recognition of the true nature of human beings in the organizational environment is necessary if the organization is to meet these objectives and if human talents and values within the organization are to be conserved.

In recent years students of organizational theory and of the behavioral sciences have attempted to approach the nature of the organization more realistically. Much has been written on the subject, but as yet there is no body of principles based on experimental findings that can be cited as definitive. The study of individual and group behavior, however, has pointed to several important variables that affect the functioning of organizations.

It is known today, largely as a result of studies in industrial leadership in the last quarter century, that the leadership function is more complex than was once realized. Earlier notions of leadership focused heavily upon the personal qualities of leaders with an implicit assumption that leaders were born, not made. More recently, however, with careful study of leadership in various contexts or situations, it has become apparent that leadership involves more than the possession of certain personal traits. The situation in which a person is assigned to lead coupled with his own behavior in relation to that situation can have a vital effect upon his success or failure as a leader.

Studies in human motivation have also made their contribution to leadership theory. They have revealed the motivational effects of employee participation in job activities, with the result that many experts in this area are enthusiastic in proposing that employees be permitted to participate in decision making as well as in other significant areas of the work.

The articles selected for this chapter cover a range of topics that will give the reader a feeling for the various facets of the organization and its functioning. The first article, *The Human Side of Enterprise,* by the late Douglas M. McGregor, is a classic that deserves first place in any listing of articles on this subject. McGregor presents a theory of motivation referred to as Theory Y which is contrary to traditional theories of motivating personnel. McGregor's theory has had considerable influence on managerial and supervisory personnel as well as on other behavioral science experts. The next article by Keith Davis expands on one of the principles of Theory Y, namely participation and consultative management, to provide encouragement to people to direct their creative energies toward organizational objectives. Davis cites classical experiments in participative management and discusses the prerequisites for participation. He discusses the problems of pseudo-participation and excessive participation which are often overlooked by enthusiasts of this approach.

One of the most significant and useful articles ever written about leadership skills is that by Robert Tannenbaum and Warren H. Schmidt. It provides useful guidance on the forces to be considered by the manager in determining the extent to which he desires to have employees participate in the decision-making process. Their stress on the manager's need to be insightful and flexible is characteristic of the sensitivity training programs with which they have been closely identified.

Early theories emphasized democratic leadership and participative management. More recently, as Tingey points out in his article *Management Today,* these earlier theories have been expanded upon and a supportive theory of management has evolved. He describes Likert's "supportive relationship" and gives a valuable comparison between autocratic and supportive managers.

Because of the technological changes that have occurred, a new type of executive is needed, according to Koprowski. In his article *Toward Innovative Leadership,* he outlines the type of training that business leaders should receive and prescribes the characteristics of an organization in which innovations may occur. Like Keith Davis, he is of the opinion that participation is an overworked word but an underworked activity.

The importance of the manager's coping effectively with change and particularly being an agent of change is the subject of the next article. Brynildsen and Wickes focus on the social rather than the technological changes and the effects that social changes have on organizations. They describe in detail the implications of the changes for management and provide several specific suggestions for managing change.

As a result of the rapid changes that have occurred and are occurring in our society, there is a need for fostering creativity in individuals. In the article *Organization Climate and the Creative Individual,* Patrick reports that there has been a slow acceptance of techniques designed to provide the type of climate required by the creative individual. He outlines the type of program needed to stimulate creative thinking which he feels is the most valuable asset of an organization and the most reliable index to its future development.

The article by our colleague, James R. Bell, focuses on the suggestion system which has long been used as an example of an activity which provides for employee participation. Bell explodes some of the myths concerning the role of the suggestion system as well as illustrating the adverse effects that the suggestion system, as typically established, can have on the morale of supervisory personnel. His critical analysis of the typical suggestion system represents the approach that all personnel workers should take toward the various personnel management programs.

The last article in the chapter by Fielden warns that the problems that have been faced by colleges and universities will eventually be faced by management. He is of the opinion that the challenge of traditional business values and authority is not all bad. It is his belief that in order to attract young people with the most promise, corporations will have to become less autocratic in decision-making processes and more responsive to social change. The companies that are open, flexible, and responsive will attract the best young people in tomorrow's managerial roles.

28—THE HUMAN SIDE OF ENTERPRISE *

Douglas M. McGregor

It has become trite to say that industry has the fundamental know-how to utilize physical science and technology for the material benefit of mankind, and that we must now learn how to utilize the social sciences to make our human organizations truly effective.

To a degree, the social sciences today are in a position like that of the physical sciences with respect to atomic energy in the thirties. We know that past conceptions of the nature of man are inadequate and, in many ways, incorrect. We are becoming quite certain that, under proper conditions, unimagined resources of creative human energy could become available within the organizational setting.

We cannot tell industrial management how to apply this new knowledge in simple, economic ways. We know it will require years of exploration, much costly development research, and a substantial amount of creative imagination on the part of management to discover how to apply this growing knowledge to the organization of human effort in industry.

Management's Task: The Conventional View

The conventional conception of management's task in harnessing human energy to organizational requirements can be stated broadly in terms of three propositions. In order to avoid the complications introduced by a label, let us call this set of propositions "Theory X":

1. Management is responsible for organizing the elements of productive enterprise—money, materials, equipment, people—in the interest of economic ends.

2. With respect to people, this is a process of directing their efforts, motivating them, controlling their actions, modifying their behavior to fit the needs of the organization.

* From *The Management Review*, Vol. 46, No. 11 (November, 1957), pp. 22-28, 88-92. Reprinted with permission. This article is based on an address by the late Dr. McGregor before the Fifth Anniversary Convocation of the M.I.T. School of Industrial Management.

3. Without this active intervention by management, people would be passive—even resistant—to organizational needs. They must therefore be persuaded, rewarded, punished, controlled—their activities must be directed. This is management's task. We often sum it up by saying that management consists of getting things done through other people.

Behind this conventional theory there are several additional beliefs—less explicit, but widespread:

4. The average man is by nature indolent—he works as little as possible.

5. He lacks ambition, dislikes responsibility, prefers to be led.

6. He is inherently self-centered, indifferent to organizational needs.

7. He is by nature resistant to change.

8. He is gullible, not very bright, the ready dupe of the charlatan and the demagogue.

The human side of economic enterprise today is fashioned from propositions and beliefs such as these. Conventional organization structures and managerial policies, practices, and programs reflect these assumptions.

In accomplishing its task—with these assumptions as guides—management has conceived of a range of possibilities.

At one extreme, management can be "hard" or "strong." The methods for directing behavior involve coercion and threat (usually disguised), close supervision, tight controls over behavior. At the other extreme, management can be "soft" or "weak." The methods for directing behavior involve being permissive, satisfying people's demands, achieving harmony. Then they will be tractable, accept direction.

This range has been fairly completely explored during the past half century, and management has learned some things from the exploration. There are difficulties in the "hard" approach. Force breeds counter-forces: restriction of output, antagonism, militant unionism, subtle but effective sabotage of management objectives. This "hard" approach is especially difficult during times of full employment.

There are also difficulties in the "soft" approach. It leads frequently to the abdication of management—to harmony, perhaps, but to indifferent performance. People take advantage of the soft approach. They continually expect more, but they give less and less.

Currently, the popular theme is "firm but fair." This is an attempt to gain the advantages of both the hard and the soft approaches. It is reminiscent of Teddy Roosevelt's "speak softly and carry a big stick."

Is the Conventional View Correct?

The findings which are beginning to emerge from the social sciences challenge this whole set of beliefs about man and human nature and about the task of management. The evidence is far from conclusive, certainly, but it is suggestive. It comes from the laboratory, the clinic, the schoolroom, the home, and even to a limited extent from industry itself.

The social scientist does not deny that human behavior in industrial organization today is approximately what management perceives it to be. He has, in fact, observed it and studied it fairly extensively. But he is pretty sure that this behavior is *not* a consequence of man's inherent nature. It is a consequence rather of the nature of industrial organizations, of management philosophy, policy, and practice. The conventional approach of Theory X is based on mistaken notions of what is cause and what is effect.

Perhaps the best way to indicate why the conventional approach of management is inadequate is to consider the subject of motivation.

Physiological Needs

Man is a wanting animal—as soon as one of his needs is satisfied, another appears in its place. This process is unending. It continues from birth to death.

Man's needs are organized in a series of levels—a hierarchy of importance. At the lowest level, but pre-eminent in importance when they are thwarted, are his *physiological needs*. Man lives for bread alone, when there is no bread. Unless the circumstances are unusual, his needs for love, for status, for recognition are inoperative when his stomach has been empty for a while. But when he eats regularly and adequately, hunger ceases to be an important motivation. The same is true of the other physiological needs of man—for rest, exercise, shelter, protection from the elements.

A *satisfied need is not a motivator of behavior!* This is a fact of profound significance that is regularly ignored in the conventional approach to the management of people. Consider your own need for air: Except as you are deprived of it, it has no appreciable motivating effect upon your behavior.

Safety Needs

When the physiological needs are reasonably satisfied, needs at the next higher level begin to dominate man's behavior—to motivate him. These are called *safety needs*. They are needs for protection against danger, threat, deprivation. Some people mistakenly refer to these as needs for security. However, unless man is in a dependent relationship where he fears arbitrary deprivation, he does not demand security. The need is for the "fairest possible break." When he is confident of this, he is more than willing to take risks. But when he feels threatened or dependent, his greatest need is for guarantees, for protection, for security.

The fact needs little emphasis that, since every industrial employee is in a dependent relationship, safety needs may assume considerable importance. Arbitrary management actions, behavior which arouses uncertainty with respect to continued employment or which reflects favoritism or discrimination, unpredictable administration of policy—these can be powerful motivators of the safety needs in the employment relationship *at every level*, from worker to vice-president.

Social Needs

When man's physiological needs are satisfied and he is no longer fearful about his physical welfare, his *social needs* become important motivators of his behavior—needs for belonging, for association, for acceptance by his fellows, for giving and receiving friendship and love.

Management knows today of the existence of these needs, but it often assumes quite wrongly that they represent a threat to the organization. Many studies have demonstrated that the tightly knit, cohesive work group may, under proper conditions, be far more effective than an equal number of separate individuals in achieving organizational goals.

Yet management, fearing group hostility to its own objectives, often goes to considerable lengths to control and direct human efforts in ways that are inimical to the natural "groupiness" of human beings. When man's social needs—and perhaps his safety needs, too—are thus thwarted, he behaves in ways which tend to defeat organizational objectives. He becomes resistant, antagonistic, uncooperative. But this behavior is a consequence, not a cause.

Ego Needs

Above the social needs—in the sense that they do not become motivators until lower needs are reasonably satisfied—are the needs of greatest significance to management and to man himself. They are the *egoistic needs,* and they are of two kinds:

1. Those needs that relate to one's self-esteem—needs for self-confidence, for independence, for achievement, for competence, for knowledge.

2. Those needs that relate to one's reputation—needs for status, for recognition, for appreciation, for the deserved respect of one's fellows.

Unlike the lower needs, these are rarely satisfied; man seeks indefinitely for more satisfaction of these needs once they have become important to him. But they do not appear in any significant way until physiological, safety, and social needs are all reasonably satisfied.

The typical industrial organization offers few opportunities for the satisfaction of these egoistic needs to people at lower levels in the hierarchy. The conventional methods of organizing work, particularly in mass production industries, give little heed to these aspects of human motivation. If the practices of scientific management were deliberately calculated to thwart these needs, they could hardly accomplish this purpose better than they do.

Self-Fulfillment Needs

Finally—a capstone, as it were, on the hierarchy of man's needs—there are what we may call the *needs for self-fulfillment.* These are the needs for realizing one's own potentialities, for continued self-development, for being creative in the broadest sense of that term.

It is clear that the conditions of modern life give only limited opportunity for these relatively weak needs to obtain expression. The deprivation most people experience with respect to other lower-level needs diverts their energies into the struggle to satisfy *those* needs, and the needs for self-fulfillment remain dormant.

Management and Motivation

We recognize readily enough that a man suffering from a severe dietary deficiency is sick. The deprivation of physiological needs has behavioral consequences. The same is true—although less well recognized—of deprivation of higher-level needs. The man whose needs for safety, association, independence, or status are thwarted is sick just as surely as the man who has rickets. And his sickness will have behavioral consequences. We will be mistaken if we attribute his resultant passivity, his hostility, his refusal to accept responsibility to his inherent "human nature." These forms of behavior are *symptoms* of illness—of deprivation of his social and egoistic needs.

The man whose lower-level needs are satisfied is not motivated to satisfy those needs any longer. For practical purposes they exist no longer. Management often asks, "Why aren't people more productive? We pay good wages, provide good working conditions, have excellent fringe benefits and steady employment. Yet people do not seem to be willing to put forth more than minimum effort."

The fact that management has provided for these physiological and safety needs has shifted the motivational emphasis to the social and perhaps to the egoistic needs. Unless there are opportunities *at work* to satisfy these higher-level needs, people will be deprived; and their behavior will reflect this deprivation. Under such conditions, if management continues to focus its attention on physiological needs, its efforts are bound to be ineffective.

People *will* make insistent demands for more money under these conditions. It becomes more important than ever to buy the material goods and services which can provide limited satisfaction of the thwarted needs. Although money has only limited value in satisfying many higher-level needs, it can become the focus of interest if it is the *only* means available.

The Carrot-and-Stick Approach

The carrot-and-stick theory of motivation (like Newtonian physical theory) works reasonably well under certain circumstances. The *means* for satisfying man's physiological and (within limits) his safety needs can be provided or withheld by management. Employment itself is such a means, and so are wages, working conditions, and benefits. By these means the individual can be controlled so long as he is struggling for subsistence.

But the carrot-and-stick theory does not work at all once man has reached an adequate subsistence level and is motivated primarily by higher needs. Management cannot provide a man with self-respect, or with the respect of his fellows, or with the satisfaction of needs for self-fulfillment. It can create such conditions that he is encouraged and enabled to seek such satisfactions for *himself*, or it can thwart him by failing to create those conditions.

But this creation of conditions is not "control." It is not a good device for directing behavior. And so management finds itself in an odd position. The high standard of living created by our modern technological know-how provides quite adequately for the satisfaction of physiological and safety needs. The only significant exception is where management practices have not created confidence in a "fair break"—and thus where safety needs are thwarted. But by making possible the satisfaction of low-level needs, management has deprived itself of the ability to use as motivators the devices on which conventional theory has taught it to rely—rewards, promises, incentives, or threats and other coercive devices.

The philosophy of management by direction and control— *regardless of whether it is hard or soft*—is inadequate to motivate because the human needs on which this approach relies are today unimportant motivators of behavior. Direction and control are essentially useless in motivating people whose important needs are social and egoistic. Both the hard and the soft approach fail today because they are simply irrelevant to the situation.

People, deprived of opportunities to satisfy at work the needs which are now important to them, behave exactly as we might predict—with indolence, passivity, resistance to change, lack of responsibility, willingness to follow the demagogue, unreasonable demands for economic benefits. It would seem that we are caught in a web of our own weaving.

A New Theory of Management

For these and many other reasons, we require a different theory of the task of managing people based on more adequate assumptions about human nature and human motivation. I am going to be so bold as to suggest the broad dimensions of such a theory. Call it "Theory Y," if you will.

1. Management is responsible for organizing the elements of productive enterprise—money, materials, equipment, people—in the interest of economic ends.

2. People are *not* by nature passive or resistant to organizational needs. They have become so as a result of experience in organizations.

3. The motivation, the potential for development, the capacity for assuming responsibility, the readiness to direct behavior toward organizational goals are all present in people. Management does not put them there. It is a responsibility of management to make

it possible for people to recognize and develop these human characteristics for themselves.

4. The essential task of management is to arrange organizational conditions and methods of operation so that people can achieve their own goals *best* by directing *their own* efforts toward organizational objectives.

This is a process primarily of creating opportunities, releasing potential, removing obstacles, encouraging growth, providing guidance. It is what Peter Drucker has called "management by objectives" in contrast to "management by control." It does *not* involve the abdication of management, the absence of leadership, the lowering of standards, or the other characteristics usually associated with the "soft" approach under Theory X.

Some Difficulties

It is no more possible to create an organization today which will be a full, effective application of this theory than it was to build an atomic power plant in 1945. There are many formidable obstacles to overcome.

The conditions imposed by conventional organization theory and by the approach to scientific management for the past half century have tied men to limited jobs which do not utilize their capabilities, have discouraged the acceptance of responsibility, have encouraged passivity, have eliminated meaning from work. Man's habits, attitudes, expectations—his whole conception of membership in an industrial organization—have been conditioned by his experience under these circumstances.

People today are accustomed to being directed, manipulated, controlled in industrial organizations and to finding satisfaction for their social, egoistic, and self-fulfillment needs away from the job. This is true of much of management as well as of workers. Genuine "industrial citizenship"—to borrow again a term from Drucker—is a remote and unrealistic idea, the meaning of which has not even been considered by most members of industrial organizations.

Another way of saying this is that Theory X places exclusive reliance upon external control of human behavior, while Theory Y relies heavily on self-control and self-direction. It is worth noting that this difference is the difference between treating people as children and treating them as mature adults. After generations of the former, we cannot expect to shift to the latter over night.

Steps in the Right Direction

Before we are overwhelmed by the obstacles, let us remember that the application of theory is always slow. Progress is usually achieved in small steps. Some innovative ideas which are entirely consistent with Theory Y are today being applied with some success.

Decentralization and delegation

These are ways of freeing people from the too-close control of conventional organization, giving them a degree of freedom to direct their own activities, to assume responsibility, and, importantly, to satisfy their egoistic needs. In this connection, the flat organization of Sears, Roebuck and Company provides an interesting example. It forces "management by objectives," since it enlarges the number of people reporting to a manager until he cannot direct and control them in the conventional manner.

Job enlargement

This concept, pioneered by I.B.M. and Detroit Edison, is quite consistent with Theory Y. It encourages the acceptance of responsibility at the bottom of the organization; it provides opportunities for satisfying social and egoistic needs. In fact, the reorganization of work at the factory level offers one of the more challenging opportunities for innovation consistent with Theory Y.

Participation and consultative management

Under proper conditions, participation and consultative management provide encouragement to people to direct their creative energies toward organizational objectives, give them some voice in decisions that affect them, provide significant opportunities for the satisfaction of social and egoistic needs. The Scanlon Plan is the outstanding embodiment of these ideas in practice.

Performance appraisal

Even a cursory examination of conventional programs of performance appraisal within the ranks of management will reveal how completely consistent they are with Theory X. In fact, most such programs tend to treat the individual as though he were a product under inspection on the assembly line.

A few companies—among them General Mills, Ansul Chemical, and General Electric—have been experimenting with approaches which involve the individual in setting "targets" or objectives *for himself* and in a *self*-evaluation of performance semiannually or annually. Of course, the superior plays an important leadership role in this process—one, in fact, which demands substantially more competence than the conventional approach. The role is, however, considerably more congenial to many managers than the role of "judge" or "inspector" which is usually forced upon them. Above all, the individual is encouraged to take a greater responsibility for planning and appraising his own contribution to organizational objectives; and the accompanying effects on egoistic and self-fulfillment needs are substantial.

Applying the Ideas

The not infrequent failure of such ideas as these to work as well as expected is often attributable to the fact that a management has "bought the idea" but applied it within the framework of Theory X and its assumptions.

Delegation is not an effective way of exercising management by control. Participation becomes a farce when it is applied as a sales gimmick or device for kidding people into thinking they are important. Only the management that has confidence in human capacities and is itself directed toward organizational objectives rather than toward the preservation of personal power can grasp the implications of this emerging theory. Such management will find and apply successfully other innovative ideas as we move slowly toward the full implementation of a theory like Y.

The Human Side of Enterprise

It is quite possible for us to realize substantial improvements in the effectiveness of industrial organizations during the next decade or two. The social sciences can contribute much to such developments; we are only beginning to grasp the implications of the growing body of knowledge in these fields. But if this conviction is to become a reality instead of a pious hope, we will need to view the process much as we view the process of releasing the energy of the atom for constructive human ends—as a slow, costly, sometimes discouraging approach toward a goal which would seem to many to be quite unrealistic.

The ingenuity and the perseverance of industrial management in the pursuit of economic ends have changed many scientific and technological dreams into commonplace realities. It is now becoming clear that the application of these same talents to the human side of enterprise will not only enhance substantially these materialistic achievements, but will bring us one step closer to "the good society."

Questions

1. In what ways can management assist subordinates in obtaining greater satisfaction of the needs for self-fulfillment?
2. What are the basic differences between Theory X and Theory Y? Why are managers often reluctant to accept the assumptions upon which Theory Y is based?
3. How does "management by objectives" differ from "management by control"? Is there any wisdom in having an employee set objectives for himself?
4. What significance does the statement "a satisfied need is not a motivator of behavior" have for the manager or supervisor in his relationship with subordinates?
5. McGregor cites decentralization and delegation, job enlargement, participation and consultative management, and performance appraisal as steps in the right direction toward applying Theory Y. Can you think of any other ways in which Theory Y may be implemented?

29—THE CASE FOR PARTICIPATIVE MANAGEMENT *

Keith Davis

Participation is an overworked word in business and government, but an underworked activity. The idea sounds good to most managers, but they are frequently unsure of what to do with it. Some grossly misinterpret what it is, so that when they say, "Participation is great," they are really talking about something else; others are not sure when to apply it or how far to go with it.

One reason for the slow growth of participation is that it is a difficult philosophy to understand, and even more difficult to develop in a group. Genuine social science skill is required to make participation work. Many supervisors get in over their heads in a burst of enthusiasm and, after experiencing a rebuff, tend to withdraw from further efforts at participation. It appears that improperly applied participation may be worse for productivity and morale than simply doing nothing. Ineffective attempts to secure participation may make a group feel manipulated, resentful, confused, or lacking in objectives.

In spite of the difficulty of developing participation, it does have enormous potential for raising productivity, bettering morale, and improving creative thinking. The need of people to participate is not a passing fancy. It is rooted deep in the culture of free men around the world, and it is probably a basic drive in man.[1] Because of its significance and permanence, participation is a method to which leaders need to devote long-range efforts. Means of tapping this source of creativity and of using its cohesive power for teamwork need to be developed. Participation affords a means of building some of the human values needed in a group. It can create an asset in morale so that when necessary orders are given, people will respond more cooperatively because they are participating in their group, although they did not participate in determining the instruction they

* From *Business Horizons*, Vol. 6, No. 3 (Fall, 1963), pp. 55-60. Reprinted with permission.

[1] Comparative studies in England and the United States suggest that participation is a basic human drive rather than a cultural acquisition. *See* N. R. F. Maier and L. R. Hoffman, "Group Decision in England and the United States." *Personnel Psychology*, XV (Spring, 1962), p. 86.

have most recently received. The importance of participation has been described as follows:

> Two thousand years ago we put participation in the religion which has come to dominate the Western world. Two hundred years ago we put this essential element in our political and social structure. We are just beginning to realize that we ought to put participation in business as well.[2]

Classical experiments

Classical experiments by Roethlisberger, Bavelas, and Coch and French confirm our belief that participation is extremely valuable. Roethlisberger and his associates originally sought to show the relationship of physical change in environment and output. In the course of their experiments, new relationships, many of them involving participation, developed between workers and supervisors, and workers and experimenters. The results convincingly showed that these social changes improved both productivity and morale. Although participation was not the whole cause of these improvements, it seemed to be a significant cause.[3]

Bavelas worked with a group of women performing a sewing operation on a group incentive basis. For his experiment, he chose a superior group whose production averaged about 74 units hourly, with a range of 70 to 78. He asked them to set their own production goal. After considerable discussion they agreed unanimously on a goal of 84 units hourly, which they exceeded within five days. A goal of 95, set at a later meeting, could not be met. The goal was then reduced to the relatively permanent level of 90 units. During the next several months, the group's output averaged about 87 units with a range of 80 to 93. The net increase after participation was about 13 units hourly.[4] Coch and French achieved similar results in experiments with sewing machine operators.[5]

[2] Ralph M. Besse, "Business Statesmanship," *Personnel Administration*, XX (January-February, 1957), p. 12.

[3] F. J. Roethlisberger, *Management and Morale* (Cambridge: Harvard University Press, 1941), p. 14.

[4] Norman R. F. Maier, *Psychology in Industry* (Boston: Houghton Mifflin Company, 1946), pp. 264-66. Lawrence and Smith have since repeated Bavelas' experiments with similar results. *See* Lois C. Lawrence and Patricia Cain Smith, "Group Decision and Employee Participation," *The Journal of Applied Psychology*, XXXIX (October, 1955), pp. 334-37.

[5] Lester Coch and John R. P. French, Jr., "Overcoming Resistance to Change," *Human Relations*, I (No. 4, 1948), pp. 512-32 and John R. P. French, Jr. and Alvin Zander, "The Group Dynamics Approach," in Arthur Kornhauser, ed., *Psychology of Labor-Management Relations* (Champaign, Ill.: Industrial Relations Research Association, 1949), pp. 73-75.

The benefits of participation are evident in the experience of a large aircraft manufacturer, who employed from 5,000 to 20,000 shopworkers during the decade following World War II. The company used a safety committee system in which each department was represented by one worker. During these ten years, not one person suffered a disabling injury while serving as safety committeeman. This record was made despite the facts that hundreds of workers served on the committee during the decade, and accident-prone workers sometimes were appointed to the post in order to make them safety conscious. Although some committeemen probably returned to work earlier than they should have after an accident in order to preserve their record, the facts still show a significant difference between committeemen and other workers. Part of the difference was surely due to the fact that the committeemen were participating in a safety program.

Participation is especially important in encouraging people to accept change, a persistent pressure on all of us in our dynamic society. Participation is helpful both in planning and installing change, because when employees understand the objectives and content of a change, they are confident that management is not trying to "pull a fast one" on them. Participation may actually improve carefully devised management plans, because it elicits the ideas of the persons who are most thoroughly acquainted with the working effects of those plans. It may cancel a poor plan and thus save management many headaches. In any case, it broadens the outlook of those involved and helps them feel that they have an active part in what is taking place.

When a change is within management's control, such as the determination of a new work method, best results are realized when the group participates in the recognition of the need for change. Participation is less effective if it begins only after management has decided that a change is necessary.

Key ideas in participation

Participation is defined as an individual's mental and emotional involvement in a group situation that encourages him to contribute to group goals and to share responsibility for them. This definition contains three important ideas.

First, participation means mental and emotional involvement rather than mere muscular activity. The involvement of a person's *self*, rather than just his skill, is the product of his mind and his emotions. The person who participates is ego-involved instead of merely task-involved.[6] Some managers mistake task-involvement for true participation. They go through the motions of participation, but it is clear to employees that their manager is an autocrat who does not really want their ideas. Employees cannot become involved in this kind of situation.

A *second* important characteristic of participation is that it motivates contribution. Individuals are given an opportunity to direct their initiative and creativity toward the objectives of the group. In this way, participation differs from consent,[7] which uses only the creativity and ideas of the leader who brings his idea to the group for their approval. Participation requires more than mere approval of something already decided. It is a two-way psychological and social relationship among people rather than a procedure imposing ideas from above.

A *third* characteristic of participation is that it encourages people to accept responsibility for an activity. Because they are self-involved in the group, they want to see it work successfully. Participation helps them become responsible citizens rather than non-responsible automatons. As individuals begin to accept responsibility for group activities, they become interested in and receptive to teamwork, because they see in it a means of accomplishing a job for which they feel responsible. A person who is actively involved in something is naturally more committed to carrying it out. Of his own free will, he creates responsibility rather than having it forced upon him by delegation. By making himself responsible, he gains a measure of independence and dignity as an individual making his own decisions, even though these decisions are heavily influenced by his group environment.

Managers often ask, "If I share decisions with my personnel, don't I lose authority? I can't afford to give up authority because I'm responsible." This is a perfectly normal worry of an executive who is considering the values of participation for the first time, but it is hardly a justifiable worry. The participative manager still retains his authority to decide. He shares his problems with the group by means of a process that may be called social delegation. Social

---

[6] Gordon W. Allport, "The Psychology of Participation," *The Psychological Review*, LIII (May, 1945), p. 22.

[7] Mary P. Follett, "The Psychology of Consent and Participation," in *Dynamic Administration: The Collected Papers of Mary Parker Follett*, eds. Henry C. Metcalf and L. Urwick (New York: Harper and Brothers, 1941), pp. 210-12.

delegation in the human relations domain is comparable to formal delegation in the organizational domain. Neither type of delegation weakens a manager's organizational authority. No manager of the future—say twenty years hence—will object to a certain amount of social delegation through participation under normal conditions. It will be as much his stock in trade as formal delegation is today.

Practice limitations

These experiments (and the conclusions drawn from them) have a number of limitations that managers cannot ignore. Their success is no guarantee that all similar practices will be successful. The experiments described were performed by professional men skilled in human relations; similar efforts by ordinary supervisors undoubtedly would not produce such consistent results. The step from experimentation to practice is a long one indeed. The experiments were mostly one-shot efforts in a narrow work situation, using small groups who were doing repetitive work and undergoing changes. Participation in large work groups may be more difficult. In any case, managers should not go overboard for participation as they once did for scientific management. The latter was a worthwhile development, but managers' failure to recognize its uses and limitations in particular situations nearly ruined it.

In developing participation, we must be able to strike a precarious balance between counterfeit participation, which would arouse distrust, and excessive participation, which would consume valuable work time and destroy unified direction. Many issues are involved. Counterfeit participation may be tinsel and ribbon to make people happy, or it may be a more insidious tool handled by skilled social scientists, the engineers of consent.

Another danger of participation—as was true of scientific management—is that practitioners will get lost in the procedures of participation and overlook its philosophy. The substance of participation does not automatically flow from its procedures; there is no such mechanistic connection. Rather, when procedures are used at the right time and in the right circumstances, they enable it to develop.

Another issue concerns a person's right not to participate. There is no evidence that advanced participation is required for everybody; there is evidence that many persons do not want to be bothered with participation. Shall we force them into a mold merely because we think it is good for them? Some persons want a minimum of interaction with their supervisor and associates. The role expectation of many employees is to work for an autocratic supervisor, and consequently they produce effectively with this type of leadership. Research shows that the more authoritarian personality derives less benefit from participative methods, while the more equalitarian personality is more favorably affected.[8] Sometimes a group can be kept participating only by pressure from above. When that pressure is released, the group reverts to patterns of less participation.[9]

Prerequisites for participation

Finally, it should be emphasized that the success of participation is directly related to how well certain prerequisites are satisfied. Some of these conditions occur in the participants; some exist in the environment. Taken together, they mean that participation works better in some situations than others—and that in certain situations, it works not at all.[10]

The first prerequisite is that ample time must be allowed to participate before action is required. Participation may not be appropriate in emergency situations. Second, the financial cost of participation should not exceed the values, economic and otherwise, that it produces. Third, the subject of participation must be relevant to the participant's organization, something in which he is interested, or he will regard it as mere busy work. Fourth, the participant should have the abilities, intelligence, and knowledge to participate effectively.

Fifth, the participants must be able to communicate in order to be able to exchange ideas. Sixth, no one (employee or manager) should feel that his position is threatened by participation. Seventh, participation for deciding a course of action in an organization can take place only within the group's area of job freedom. Some degree of restriction on subunits is necessary in any organization in order to maintain internal stability; subunits cannot make decisions that

---

[8] Victor H. Vroom, "Some Personality Determinants of the Effects of Participation," *Journal of Abnormal and Social Psychology*, LIX (November, 1959), pp. 322-27.

[9] Robert N. McMurry, "The Case for Benevolent Autocracy," *Harvard Business Review*, XXXVI (January-February, 1958), pp. 82-90.

[10] For further explanation, *see* Robert Tannenbaum, Irving R. Weschler, and Fred Massarik, *Leadership and Organization: A Behavioral Science Approach* (New York: McGraw-Hill Book Company, Inc., 1961), pp. 88-100.

violate company policy, collective bargaining agreements, or similar restraints.

Since participation is a deep-seated need of man, it is worth trying: (1) if the manager understands what he is doing; (2) if he has developed some social science skill; (3) if he will meet the prerequisites; (4) if he will respect the role expectations of his people; and (5) if he will begin in a small way, rather than shooting for the moon in the first few months. Managers should proceed with caution, building each improvement upon past successes—but by all means, they should proceed.

Questions

1. How does Davis define "participation"? In what way does it relate to the continuum of leadership by Tannenbaum and Schmidt (Article 30)?
2. Will the composition of the work group affect the extent to which its members will accept responsibility for group activities? Explain.
3. Is there a relationship between participation and employee motivation? Explain.
4. Why do managers sometimes resist sharing decision making with subordinates? How can this resistance be overcome?

30—HOW TO CHOOSE A LEADERSHIP PATTERN *

Robert Tannenbaum and Warren H. Schmidt

- "I put most problems into my group's hands and leave it to them to carry the ball from there. I serve merely as a catalyst, mirroring back the people's thoughts and feelings so that they can better understand them."
- "It's foolish to make decisions oneself on matters that affect people. I always talk things over with my subordinates, but I make it clear to them that I'm the one who has to have the final say."
- "Once I have decided on a course of action, I do my best to sell my ideas to my employees."
- "I'm being paid to lead. If I let a lot of other people make the decisions I should be making, then I'm not worth my salt."
- "I believe in getting things done. I can't waste time calling meetings. Someone has to call the shots around here, and I think it should be me."

Each of these statements represents a point of view about "good leadership." Considerable experience, factual data, and theoretical principles could be cited to support each statement, even though they seem to be inconsistent when placed together. Such contradictions point up the dilemma in which the modern manager frequently finds himself.

New Problem

The problem of how the modern manager can be "democratic" in his relations with subordinates and at the same time maintain the necessary authority and control in the organization for which he is responsible has come into focus increasingly in recent years.

Earlier in the century this problem was not so acutely felt. The successful executive was generally pictured as possessing intelligence, imagination, initiative, the capacity to make rapid (and generally wise) decisions, and the ability to inspire subordinates. People tended to think of the world as being divided into "leaders" and "followers."

* From *Harvard Business Review*, Vol. 36, No. 2 (March-April, 1958), pp. 95-101. Reprinted with permission.

New focus

Gradually, however, from the social sciences emerged the concept of "group dynamics" with its focus on *members* of the group rather than solely on the leader. Research efforts of social scientists underscored the importance of employee involvement and participation in decision making. Evidence began to challenge the efficiency of highly directive leadership, and increasing attention was paid to problems of motivation and human relations.

Through training laboratories in group development that sprang up across the country, many of the newer notions of leadership began to exert an impact. These training laboratories were carefully designed to give people a first-hand experience in full participation and decision making. The designated "leaders" deliberately attempted to reduce their own power and to make group members as responsible as possible for setting their own goals and methods within the laboratory experience.

It was perhaps inevitable that some of the people who attended the training laboratories regarded this kind of leadership as being truly "democratic" and went home with the determination to build fully participative decision making into their own organizations. Whenever their bosses made a decision without convening a staff meeting, they tended to perceive this as authoritarian behavior. The true symbol of democratic leadership to some was the meeting—and the less directed from the top, the more democratic it was.

Some of the more enthusiastic alumni of these training laboratories began to get the habit of categorizing leader behavior as "democratic" or "authoritarian." The boss who made too many decisions himself was thought of as an authoritarian, and his directive behavior was often attributed solely to his personality.

New need

The net result of the research findings and of the human relations training based upon them has been to call into question the stereotype of an effective leader. Consequently, the modern manager often finds himself in an uncomfortable state of mind.

Often he is not quite sure how to behave; there are times when he is torn between exerting "strong" leadership and "permissive" leadership. Sometimes new knowledge pushes him in one direction ("I should really get the group to help make this decision"), but at the same time his experience pushes him in another direction ("I really understand the problem better than the group and therefore I should make the decision"). He is not sure when a group decision is really appropriate or when holding a staff meeting serves merely as a device for avoiding his own decision-making responsibility.

The purpose of our article is to suggest a framework which managers may find useful in grappling with this dilemma. First we shall look at the different patterns of leadership behavior that the manager can choose from in relating himself to his subordinates. Then we shall turn to some of the questions suggested by this range of patterns. For instance, how important is it for a manager's subordinates to know what type of leadership he is using in a situation? What factors should he consider in deciding on a leadership pattern? What difference do his long-run objectives make as compared to his immediate objectives?

Range of Behavior

EXHIBIT I presents the continuum or range of possible leadership behavior available to a manager. Each type of action is related to the degree of authority used by the boss and to the amount of freedom available to his subordinates in reaching decisions. The actions seen on the extreme left characterize the manager who maintains a high degree of control while those seen on the extreme right characterize the manager who releases a high degree of control. Neither extreme is absolute; authority and freedom are never without their limitations.

EXHIBIT I. CONTINUUM OF LEADERSHIP BEHAVIOR

Boss-centered leadership						Subordinate-centered leadership
Use of authority by the manager				Area of freedom for subordinates		
Manager makes decision and announces it.	Manager "sells" decision.	Manager presents ideas and invites questions.	Manager presents tentative decision subject to change.	Manager presents problem, gets suggestions, makes decision.	Manager defines limits; asks group to make decision.	Manager permits subordinates to function within limits defined by superior.

Now let us look more closely at each of the behavior points occurring along this continuum:

The manager makes the decision and announces it.

In this case the boss identifies a problem, considers alternative solutions, chooses one of them, and then reports this decision to his subordinates for implementation. He may or may not give consideration to what he believes his subordinates will think or feel about his decision; in any case, he provides no opportunity for them to participate directly in the decision-making process. Coercion may or may not be used or implied.

The manager "sells" his decision.

Here the manager, as before, takes responsibility for identifying the problem and arriving at a decision. However, rather than simply announcing it, he takes the additional step of persuading his subordinates to accept it. In doing so, he recognizes the possibility of some resistance among those who will be faced with the decision, and seeks to reduce this resistance by indicating, for example, what the employees have to gain from his decision.

The manager presents his ideas, invites questions.

Here the boss who has arrived at a decision and who seeks acceptance of his ideas provides an opportunity for his subordinates to get a fuller explanation of his thinking and his intentions. After presenting the ideas, he invites questions so that his associates can better understand what he is trying to accomplish. This "give and take" also enables the manager and the subordinates to explore more fully the implications of his decision.

The manager presents a tentative decision subject to change.

This kind of behavior permits the subordinates to exert some influence on the decision. The initiative for identifying and diagnosing the problem remains with the boss. Before meeting with his staff, he has thought the problem through and arrived at a decision—but only a tentative one. Before finalizing it, he presents his proposed solution for the reaction of those who will be affected by it. He says in effect, "I'd like to hear what you have to say about this plan that I have developed. I'll appreciate your frank reactions, but will reserve for myself the final decision."

The manager presents the problem, gets suggestions, and then makes his decision.

Up to this point the boss has come before the group with a solution of his own. Not so in this case. The subordinates now get the first chance to suggest solutions. The manager's initial role involves identifying the problem. He might, for example, say something of this sort: "We are faced with a number of complaints from newspapers and the general public on our service policy. What is wrong here? What ideas do you have for coming to grips with this problem?"

The function of the group becomes one of increasing the manager's repertory of possible solutions to the problem. The purpose is to capitalize on the knowledge and experience of those who are on the "firing line." From the expanded list of alternatives developed by the manager and his subordinates, the manager then selects the solution that he regards as most promising.[1]

---

[1] For a fuller explanation of this approach, *see* Leo Moore, "Too Much Management, Too Little Change," HBR (January-February, 1956), p. 41.

The manager defines the limits and requests the group to make a decision.

At this point the manager passes to the group (possibly including himself as a member) the right to make decisions. Before doing so, however, he defines the problem to be solved and the boundaries within which the decision must be made.

An example might be the handling of a parking problem at a plant. The boss decides that this is something that should be worked on by the people involved, so he calls them together and points up the existence of the problem. Then he tells them:

> "There is the open field just north of the main plant which has been designated for additional employee parking. We can build underground or surface multilevel facilities as long as the cost does not exceed $100,000. Within these limits we are free to work out whatever solution makes sense to us. After we decide on a specific plan, the company will spend the available money in whatever way we indicate."

The manager permits the group to make decisions within prescribed limits.

This represents an extreme degree of group freedom only occasionally encountered in formal organizations, as, for example, in many research groups. Here the team of managers or engineers undertakes the identification and diagnosis of the problem, develops alternative procedures for solving it, and decides on one or more of these alternative solutions. The only limits directly imposed on the group by the organization are those specified by the superior of the team's boss. If the boss participates in the decision-making process, he attempts to do so with no more authority than any other member of the group. He commits himself in advance to assist in implementing whatever decision the group makes.

Key Questions

As the continuum in EXHIBIT I demonstrates, there are a number of alternative ways in which a manager can relate himself to the group or individuals he is supervising. At the extreme left of the range, the emphasis is on the manager—on what *he* is interested in, how *he* sees things, how *he* feels about them. As we move toward the subordinate-centered end of the continuum, however, the focus is increasingly on the subordinates—on what *they* are interested in, how *they* look at things, how *they* feel about them.

When business leadership is regarded in this way, a number of questions arise. Let us take four of especial importance:

Can a boss ever relinquish his responsibility by delegating it to someone else?

Our view is that the manager must expect to be held responsible by his superior for the quality of the decisions made, even though operationally these decisions may have been made on a group basis. He should, therefore, be ready to accept whatever risk is involved whenever he delegates decision-making power to his subordinates. Delegation is not a way of "passing the buck." Also, it should be emphasized that the amount of freedom the boss gives to his subordinates cannot be greater than the freedom which he himself has been given by his own superior.

Should the manager participate with his subordinates once he has delegated responsibility to them?

The manager should carefully think over this question and decide on his role prior to involving the subordinate group. He should ask if his presence will inhibit or facilitate the problem-solving process. There may be some instances when he should leave the group to let it solve the problem for itself. Typically, however, the boss has useful ideas to contribute, and should function as an additional member of the group. In the latter instance, it is important that he indicate clearly to the group that he sees himself in a *member* role rather than in an authority role.

How important is it for the group to recognize what kind of leadership behavior the boss is using?

It makes a great deal of difference. Many relationship problems between boss and subordinate occur because the boss fails to make clear how he plans to use his authority. If, for example, he actually intends to make a certain decision himself, but the subordinate group gets the impression that he has delegated this authority, considerable confusion and resentment are likely to follow. Problems may also occur when the boss uses a "democratic" facade to conceal the fact that he has already made a decision which he hopes the group will accept as its own. The attempt to "make them think it was their idea in the first place" is a risky one. We believe that it is highly important for the manager to be honest and clear in describing what authority he is keeping and what role he is asking his subordinates to assume in solving a particular problem.

Can you tell how "democratic" a manager is by the number of decisions his subordinates make?

The sheer *number* of decisions is not an accurate index of the amount of freedom that a subordinate group enjoys. More important is the *significance* of the decisions which the boss entrusts to his subordinates. Obviously a decision on how to arrange desks is of an entirely different order from a decision involving the introduction of new electronic data-processing equipment. Even though the widest possible limits are given in dealing with the first issue, the group will sense no particular degree of responsibility. For a boss to permit the group to decide equipment policy, even within rather narrow limits, would reflect a greater degree of confidence in them on his part.

Deciding How to Lead

Now let us turn from the types of leadership that are possible in a company situation to the question of what types are *practical* and *desirable*. What factors or forces should a manager consider in deciding how to manage? Three are of particular importance:

- Forces in the manager.
- Forces in the subordinates.
- Forces in the situation.

We should like briefly to describe these elements and indicate how they might influence a manager's action in a decision-making situation.[2] The strength of each of them will, of course, vary from instance to instance, but the manager who is sensitive to them can better assess the problems which face him and determine which mode of leadership behavior is most appropriate for him.

Forces in the manager

The manager's behavior in any given instance will be influenced greatly by the many forces operating within his own personality. He will, of course, perceive his leadership problems in a unique way on the basis of his background, knowledge, and experience. Among the important internal forces affecting him will be the following:

(1) *His value system.* How strongly does he feel that individuals should have a share in making the decisions which affect them? Or, how convinced is he that the official who is paid to assume responsibility should personally carry the burden of decision making? The strength of his convictions on questions like these will tend to move the manager to one end or the other of the continuum shown in EXHIBIT I. His behavior will also be influenced by the relative importance that he attaches to organizational efficiency, personal growth of subordinates, and company profits.[3]

(2) *His confidence in his subordinates.* Managers differ greatly in the amount of trust they have in other people generally, and this carries over to the particular employees they supervise at a given time. In viewing his particular group of subordinates, the manager is likely to consider their knowledge and competence with respect to the problem. A central question he might ask himself is: "Who is best qualified to deal with this problem?" Often he may, justifiably or not, have more confidence in his own capabilities than in those of his subordinates.

(3) *His own leadership inclinations.* There are some managers who seem to function more comfortably and naturally as highly directive leaders. Resolving problems and issuing orders come easily to them. Other managers seem to operate more comfortably in a team role, where they are continually sharing many of their functions with their subordinates.

(4) *His feelings of security in an uncertain situation.* The manager who releases control over the decision-making process thereby reduces the predictability of the outcome. Some managers have a greater need than others for predictability and stability in their environment. This "tolerance for ambiguity" is being viewed increasingly by psychologists as a key variable in a person's manner of dealing with problems.

The manager brings these and other highly personal variables to each situation he faces. If he can see them as forces which, consciously or unconsciously, influence his behavior, he can better

---

[2] *See also* Robert Tannenbaum and Massarik, "Participation by Subordinates in the Managerial Decision-Making Process," *Canadian Journal of Economics and Political Science* (August, 1950), pp. 413-418.

[3] *See* Chris Argyris, "Top Management Dilemma: Company Needs vs. Individual Development," *Personnel* (September, 1955), pp. 123-134.

understand what makes him prefer to act in a given way. And understanding this, he can often make himself more effective.

Forces in the subordinate

Before deciding how to lead a certain group, the manager will also want to consider a number of forces affecting his subordinates' behavior. He will want to remember that each employee, like himself, is influenced by many personality variables. In addition, each subordinate has a set of expectations about how the boss should act in relation to him (the phrase "expected behavior" is one we hear more and more often these days at discussions of leadership and teaching). The better the manager understands these factors, the more accurately he can determine what kind of behavior on his part will enable his subordinates to act most effectively.

Generally speaking, the manager can permit his subordinates greater freedom if the following essential conditions exist:

- If the subordinates have relatively high needs for independence. (As we all know, people differ greatly in the amount of direction that they desire.)
- If the subordinates have a readiness to assume responsibility for decision making. (Some see additional responsibility as a tribute to their ability; others see it as "passing the buck.")
- If they have a relatively high tolerance for ambiguity. (Some employees prefer to have clear-cut directives given to them; others prefer a wider area of freedom.)
- If they are interested in the problem and feel that it is important.
- If they understand and identify with the goals of the organization.
- If they have the necessary knowledge and experience to deal with the problem.
- If they have learned to expect to share in decision making. (Persons who have come to expect strong leadership and are then suddenly confronted with the request to share more fully in decision making are often upset by this new experience. On the other hand, persons who have enjoyed a considerable amount of freedom resent the boss who begins to make all the decisions himself.)

The manager will probably tend to make fuller use of his own authority if the above conditions do *not* exist; at times there may be no realistic alternative to running a "one-man show."

The restrictive effect of many of the forces will, of course, be greatly modified by the general feeling of confidence which subordinates have in the boss. Where they have learned to respect and trust him, he is free to vary his behavior. He will feel certain that he will not be perceived as an authoritarian boss on those occasions when he makes decisions by himself. Similarly, he will not be seen as using staff meetings to avoid his decision-making responsibility. In a climate of mutual confidence and respect, people tend to feel less threatened by deviations from a normal practice, which in turn makes possible a higher degree of flexibility in the whole relationship.

Forces in the situation

In addition to the forces which exist in the manager himself and in his subordinates, certain characteristics of the general situation will also affect the manager's behavior. Among the more critical environmental pressures that surround him are those which stem from the organization, the work group, the nature of the problem, and the pressures of time. Let us look briefly at each of these:

Type of Organization. Like individuals, organizations have values and traditions which inevitably influence the behavior of the people who work in them. The manager who is a newcomer to a company quickly discovers that certain kinds of behavior are approved while others are not. He also discovers that to deviate radically from what is generally accepted is likely to create problems for him.

These values and traditions are communicated in many ways—through job descriptions, policy pronouncements, and public statements by top executives. Some organizations, for example, hold to the notion that the desirable executive is one who is dynamic, imaginative, decisive, and persuasive. Other organizations put more emphasis upon the importance of the executive's ability to work effectively with people—his human relations skills. The fact that his superiors have a defined concept of what the good executive should be will very likely push the manager toward one end or the other of the behavioral range.

In addition to the above, the amount of employee participation is influenced by such variables as the size of the working units, their geographical distribution, and the degree of inter- and intra-organizational security required to attain company goals. For example, the wide geographical dispersion of an organization may preclude a practical system of participative decision making, even though this would otherwise be desirable. Similarly, the size of the working units or the need for keeping plans confidential may make it necessary for the boss to exercise more control than would otherwise be the case. Factors like these may limit considerably the manager's ability to function flexibly on the continuum.

Group Effectiveness. Before turning decision-making responsibility over to a subordinate group, the boss should consider how effectively its members work together as a unit.

One of the relevant factors here is the experience the group has had in working together. It can generally be expected that a group which has functioned for some time will have developed habits of cooperation and thus be able to tackle a problem more effectively than a new group. It can also be expected that a group of people with similar backgrounds and interests will work more quickly and easily than people with dissimilar backgrounds, because the communication problems are likely to be less complex.

The degree of confidence that the members have in their ability to solve problems as a group is also a key consideration. Finally, such group variables as cohesiveness, permissiveness, mutual acceptance, and commonality of purpose will exert subtle but powerful influence on the group's functioning.

The Problem Itself. The nature of the problem may determine what degree of authority should be delegated by the manager to his subordinates. Obviously he will ask himself whether they have the kind of knowledge which is needed. It is possible to do them a real disservice by assigning a problem that their experience does not equip them to handle.

Since the problems faced in large or growing industries increasingly require knowledge of specialists from many different fields, it might be inferred that the more complex a problem, the more anxious a manager will be to get some assistance in solving it. However, this is not always the case. There will be times when the very complexity of the problem calls for one person to work it out. For example, if the manager has most of the background and factual data relevant to a given issue, it may be easier for him to think it through himself than to take the time to fill in his staff on all the pertinent background information.

The key question to ask, of course, is: "Have I heard the ideas of everyone who has the necessary knowledge to make a significant contribution to the solution of this problem?"

The Pressure of Time. This is perhaps the most clearly felt pressure on the manager (in spite of the fact that it may sometimes be imagined). The more that he feels the need for an immediate decision, the more difficult it is to involve other people. In organizations which are in a constant state of "crisis" and "crash programing" one is likely to find managers personally using a high degree of authority with relatively little delegation to subordinates. When the time pressure is less intense, however, it becomes much more possible to bring subordinates in on the decision-making process.

These, then, are the principal forces that impinge on the manager in any given instance and that tend to determine his tactical behavior in relation to his subordinates. In each case his behavior ideally will be that which makes possible the most effective attainment of his immediate goal within the limits facing him.

Long-Run Strategy

As the manager works with his organization on the problems that come up day by day, his choice of a leadership pattern is usually limited. He must take account of the forces just described and, within the restrictions they impose on him, do the best that he can. But as he looks ahead months or even years, he can shift his thinking from tactics to large-scale strategy. No longer need he be fettered by all of the forces mentioned, for he can view many of them as variables over which he has some control. He can, for example, gain

new insights or skills for himself, supply training for individual subordinates, and provide participative experiences for his employee
group.

In trying to bring about a change in these variables, however, he
is faced with a challenging question: At which point along the continuum *should* he act?

Attaining objectives

The answer depends largely on what he wants to accomplish.
Let us suppose that he is interested in the same objectives that most
modern managers seek to attain when they can shift their attention
from the pressure of immediate assignments:

1. To raise the level of employee motivation.
2. To increase the readiness of subordinates to accept change.
3. To improve the quality of all managerial decisions.
4. To develop teamwork and morale.
5. To further the individual development of employees.

In recent years the manager has been deluged with a flow of
advice on how best to achieve these longer-run objectives. It is little
wonder that he is often both bewildered and annoyed. However,
there are some guidelines which he can usefully follow in making a
decision.

Most research and much of the experience of recent years give
a strong factual basis to the theory that a fairly high degree of
subordinate-centered behavior is associated with the accomplishment
of the five purposes mentioned.[4] This does not mean that a manager
should always leave all decisions to his assistants. To provide the
individual or the group with greater freedom than they are ready
for at any given time may very well tend to generate anxieties and
therefore inhibit rather than facilitate the attainment of desired
objectives. But this should not keep the manager from making a
continuing effort to confront his subordinates with the challenge of
freedom.

Conclusion

In summary, there are two implications in the basic thesis that
we have been developing. The first is that the successful leader is

---

[4] For example, *see* Warren H. Schmidt and Paul C. Buchanan, *Techniques
that Produce Teamwork* (New London, Arthur C. Croft Publications, 1954); and
Morris S. Viteles, *Motivation and Morale in Industry* (New York, W. W. Norton
& Company, Inc., 1953).

one who is keenly aware of those forces which are most relevant to his behavior at any given time. He accurately understands himself, the individuals and group he is dealing with, and the company and broader social environment in which he operates. And certainly he is able to assess the present readiness for growth of his subordinates.

But this sensitivity or understanding is not enough, which brings us to the second implication. The successful leader is one who is able to behave appropriately in the light of these perceptions. If direction is in order, he is able to direct; if considerable participative freedom is called for, he is able to provide such freedom.

Thus, the successful manager of men can be primarily characterized neither as a strong leader nor as a permissive one. Rather, he is one who maintains a high batting average in accurately assessing the forces that determine what his most appropriate behavior at any given time should be and in actually being able to behave accordingly. Being both insightful and flexible, he is less likely to see the problems of leadership as a dilemma.

Questions

1. Why should the manager make it clear to his subordinates just what authority he is keeping and what role he is asking his subordinates to assume in solving a particular problem?
2. What risks are involved when a manager delegates decision-making power to his subordinates? Is this type of delegation a form of buck passing?
3. If you as a manager were somewhat skeptical of using the most extreme type of subordinate-centered leadership, what types of problems might you try to solve by this approach?
4. Do you feel that the pressure of time is usually a valid reason for a manager not using more democratic (subordinate-centered) leadership approaches?
5. The authors characterize the successful leader as one who is both insightful and flexible. What is meant by these characteristics and can they be learned?

31—MANAGEMENT TODAY *

Sherman Tingey

Traditional management has been defined as the planning, organizing, directing, and controlling of operations so that organization objectives can be effectively and efficiently achieved. For many management theorists, particularly those with a behavioral science background, this definition is insufficient because it does not give strong enough emphasis to the most important variable with which a manager deals—the variable of *people*. Managers plan activities for people. Of the various resources which require organizing, the organization of people is the most important. Direction is the process of leading people. And in controlling operations, the manager attempts to control the activities of people. Therefore, many modern management theorists have preferred a definition of management that emphasizes the integration of people in a work environment.

The basic components of an organization with which a manager works are (1) people; (2) functions or jobs; and (3) capital and capital goods (money and physical assets). The successful manager integrates these three into an effective producing organization. Of the three components, managing the human element in organizations is the central and most important managerial task, because it is the major determinant in how effectively and efficiently organization objectives will be achieved. Even the newest capital equipment and best possible arrangement of functions or jobs will be of little value if the enthusiastic cooperation and effective coordination of personnel is not attained. The following discussion will help illustrate how the traditional concept of management—wherein management is viewed as a process of planning, organizing, directing, and controlling—can be integrated with the behavioral approach which emphasizes the human factor in organizations.

---

* Reprinted with permission from *Hospital Administration*, the quarterly journal of the American College of Hospital Administrators (Spring, 1969, Vol. 14, No. 2, pp. 32-41).

Integrating the concepts—objectives

One of the first and most important functions of a manager is to establish clear cut objectives. Professor Mee has underscored the importance and primacy of objectives by identifying what he has termed the "principle of the objective," which states: "Before initiating any course of action, the objectives in view must be clearly determined, understood, and stated." [1]

In *Management by Objectives,* Dr. George S. Odiorne emphasizes the importance of periodically establishing objectives for the organization as a whole and for every subunit of the organization down to and including each individual. [2]

The advantages of determining and communicating objectives are many and include the following. First, objectives *provide the basis for cooperation* in the organization. When all objectives are dovetailed toward achieving the common organization objectives and each organization member is working toward his specific objective, greater coordination should result and the successful accomplishment of goals be enhanced.

Second, objectives *indicate the proper course of action* to follow. They provide criteria for determining whether or not action which is not specified in the directions of a superior should be taken. Tasks which will not help achieve objectives can be eliminated more easily. Therefore, objectives help develop self-direction and improve the decision-making abilities of organizational members.

Third, objectives *establish standards for control.* Well-defined goals which are broken down into production targets, quality standards, time deadlines, and other similar quantifiable specifics result in yardsticks for measuring accomplishments and progress. Such yardsticks provide incentive and motivation toward work accomplishment.

Fourth, proper utilization of objectives enables *"management by exception,"* which refers to a management approach that requires feedback only when actual performance is different from planned performance. In application, attention is directed at significant deviations—whether especially good or bad. Rather than spend valuable time leafing through voluminous reports covering all the activities which have occurred, a manager using this concept would receive

---

[1] John F. Mee, "Principle of the Objective," reprinted in Max D. Richards and William A. Nielander, *Readings in Management*, 2nd Edition (Cincinnati, Ohio: South-Western Publishing Co., 1963), pp. 335-336.

[2] George S. Odiorne, *Management by Objectives* (New York: Pitman Publishing Company, 1965).

information which reports only deviations from predetermined objectives or standards. Some deviations may indicate a need for corrective action while others may indicate a need for a change in the objectives. A simple example of management by exception is the elimination of daily records on number of hours worked and the substitution of less frequent reports showing only absenteeism or overtime.

Opposition of organizational/individual

At first glance, it would appear that if a manager establishes and communicates clear-cut objectives directed toward the achievement of organization goals, most of his worries are over. However, organization psychologists have identified a major stumbling block in trying to achieve goals (or objectives) in organizations. Their research has shown that *the goals and needs of individuals in organizations are different from the goals and needs of the organization!* This results in inescapable tension between individual and organizational goals.

Individuals join organizations in order to satisfy certain needs such as physiological, safety, social, and esteem needs. What an individual wants from the organization is an opportunity to receive enough wages and income to provide for his family; a certain amount of security in continued employment; satisfying interpersonal relations with peers and colleagues; recognition of accomplishments; the esteem of the organization through his superiors; and an opportunity to perform work which is worthwhile and beneficial.

The organization's needs are not identical to the individual's needs. The organization has specific goals to accomplish—usually economic in nature—which require the productive efforts of the individual. The organization needs the individual to contribute his physiological, psychological, and intellectual efforts toward the accomplishment of organizational goals. In effect, the organization is trying to satisfy its needs through the individual while the individual is trying to satisfy his needs through association with the organization. The organization asks for energy, work, and commitment, while the individual asks for satisfaction of physiological and sociological needs.

The exchange process

This becomes an "exchange process" wherein the individual must perceive he receives an equal payment in need satisfaction for the efforts he contributes toward the organization goals. If the individual goals are not being met satisfactorily, then he will discontinue contributing toward the accomplishment of organizational goals by either leaving the job and going to work elsewhere or by withholding his potential contributions and performing only minimally on the job.

We are all familiar with the many individuals who are not receiving what they perceive to be "equal payment" from the organization in the satisfaction of their personal goals. Usually they receive high enough incomes to satisfy their physiological needs (although they often verbalize their dissatisfaction in terms of wanting even higher wages). The real problem is usually found in the work itself or the work environment. The work "isn't challenging enough" or "could be accomplished by one with half my skills" are typical complaints.[3] Managers have often been to blame in failing to provide an environment which (1) challenges the individual to utilize his intellectual abilities, (2) gives proper recognition to accomplishments, or (3) enables the individual to develop satisfying social relations with others on the job.

The typical example is the manager who takes every opportunity to break up the association of his subordinates by changing their work assignments or locations whenever he sees the first signs of close social interaction developing. He seriously believes that individual performance will suffer if informal organizations and satisfying interpersonal relationships develop among subordinates. This belief is understandable, since such groups may become power centers which may thwart the goals of the manager. However, recent research has shown that the opposite result is more often true. By assisting organization members to develop satisfying social relationships and by thinking of employees as human beings rather than as tools to get the work done, the productivity and effectiveness of the group will be enhanced.[4]

Dealing with conflicting goals

Attempts have been made to modify traditional management concepts and integrate some of the research findings of the behavioral

---

[3] Research has shown that mentally retarded persons can perform more effectively in some work situations than "normal" people. There have even been experiments where monkeys and pigeons have done the same. For an interesting discussion of the problems in making work satisfying, see Chris Argyris, "We Must Make Work Worthwhile," *Life* (March 5, 1967), p. 56.

[4] An excellent source which reports the summaries of many research efforts, including his own, on the general topic of leadership behavior and organizational performance is found in Rensis Likert, *New Patterns of Management* (New York: McGraw-Hill Book Company, Inc., 1961). See especially Chapter 2.

sciences into modern management theory. Not only is this being done by writers in the management field, but also by practitioners. For example, the problem of conflicting goals between the organization and the individual organization members is now recognized and accepted by forward thinking managers.

Several frameworks for dealing with this problem and under-standing the exchange process have been developed and experimented with. Some of the early frameworks presented emphasized "demo-cratic leadership" and "participative management" or "consultative management." These approaches stressed the positive effects of greater employee participation in decisions that affect him.

EXHIBIT I. LIKERT'S "SUPPORTIVE RELATIONSHIP" ILLUSTRATED

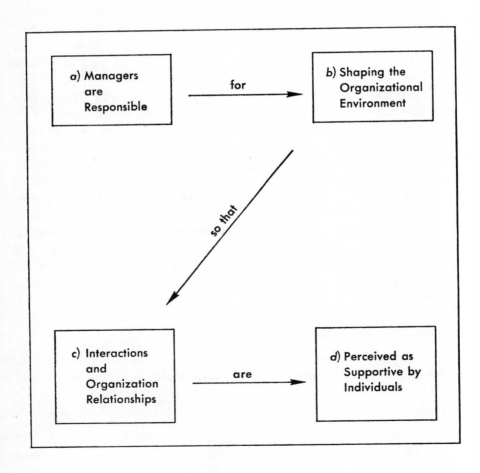

The constant plea for greater use of participation appears throughout the early writings of the behavioralists.[5] Studies showed that greater participation tends to:

1. Increase the understanding of the problems and alternatives being considered.
2. Give the individual a better understanding of the other person's point of view.
3. Increase the degree of cohesiveness between participants and the organization.
4. Instill a sense of responsibility for the success of the decision.
5. Develop a broader, overall organizational point of view.

Most of the early efforts to integrate behavioral theories with traditional management concepts tended to emphasize only one aspect of the problem, e.g., leadership style or participation in decision making. Recent efforts have been more comprehensive in scope. For example, Argyris and Bakke have developed a theory called the "fusion process" which attempts to integrate the needs of the individual with those of the organization.[6] Several others, including such noted writers as Keith Davis and Rensis Likert, have contributed to a management theory now termed "supportive management."

Supportive management

Essential to the theory of supportive management is the idea that the manager's role should be one of providing an organizational

---

[5] See, for example, George B. Moser, "Consultative Management" in *Management Record*, Vol. XVII, No. 11 (November, 1955), pp. 438-439, National Industrial Conference Board. Countless studies have shown, according to Moser, that increased morale and productivity result from the application of consultative management.

Whyte's interaction method of analyzing organization behavior calls for more subordinate participation. See William Foote Whyte, *Men at Work* (Homewood: The Dorsey Press, Inc., and Richard D. Irwin, Inc., 1961).

Another example, although somewhat different in technique, includes the multiple management concepts espoused by Charles T. McCormick in *The Power of People* (New York: Harper & Brothers, 1949).

[6] Several original sources are available which describe the fusion process, including E. Wight Bakke and Chris Argyris, *Organization Structure and Dynamics* (New Haven, Connecticut: Yale Labor and Management Center, 1954), or E. Wight Bakke, *The Fusion Process* (New Haven, Connecticut: Yale Labor and Management Center, 1953). For a brief summary of the most important points of the fusion process and a summary write-up of an effort to test the theory of the fusion process in a bank, see John M. Pfiffner and Frank P. Sherwood, *Administrative Organizations* (New Jersey: Prentice-Hall, Inc., 1960), pp. 375-383.

environment which supports the individual's efforts toward the fulfillment of his personal needs. Likert describes this supportive relationship as follows:

> The leadership and other process of the organization must be such
> as to insure a maximum probability that in all interactions and in all
> relationships within the organization, each member, in the light of his
> background, values, desires, and expectations, will view the experience
> as supportive and one which builds and maintains his sense of personal
> worth and importance.[7]

As illustrated in Exhibit I, an analysis of this definition emphasizes the following points:

a) The manager's responsibility for providing appropriate leadership
   style and influencing various organizational processes so that
b) interactions and organizational relationships
c) will be *perceived* by each organization member
d) as *supportive* of his own psychological growth needs.

How does the role of the supportive manager differ from the
management pattern of the autocratic manager? The following comparison will be helpful in identifying the major differences.[8]

Autocratic vs. supportive managers

Direction. Although autocratic managers can be dictatorial or benevolent, they direct activities from a position of organizational
power. The formal organization *authority* which he possesses gives
him the right to command subordinates. He depends upon and uses
this authority to get performance. In contrast, the supportive manager depends upon his leadership abilities to structure an organizational environment which supports the subordinate's efforts to contribute to the organization and maintain a sense of personal worth.

Motivation. The autocratic boss uses a negative motivation pattern.
Such penalties as loss of job, reprimand in the presence of others, and
demotion are employed as a means of frightening subordinates into
productivity. Although the benevolent autocratic would be an exception, most autocratic managers tend to utilize negative patterns of
motivation with subordinates.

---

[7] Rensis Likert, *The Human Organization* (New York: McGraw-Hill Book
Company, Inc., 1967), p. 47.

[8] The primary source of the concepts presented in this section of the paper,
including the table, is Keith Davis, "In the Spotlight: The Supportive Manager,"
Arizona Business Bulletin, Vol. XIV, No. 10 (December, 1967), pp. 252-256.
For an expansion of these ideas and further materials on the underlying concept of supportive management, the reader is referred to Davis' article, also
Keith Davis, *Human Relations at Work: The Dynamics of Organizational Behavior*, 3rd Edition (New York: McGraw-Hill Book Company, Inc., 1967).

Exhibit II

A Comparison of Autocratic and Supportive Managers

	Autocratic	Supportive
Depends on	Power	Leadership
Managerial orientation	Authority	Support
Motivational pattern	Negative	Positive
Employee orientation	Obedience	Performance
Employee psychological result ...	Personal dependency	Participation
Morale measure	Compliance	Motivation
Employee needs met	Subsistence	Higher-order
Performance result	Minimum	Awakened drives
Abilities primarily used	Manager only	Whole group

Source: Keith Davis, "In the Spotlight . . . ," *op. cit.*, p. 253.

Supportive managers use rewards to create a positive motivation pattern. His study of human behavior has taught him that people in organizations today respond more effectively to positive incentives—particularly psychological rewards, such as recognition, advancement, and responsibility.

Effect on Employees. An employee finds it necessary to adopt an attitude of obedience to his autocratic boss. The constant reminder of his boss' power to hire, fire, and "perspire" him forces him into a condition of personal dependency on his boss. In contrast, under supportive management the orientation is toward achievement and responsibility. An employee in this environment is oriented toward performance in his work. He shares in decision making and develops a feeling of participation in the overall accomplishments of his work group.

Morale and Need Fulfillment. Under autocratic management the employee is expected to take his orders and follow them. Usually the level of morale attained is unenthusiastic compliance with rules and directives. As a result only the lower level or subsistence needs of the employee tend to be satisfied. He puts in his eight hours and makes enough to live on.

Under supportive management, morale is measured in terms of the individual's motivation to contribute his talents to the achievement of organization goals. Because he feels the support of the organization, his higher-order needs are challenged. He works toward recognition, the esteem of others, and self-fulfillment.

Performance. Because of the lack of motivation under autocratic management, the employee reluctantly gives only minimum performance and hopes for better things to come. The autocrat has centralized many functions in himself and thus usually works hard to keep ahead. Less than optimal goals are achieved, however, because the resources utilized are primarily those of the manager only.

Performance of employees in a supportive organizational environment is characterized by awakened drives. Individuals are highly stimulated to participate in and contribute to the accomplishment of common goals. High achievement levels are attained because the resources of the whole group are utilized, rather than those of the manager only.

Organizational psychologists have identified an important organizational problem. The goals and needs of the organization are different from the goals and needs of the individuals in organizations. Traditional management theories do not provide for such a problem. Based upon recent behavioral science research of people in organizations, management theorists have attempted to develop frameworks which enable practicing managers to understand and deal effectively with the situation. These frameworks are usually based on the concept of the "exchange process." This concept implies that the individual must receive an equal payment in *need satisfaction* for the efforts he contributes toward accomplishment of organizational goals.

Summary

Early theories emphasized democratic leadership and participative management. More recent writers have contributed to a more comprehensive and a more promising theory called supportive management. This supportive theory of management identifies the manager's role as one of providing an organization environment which supports the individual's efforts toward the fulfillment of his personal needs—particularly his psychological growth needs. In turn, the individual is more highly motivated toward accomplishing organizational objectives.

Supportive management concepts are not easy to master and require a substantial amount of education and training prior to full application. However, even small efforts toward the use of supportive management can be richly rewarding.

Questions

1. Why is it not enough for the manager to state the objectives for the organization as a whole, for its subunits, and individual members?
2. What does Tingey mean by the "exchange process"? How is it related to the achievement of organizational goals?
3. How does the principle of supportive management relate to the earlier concepts of democratic leadership and participative management?
4. Contrast the attitudes and behaviors of autocratic and supportive managers.

32—TOWARD INNOVATIVE LEADERSHIP *

Eugene J. Koprowski

What I need is a new breed of executive. The "shopkeeper" variety is on his way out. Give me a man who can stand toe-to-toe with the Ph.D. chemist or the operations research mathematician and know the right questions to ask at the right time. Add to that international sophistication, a flair for creative thinking, courage, common sense, and the ability to lead and inspire the smart, young, energetic people who are entering our organization, and I think we'll be well on our way.

The name of the executive who made that statement is unimportant. What is important is that the focus of the management game is rapidly changing, and innovation holds the spotlight. Unfortunately, much of what has been written treats the subject generally or deals with innovation as it pertains to specific functions such as research and development or marketing. There is an important distinction between this type of innovation and innovative leadership. In the first case, the results are new or better processes or products. In the latter, the desired ends are new or better goals and organizational arrangements to achieve these goals. For as we move from mass production to an automated technology, the type as well as the amount of change required will be dramatically altered.

There is mounting evidence, for example, that business leaders will be called upon to assume an increasingly important role in solving many of our nation's social problems, such as air and water pollution, poverty, crime, transportation, unemployment, and civil rights.[1] Pressures in this direction will become heavier as our computers force us into new patterns of thinking and interacting. As a result, in the future the trend will be toward a growing interdependence of the various subsystems of our society. Within this

* From *Business Horizons*, Vol. 10, No. 4 (Winter, 1967), pp. 79-88. Copyright, 1967, by the Foundation for the School of Business, at Indiana University. Reprinted by permission.

[1] Kenneth Galbraith, *The New Industrial Society* (Boston: Houghton Mifflin Company, 1967); F. Bradford Morse, "Private Responsibility for Public Management," *Harvard Business Review* (March-April, 1967), pp. 6-21; Robert F. Kennedy, "What Can the Young Believe," *The New Republic* (March 11, 1967), pp. 11-12.

context, innovative leadership becomes something more than a new fad. It becomes the primary requisite for survival in a world that is rapidly being redefined by a new technology.[2]

This leads to two basic questions: Where do we find this special brand of leadership? What can we do to increase the creative output among our present staff? The balance of this paper will attempt to answer these questions by proposing a series of specific strategies and techniques that should find application in a wide range of organizations.

Input Strategies

Business organizations look to our colleges and universities as the primary source of future leaders, yet they are concerned because many of the most talented and creative graduates seek careers elsewhere.[3] This has prompted concerted attempts to change the business image in the academic community. Sophisticated advertising campaigns that stress the challenging nature of business, student summer work programs, and various types of scholarship programs are examples of these efforts. The assumption is that if graduates have a realistic understanding of the business world, they are more likely to choose business careers. Unfortunately, the problem is much more complex than this.

Research studies show, for example, that (1) the most creative students attend liberal arts colleges [4] and (2) that their interests and values are dissimilar to those of successful business executives.[5] Despite the evidence, many organizations persist in saying they want innovative people while employing self-defeating recruiting strategies. Carried down to a practical level, organizations attempting to increase their innovative inputs should:

1. Do more undergraduate recruiting in the liberal arts colleges. According to the University of California Studies, creative individuals

---

[2] Marshall McLuhan, *Understanding Media: The Extensions of Man* (New York: McGraw-Hill Book Company, 1964).

[3] Peter F. Drucker, "Is Business Letting Young People Down?" *Harvard Business Review* (November-December, 1965), pp. 49-55; Roger M. Blough, "Business Can Satisfy the Young Intellectual," *Harvard Business Review* (January-February, 1966), pp. 49-57; and John S. Fielden, "The Right Young People for Business," *Harvard Business Review* (March-April, 1966), pp. 76-83.

[4] Timothy W. Costello and Sheldon S. Zalkind, *Psychology in Administration: a Research Orientation* (Englewood Cliffs, N. J.: Prentice-Hall, Inc., 1963), p. 420.

[5] Victor H. Vroom, *Motivation in Management* (American Foundation For Management Research, 1965), pp. 22-26.

are most likely to have interest patterns similar to those of psychologists, architects, writers, physicists, and musicians.[6]

2. Advertise in magazines and periodicals that appeal to the "intellectual" as well as to the business student.

3. Minimize the "Wine 'em, dine 'em, money is no object" recruiting approach. Remember that creative students are likely to be more interested in the challenge of their work and where they will live than with symbols of status and power.

Even if business organizations redirect their advertising efforts and recruiting strategies to fit the interests and values of creative individuals, there is still the problem of how to reconcile conflicting goal systems. It is foolish to assume that businesses can ever adopt the pursuit of truth, beauty, and harmony as their primary objectives. Yet, it is probable at this level that industry is losing the major battle for creative talent, since these types will seek careers with organizations and groups whose goals and values are more compatible with their own. As a result, the academic world, the arts, and the professions end up with the lion's share of innovative leaders.

Three alternatives

Fortunately, there are alternatives to employing this kind of talent; organizations can develop strategies to introduce innovation in other ways. Three alternate methods are based on the alter ego, the task force, and the research models. Each allows the innovator to contribute toward practical business objectives and still retain his primary identification outside the business world.

Alter Ego Model. The primary purpose of this model is to introduce creative leadership into the organization by providing an alter ego for the line or staff manager already in a high-level policy-making position. Since creative ability and leadership are rarely found in the same person, it may take the combined talents of a leader and an innovator to get the job done. In practical operation, here's how such an arrangement might work.

Company A is in a highly competitive cosmetic industry where novel marketing is one of the primary keys to success. To assure creative thrust, the president engages the services of a top-flight research anthropologist from a local university to spend four hours a week with the marketing vice president. The anthropologist knows

---

[6] *Psychology in Administration: a Research Orientation*, p. 420.

nothing about the cosmetics business, but is highly regarded among his colleagues as an original and creative thinker. In his relationship with the marketing vice president, he does not serve in the traditional capacity of a consultant in terms of giving advice; instead, he serves as a catalyst and a sounding board for new ideas and approaches to marketing.

Task Force Model. This method is used when there is need to solve some specific organizational problem that calls for original ideas. The job of problem solving is assigned to an in-company task force, which is provided an outside resource person or persons of acknowledged creative ability. For example, a chemical company might engage the services of an eminent research chemist employed by a nonprofit foundation to help the development group work out the problem of excessive corrosive salts in one of their major product lines.

Research Model. In this situation, top management of a manufacturing company might be interested in improving worker motivation through the application of job enlargement in a particular plant. To guide this project, the company retains the services of a team of local college professors of recognized ability and interest in this area. In this case, the research team would work with local line-and-staff management to formulate new concepts and ideas and to engineer the required change.

The cards appear to be stacked against staffing our business organizations with sufficient numbers of innovative leaders. Although improving the business image on college campuses might produce some positive results, the personality dynamics that lead young men to choose business careers usually are not the same ones that are found in creative individuals. The strategies that have been mentioned would allow business organizations to tap innovative talent in a way that would be compatible with the value orientations of creative individuals.

Organizational Strategies

Innovation can flourish only in an environment that supports and encourages it. Much of our thinking about innovative organizational climate comes from studies of creative individuals. Once we know their characteristics, we can ask in what organizational setting this type of person will be most productive.

While prescriptions vary, most knowledgeable observers agree that an innovative organization will have these essential characteristics: [7]

> Authority and decision making will be distributed as widely as possible. Risk taking will be a recognized component of innovation. Communications systems will be planned to work effectively in all directions. The burden of formal structure will be minimized as much as possible. Innovative behavior will be appropriately rewarded.

Although these prescriptions may sound practicable, many organizations will find them difficult to put into effect. Most American business corporations are organized around a set of assumptions about people that discourage rather than encourage innovation.[8] Change involves risks and fear, and establishing a system conducive to innovation and creativity will be marked by many false starts, anxieties, and disillusionments. Old ways of looking at things and getting things done must be replaced with something of value to the individual who is involved. A brief look at some of the patterns typically utilized by some businesses will be helpful in clarifying possible alternatives for establishing more innovative organizational climate.

First, it is not unusual for a corporate president to attempt to increase innovation through proclamation. He does this by calling his immediate staff together, eloquently championing the cause of innovation, and explaining a specific course of action. The implementations usually involve a company policy, articles in the various company publications, and increased participation of the president's staff in seminars and conferences on creative problem solving and related areas. Sensitive subordinates quickly pick up a new set of buzz words and dutifully turn their attentions to this new dimension of "playing organization."

Another typical approach is to delegate the responsibility for change to a staff group. In this case, they develop the strategy, attempt to sell the program to the line executives, and are often held responsible for the results. Traditionally, one of the characteristic methods used by such a group is training and development. And, in the case of creating an innovative climate, one would expect that a staff-directed program would have an ample sprinkling of seminars,

---

[7] Chris Argyris, *Organization and Innovation* (Homewood, Ill.: Richard D. Irwin, Inc., 1965); John W. Gardner, *Self-Renewal: The Individual and the Innovative Society* (New York: Harper & Row, Publishers, 1964); and Gary A. Steiner, *The Creative Organization* (University of Chicago Press, 1965), pp. 37-45.

[8] *Psychology in Administration: a Research Orientation*, pp. 414-15.

conferences, and various manuals on innovation. All this would be done with great finesse and sophistication. Again, managers down the line would dutifully play the game.

The third variation is to bring in an outside consulting group. The contention here is that, if these consultants are really worth their salt, they'll be able to stimulate innovation in the organization. This, of course, is not necessarily true. Much depends upon the degree of acceptance and commitment on the part of the chief executive and the actual pressures to change. The chief executive sets the pace and the tone in his company. He must be willing to take risks and to change his own behavior. If these conditions are met, there is some hope that innovation will be more than a new variation of an old organizational game.

Unfortunately, innovation cannot come through proclamation or administrative ostentation and display. It must come from the careful engineering of social change and with the use of all the means available to the company—internal and external. Although there is no foolproof theory for implementing this kind of change, there are a few specific strategies that can prove useful.

Authority revisited

Traditional organizational theory specifies that authority flow from the owners through the chains of command, and that power is derived from the structure. This is the first roadblock to innovation. Creative people may have their own ideas about authority—they see conventional authority as arbitrary, temporary, and restrictive. For these people, power does not flow from the hierarchy, but from personal expertise and demonstrable superiority in a given knowledge area.[9]

This suggests a number of dimensions for change. One obvious step top management can take is to give members of organizational groups some voice in choosing their leaders. Revolutionary as this may sound, a number of organizations are experimenting with this approach and are finding that it works. Despite the fact that such notions are contrary to ingrained ideas about prerogatives of command, a leader is not someone superimposed on a group—he is an integral part of it.

---

[9] Gary A. Steiner, *The Creative Organization* (Chicago: University of Chicago Press, 1965), p. 8.

A second alternative is to rotate the leadership function. In group problem-solving situations, this is what actually happens on an informal basis.[10] Why not carry this one step further and let the problem to be solved, rather than the arbitrary notion of hierarchy of command, determine who will serve as leader Alternating the leadership role in this way is not only more realistic, but it has the additional advantage of increasing the range of informational inputs for the various participants.

A third strategy is to seek ways and means of increasing participation in the management process. Participation, like innovation, is currently a potent term—or, in corporate parlance, a buzz word. Unfortunately, many managers either use participative approaches to manipulate subordinates or in abortive ways that dilute their value. This is regrettable, since participative techniques can be very powerful management tools if used properly.

For example, I was recently called upon by a sales vice president of a leading manufacturing organization to suggest ways and means of improving morale among career salesmen. Rather than begin with a series of a priori assumptions about the morale of salesmen in general, I visited the regional offices to find out what problems faced the salesmen from their point of view. The information generated was quite different from the assumptions that were originally made at corporate headquarters. This method of gathering information not only provided a more realistic basis for designing strategies to increase motivation but it also gave the salesmen a feeling of participation in the management process.

Risk taking

Innovation is inconceivable without risks. Yet many businesses try to minimize the risks of operation by careful planning. Fortunately, the two ideas are not as incompatible as they seem. It is possible to use an innovative approach to management and still minimize risk. Take, for example, an organization that wants to test the notion that job enlargement increases motivation and production among workers. This could be approached in a number of ways. The company could establish a formal policy that job enlargement is the direction in which the organization intends to move, and the full weight of

---

[10] Robert F. Bales, "In Conference," *Harvard Business Review* (March-April, 1954), pp. 44-50.

corporate authority could be brought to bear implementing this new philosophy. If the assumptions behind job enlargement are correct and if every supervisor and worker is committed to these assumptions, the new approach might work.

Another strategy is to gradually move into job enlargement. This would involve a pilot study in a segment of the organization where the supervisor is enthusiastic about the possibilities, the jobs lend themselves to combination, and failure to the project would be least harmful to the total organization. Planned risk taking of this variety can actually increase an organization's capacity to absorb failure and thus stimulate attempts at innovation.

Communications networks

One of the reasons that creative people are able to combine outputs in novel ways is that usually they have greater access than the average person to their inner resources or emotional life. Many are more honest with their feelings and are better able to tolerate unpleasant aspects of their personalities; as a result, they may allow for a greater range of perceptual inputs from the outside.[11] The same could be said for innovative organizations. Here communications means something more than the traditional suggestion system, house organ, and staff meeting. Such devices contribute little to the brand of communications necessary for innovation. What appears to be most needed are new patterns of informational inputs that differ not only in quantity but also in quality from those conventionally fostered.

A growing school of behavioral scientists feel that T-group methods hold considerable promise in changing qualitative aspects of interpersonal communications networks.[12] One of the basic goals of these approaches is to reduce communications game playing and to move individuals in the direction of more authentic relationships. The contention is that traditional organizational structure encourages various disruptive communications patterns. Typical examples are "yea saying" (saying what the boss wants to hear), "clay pigeoning" (setting up an opponent, only to shoot him down when some flaw

---

[11] *The Creative Organization*, pp. 8-9.
[12] Chris Argyris, "Interpersonal Barriers to Decision Making," *Harvard Business Review* (March-April, 1966), pp. 84-97; Edgar H. Schein and Warren G. Bennis, *Personal and Organizational Change Through Group Methods— The Laboratory Approach* (New York: John Wiley & Sons, Inc., 1965).

in his proposal is fully exposed), "gloss jobbing" (killing a good idea in order to avoid unpleasant interpersonal conflicts), and "smoke screening" (diverting attention from real issues to gain personal advantage).

Developmental Strategies

Movement toward innovation also requires quantitative informational input changes. These must occur on an individual as well as an organizational level. At the individual level, three specific strategies will be discussed. Each has a unique potential for developing innovative leadership patterns by increasing the range of inputs. For lack of better labels, these will be called developmental jobs, developmental bosses, and new-view exposure.

Developmental jobs

Most organizations have certain jobs that are especially rich in potential for developing innovative patterns of behavior. Overseas assignments are one example. Executives forced to make decisions in an unfamiliar environment thousands of miles from corporate headquarters must innovate to survive. In such a setting, they are also provided alternate frames of reference by the local culture. Companies without foreign operations might negotiate executive exchange programs with their industrial counterparts in other countries and achieve similar results.

On the domestic scene, exposure to profit center management provides an excellent opportunity for individuals to see the complex interrelations of production, sales, and community relations. In smaller companies, executive inputs can be increased by rotating these people through a high-level administrative assistant's job.

Another promising approach is to rotate line-and-staff executives. Specialization, which gave rise to the line-staff concept in organizational theory, has the distinct disadvantage of reinforcing provincialism among executives. Putting an up-and-coming production manager in a staff position such as manpower planning and development not only forces him to broaden his perspectives, but it also requires him to exercise organizational influence without formal line authority. This type of line-staff rotation also can do much to improve communications patterns between these two sometimes hostile groups.

It is important that the use of developmental jobs is not left to chance. Organizations should carefully identify these positions and make a special effort to keep them free of deadwood.

Developmental bosses

The notion of developmental bosses is based on the assumption that there are many ways to skin a cat, and the more of these an executive knows, the better the odds that he will adapt innovative solutions to his problems. In actual practice, this means being exposed to bosses who are either highly innovative or whose style of management is substantially different from the rotating subordinate's. This kind of personal contact helps build tolerance, flexibility, and perspective. The key to making this approach work is carefully identifying innovative qualities and styles of management among the existing executive group and following up with planned sequences of rotation.

New-view exposure

It is common practice for companies to belong to various industry-type membership organizations that conduct seminars and conferences, provide research services, and publish information of common interest. While such communications exchange has obvious benefits, there is the danger of becoming locked into a particular industrial point of view. Therefore, to maintain balance, there should be planned exposure to the ideas, methods, and problems of other industries. Examples would include university executive development courses, broad-based management seminars, conferences, work shops, and visits to other companies.

Both qualitative and quantitative changes in communications patterns are necessary ingredients for an innovative organizational climate. Qualitative changes should be in the direction of minimizing communications game playing and maximizing honest confrontation. Quantitative changes should be in the direction of broadening the range of inputs both for the individual executive and for the organization as a whole.

Structure and Innovation

Excessive numbers of policies, rules, manuals, guidelines, descriptions, and prescriptions all tend to have an inhibiting effect on innovation.[13] This is especially true when these are written. There is something about the written word that is like a message chipped in stone. Companies interested in more innovative patterns of management should periodically review all written policies and rules at least once a year with the object of ruthlessly eliminating at least 10 percent of the "stone tablets" at each sitting. Even so, many organizations would find that, at the end of five years, they still would have more policies and rules than were needed.

These rather flamboyant prescriptions are based on at least two important observations about organizational behavior. The first is that often the most effective managers are those who break the most "rules." The second is that the organizations with the thickest organizational manuals are usually the least adaptive to change. This does not mean that all rules and regulations should be outlawed; it simply means that active steps should be taken to minimize their number.

Another organizational refinement of structure is the ever popular position description. The thinking here is that a man who knows his responsibilities and authorities will operate more effectively than one who doesn't. This, however, is not necessarily true. A study of the relationship between perceived degree of decision-making authority and rated effectiveness has revealed that the most highly-rated managers assumed they had more authority than either their position description or their superior prescribed.[14] This suggests that traditional position descriptions, logical as they appear, have questionable value outside of making managers feel good about precise assignment of responsibility and authority. More serious is the fact that they tend to inhibit innovative behavior by drawing a restrictive circle around the individual. An alternate approach is to focus on goals and allow the manager to choose his own means of implementation. The result would be goal descriptions rather than position descriptions.

Rewarding Innovation

It is a well-established principle of learning that, to change people, the new desired patterns of behavior must be appropriately rewarded. It follows that to make an organization more innovative, innovation

---

[13] John W. Gardner, *Self-Renewal: The Individual and the Innovative Society* (New York: Harper & Row, Publishers, 1964).
[14] Unpublished study by the author conducted in 1965 in an international primary metals manufacturing organization.

must be rewarded. Unfortunately, it is not that simple. Vroom points out that "explanations of motivated behavior require at least two sets of variables—preferences among outcomes and expected relations between actions and outcomes." [15]

In terms of preferences, reward systems are based on the assumption that executives prefer money, status, and power to other possible rewards. These in turn are linked to actions that increase profitable productivity. Certainly, no business organization can simply substitute its profitable productivity goal for an increased innovation goal. To further complicate matters, not all members of the organization prefer money, status, and power to other incentives such as feelings of personal growth, independence, and meaningful work. This means that motivational strategies to increase innovative output must answer two basic questions: (1) What is an appropriate balance between profitable productivity goals and innovation goals? (2) How can incentive systems be administered to recognize individual differences in reward preferences?

The first question depends to a very large degree upon the competitive environment in which the organization finds itself. Some companies will find that imitation is more appropriate than innovation.[16] Others will be forced to innovate by highly innovative competitors. While this question can be answered only by the top management of any particular company, it is one which should be formally asked and thoughtfully discussed.

Once there is reasonable agreement on the degree of innovation that is needed or can be tolerated by the organization as a whole, the next step is to relate this to specific departments. The balance between the profitable productivity goal and the increased innovation goal would not and should not be the same for a research and development department as for a production department. Yet, many organizations assume the same goal mix. This is seldom done by formal proclamation, but it is understood by both groups. Again, there is a definite need for business organizations to decide within some broad limit the proper combination of goals for each department. This in turn must be communicated to the members of those departments not only in words but by the appropriate administration of the reward system.

---

[15] *Motivation in Management*, p. 13.
[16] Theodore Levitt, "Innovative Imitation," *Harvard Business Review* (September-October, 1966), pp. 63-70.

Finally, there is the question of individual differences in reward preferences. For once the goal mix is decided, it is not simply a matter of linking rewards to goals, since not all members of the organization will respond to the same rewards. While many business executives are motivated primarily by incentives that stress money, status, and power, the more creative members of the organization are probably more interested in feelings of personal growth, independence, and meaningful work. Rewarding innovative behavior of such people only with money, status, and power is likely to produce diluted results. What, then, are some ways that differential rewards can be administered to take this into account?

Personal growth needs of creative individuals can be satisfied in a variety of ways. Examples are visits to other organizations, attendance of professional meetings, and periodic "sabbaticals." There are also a number of ways in which organizations can appeal to the relatively greater need for freedom and independence among their more creative members. Take the matter of hours of work and physical location of the work place—innovation is not limited to conventional working hours or to a specific physical location. As a matter of fact, most business locations were designed for profitable productivity goals, and many of the physical arrangements actually inhibit creativity. Stereotyped offices, constant phone calls, and visitor interruptions are hardly conducive to innovation, which is often a solitary process.

In one organization with which I am familiar, a highly creative writer and editor is allowed to do much of his work away from the office and at his own pace. One of his most recent achievements was a company publication that won nationwide recognition. Much of the work was not conceived or produced in the corporate headquarters building, but at a small cottage on the seashore. Approaches of this type certainly seem to be more in harmony with what we know about innovation and innovative people than attempting to cast every member of an organization into the same mold just because it is easier to justify from an administrative point of view.

The need for creative leaders is being emphasized by our rapid movement from a mechanical to an electronic technology. Computers have done far more than give us an amazingly fast and accurate tool for analyzing, processing, and controlling the flow of information; they have created new patterns of thinking and new pressures in our society. The very existence of this powerful tool poses the question, what do we do with it now that we have it? Thus, our attention is shifted from the techniques by which we reach goals to the goals themselves. Computers also focus on the need for understanding how various subsystems link together to make the total system function more effectively. No longer can the thoughtful businessman view the goals of his employees as different from those of the organization, nor can he view the goals of his organization as separate from those of society. Instead, they are all interdependent. A breakdown in one has system-wide implications. This, then, is the context within which the innovative leader must make his contribution.

Many questions about innovation and creativity are still unanswered; any organization wishing to attract innovative leadership will find it a long and difficult road to travel. Notions about authority, commitment, and control will have to be closely scrutinized in terms of what is currently known about the creative process. None of this can be accomplished through presidential proclamation or by passing the buck.

But once there is genuine conviction that innovative leadership is something more than a fashionable frill, there are a number of specific steps that can be taken to improve the situation. In terms of staffing strategies, three key questions must be carefully pursued: Is sufficient recruiting being done in liberal arts colleges? Are recruiting policies and practices consistent with the theoretical, aesthetic, and humanitarian values of creative people? Is full use being made of innovative resources outside of the organization?

The second, more difficult step requires developing organizational strategies that will increase innovative output among the current work force. It seems logical at this point to assume that the model for the creative organization must be found in the creative individual. Just as the creative individual is more "open" to inner and outside experiences, so must be the creative organization. Excessive structure, too many rules, inbreeding, and provincialism all inhibit innovation. Accompanying this "openness" must be the willingness to take risks. For without risk taking and experimentation, there can be no change. Finally, innovation must be rewarded with appropriate incentives. These incentives must be consistent with the values of the contributor and not based on the false assumption that status, power, and prestige are equally appealing to all members of the organization.

An attempt has been made to show how many of these ideas could be translated into specific action, but their effective application in any organization will require a liberal dose of what this article is all about—innovative leadership.

Questions

1. The author states that "It is foolish to assume that businesses can ever adopt the pursuit of truth, beauty, and harmony as their primary objectives." Is this a foolish assumption? Why?
2. Under what circumstances may the alter ego, task force, and research models be used to introduce innovation into an organization?
3. What types of social changes within an organization are needed to stimulate innovation? In what ways do the changes conflict with traditional attitudes and approaches?
4. According to the author, written policies and rules tend to restrict innovation. Would you agree? Why?

33—AGENTS OF CHANGE *

R. Douglas Brynildsen and T. A. Wickes

Over the past two decades, rapid and drastic changes have taken place in society and technology. These transformations have necessitated significant changes in the nature of organizations, the demands placed on managers, and the needs and motivations of organization members. Organizations which have survived and are growing are those which have learned to cope effectively with this accelerating pace of change. Successful managers are those who have learned to understand and cope with change.

The not so successful breed has relinquished the initiative and merely reacted to change. If today's and tomorrow's managers are to truly function as agents of change—rather than reactors to change— they must fully understand the critical changes occurring and their implications for management strategies.

Of the major pressures affecting organizations today and which underlie management's challenge of change, three deserve special note: the organization's emerging role as an involved, concerned element of society; the growing complexities of today's organization; and the ongoing shifts in professional values of individuals.

The Organization and Society

Industry is becoming increasingly involved in society's larger problems because of society's growing awareness of its problems and recognition of industry's capacity—and obligation—to provide solutions. These "problems" range through environmental pollution; poverty; civil rights; religious, sex, and ethnic equality; and health and education—just to mention the main ones.

Industry's necessary involvement can be argued from two points. One says that helping solve these problems is the correct ethical and responsible course of action (this assertion, often made in the past, has not always impressed businessmen). The second says that if business and industry do not get busy and help, John Q. Public will

* From *Automation*, Vol. 17, No. 10 (October, 1970), pp. 36-40. Reprinted with permission.

313

ask for and support legislation forcing them to help (this assertion tends to impress the businessmen not receptive to other lines of reasoning). Here are some trends that can affect the role of business organizations:

- Our population is becoming more educated.
- Forecasters tell us that within 15 years two-thirds of our population living in metropolitan areas will have attended college.
- Adult education programs are experiencing rapid expansion.
- Changes in transportation systems have drastically altered life styles and affected mobility alternatives.
- Some twenty percent of our population currently move at least once a year.
- Industrial organizations are increasingly faced with a bimodal age distribution among employees. This division of young vs. old is producing two sets of management philosophies and strategies. One tends to protect the status quo—looking toward pension and vacation problems—while the other strives toward change—looking toward higher immediate pay and greater use of skills. These are only samples and are not, of course, based on mutually exclusive philosophies.

Such trends as these affecting the role of business organizations in society make it clear that managers will need a broader perspective and will need to see themselves as responsible human beings functioning within an industry which, in turn, draws its fundamental support from a particular society.

Organization Complexities

Diversification will continue to pervade organization life. Large scale, complex organizations will tend to replace smaller scale enterprises. Tasks will become more technical, complicated, automated, and shorter lived. There is evidence to suggest that the rate of technological innovation can cause scientists' and engineers' knowledge to be obsolete in 10 years if further education is not pursued.

The increased complexities and technological changes will create continued inefficiencies in the traditional bureaucratic organization. Temporary and short-term projects will become the order of the day. Individuals from various specialties will be brought together from different parts of the organization to accomplish tasks and then be dispersed. The traditional mode of operation will become less and less able to quickly pull together the necessary resources to get a job done.

Shifts in Value

One of the most significant and fast moving changes facing organizations is the shift in individual values. Many of the traditional values and ideals seem threatened. Commitment will be more in terms of the task, job, or profession rather than loyalty to a company. New criterion beyond pay and job content are beginning to determine job choice. Examples are the kind of business (defense vs. nondefense), management philosophy (autocratic-participation), experimental outlook, physical location, and many others.

Perhaps even more notable is the high premium being placed on autonomy. Individuals want to have more and more impact on their work and environment—to control it, not to be controlled by it. Acceptance of the status quo is being replaced by comparing oneself or the organization to its potential. The result is a kind of giant dissatisfaction with what is versus what could be.

These shifts in values affect the philosophies and assumptions under which organizations operate, their styles of management, policies and procedures, boss-subordinate relationships, employment and compensation practices, and even the kinds of business that organizations decide to enter.

Implications for Management

The increased interdependence of organizations and their relation to society require a broader knowledge base in the behavioral, social, and political sciences. Managers need to become more knowledgeable about community affairs, government trends and contracts, world affairs, international practices and procedures, the changing nature of individual needs, and group motivations.

Further, keeping up with technological developments in fields related to one's specific specialties is becoming more critical. Knowledge and understanding of the computer and its applications, new integrative planning systems, business systems, changing accounting and control systems, and marketing innovations are fast becoming relevant to general management personnel. Gaining knowledge in these areas will assist managers to realize what they don't know and what is critical that they should know more about. Equally important is openness and receptivity to new ideas and a willingness to learn about and experiment with new processes and operations.

Managers should also understand that the nature of power is changing. Regimentation, competition, sometimes coercion, and simple reward-punishment systems were hallmarks of earlier managerial styles. They were based in large measure upon the fact that men and women, through their own thinking processes or through environmental reality, could not move from one location to another. Even after the depression faded and jobs were easier to come by, people remained in their own psychological isolation cells. They feared losing their jobs or risking their livelihood by moving from one plant to another in the same town where the "bosses all talk to one another." Nothing less than a natural catastrophe could drive them out.

Not so today. Younger people are mobile. Their skills—from master mechanic to astronautic engineer—are salable all over the nation. They want to work—but where work is not all humorless attention to detail. They want to use all of their skills and they will leave, easily and continuously, until they find a place where they are satisfied. Thus, the new managers need to behave differently. Collaborative and more democratic styles are replacing coercive and bureaucratic tactics. Managers are trying to be more participative, work toward consensus, and gain personal commitment to tasks.

To gain this commitment, more time and energy are being spent on developing ways for individuals to satisfy their needs through accomplishing organization tasks. Managers are learning about their own personal styles and how a style affects others. They are becoming more flexible and individualistic in their interactions with others.

More participative forms of managing are too often thought of as "soft" management. In fact, however, such a management strategy requires a high task orientation wherein conflict is worked through and not evaded. Confronting conflict, being open to alternative ways to solve problems, and high task orientation require significant trust and openness in interpersonal and intergroup relationships. Managers need to be more open with themselves and with others. Openness refers to being open to influence from others as well as expressing more of their feelings, thoughts, and reactions to others. The task is to create an environment which prizes and nourishes the ideas of all people, encourages attentive listening, and rewards personal involvement and commitment to the work being done.

Multiple Managerial Roles

Increasingly, organization complexities and interdependence—combined with scarce human resources—are forcing managers to assume multiple roles. Often, a manager must be a member of several groups accomplishing different kinds of tasks. Assumptions about working with one work unit for one boss are becoming untenable.

Many organizations are moving toward structures involving multiple managerial roles, not only to facilitate resource allocation but to speed effective problem-solving. The matrix organization and program management are perhaps the most typical. Many people in matrix organizations will have multiple bosses and be involved with several major tasks at a given time.

An individual may be a leader in one group, a working member in another, and a consultant in another. In the same day he may be designing in one group, coordinating in another, and recording in a third. Functioning in multiple roles necessitates flexibility in behavior. The need is to adapt quickly to changing situations and behave in ways appropriate to the task at hand—not remain rigid and fixed.

Under these conditions, problem-solving and decision-making processes are more pressured and less certain than ever before. The range of available alternatives for solving problems is greater than ever. Short vs. long-range trade-offs are now more difficult to evaluate. More intangibles and organization interdependencies need to be considered. Shorter turnaround time and precise planning are vital. While managers are better trained and more informed than ever before, they are required to work and make decisions in environments which are more ambiguous.

Organizations will need to reinforce changes in management thinking and behavior by developing suitable formal and informal rewards. The compensation system (including more than just monetary rewards) must reflect the new values of the organization. For example, many organizations now reward broadly for accomplishing results and punish narrowly for visible mistakes. In the future, organizations will have to reward for preventing mistakes as well as for broadly accomplishing results.

Today, some organizations talk about the need to be responsive, have integrated planning, modern management thinking and behavior, etc.—yet reward only for short-term profit and loss. One example can be seen in the "monthly top management" meetings where financial results alone are discussed with little mention of manpower problems, facilities planning, training, and R & D innovations. In other words, only short-term progress to financial forecast is seen as truly relevant. While such a process has value, the lack of additional kinds of meetings focuses the reward system only on monthly profit and loss on investment. Thus, the total reward system, including monetary compensatory practices, needs to be analyzed for consistency with its values or change directions.

Suggestions for Managing Change

Creating the kinds of managerial, attitudinal, and behavioral changes which have been described is a long-term process. About five years of planned change activities are required to develop an organization climate really conducive for growth. This change process involves *unfreezing* (casting doubt at existing modes of operation), *changing* (trying new behaviors or modes of operation), and *refreezing* (reinforcing the new, more desirable changes). Moving through this process is difficult.

All human systems interact in ways which make them hard to change—let alone change rapidly. However, following are some suggestions for managing change and creating healthy organizations. Some of the suggestions require involvement of top managers, others require the involvement of several managers from different professions, while still others require changes in some specialty areas such as training and development.

Employ professional assistance

To manage change, organizations should consider employing people who are trained in this area. Typically, these individuals are known as "organization development" or "organization improvement" specialists. Though this professional resource is limited, full-time as well as part-time consulting help can be acquired.

Consultants can be useful in such areas as organization diagnosis, developing training and education programs, planning change strategy, developing more effective interpersonal and intergroup working relationships, and working with units where internal personnel have a difficult time gaining acceptance. In this way, managers can be agents of planned change. Systematic planned change can help create more flexible organization forms (such as matrix organizations), more effective ways of achieving organization objectives, and the kind of organization climate which facilitates growth and increased productivity.

Be consistent in compensation

Compensation, in its broadest sense, is a fundamental aspect of change. To be really effective, compensation systems should be analyzed periodically in terms of policy, philosophy, and application. Some compensation areas regularly need change. For example, fringe benefit programs need to provide more alternatives and better links to old, young, women, minority group members, rural, and secondary wage earners. All have somewhat different needs. As another example, the requirement for more group work and the need to continue to encourage individual contributions should be reinforced by special awards programs.

Programs need to be developed which recognize collaborative group task accomplishments as well as outstanding individual performances. Also, special compensation programs need to be pushed further down in the organization structure. Most organizations tend to reward the top and bottom levels but spend minimal energy in the middle. It is this large middle-lower management grouping that should be considered for additional kinds of compensation—whether it be stock options, annual awards, or nonfinancial rewards.

Managers need to view compensation in a broader perspective. Activities such as sabbaticals, more flexibility in ways to provide salary increases, special individualized R & D allocations, more freedom to work on personal projects which may have only an indirect relation to current product lines, and for some, perhaps, special working hours, etc. All need to be explored for their relevance to individual managers and specialists.

Various organizations have little differentiation in merit increases. They rely on market surveys and budgets and not on results, winding up with a standard or average year increase. Managers need to become more discriminate in rewarding results and not be so polarized by the averages. This implies that the annual performance appraisal/salary reviews should be discarded and replaced by more frequent discussions geared to performance. Salary discussions would then, whenever they did occur, take very little time, and the basis for any action would be clearly understood by both man and manager.

Set goals

Goal-setting, or management by objectives, is a management tool which has received mixed reactions from industry for years. Many of the reasons for its failure are well known. However, using this tool for integrated planning, channeling of energies, and evaluation of performance based on results is both viable and useful. While it requires skillful application and an open and trusting climate, there is evidence that it can work and work well. And, even though desirable, it does not have to start at the top of the organization. Any manager, at any level, can initiate his goal-setting as a way to help manage his work units.

Develop data

Using vertical or horizontal or perhaps random sampling techniques, managers should gather data on their organizations. Data can be in terms of general problems, interdepartmental problems, specific areas of concern, or whatever. Such a process enables the top of a work group to meet with the middle or bottom in small groups for direct interchange and diagnosis of data.

Train for change

Managers need to train and educate themselves in change and change techniques in the same way they need to know budgets, the dynamics of forecasts, standard hours, and cost control. Training programs and seminars need to be established which deal with interpersonal and intergroup relations, the nature of change, additional requirements on managers, the use and misuse of competition and collaboration, appraisals, understanding managerial styles, and increased impact of new technologies. Training specialists need the ability to integrate change knowledge with the problems confronting managers in their unique environments. Training, therefore, becomes relevant to the problems at hand but draws upon the latest management change tools and theory.

Utilize manpower

In support of the need for more effective internal job mobility, top management must spend a larger portion of its time on the area of manpower planning and utilization. Activities in this area include more definitive translation of business plans into manpower requirements, personnel assessment, coping with problem cases, more detailed manpower planning, appropriate action planning, integrating career plans and jobs, and sharing appraisals of subordinates.

Traditionally, the Personnel Department has dealt with these kinds of issues. This treatment often results in a nonsystematic, uncommitted, uninvolved plant management group which pays little attention to developing people. The Personnel Department then becomes the scapegoat for people problems. While this department may serve as a staff resource and facilitator, the top management group must "own" the problem of people utilization and development in the same way they "own" the sales forecast and budget.

Another area which can have significant payoff involves manpower balancing between separate organizations. Rapid changes make it difficult to effectively plan future manpower requirements. In some smaller or less sophisticated organizations, rapid change makes it hard to provide growth promoting job opportunities for employees.

In the future, separate organizations—especially within a community—may well work together on the transfer of personnel to provide more job security and growth opportunities for its people. Perhaps special contractual arrangements will need to be developed; but for the most part such a transfer technique would keep manpower planning from becoming "inbred," provide new and more challenging work assignments, expand job alternatives, and increase basic security at all levels. This area is ripe for truly creative and rewarding developments.

Create interdisciplinary task teams

Many organizations do not know how to pull together or apply the creative problem-solving ability they have within their own systems. Properly prepared interdisciplinary task teams can supply the integration of thinking and creativity necessary for quantum leaps on organization effectiveness. Pulling specialists together to accomplish a short-term task not only condenses the time necessary to get results but also provides opportunities for optimum interchange and spread of ideas.

Improve teamwork

The focus, in permanent or temporary work teams, is on the identification and solution of work group problems, particularly across

interpersonal and organization barriers. While solving real problems, natural work teams become more effective and cohesive and
learn more about working well together by diagnosing their own
mode of operation.

Facilitate job movement

Increased job mobility is a prime means for keeping men challenged. Job posting and similar activities that move in this direction
are not sufficient. Policies and mechanisms need to be established
which facilitate career movement. One of the bases on which managers need to be evaluated is how well they have developed subordinates.

Individuals need to move through jobs quite rapidly, yet stay long
enough to make a contribution and prepare for the next job. Activities
to help condense this time include frequent performance reviews,
career discussions and reviews, special meetings to review problem-
solving and decision-making strategies of individual managers, job
enrichment and redesign activities, tutoring relationships, and peer
feedback discussions. These are not entirely new to managers—yet
managers don't devote sufficient energies in these areas. As agents of
change they will have to arrange their priorities to include these
activities.

Hold intergroup meetings

When problems between work groups become acute and there is
mutual commitment to deal with them, intergroup meetings are a
highly relevant change suggestion. Departments such as Manufacturing and Quality, line and staff relations, and even relations with
customers can employ this technique.

Use a third party critic

Use of a knowledgeable and skilled third person for diagnosis and
problem resolution can be a highly advantageous way to bring about
constructive change. Third parties can provide feedback on a manager's style, function as a catalyst to improve interactions of a management team, develop more effective staff meetings, and assist in
working through difficult one-to-one problems.

Enrich jobs

Any manager can improve his work unit by collaboratively changing job content to better suit the unique skills of his subordinates or by changing the job tasks to provide more satisfaction of the needs of individuals.

Self-development

Individual contributors need to be more initiating and aggressive in developing their own development programs. Based on what an individual wants and his understanding of himself, he can develop activities to close the gap between what he desires and the present. This may mean taking special courses in unrelated fields, tutoring programs, attending human relations laboratories or AMA seminars, or even taking time off from work for a course he considers important. Hopefully, the organization will support such activities. But it may be necessary for the individual to get busy and do it, not sit around waiting for the organization to develop him.

Questions

1. What are some of the changes in the nature of the population and the experiences that people have that are likely to force organizations to become increasingly involved in the larger problems of society?
2. The authors mention that the nature of power in organizations is changing. How is it changing? What will be the nature of power in the future?
3. Why should an organization use outside organizational development specialists? Should the managers ever become involved in organizational development activities? Why?
4. It is suggested that organizations within a community work together on the transfer of personnel to provide more job security and growth opportunities for its people. Of what value would this be to the organizations, to the community?

34—ORGANIZATION CLIMATE AND THE CREATIVE INDIVIDUAL *

John F. Patrick

The development of our present civilization can be credited, in great part, to man's ability to produce new ideas through creativity. Today the need for creative people in our complex society is greater than ever before. If living standards are to continue to rise, more and more creative solutions to the diverse problems facing the world must be found.[1]

Creativity has been defined in a number of ways in the psychological literature, in business seminars, and by various authors. Because of its flexibility, it is not easily defined. Creativity has to do with the development, proposal, and implementation of new and better solutions.[2]

The intense interest in creativity in recent years has led to research concerned with the identification of creative individuals and the promotion of thought processes. However, relatively little attention has been given to the more important topic of how to establish an organizational climate which maximizes the production of creative ideas.

It is the task of management to recognize the qualities of creative minds and to establish the climate in which they are most likely to flourish. A management philosophy that stresses creativity as an organizational goal, that encourages and expects it at all levels, will increase the chances of its occurrence.

The general objectives of a creative climate are to encourage more creative thinking about organizational problems; insure that new or original ideas are never turned away without serious consideration; and provide the training, indoctrination, and encouragement necessary to assist individuals in thinking creatively about everything the organization does or may do. Building this climate will serve the needs

* From *Public Personnel Review*, Vol. 31, No. 1 (January, 1970), 31-35. Reprinted with permission.
    [1] Pierre Cros, *Imagination—Undeveloped Resource. A Critical Study of Techniques and Programs for Stimulating Creative Thinking in Business* (Cambridge: Harvard Graduate School of Business Administration, 1955), p. 1.
    [2] Gary A. Steiner, *The Creative Organization* (Chicago: The University of Chicago Press, 1965), p. 4.

of both the organization and the individual. A number of goals are suggested for management desiring to establish a climate that will encourage creativity.

Organization

An organization can be set up in such a way that creativity is either encouraged or discouraged. A manager who desires to plan his operations to facilitate creativity will have a wide span of control rather than a narrow one. In an organization where each layer of supervision has only three or four subordinates, the result may be over-management. Since each manager has so few subordinates, he is free to direct and control all aspects of his subordinates' actions. In contrast, the supervisor who has eight or ten subordinates is forced to delegate authority and responsibility to them and to leave them relatively free to make their own decisions. An arrangement of this type encourages creativity rather than the conformity that results from a narrow span of control.

Strong staff groups in an organization can make significant contributions toward the identification and solution of problems. Creativity results from the cooperation of line managers with staff groups. Since they are not burdened with the day-to-day problems imposed on line managers, staff personnel sometimes have more opportunity to develop solutions to problems. The solutions proposed by staff departments can be evaluated and modified by line managers.

Management support

In order to clarify the essential problems involved in the creation of a favorable climate in industry, *Industrial Relations News* (an affiliate of Deutsch and Shea, Inc., technical manpower consultants) surveyed 105 scientists and administrators who had either made distinguished contributions to their fields or had been active as administrators, teachers, or researchers in encouraging the creativity of others.[3]

There was nearly unanimous agreement among the experts participating in the survey that top management levels set the climate for creativity in the organization. The values and operating philosophy of

[3] Deutsch & Shea, Inc., *Company Climate and Creativity* (New York: Industrial Relations News, 1959), p. 1.

management in regard to creative research they saw either as catalysts that release or as blocks that stifle potential creativity in an organization. This is attributed to the fact that management's basic philosophy and attitudes influence the attitudes of all intermediate management levels under whom creative researchers work. In addition to favorable management attitudes, however, there must also be a responsive attitude on the part of research workers toward the positive climate created by management.

The supervisory role

In the survey conducted by *Industrial Relations News,* panelists were asked to list the attitudes and attributes of the ideal supervisor. While these are difficult to attain in practice, they can serve as a goal toward which the supervisor can strive.

The supervisor himself should be creative in order to inspire creativity through identification. He should be creative in the sense that he is free from the biases brought about by the need to conform. The ideal supervisor should have active, technical imagination, which should express itself in an ability to detect and offer creative challenge to his group.

He should have insight into the creative process. He must attempt to understand the experiments and frustrations of the creative cycle, promote the research projects, and give the proper measure of encouragement at the right time. He should understand the basic psychological characteristics of creativity, some of the blocks which discourage it, and some of the methods which can be used to release creative approaches in his employees.

The ideal supervisor should inspire and encourage. He provides encouragement and stimulation, and demonstrates interest in the scientific achievements of his group. He should be an individual who stimulates his employees to develop new imaginative approaches, who encourages innovation, and who takes an active interest in their efforts and problems.

In order to insure sustained effort on the part of his group members, the supervisor should bolster self-confidence through his supportive role. Fear of criticism or disapproval can inhibit creativity. Although his optimism should be tempered with reality, it would benefit the supervisor if he could be more optimistic than realistic during the earlier stages of the project. Since creative people are often extremely sensitive to any actual or implied criticism of their ideas, the supervisor should administer any criticism with skill and tact.

Permissive atmosphere

Another factor that greatly encourages the desire to be creative is a permissive atmosphere. Basically, a permissive atmosphere is one that is receptive to new ideas.[4] A few of the elements that assist in creating a permissive atmosphere are: freedom of expression, encouragement by superiors and colleagues, and mutual trust and respect.

The term "permissive" originated with the work of Carl Rogers in psychotherapy. He discovered that to successfully uncover and understand the psychological defenses a patient uses to solve his emotional problems, the therapist must create a warm, accepting relationship between himself and the patient. This relationship is harmed when the therapist judges the patient, laughs at him, or even offers him readymade solutions to his problems.[5]

Permissiveness in top management is demonstrated by insistence that research be represented at a relatively high organizational level. This is necessary because of the danger that ideas can be destroyed if forced to travel through too many channels of management. Another example of permissiveness on the part of top management is the willingness to share future planning with other management personnel on a timely basis. This results in a sharing of ideas at a point where suggestions from other sources can be given.

Communication

Creativity is encouraged by free and open channels of communication. Employees must feel free to use the existing channels and should be encouraged to communicate with colleagues and associations outside the organization. The publication of research findings in professional and technical publications is helpful in gaining recognition for creative individuals.

Rewards and compensation

One of the most difficult tasks in establishing formal programs to stimulate creativity is that of determining suitable rewards and incentives. There may be a genuine need for a tangible reward structure in order to motivate individuals to contribute more than merely a

---

[4] Cros, *op. cit.*, p. 12.

[5] American Management Association, *Creativity: Key to Continuing Progress* (New York: American Management Association, 1960), p. 19.

minimum effort. However, there are often complications which include the equitability of the reward, and the organization's ability to pay.

With the emphasis on monetary rewards for new suggestions, methods, and patents in the past, management has tended to overlook other ways of motivating people. If organization morale is high, for example, an effective reward system might include recognition and praise for the creative individual. It is necessary that rewards made for ideas or creativity receive wide publicity throughout the organization.

At Lincoln Electric Company, the creative contribution made by each worker is one of the basic factors in determining the amount of annual incentive bonus he earns. Lincoln evaluates each person's contribution in new ideas, new methods, and thinking. Although rewards are monetary in nature, the plan is used in connection with profit sharing, a less costly method, and provides a direct reward to the worker who has ideas that can help the company reduce costs, increase output, improve quality, or assist the company in its relations with its customers and the public.[6]

There is a growing recognition that creative accomplishment and invention are very responsive to both the tangible and intangible motivating factors in company climate. Although the incentive award or bonus system has been effective in motivating factory workers to greater productivity, it has not found widespread acceptance among scientists and engineers.[7] Historically, there has been considerable resistance in many companies to instituting a special bonus or a rewards system for creative research and inventions.

The general preference and necessity for teamwork in modern organizations complicates the task of establishing an equitable system of rewards. Any real or imaginary inequity in distributing additional compensation for ideas or inventions could easily disrupt the team. Opposition to special awards or bonuses is also based on the difficulty of deciding fairly which team member is responsible for the idea or invention. Many scientists feel that monetary considerations play only a minor role in motivating the creative individual. A truly creative person, they feel, has other more career-oriented motives that function as his prime incentives.

---

[6] Joseph G. Mason, *How to Be A More Creative Executive* (New York: McGraw-Hill Book Co., 1960), p. 33.

[7] Deutsch & Shea, Inc., *op. cit.*, p. 61.

Channels for advancement

The organization should provide formal channels for advancement and status within the area of creativity. The creative scientist should be offered a clear alternative to becoming a manager. In a number of cases, the only avenue of advancement has been a promotion to the management field, thus converting, in some cases, an excellent scientist or engineer to a poor administrator.[8] The greater monetary and status rewards available in a management position have been very attractive to the creative individual. In recent years, the senior scientist career ladder has provided a second path toward progression.

Training and development

Another tool for building a creative climate in an organization is training for creativity. Creative training is designed to teach the worker to use his own mind to develop better ways of handling standard tasks or assignments.

The employee is exposed to information that will enhance his ability to think in creative ways. A conference on methods, for example, will include background on the development of the method as well as the reasons behind it. Specialized reading material, such as booklets on idea-production methods, are provided. Outside speakers or instructors are used to conduct indoctrination sessions on principles, practices, and methods of solving problems creatively. Many organizations effectively rotate their trainees through a variety of on-the-job assignments.

A number of organizations have taken steps to stimulate creativity among their employees. Early in 1954, B. F. Goodrich organized a pilot group of twenty technical personnel, predominately engineers, to attend fourteen sessions on the subject of creative thinking.[9]

The course was primarily an educational program designed to reduce barriers to creativity and thus make it easier for the men to solve problems. The A. C. Spark Plug Division of General Motors also established a creative training program. The program began with a series of seminars conducted by Professor John Arnold of the Massachusetts Institute of Technology for a dozen members of A.C.'s top

---

[8] John W. Haefele, *Creativity and Innovation* (New York: Reinhold Publishing Corporation, 1962), p. 181.

[9] Cros, *op. cit.*, p. 20.

management.[10] After they were convinced of the value of such a program, management extended the program to the lower echelons.

In addition to a training program, some form of development program is helpful in promoting creativity. It is usually designed to assist the employee in gaining self-confidence and developing as a person. Although the employee can be channeled into a development program, there is normally less control than in a training program. He is encouraged to study organization problems and try out new ideas. Other development devices include membership in job-related organizations and participation in outside study courses. Through these media the employee is exposed to a diversity of backgrounds and other ideas, methods, and thought processes useful in solving problems on the job.

Other techniques

Other techniques useful in fostering a creative climate include flexible laboratory facilities, organization libraries for use as reference sources, and a model shop where technicians can perform some of the basic testing that is an integral part of sound research. Privacy is an important factor since creativity usually requires a withdrawal as well as a relatively extended period of concentration. The noise created by typewriters and telephones as well as interruptions can reduce the creative flow. By providing many services of a routine nature, the organization eliminates blocks to creativity, decreases interruptions, and removes things which limit opportunity for reflective thought. A list of helpful services could include stenographic support, efficient filing systems, easy procurement of materials, and contacts with universities.

Conclusion

The relative newness of the idea of stimulating creativity has led to a slow acceptance of techniques designed to provide the organizational climate required by the creative individual. One of the difficulties in gaining acceptance stems from the fact that many people fail to realize the importance of new ideas. A similar obstacle is the complacent attitude characterized by the belief that individuals are naturally creative and do not require programs to

---

[10] Cros, *op. cit.*, p. 21.

stimulate them. In addition, it is difficult to assess the dollar values of the results achieved through the use of techniques to promote creativity.

The type of program designed to stimulate creative thinking and its extent depend upon the particular organization and its objectives. Although the job of building a more creative climate is a difficult task for an organization, the rewards are impressive. The creative talents of an organization are its most valuable asset as well as the most reliable index to its future development.

Questions

1. What role does top management play in determining the extent to which members of the organization will be creative? What role should supervisors play in the process?
2. How do you account for the resistance of many companies to have a special bonus or reward system for creative research and inventions?
3. Why is it risky to reward the creative scientist with a promotion to a managerial position? What alternatives are there to this approach?

35—A RE-EXAMINATION OF SUGGESTION SYSTEM PHILOSOPHY *

James R. Bell

In a rapidly changing technological society where social values are constantly being modified we need frequently to re-examine and restate the basic assumptions or philosophy underlying our personnel management programs. We need to follow this re-examination with appropriate revisions of our personnel practices and procedures. This paper is an attempt to examine the validity of suggestion system philosophy to see how well it accords with suggestion system practice and to propose changes in both to accord with the realities and needs of the work place.

The following propositions regarding suggestion systems are those regularly encountered in the literature of personnel. They have been drawn at random from current texts on personnel management. The evaluation of them will disclose that certain familiar postulates relating to suggestion systems are either lacking in factual support or are actually contradictory to the assumptions which underline other well-established personnel practices. The conclusion recommends a single guiding postulate for suggestion systems and proposes some changes in suggestion system practices.

Proposition no. I

Employees have a vast reservoir of good ideas for improving their work and need only the encouragement of management and systematic procedures to release a flood of beneficial suggestions.

The basis for this assumption is hard to identify. Extended observation of almost any ordinary work group will reveal just the contrary. Most employees are trained to do their jobs in certain ways; they accept this training and their work methods uncritically and most of them go about their work for years on end without giving very much thought to change. Most of us like the status quo. Well-formed habits and routines are comfortable and reassuring.

* From *National Association of Suggestion Systems Quarterly*, Summer, 1965, pp. 15-20. Reprinted with permission.

332

Change is upsetting. Some contemporary research causes us to doubt that creativity is characteristic of the average American adult male. Many employees sincerely believe that management has worked out how it wants the work done and has devised the best ways for doing it.

There are additional reasons for doubting that suggestion systems will really unleash employee creativity. Because of the routine character of much of today's work in business and government, the employee's time-saving idea of today may put him out of a job tomorrow. It is unlikely that employees, in great numbers, are going to come forward enthusiastically to present ideas which may one day result in their own unemployment. Some unions resist suggestion systems for this reason.

Suggestion system statistics belie the proposition. Thirty-three suggestions per 100 employees per year is considered a good rate of submission. One hundred ninety-seven National Association of Suggestion Systems members reported for 1963 that among each 100 eligible employees 25 submitted suggestions. Adopted suggestions, the better ideas, number about one-fourth to one-third of those submitted. This means that the pool of ideas is to be found among only four or five per cent of the employees. Some large governmental merit award programs have submission rates as low as five to ten per cent which means that only one to three per cent of the employees are submitting acceptable suggestions. These data hardly support proposition No. 1 that there is a good pool of untapped worthwhile ideas among employees.

Finally, if employees have a genuine "need" for creative expression, why is it that suggestion system managers must devote so much time and money to promotion, publicity, urging, coercing, pleading to get so few good suggestions from so few employees?

Proposition no. 2

With a good suggestion system, employees will have a "sense of participation" and this is good for employee relations generally.

This proposition is one of those bits of folklore which has been responsible for the uncritical establishment of not only idea award programs, but numerous "employee relations" gimmicks. No one has determined just what constitutes a "sense of participation"; how you

determine its presence; and if it is present (which no one can establish) what contribution it may be making to the attainment of the
goals of the organization.

Brushing aside these substantial questions however, it is clear
from the statistics that so few employees submit suggestions that the
sense of participation can hardly extend widely within the work
force. A recent Air Force study revealed that 73 per cent of the
employees had never submitted a suggestion. NASS members with
a total of over one-half million employees reported for 1963 that less
than 10 per cent of the eligible employees submitted suggestions.
Only eight per cent of the eligible employees received awards for
adopted suggestions. Where and how does this sense of participation
arise and who feels it? Put directly: how, under these circumstances,
can an idea award program make a substantial contribution to the
improvement of general employee relations?

Proposition no. 3

Suggestion systems are a means of communication between employees and management. Employees will feel that they are closer
to and in a sense participating in management.

An obvious first question: who is management? In training
courses we tell first-line supervisors and middle management that
they are the foundations of the management structure: "on the
management team" is the way it goes. The foreman and supervisor
are exhorted to make the "vital shift" from worker to manager.
Job descriptions spell out in detail the managerial responsibilities.
Yet in spite of all this, suggestion systems are designed to by-pass,
and to obviate communication with this "key" level of management.
How can employees communicate with management under these
circumstances?

It is doubtful that the suggester is really communicating with
line management at any level. He is provided a channel for, in effect,
saying to a non-line management agency (award board, suggestion
monitor or whatever it may be called), "I don't trust the management
here so I'm sending my idea to you. I think you will both protect my
identity (until it has to be revealed) and see that my suggestion gets
fair consideration."

The general literature on organization communication stresses the
need and the means of maintaining two-way free communication
between employees and management, not excluding lower and middle

management. The mechanics of many suggestion systems are clearly counter to this philosophy. The consideration of employee ideas as they are forced back down the management chain from the impersonal suggestion office can hardly be claimed either to give employees a sense of participating in management or to improve employee-management communications. Discussions with many supervisors have convinced the author that the established procedures more often antagonize supervisors than improve their communication with employees. The suggestion system procedure as generally established assumes that the formalized systematic by-passing of management is better than using management channels for the discussion by employees and managers of problems of work which should be of mutual concern.

Proposition no. 4

Even though there may be serious flaws in the suggestion system philosophy as now expressed, it cannot be denied that the good suggestions, although comparatively few in number, do result in tremendous savings.

This assertion can neither be proved nor disproved. No comparative studies have been made (so far as the author can determine) which reveal how many employee suggestions were made before an idea award system was established, how much was saved thereby, and how that compares with the results after a system has been installed.

No responsible personnel man or manager would deny however that over the last 50 years a great deal of our progress in technology and in operating practices and mechanics in government and business has been due to employee ideas freely contributed without expectation of payment or other award. Did employees have no ideas before the advent of suggestion systems? And did they hold their ideas back because no pay was offered for them? Even the most ardent supporter of suggestion systems would not contend this. We will never know how much clear gain in operational savings arises from idea award plans.

Once a system is established a valid criticism is that the savings are overstated. What factors should go into estimating them? First, there should be the amount of the award; second, the costs of operating the systems; third, the full costs of investigating the idea; fourth, the full costs of experimentation and installation of the idea; and fifth, the full costs of developing the suggestion initially to the extent that it is done on time taken from the job. The first and second items are easily identified and no doubt are fully stated. The full costs of investigation are rarely charged and in many cases not at all. One company calculated that an average of two hours time was given to considering each suggestion submitted. At ten dollars per hour each submitted suggestion would cost twenty dollars to investigate. The fourth item, costs of experimentation and installation, are usually included but how fully is unknown. It may be that managerial resistance to suggestion systems and to the notion of paying for employee ideas results in these costs often being overstated. The last cost, time taken from the job by the suggester and his collaborators in developing the idea, is rarely, if ever, stated.

One other reservation regarding purported savings must be expressed. It has to do with long-run savings. Many awards are based on the first year savings. Some systems arbitrarily assume that the saving will continue undiminished for a given period of time, say five to ten years and the system is entitled therefore to claim savings of five to ten times the first year's savings. Some long-run savings can legitimately be claimed. Exactly how much could only be determined by a laborious and costly follow-up to determine how much each suggestion did in reality save. Because of the rapid changes in modern technology and procedures and considering the minor nature of most of the suggestions, there is good reason to suspect that long-run savings may be overstated. In any case there is no doubt that costs are not fully stated and that suggestion system initial savings may well be overstated.

The foregoing evaluation of suggestion system philosophy and practice does not argue for the abandonment of such systems. It does argue for a reappraisal of philosophy and practice and an attempt to bring both into conformity with the reality of modern organization life. There are inconsistencies between claims for and performance of such programs. Far too much has been assumed for too long without critical analysis simply because spectacular savings could be claimed as against awards made.

It is proposed that a single principle, namely monetary gain to the organization, be the basis for establishing employee suggestion plans: that they be viewed purely and simply as a method for buying employee ideas—for that is what they are. Drop all pretense that they "give a sense of participation," "improve communication," "stimulate employee creativity," and so on. If such by-products result, so much the better, but the system should not be founded on such unprovable and in some cases, unlikely propositions.

If the suggestion system is an organized way of buying employee ideas to improve productivity and to save money, then the whole matter of procedures can be faced up to squarely. New attitudes toward management participation and communication will emerge and the hypocrisy in the present systems can be swept away. But here, we encounter perhaps the most serious contradiction and obstacle of all—the matter of supervisory participation.

We shall have to reconcile basic conflicting ideas regarding supervisors and their functions. On the one hand we claim that a supervisor is paid to improve methods—he is among other things an innovator. That is why he cannot receive awards for suggestions affecting his own unit. On the other hand many supervisors are actually controllers, inspectors, expeditors, stabilizers if you will, guardians of the status quo. Most supervisors are neither paid to nor especially encouraged to innovate. Simple proof that the supervisor is not really viewed as an innovator is seen in the deliberate building of the suggestion system channel around him because it is believed that he fears new ideas and will suppress them. This conflict regarding supervisory attitudes and performance must be resolved before suggestion system procedures can be reconstructed within a new philosophy.

It is proposed that lower and middle managers be brought into full partnership in award plans and that they share equitably in suggestion awards applicable to their work and which originate in their units. Supervisors must be given an incentive to promote new ideas. Various schemes can be developed and different bases of compensation can be established. Perhaps supervisory awards can begin with a 15 per cent sharing at the first level and scale down to 10 and 5 per cent for the next two levels above. Fuller participation by the supervisor in idea development will result in more good suggestions, result in higher awards, and reduce the large number of poor suggestions. Supervisory payments must be over and above, not taken from, the employee's award.

The proposed procedure means that all suggestions must be initiated and perfected in the line as a part of normal work activity. They will be routed around management and back down as at present. Line management must have the last word in the matter of work improvements which are essential to the management function. What is offered is a kind of profit sharing plan based on operational savings. In larger organizations a high-level committee may be desirable to review accepted suggestions, to examine the basis for estimated savings, and to maintain reasonable uniformity of standards. With this different philosophy the suggestion system coordinator's function should change. He can become a man whose duty is to help management identify "problem areas" and to stimulate employees and supervisors to develop solutions to them.

In summary, what is proposed here is a clarification and simplification of suggestion system objectives and the creation of a simple line system for stimulating, perfecting, and installing money-saving operational improvements. It is a plan for buying the good ideas and the creativity of all employees: non-supervisors and managers alike.

Questions

1. What effects, if any, is the typical suggestion system likely to have on the supervisor's promotion of new ideas? Does the system usually provide for his participation?
2. Bell concludes that even a good suggestion system does not give employees a sense of participation. Do you agree? Why?
3. What are some of the problems encountered in estimating the financial savings that accrue from a suggestion submitted by an employee?
4. Do you believe that employees should be financially rewarded for suggestions concerning the improvement of their own job procedures? Why?
5. The author reexamines the basic assumptions of philosophy which he believes underlie the typical suggestion program. Would this be a desirable procedure to follow in other areas of personnel management? Why?

36—TODAY THE CAMPUSES, TOMORROW THE CORPORATIONS *

John S. Fielden

Top managers today are talking the way academic deans and university presidents talked ten years ago—it can't happen here. At that time, students were criticized for being apathetic; student activities were poorly attended, student governments were foundering, and student rallies were nonexistent. As we all know, things have changed, and the change took place quickly. Interviews with top executives of major companies, however, show that management feels safe from the problems of youth's upheaval: "You're crazy; it can't happen here. We in management aren't as soft as you in academic circles. We know how to deal with loud-mouthed kids!" My own feeling is that what has happened to us on the campuses is going to happen to the corporations tomorrow.

One of our interviews was with the publisher of a large number of magazines in the electronics field. About a week before the October 15 Moratorium, his secretary told him that one of the editorial assistants way down the line had requested an interview with him. All smiles, especially since she was a curvaceous young lady, he ushered her in. She informed him that she felt his publishing company should take a stand against the war in Vietnam and that the company ought to take a full-page ad in *The New York Times* letting the world know that it strongly endorsed the Moratorium and calling for an immediate withdrawal of United States troops. He looked at her and said, "Do you realize this would cost approximately $15,000 to $16,000?" Her reply was, "Oh, that's a relief. I thought it would cost $25,000!"

That argument shot down, he tried another: "How can my publishing company take a single posture that speaks for all its members?" "Oh, I've taken care of that," she replied. "I have a petition here that I've put together." Naturally, he expected to find the petition had been signed by most of the lower level clerical help,

* From *Business Horizons*, Vol. 13, No. 3 (June, 1970), pp. 13-20. Reprinted with permission.

eager for a day off. But, to his astonishment, he found that about 80 percent of his key editorial people had signed up!

Suddenly the fun went out of it. He then had to hold a mass meeting and decide on the proper posture for the company. Debate raged. Fortunately for his budget, the idea of the *Times* advertisement was scuttled. Instead, the company managed to get by with time off during the day for those who wanted to march with the demonstrators in New York City. But even so, the publisher was deeply shaken.

Is this an isolated example? No, it is not! Can the traditional hierarchical organization of big business be seriously threatened in the years to come? Most definitely. We have only to look at what is happening in the world's oldest hierarchical organization, the Roman Catholic church, which for 2,000 years has managed to make authority and rank stick. As managers, we ought to keep our eyes on what is taking place within church management. Much of modern corporate organization—indeed, our whole management concept of line-and-staff—is patterned after the Roman Catholic church's organization chart. Hence, evidence of breakdowns in the authority of church management, which are becoming more and more frequent, should be of real concern to business managers.

Opposition to the Pope's authority has become more outspoken. The liberal wing of cardinals holds that modern times require decision making not with and under the Pope but in a spirit of cooperation and coresponsibility. Large numbers of cardinals are urging a quick and broad implementation of collegiality or shared authority. And they are getting it. Early this year, the Pope hinted at the possibility of another Protestant Reformation, similar to the break 400 years ago, which could split the Christian world. For the first time he compared Catholic rebels to Protestants. The Pope, sounding much like a beleaguered university president, cried out that the present generation was on what he called an intoxicated quest for novelty. In the name of progress, he charged, the past was being forgotten, tradition disrupted, and habits abandoned:

> Innovation, innovation. Everything is being questioned, everything is in a state of crisis. Man is no longer calm. He is seized by a frenzy, a dizziness, and sometimes madness which makes him want to turn everything upside down in a blind trust that a new order, a new world, a regeneration still not clearly forseeable is about to emerge.[1]

---

[1] *The Boston Globe*, Jan. 16, 1969.

That is a perfectly accurate statement. That, as I see it, is precisely what is happening in our society, and I predict that corporations will be drawn into it too. People have become distrustful of representative government and are reluctant to delegate decisions. This thrust of self-expression has been felt in the labor unions. Recently, in the case of a large company in Boston, the union's negotiating committee recommended a wage package to its membership, only to be voted down 7 to 1. The same happened in the New York mail strike, and similar examples are occurring all over the country.

Some business leaders are amused when an academic administrator, the Pope, or a labor leader has his troubles because everybody demands a personal part in the decision-making process, but the businessmen we interviewed did not think it half so much fun when we implied that they are next on the list. But they are. Man is no longer calm. Man has lost his trust. A recent *Newsweek* survey entitled "The Troubled American" shows that 46 percent of the United States' population feels that the nation is likely to change for the worse over the next decade, and 40 percent feel that we are less able to solve our problems than we were five years ago. Higher education and greater freedom has led more people to come to the conclusion that, since they trust no one else, they have the right to participate in decisions affecting their lives.

Is this all bad? Is our society so perfect that we want to preclude protest against that which is highly mechanistic and impersonal? We must be able to make a virtue out of this demand for greater participation. We must respect the desires of all those in the Western World who reject the benefits of the computerized society, those who demand that the human element be retrieved from the mechanistic, and that the benefits of this affluent nation be made available to everyone. If we overreact, we may undermine one of the most important constructs of the democratic system: the right and obligation of everyone to express his opinions, however outrageous.[2]

The dissidents of the sixties have performed a service by questioning the values, assumptions, and institutions of American society; and they should, difficult as it may be, be respected. After all, these dissidents have not "copped out." The real danger to our children is not that they will be young and idealistic and *care*, want to stop

---

[2] Compare *The Annals of the American Academy of Political and Social Science* (March, 1969), pp. *ix-x.*

constant wars, and want to help the poor of our country and of the world. The real danger is that they will say, "The hell with it! The whole system is so fouled up, we might as well take drugs and drop out. Stop the world, I want to get off." The young people who care enough to put down their transistor radios, uncork their eyes from the TV, raise Cain about social ills, and hold whole universities hostage for war and the ills of our violence-ridden society— these are the young people who are going to build fires under corporate managers.

Business Next

Many of the top managers we interviewed rejected the possibility of challenge. Nevertheless, I see it as inescapable that American business organizations are going to be part of the world-wide breakdown of hierarchical authority that is taking place. Many managers I have talked with have wondered why university presidents and deans have not turned the hose on "loud-mouthed" demonstrators. They forget that these people are our "customers." They forget that, in the early part of this century, they too buckled under pressure when labor demanded a voice in management decisions. If they did not have the muscle to put down labor unions, which were made up of employees rather than customers, they are hardly in a position to criticize universities for reluctance to call the cops on their children. Because that is who they are—their children and mine.

Labor won its voice and its peace with management. Students are winning—and I think rightfully so—a voice in decisions affecting their academic lives. And I think that today's managers are going to experience in their lifetime a similarly greater demand for increased participation by lower managers.

It is already coming to pass. We found in our interviews that subordinates can no longer be pushed around the way they once were. Today when a valuable young man is told to pack up his family and move from Schenectady to Pasadena, then three years later back to Waltham, he objects and gets away with it. Today when a young man is told to drop whatever he is doing, say, in finance, and move to a staff job in marketing, he objects if he does not want to do it and gets away with it. In the past the argument has been, if you do not like it, quit. That argument was used against rebelling preunion workers and is used against today's rebelling student. It did not work then, and it does not work now. Valuable employees will not take it; poor ones will—and managers know it.

I think that for extremely complex reasons we are entering a period of increased corporate democracy with all that will be good and bad about it. But it will be coming. For example, I think that salary ranges will shrink, that in this corporate democracy it will be much more difficult to justify a salary for the president of a company that is infinitely greater than that received by the President of the United States. I think that we will find more meaningful boards of directors being truly responsive, not only to the wishes of the stockholders but to the needs of the employees. I think that super-remunerative stock options will disappear or at least be made available to more than just a favored few.

Corporations, if they are to survive, will be dramatically more responsive to the needs of society. Like universities, they will be forced to examine more closely their relationships with the military and with political groups. Corporate presidents will have to face head-on the question of whether their corporations can afford a social conscience and whether maximum returns to stockholders is the ultimate goal. Even now, for example, in the annual shareholders' meeting of the United Fruit Company last year, John Fox, chairman of the board, began his remarks by examining the role of business in social programs:

> All business has a tremendous stake in the solution of urban problems. Furthermore, private enterprise, in my opinion, holds the keys to the problem. Jobs must be found for the hard-core, so-called unemployables of the ghetto. By jobs I mean productive, useful, self-confidence-building jobs, not WPA shovel-leaning, soul-destroying activities.
> The corporations of this country are being called upon to use their skills in training and their ingenuity in supervision to find a way of gainfully employing a half million of these people who, ordinarily, would not qualify for employment under industry's rigid job standards.
> It will be a difficult task and an expensive one. The cost will be borne by the shareholders of our major corporations . . . I can only say that we must carry our share of this program. The price for *not* doing so is beyond calculation.

Managers of the future will have to face, just as university administrations have done, the challenge of coping with social change and a redefinition of the decision-making processes. They will have to be less the autocrats and more the politicians in the best sense. They will have to be more liberal in their thinking, not clinging blindly to socially outmoded ways of arriving at decisions and getting jobs done. I say that no generation of Babbitts today can hope to keep our nation together in moving toward decency in standards of living and equality of opportunity for all. I say that managers of the future are going to have to participate vigorously and whole-heartedly in the task of making our nation in actuality what it can be in its promise.

The new breed

Most businessmen will not reject everything that has been said. But what they do say is that they will not have any trouble in dealing with demands by lower-level employees to participate in significant decisions because their hierarchical systems are attractive only to those who like authority. SDS types will not apply; those who do apply will be organizational types who will be quite comfortable within the system because it has defined limits, because it has rules, because it is law and order and rationality personified.

But there are some flaws in this argument. First, it is true, according to Daniel Yankelovich who has done some first-rate research in this area, that radical students make up only about 3 percent of our college population.[3] And probably at any time in our history we would find 3 percent of our population wildly radical in one direction or another. But the important thing Yankelovich's research indicates is that 41 percent of the current academic population falls into what he called the forerunner group. This group, he feels, points out the future direction for our society. They are young men and women who come mainly from affluent middle-class families, the first depression-free generation.

Unlike past generations, they do not seek the traditional benefits of a college education—earning more money, having a better career, and enjoying a higher status in society. All this they take for granted and minimize. Rather, they are searching for something far more intangible—they want to change society, rather than make out well within the existing system. They believe in draft resistance and civil disobedience. They are against the Vietnam war, against the military, against the police, against restrictions on marijuana, against conventional sex morality, and against other forms of

---

[3] Daniel Yankelovich, "Karl Marx vs American Business: Round 2," *Bell Telephone Magazine* (September-October, 1969).

restraints. They believe that something fundamental is wrong with American society, and they enthusiastically support radical reform of our most cherished institutions.

The campus radicals are not traditional Marxists; many of them are truly anti-intellectual and pick up their notions second-hand. But they get Marxist theory, filtered down through pamphlets, articles, and speeches. Thus, as Yankelovich points out, the New Left has absorbed, as if by osmosis, a number of premises with a Marxian flavor. First of all, the New Left believes that economic motives dominate other people and institutions, but not themselves; the New Left underscores the importance of power and views society in terms of social class. It believes that our society concentrates its power and resources in profit-making institutions, and thus feels that large-scale social and economic inequities are inevitable in a capitalistic society, so much so that the average person is doomed to exploitation by the capitalistic system.

At this point, most managers will be hoping that Yankelovich is right, that only 44 percent of the college population is threatened with indoctrination in beliefs such as these. Such a hope is dimmed by another statistic from the same source: college students are not alone in their conviction that business is overly concerned with profits and not sufficiently concerned with public responsibilities. Ninety-four percent of all college students endorse this view strongly or partially, but so do 92 percent of the noncollege youths. Furthermore, 79 percent of the parents of college students and 84 percent of the parents of noncollege youths also believe that business is overly concerned with profits. In other words, the view that business is excessively profit-minded is spread throughout our society—and perhaps may even include businessmen.

If it is true that most Americans want decreased emphasis on profits and increased emphasis on social responsibility, then companies may not easily hire, as they claim, employees who readily accept the values and hierarchical organization of business. Admittedly, one is unable to prove that young people hired into management, even though more socially minded than their elders, will chafe at serving under them in the corporate hierarchies. It seems obvious, however, that this clash of values will be disruptive of the ongoing activities of the corporation—at least that is what has happened so far in the church and on the campuses.

Is it so bad?

But why is the possibility of such challenging of values and authority by youth so bad? Does business really want to hire young people who are dependent personalities, who enjoy working within rigid, seniority-ridden, arbitrary, and hierarchical structures? Does business really want young people who do not question, who do not probe the system, who do not think up new ways of doing things? I do not think so. In the past, too many people like this have worked to the detriment of business, especially if they were in managerial positions. Government has no monopoly on bureaucrats. Top executives are always complaining about their company's need for managers with entrepreneurial drive. Without entrepreneurs the game will be over.

One of Harvard's great economists, Joseph Schumpeter, predicted that the fall of big-business oriented capitalism would come not from the challenge of any other ideology but from the death of the entrepreneurial spirit.[4] Entrepreneurs are rebels, in a sense, against bureaucracy, bigness, and hierarchical structures. A viable free enterprise system needs challenges, and these challenges have usually come from youth.

Recently, many emotional accolades have been paid to our successful moon shot. Original plans, however, called for a direct flight to the moon. One man about five steps down in the hierarchical structure of NASA felt that a different plan was essential. This was to go into moon orbit and launch a ship from that position. To make his opinion heard, he went around to superiors and spoke to the head of the program. In many large companies, stubbornness of this kind is simply not tolerated, and the pride of senior executives can lead to the failure of the company or cause good people to leave. Some corporations would have fired an employee for such an action.

Many young people are becoming more aware of the fact that few innovations in business come from the senior people. For example, the modern supermarket as we know it was not developed by an established chain such as A&P or First National; A&P, in fact, has had a hard time maintaining its position. The modern supermarket has evolved through the efforts of small independents and younger men. The big, old organizations resisted this movement for years and

---

[4] Joseph Schumpeter, *Capitalism, Socialism, and Democracy* (New York: Harper & Row, Publishers, 1942).

were almost forced out of business because of their stubbornness. Similarly, the discount stores were developed by independents— Korvettes, Masters, and the rest—not by the established stores like Macy's, Gimbel's, or Filene's. In every case, young men were instrumental in beginning these ventures and in making them successful. Older organizations were threatened, were forced to change their practices, and to go along with the new trends.

The facts of life, the facts of business, and the facts of organizations are being taught at business schools today. Students are learning that major innovations are being made by young businessmen. They also learn that recognized institutions with senior executives often turn down exciting new ideas. For example, when Edwin Land was a sophomore at Harvard he went to Eastman Kodak with his now famous Polaroid camera. Kodak refused him on the grounds that, through their experience, the public would not be interested in such low-quality pictures. As every business school student knows, Land went out, started his own company, and became fabulously successful.

Another promising young man with a brilliant new idea was turned down by a large corporation. Joseph Wilson, believing in the Xerox technique as a new copying procedure, could not find anyone to support him. No established company would pick up his idea, so he developed it on his own and created a dazzlingly successful company without the financial backing of any large, reputable established organization. Another example is the development of the Cassette, a relatively new arrival on the corporate market. Companies such as RCA and CBS refused to touch the idea. As a result, it finally came out of a smaller, independent company in Europe and had to be exported to the United States.

Older people, if progressive, may go so far as to say to a young person with a new idea that, if the market research can support it, they will go along. Young people know, however, that one cannot market research a new idea. For example, who would have bought a Polaroid camera ten years ago before anyone knew anything about it? People cannot imagine new things.

To get ahead in business today certain qualities are required: courage and willingness to take a risk. But these are not qualities of the typical senior business executive. The outstanding business successes of the past few years have all been men who started their own organizations at a relatively early age and who have acted in ways the Establishment considers unconventional and unacceptable.

Some examples are Jim Ling of Ling-Temco-Vought; Saul Steinberg of Leasco; H. Ross Perot of Electronic Data Systems Corporation of Dallas who quit as a salesman for IBM when the company wouldn't listen to his ideas, formed his own company, and now has an estimated net worth of over $300 million. In all these cases, each businessman was turned down by big corporations and well-known executives. Also worth noting is the fact that these newly formed companies have made more money and grown more phenomenally than have such corporate giants as Ford and General Motors.

Every argument has its rebuttal, of course. Cases like Land, Ling, and Steinberg and the rest still refer to people who accept the values of our capitalistic society. But many of the young people I am concerned with are rebelling against these values. And these youngsters may, indeed, be the brightest and most valuable people entering adult society today. Thus the vital question facing corporate managers is this: can you afford the risk of acquiring young people with a capacity for creative new thinking, who also carry with them the seeds of a challenge to, if not the destruction of, the traditional hierarchical structure of American business?

I think that business needs these bright, original people; and I think if they understood the potential for change within American business practices, they would want business. The situation resembles Freud's description of the two cold porcupines who wanted to huddle together for warmth. The closer they got, the more they stuck one another. This dilemma in human interrelations is going to trouble management ever more deeply in the future. What we need is to have the battle cry ring out and have everyone rush to the barricades— and, somehow, in some miraculous way, find that all of us are on the same side of the barbed wire. Making this miracle come to pass should be an important challenge to advertising executives who are used to solving problems of communication between groups of people who seemingly have nothing in common.

Research has proven that if senior executives want their employees to be innovative, creative, and responsible and to make contributions they must encourage participation in management decisions; otherwise, they only invite passive obedience and sycophancy. But if middle management allows lower management freedom, then top management must also allow middle management freedom. There is no evidence that age necessarily means better decisions, nor that more imposing titles mean better work.

We are now at the point where middle managers are managing lower managers, who know more than the middle managers. And top managers are managing people who know more than they do. This is due to the rapid advance of technology. As a result, top management people are twice removed from the young M.B.A. graduates, and the business pace is becoming more and more accelerated. Somehow these groups have to be brought together, but to do so deeply threatens seniority, which is the heart of all hierarchical organizations.

But to acquiesce to more participation in management decision making means that older executives in corporations must recognize the gap between their profit-oriented values and the ever-increasing social consciousness of our people. Senior executives must recognize the idealism of today's youth, their reluctance to simply "chase a buck." The Puritan ethic that motivated us is being rejected. When young people say that someone comes from a "good" family today, they do not necessarily mean he comes from a rich family. Our children's heroes are not Horatio Algers.

The Corporate Plan

If by this time a businessman remains convinced that it will be business as usual in the future, that the increasing social consciousness of the brightest young people today and its impact on corporations is a myth and a straw man, then he has nothing to worry about. If he thinks that even bright young M.B.A.s, whom he would have every reason to believe would be more tolerant of business values, will not increasingly chafe in the future over lack of participative opportunities, then full speed ahead. But if a businessman is willing to consider the possibility that corporations lead no charmed life in our society, if he suspects that they will be caught up in social change as much as—if not even more so—other institutions, then what should he do about it?

It seems to me that corporations are fortunate in not having to repeat the mistakes made in the past by other institutions, such as education and the church, which have borne the first brunt of questioning. First of all, top executives in corporations must, I feel, compromise on the position that their responsibility to return maximum profits to shareholders means that they must not divert significant corporate resources to the alleviation of social problems. They must recognize the fact that what is good for the nation is in the long run good for General Motors—that if our free enterprise system cannot divert resources to the have-nots of our population, the price may be constant turmoil in our streets.

Corporations must also reexamine their part in a world-wide social system that has led to constant warfare. I know of no executive who, as the SDS claims, wants warfare as a means of making profits. But we are all caught up on a mad merry-go-round offering no brass rings for mankind. If big business is truly influential in our country and throughout the world, surely we must learn how to force an outbreak of peace.

Corporations must face up to and eradicate racial and religious prejudice operative even implicitly in the organization's behavior. If we are a business-oriented society, then business must intensify its already impressive beginnings.

Corporations must learn to seek commonly shared values through greater permissiveness and participation. As M.I.T. did last year, corporations may have to call a pause in ongoing operations and allow lengthy, fully participative meetings to occur among all segments and levels of persons in the organization, to allow all to ventilate feelings relative to the corporations' posture vis-a-vis self-interest and societal responsibility. Through greater participation, more shared values must result, and even those whose ideas are not adopted should at least feel they had a free voice prior to the decision.

Corporations therefore must have flatter organization charts, and a greater sense of community and dedication to achievement of mutually accepted goals should result. It is more than possible, I think, that if a corporation decided that it must both be fair in returning adequate dividends to stockholders and in contributing corporate resources toward the cure of society's problems, then it is reasonable for all members of that corporation to be willing to make the extra effort to generate the extra profits required.

From my talks with a wide range of young, bright people considering careers in business, I have come to the conclusion that it will be companies this open, this flexible, and this responsible that will attract the best young people into tomorrow's top managerial roles. Age makes us cynical. Experience tells us that the world is gray, not black and white. But let us do the best we can for this country. By our actions, we must help America's youth recover some of the lost idealism we felt about our nation when we were young. Let us rebuild and emphasize social responsibility as *part of*—instead of *an alternative to*—the free enterprise system.

Questions

1. Why are more people questioning the authority of managers in all types of organizations? What effect will this questioning have on managers? on organizations? on society?
2. Do you believe that business organizations are overly concerned with profits? How do your opinions compare with others? How far can a business organization go in decreasing its emphasis upon profits?
3. Does the use of computers necessarily result in depersonalization and a mechanistic approach to people?
4. The author states that today's youth want to change society rather than make out well within the existing system. Assuming this statement to be true, what long-range impact could this have on business organizations?
5. What would be achieved if corporations had flatter organizational charts? Can you cite any examples of companies that have flattened their organizational structures?

CHAPTER 5

Union Relations

The right of employees to organize and to bargain collectively with employers over the conditions of their employment is not only accepted by our society but is also guaranteed by legislation. Although only approximately a quarter of this nation's work force is unionized, the influence of the portion that is organized and the labor agreements negotiated by it exert a very significant effect upon personnel management. The bargaining agreements that a union negotiates with an employer establish the pattern of employment relations and conditions for those employees who are its members. The bargaining agreements also establish the pattern for any of the company's personnel who are not unionized, if they are to be given comparable treatment. Companies that are not unionized must also provide treatment and employment conditions that are comparable to those provided for in union agreements if they are to recruit and to retain competent employees and not become the subject of a union organizing campaign.

In spite of the significant impact that unions have had upon our industrial society and upon personnel management policies and practices, they have had their share of internal problems. Unions are confronted not only with the threat of automation upon the jobs of members but also with a condition of apathy and lethargy among these members. The article by Bernard Karsh discusses this apathy and the problems which it creates for the local union and for organized labor in general. The article *The Union Challenge to Management Control* by Neil W. Chamberlain, on the other hand, points up some of the problems confronting the employer as the result of union challenges to what management once considered to be its exclusive prerogative.

The extent to which an employer is able to achieve a labor agreement under which he can manage his business effectively is dependent, among other things, upon his negotiating ability. The article by Thomas G. Downing discusses the strategy and tactics that can be used in achieving collective bargaining objectives. In administering the agreement that has been negotiated, it can be expected that some differences may arise between the employer and the union over the interpretation of certain provisions of this agreement. Those differences that cannot be resolved by the two parties generally must be settled by an arbitrator. The article *Is the Arbitrator Your Friend?* by Laurence Stessin reveals the position that the arbitrator is likely to take when called upon to hear and to rule upon union-management disputes. This article discusses some of the precautions that management can take to insure that it will have a strong case to present to the arbitrator should it be necessary to take a dispute to him for settlement.

One of the areas in which unions are experiencing the greatest success in their efforts to increase membership is in public employment. Public employees in the various branches of local, state, and federal government after having witnessed the gains achieved by union members in private employment are turning to unions for help. Goldberg's article discusses some of the legislation that has been passed to improve the bargaining rights of public employees as well as the changes that are occurring in the relationship between government employers and the unions or other organizations representing their employees.

The final article in the chapter discusses a new area in which some unions have become involved, namely, that of manpower development. As the title *Union Connects Jobs and Workers* would indicate, this article describes the experiences of one union in helping workers improve their skills and qualify themselves for employment in higher paying jobs. These experiences indicate what union-management cooperation can accomplish in coping with a very acute problem previously considered to be the responsibility of employers and/or government agencies.

37—UNION TRADITIONS AND MEMBERSHIP APATHY *

Bernard Karsh

The author is with the Institute of Labor and Industrial Relations, University of Illinois. He is grateful to Joel Seidman, Jack London, and Daisy Tagliacozzo for many of the ideas presented here. An elaboration of this material is contained in *The Worker Views His Union* (University of Chicago Press, 1957), on which he worked with the above.

The assertion that membership apathy is one of the determinants of the local union's power potential needs no documentation here. The ability of the local to achieve its formal objectives, it is said, is bound up with the support which the local's formal leadership receives from the membership. A measuring rod, often used by management and other students of industrial relations to gauge membership support, is attendance at membership meetings—and the universal cry in the labor movement is that attendance is poor. Some legislators, as well as others, assert that rank-and-file apathy leads to the monopolization of power by a handful of leaders and, therefore, increases the possibility that these leaders will abuse their power grant. Corruption, racketeering, and undemocratic practices are seen to be the result, at least in part, of membership apathy.

I propose here to examine some implications of such assertions by taking a look at a few aspects of the composition of the local union, its leadership, membership, and functions. My remarks may be most applicable to the local in the manufacturing industry, particularly the large one, though I think a good case can be made for applying these comments to many building trades locals.

The word "apathy" carries a number of implications, at least as applied to understanding the operations of the local union. To describe the membership as apathetic is to assume, in the first place, that the membership is a relatively homogeneous mass with respect to their conception of the union and of unionism. It assumes that

* From the *Labor Law Journal*, Vol. 9, No. 9 (September, 1958), pp. 641-646. Copyright 1958, Commerce Clearing House, Inc. Reprinted with permission.

all members, by virtue of their status as members, have or should have an equal or relatively equal set of reasons for becoming members and, therefore, should have an equal or relatively equal obligation to take an active role in the government of the union, the formation of its policies and programs, and the successful achievement of the local's professed objectives. In short, we often assume, and certainly the typical set of local union leaders assume, that local union members have or should have an undifferentiated set of motives for membership and obligations as members, and a uniform conception of an abstract union or unionism.

Rather than being a body of relatively undifferentiated individuals, each having by virtue of his status as a member a similar conception of what the union is all about and, therefore, relatively equally motivated in his behavior toward it, membership is differentiated in a number of ways. Obvious differences occur on the basis of age, skill, occupation, seniority, sex, family background, information about and experience with unions, and similar variables. These factors get summarily combined to produce a number of fairly distinct types of members, each differentiated from the other on the basis of differing sets of values with respect to unionism.

Seven types of local union members can be distinguished: (1) a fairly insignificant number of ideological unionists who see the labor movement as a vehicle for fundamental social, political, and economic change in society; (2) a solid core of "good union men" with whom I will shortly deal at some length; (3) a small group of members who, in most respects, are like the good union men but critical of either incumbent leaders and present policies or both; (4) a large proportion of "crisis activists" who, though accepting the union, by and large see it in a personal way as an agency to be used to protect and advance self-interest; (5) a relatively few members, in most part drawn from the skilled craftsmen, who accept the union but who adopt management's point of view to criticize some of its programs and practices; (6) a substantial number of "card carriers" or totally indifferent members; (7) on the outer fringe, a few unwilling unionists who, if left to their own devices, would not join a union, and if compelled to join would get out at the first opportunity.

Each of these types, and there may be still others, are ideal constructs or models and they differ from each other in their basic conceptions of an abstract union and the meaning which this word has for them. The crisis activist, probably constituting the largest proportion, is the fellow who hardly ever comes to meetings or volunteers for picket duty or committee work. He may or may not vote in elections, but he can be counted upon to present himself to his departmental steward when he has a complaint to make or to turn up at a meeting whenever an issue arises that he feels affects him directly and immediately. He would deny that his membership in the union obligates him to the same degree as the obligation faced by the leaders whom he elected. Like the card-carrier, or indifferent type, he may have come to the union movement almost completely ignorant about it or hostile towards it. He may subsequently learn that the union performs a set of functions which are useful to him, not in his status as a *union member*, but in his status as an *employee* of the company. He is interested in the union almost exclusively because it is for him an insurance policy against the day when he may get into trouble on the job.

The union, for this type of member, is essentially a policeman— a "cop on the beat" who is there in order to "keep the boss honest." He supports the union but without any kind of emotional involvement; he pays his dues willingly but views dues in the same way he views taxes which are collected to pay the police and fire departments. He hopes that he'll never have to call the cop (and even goes out of his way to avoid contact with him except when he's in trouble) and, similarly, he hopes that he'll never have need of the fire department. Essentially, he supports both as kinds of necessary evils.

The second most numerous type found in the local union membership is the card-carrier, the worker whose union membership is a matter of almost complete indifference. He is neither prounion nor antiunion; he joins because he has to. A compulsory membership clause or the pressure of co-workers has brought him in it. He carries a union card but has no sense of duty or obligation; he is both indifferent and uninformed.

Unlike these types, which probably comprise the largest proportion of members, the good union man (usually the elected officer or steward) is devoted to the union. He understands its generalized goals in a historical perspective and accepts them fully. Ideally, he tries at all times to protect and advance the union's prestige and power. More than anybody else, he disparages those who are critical of the union or view it as an agency through which their own self-interest may be enhanced, or who are indifferent toward it. He particularly discredits fellow members who do not "assume their union responsibilities as I do." He, more than any other type, considers that all members have an equal obligation to be good union men.

He often views the crisis activist or the card-carrier as somehow disloyal. In substance, he measures all other union members by his own standards, and when they fail to qualify he denounces their irresponsibility.

The good union man is the primary link between the historical tradition and values of the union movement and the present and future generations of workers and members. If the rank-and-file member knows any of his union officers, he is most likely to know his local union leaders, particularly his steward or grievance committeeman. Whatever sympathetic understanding he may have of the union movement is most likely to come in his contact with the good union man in his department. The good union man may have learned trade union values on a picket line or at the end of a policeman's billy club, or from an employer who paid substandard wages in exchange for a continuous speed-up and abusive treatment. It is in terms of these experiences that he came to the union movement and adopted its values. However, with the submergence of the depression-born militant unionism in the economic boom of the past decade and a half, the core of good union men is increasingly becoming smaller and increasingly ceases to be the transmitter of the union's heritage.

Consider what has arisen in many places to substitute for the abusive employer or the good union man in recruiting and proselytizing the new worker, the young fellow just out of school. Presently when the young worker enters an employment office to apply for his first job (and this experience may be repeated on subsequent occasions), he is typically given a number of forms to fill out by the employment officer—the personnel man or clerk. Among these forms may be an application for employment, a social security form, workmen's compensation or other health or insurance forms, an application for membership in the union and a dues checkoff authorization card. He will probably be told that his application for union membership will take effect 30 days hence and that he must pay $5 a month to belong to a union he never heard of and, at best, cares nothing about. However, he may be told that he has to join and to pay in order to work. The personnel clerk may also give him an elaborate multicolored, very attractively designed brochure which contains a list of the many benefits he will enjoy as an employee—the insurance program for himself and his family (company paid, perhaps), a comprehensive medical program, a pension plan, a cafeteria where he can buy his meals at reasonable prices, a plan which pays him benefits supplementary to the regular state unemployment com-

pensation should he ever be laid off, paid vacations and holidays, and
so forth and so on. He is probably not told that many of these
benefits may have been the result of a long strike which the union
mounted five years ago. He may be shown the clean locker rooms
and washhouses but is probably not told that these kinds of improvements may have been the result of the constant pressure of the union.
He is merely asked, as a condition of employment, to sign an application for membership in the union and a dues checkoff card. He has
as yet no knowledge of the struggles and sacrifices which good union
men may have made to win these benefits for him.

This is quite different from an earlier time when the newly hired
was recruited to the union by a good union man. Nowadays, it is
more likely that he'll be recruited to union membership by the company, not the union. Thus, there may be an immediate identification
of the specific company as the bestower of all that is good, and of an
abstract union that requires that he pay tribute for reasons which
are not explained other than to join up and pay or look for a job
elsewhere. At least two effects may result: (1) Our young worker
gets the idea that the company is really a good outfit because of the
high wages it pays and the many fringe benefits it gives and (2) in
order to enjoy the company's beneficence, he must contribute to a
union whose history, program, structure and function is vague, unde-
fined and provides him with no specific guides for action. He may
also get the notion that there is really no distinction between the
union and the company anyway, since it was in fact an agent of the
company that recruited him to the union.

The good union man in his department, as the principal link in
the transmission of the union's values and accomplishments, is almost
the only source of information that the new recruit has to establish
the connection between the company's benefits and the payment of
dues. However, our young worker's opportunity to interact with the
good union man is infrequent and often ephemeral. It may only
come when the new worker gets into trouble on the job. Since the
cash nexus has already been established, he demands that the steward
—the good union man—come through with a payoff for dues collected. If the steward is unable to get him out of trouble, the new
worker's identification with the union is even more tenuous than
before. He pays his dues for nothing, he may feel. If the new recruit
feels sufficiently disturbed, he may attend the next membership
meeting only to be confronted with a bewildering display of what
appears as endless wrangling, parliamentary confusion, long and

irrelevant reports and communications, and maybe even a heated debate between factional opponents about an issue which he doesn't understand and is even less interested. An initial indifference or apathy may be re-enforced.

Good union men are among the first to hold that members should play more active roles in policy formation and execution, and that this would make the union somehow more effective. Attendance at meetings is the crucial test. "He has as much of a duty to attend meetings and keep informed as I do," the local leader is apt to assert. "If he doesn't come to meetings, I'm not going to tell him what went on because then he'd know and he'd never come around." When the good union man is pushed to suggest some number of members which is required to have a good meeting, his estimate is apt to vary anywhere from 20 per cent, rather than the present 3 or 5 per cent, to 40 or 50 or 60 per cent. When he's asked to explain why 30 per cent of the members, for example, is needed to have a good meeting (rather than some other figure), he runs into a wall. There seems not to be any logical reasons. "It just seems good," he may say.

The problem of local union power does not turn on the number of people at a meeting but on *whom* they are. There is no magic in playing this "numbers game." The traditional value of participation is achieved if the *interests* of *all* of the members are represented. By and large this is what actually occurs.

The typical membership meeting is attended regularly by the elected officers, stewards, executive board members and committee chairmen. In the ordinary case, particularly when the local is composed of a heterogenous membership, many of the diverse membership interests are represented among the officers. Where local union elections are conducted on the basis of slates of candidates, the slate-makers are very likely to deliberately select candidates as representatives of particular interest groups. The political process in a local union is essentially no different in this respect from what occurs on our larger political scene. Thus, the solid core of routine meeting-goers is typically composed of the representatives of special interests inside the shop. Additional meeting-goers are typically drawn from the personal following of the elected leaders, a small number of workers who come to the meeting to plead special causes, and an occasional chronic dissenter or curiosity seeker.

When a contract or collective bargaining item is scheduled to come before the meeting, the number present grows substantially. However, it is generally the crisis activists who now come. They do so in order to protect or advance their status as *workers*, not necessarily as union members. The point here is that the union, as an institution, has the professed goals of serving the interests of its members as union members and as employees. However, the rank-and-file member is not much interested in the professed goal of service to him in his status as a member. He is much more interested in the service he gets by virtue of his status as an employee of the company.

There is a real question as to whether the democratic ideology of the trade union movement, as expressed in its rhetoric, is compatible with its function in an age of mass unionism—of locals with many hundreds of members and diverse interests. In such locals the meeting of all members is as poorly adapted to an effectively functioning decision-making body as the New England town meeting is to the needs of the modern metropolis. Once more then, several hundred persons and a large number of different interests are involved, it is no longer efficient—indeed, often impossible to transact business through mass meetings. The meetings of hundreds of people may serve other functions, like generating enthusiasm, demonstrating needs and loyalties, or transmitting information, but it is not a useful device for transacting business.

The simple fact is that a large proportion of members will not attend routine meetings because they feel no obligation to do so. The fact is that there would be no place to put them if they came, and that if a place were available the proper conduct of business would be impossible. The nature and function of the union meeting, shaped when the membership groups were small and homogeneous, need redefinition in an age of mass unionism. Indeed, it can be argued that the formal structure of government in the local union is a carry-over from an earlier time and is no longer appropriate.

One can conceive of the local union as embodying not one but two distinct governments, each performing a different function for which an appropriate structure has been built. One government, concerned with relations *within* the union, is formed to control the relationship between member and member. Its rules and regulations are provided in the constitution and bylaws. An executive board is elected to administer these rules and regulations. This government is essentially concerned with the worker in his status as a union member. The other government, concerned with relations with the employer, is symbolized by the collective bargaining agreement and the grievance procedure. Its functions are carried out by the stewards and the grievance committeemen who carry on collective bargaining. Essentially, this government seeks to establish rules and regulations for the worker in his status as an *employee*. Though the personnel executing these two functions may overlap, their roles are different. The second government, for the most part, carries on its business at the work place where the members are found, and is structured formally as a representative government and enlists the support, participation and interests of the workers to a far greater degree than does the first government.

The local of such size that its members can no longer interact as members of face-to-face groups might do well to abandon the rhetoric of the mass business meeting, based as it is on the assumption of a homogeneous membership and equal or relatively equal identification with, conception of and obligation toward the union in all matters. Rank-and-file control and, accordingly, leadership responsibility to an electorate can better be achieved if workers meet for the discussion of issues in relatively small and homogeneous units such as departments. Action on the discussed issues could be taken through a body of representatives, each of whom was chosen by and responsible to a constituency of fellow workers. Since those who attend routine meetings are usually stewards or other active members who legislate with the interests and views of the workers in their departments in mind, why not recognize this and accordingly, change the structure of the meeting. A formally constituted representative internal government, structured similarly to the formally constituted representative collective bargaining government, would not guarantee greater participation in decision-making. However, it might tend to safeguard the local against legislation enacted by a special interest group that packed the meeting or the domination by an organized minority that attended meetings regularly. It might also build into the system a formal channel of communication between the leaders and the members that is not now present except informally.

This raises the importance of keeping the membership informed of developments in the local. Often the officers insist that the meeting is designed to perform this function and that they have no further responsibility to members who fail to attend. This is another variation on the theme that members are undifferentiated and, accordingly, have equal responsibilities as members. Leaders who see the membership in their own image will usually insist that they have no further responsibility to members who do not come to meetings. Since few members do attend routine meetings, the result is usually a membership that is uninformed as well as inactive. Many devices are available to inform the rank and file—a local union paper which may be no more than a one-page mimeographed sheet, departmental meetings, locker room and lunch room informal discussions, and simply talking up the union in the shop might provide the member with an intelligent basis for re-electing or defeating officers at the next election. It may even persuade a card-carrier to become a crisis activist, on the whole a net gain. However, sometimes the good union man, in his zealous effort to safeguard the security of the union, as he sees it, is afraid to open channels of communication with his members outside the local meeting on the ground that the employer would learn too much about internal union affairs. However, the chances are that an alert management, with its many and diverse lines of communication, knows as much about what goes on inside the local as the leader does—maybe even more when his communication channels include a pipe line into the opposition group where it exists. The good union man might even be an officer in a local which elects inner and outer guards to the executive board, and he may still view the union as the semisecret body which in an earlier time required such guards to protect the business of the local from hostile eyes and ears. However, the business of the local union is now public business which operates with a grant of authority from a larger public body—a law.

When the good union man takes the position that the inactive or apathetic member can "stew in his own ignorance," he is likely to confirm the suspicion of the crisis activist or the card-carrier, however mistaken, that the local is a tightly controlled, close corporation, run by and for the "elite," the officers who have the company agents recruit him to membership, force him to pay dues to an institution he knows little about and doesn't understand, and who won't tell him when he does ask. The result, again, may be increasing indifference or increasing hostility.

The problem of communications and participation in the local's power structure and the matter of apathy all involve the following question: What kind of loyalty does the ordinary rank-and-file member have toward the union or the company? Rather than possessing loyalty to both institutions, as some writers have concluded, a large number of ordinary members, labeled apathetic, may possess dual apathy. The crisis activist or the card-carrier, not to speak of the unwilling unionist, may see the union as an agency seeking to impose a set of values upon him and the company similarly engaged.

He internalizes the original and professed goals of neither institution. A large proportion of factory employees work for the company because by doing so they are able to satisfy needs which arise outside the work place. Work is seen merely as a way to escape from the boredom of routinized, trivialized and repetitive labors. The worker who has this view, and the proportion is probably very substantial, may belong to the union because he is compelled to belong by the language of a contract whose meaning to him is obscured in complicated and legal terminology. He may belong simply because his fellow workers do and he doesn't want to be a deviate. In neither case does such a worker internalize the values of the union or the company. Each institution provides a different set of satisfactions for him; neither provides a value system with which he identifies himself or which he understands and accepts. However, he puts up with them and, hence, accepts them for reasons which are different from the values which each professes.

Studies of organization life have shown that running an organization generates problems which are not necessarily related to the professed or original goals of the organization. Indeed, the day-to-day behavior of individuals in groups becomes centered around specific problems and the achievement of immediate goals. These goals may often be different from the professed and original goals of the organization. Then, since these day-to-day activities come to consume an increasing proportion of the time and thoughts of the actors, from the point of view of actual behavior, the day-to-day activities become substituted for the intended goals. The highly abstract ideas intended to be conveyed by the notion of "unionism" simply do not specify sufficient concrete behavior to have very direct influence on the bulk of union members. The general idea of "union" may influence the action of members by setting the limits and defining the context for action, but only in a very general way. This is true not because the leaders or the ideals are evil or unintelligible, but because the ultimate ideals and the formal structures initially erected to effect the ideals are not very helpful in the constant effort of the worker to find proximate and immediate solutions to the specific problems which day-to-day factory living poses. Phillip Selznik has put it this way:

> Besides those professed goals which do not specify any concrete behavior . . . there are other professed goals which require actions which conflict with what must be done in the daily business of running an organization. In that conflict the professed goals will tend to go

down in defeat, usually through the process of being extensively ignored.[1]

How many of the newer entrants into factory employment will develop the attitudes and ideal characteristic of trade union traditions? The union movement of the future will be but a pale image of the present one, let alone of the new unionism of the middle and later 1930's, unless ways can be found to reach the large proportion of members, presently discredited as apathetic, who operate with a value system which is a departure from the intended or original values of the trade union movement. These are workers who see the union not as an abstract ideal, but through the cash nexus of the union shop, the checkoff and the payoff, that is, the satisfaction of personal and immediate shop problems. The professed ideals of trade unionism will disappear through ignorance or become transformed to make them compatible with the value system of the apathetic—or local union power will increasingly depend upon the formal structure of authority and the appointed or elected officials who exercise that authority from points of power which may be even more distant to the rank and file than the local union.

Questions

1. What bearing, if any, are differences in the members' background likely to have upon their enthusiasm or their apathy toward union administration?
2. How does the background of the typical "union activist" member differ from that of the "good union man"?
3. What are some of the reasons why many members today fail to develop any sense of loyalty toward their union?
4. What is the reason why a large portion of union members fail to attend their union meetings?
5. What effect, if any, does the support or the apathy exhibited by its members have upon the degree of democracy that exists within the union?
6. What changes in the traditional organization and administration of unions might help to reduce apathy on the part of their members?

---

[1] Phillip Selznik, "An Approach to a Theory of Bureaucracy," *American Sociological Review*, 47-54 (1943).

38—THE UNION CHALLENGE TO MANAGEMENT CONTROL *

Neil W. Chamberlain

One recent day at a small cement plant near Palo Alto, Calif., the boss strode up to one member of a two-man crane-operating crew. The boss asked if he'd step down off the giant machine now and then, walk a few paces to the side, and punch a button that would start or stop the conveyor belt being used to haul sand and gravel into the plant. The oiler complied.

A couple of days later, this matter came to the attention of a business agent for the International Union of Operating Engineers in San Francisco. The union speedily dispatched a representative to the scene. He instructed the oiler that henceforth he wasn't to set foot off the crane while on duty. Next morning an additional man appeared on the job to run the conveyor belt.

Incidents such as this—in which unions, rather than management, decide where workers are to work, and what they're to do—are provoking a management counterattack that's far broader than generally realized. While the battles over "featherbedding" in the steel industry, the railroad industry, and on the East coast docks have been grabbing the headlines, the fight also is being waged in a variety of other businesses, large and small across the country.[1]

The interpretation of management rights has become important as an arbitrable matter and the management rights issue is rising in prominence. In the immediate postwar days, when management rights clauses were being introduced in contracts, many observers believed these clauses to be window dressing. It seemed that acknowledged rights of management were being formally put into words, and this formalization had no value except possibly for public relations purposes.

Now it is being realized that perhaps there is greater substance in these clauses than was thought and that they do have a bearing on the interpretation of other clauses in the contract. Consequently, we may need to take a new look at what they mean. Indeed, there seems to be a feeling across the nation that rights which had once been conceded to the union are again under scrutiny, that privileges which unions thought had been won in the postwar decade are being

* From *Industrial and Labor Relations Review*, Vol. 16, No. 2 (January, 1963), pp. 184-192. Copyright © 1963 by Cornell University. All rights reserved.
[1] James R. MacDonald, "Work Rules Battles," *The Wall Street Journal*, November 4, 1959, p. 1, col. 1.

re-examined and subjected to hard bargaining. Assignment of work and subcontracting are just two of these controversial areas, areas which in their larger setting are generally referred to as disputes over managerial prerogatives and the unions' attempted invasion thereof.

What is involved here is a power struggle, a conflict of relationships which has gone on over the years, perhaps over the centuries. This phenomenon should be viewed in historical and philosophical perspective.

From this perspective what we are interested in are the points of similarity between the situation today and situations in the past. We are also interested in the ways in which today's situation may be distinguished from those involving the same kind of dispute, the same kind of argument over prerogative power relationships in previous years.

The issue of prerogatives

At the outset, it may be suggested that the issue of management prerogatives, of authority prerogatives, is as old as the master-servant relationship, and goes back a good many centuries. In fact, it might be fair to say that this issue of prerogatives is as old as the parent-child relationship. Wherever there is an authority which presumes to direct a subordinate and to determine paths of conduct and routines of behavior, and wherever this kind of authority is assumed, there will inevitably be protest from those to whom the assignment is made. There will be questioning by the subordinates of the basis for the authority, and of the reasonableness of its exercise. So let us not assume that this is an issue which somehow has suddenly been precipitated into our midst. It is one which has been experienced in human relationships in a variety of forms over hundreds and thousands of years.

This issue, too, studs the history of the union-management relationship. Every bit of progress the unions have made, every achievement they have won, has been realized in the face of charges that they were invading the prerogatives of others, that they were assuming authority which should be the proper preserve of some other group, generally a managerial one. Unions have become somewhat inured to this charge of invasion of others' prerogatives.

They were so charged when they sought to reduce the twelve-hour, indeed even the sixteen-hour, workday. They were so charged when they first attempted to have some say on so elementary a matter as wages. When they first attempted to bargain on these matters they were met by the counter-offensive that such matters were really in the hands of those who represented the workings of a systematic order, perhaps even in the hands of God. One need but remember some of the quotations which are part of the lore of labor relations from those who presumed that they were spokesmen of higher order, vessels of an authority which was greater than their own, and whose righteous position was being challenged by renegade, upstart, rebellious groups who really had no ground for such a challenge.

A typical illustration of this can be found in an editorial which appeared a little more than a hundred years ago, in the *Journal of Commerce* published in New York City.

On an occasion when the printers' union was attempting to negotiate on such matters as restriction of number of apprentices, the employment of women as compositors, child labor, and female labor (viewed as a threat to the position of the old established compositors), the editorial attacked the union in this fashion.

> Who but a miserable craven-hearted man would permit himself to be subjected to such rules, extending even to the number of apprentices he may employ, and the manner in which they shall be bound to him; to the kind of work which shall be performed in his own office, at particular hours of the day, and to the sex of the persons employed, however separated into different apartments or buildings. For ourselves we never employed a female as compositor, and have no great opinion of apprentices; but sooner than be restricted on these points, or any other, by a self-constituted tribunal outside of the office, we would go back to the employment of our boyhood and dig potatoes, pull flax, and do everything else that a plain honest farmer may properly do on his own territory. It is marvelous to us how any employer having a soul of a man within him can submit to such degradation.[2]

This is characteristic of the heights or the depths of feeling which can be stirred by such challenges to one's authority. It is interesting to note how this reference to the position of the plain honest farmer who controls his own destiny has always seemed to be an escape hatch for managements beset in this fashion. About a hundred years after the appearance of this editorial, Charles E. Wilson, then president of General Motors, was faced with a demand from his union for a union security clause. He replied: "I would not have a closed

---

[2] George A. Stevens, *New York Typographical Union No. 6*, Annual Report of the Bureau of Labor Statistics, New York State Department of Labor, 1911, Part 1, pp. 240-241.

shop. I am never going to sign one. When it gets around to that, it will make a farmer out of me." This thought of a return to the soil as a means of escaping the depredations of unions seems to have persisted over the years and has perhaps been a comforting reassurance to management that if the unions become too persistent, there is always a way out.

In certain respects the issues we are examining have continuities with the past and ties to history of which we can remind ourselves. But there are also elements of difference. One peculiarity of the present labor-management relationship is that, so far as I know, for the first time in history our society has given, not only legal sanction, but a measure of encouragement to those whose very function is to challenge a vested authority.

We realize that the very role of unions is to act as a challenge to management. Nonetheless, our society has since 1935 given legal protection to those seeking to attack the wielders of established authority in the business setting. This has been forcefully brought home to many managements in the form of NLRB decisions dealing with the duty to bargain over a large variety of issues.

We may recall the Circuit Court decision which upheld the National Labor Relations Board in its ruling with respect to the Phoenix Mutual Life Insurance Company.[3] In that case, a group of insurance salesmen had decided that the frequent turnover of the cashier in the office was a handicap to them. Consequently, they banded together in order to support the appointment of a new cashier after the latest one had left the company. They prepared a petition in which they urged the appointment of the person who was then acting as assistant cashier. This came to the attention of the office manager before the petition was formally presented, and the two ringleaders were fired.

This was an informal kind of action. No union was involved. But because it was considered concerted activity, a charge was filed with the National Labor Relations Board. The Board supported the two discharged men and ordered their reinstatement. A majority of the Circuit Court upheld the Board and said that the salesmen's interest in the appointment of the cashier was reasonably related to the conditions of their employment. This evoked a very strong dissent from one judge who said that the choice of a cashier was purely a management affair and that: "To put it bluntly, their grievance was directed

---

[3] *Phoenix Mutual Life Insurance Co.*, 73 NLRB 1463 (1947).

at a matter which was none of their business or concern." [4] He then went on to say that he supposed, under the construction given by the majority, the employees would have been protected if they had concerted regarding the naming of the company president, or directors of the company, or the general counsel of the company, or other officials who were important to the conditions of their employment. This is an interesting example of a case in which an arm of the government is protecting a group of employees who are contesting a managerial right or are at least seeking to influence a managerial prerogative of appointing company staff.

The issue has come up in numerous other ways. The appropriateness of stock options as a subject of mandatory bargaining has been upheld. The cases in which the Board has held a subject non-bargainable are surely rare.

Conflict in values

Now to examine the underlying value conflict that permeates this kind of relationship. Sometimes we feel that this attempted union invasion of management rights represents an aggressive, a novel, an intruding, a radical kind of approach—that it puts the unions in the position of urging radical institutional reforms. To some degree and in some respects one might defend that argument.

It could be said, using a sociologist's phrase, that this is an unintended consequence of purposive action. In fact, the union's actions have been motivated by a conservative point of view. The underlying rationale is one, usually, of trying to preserve a relationship rather than trying to establish a new one. The latter is sometimes present, but the former is much more prevalent.

This reminds us of the functions performed in this sort of controversy by management and union, and the conflict of values represented in their very functional roles. What I am suggesting is the conflict which is engendered by disputes over managerial prerogatives is not simply one of a right or a wrong in a particular situation, but is a conflict of values which is virtually inherent in the very functional roles which are played by the two parties.

We must remember that management in the performance of its function is necessarily an instigator of change, a responder to change. Management is operating in an economic environment within which

---

[4] *NLRB* v. *Phoenix Life Insurance Co.*, (C.A. 7th, 1948), 22 LRRM 2089 at 2095.

change is the rule. The pressures of economic competition force it to be responsive to changes that are occurring around it. Thus, for management, change is the law of life, whereas unions, on the other hand, very frequently are cast in the roles of forestallers of change. They are seeking to preserve positions involving security for their members.

In its role, management, almost of necessity, seeks to achieve certain well-focused objectives. It may be seeking to pass a competitor in total sales. It may be trying to bring a new product to the market before a rival does so. It may be trying to open up new territory, establish a new plant, or effect a merger with another company. These can be fairly large objectives, but they are almost always quite concrete in their execution.

On the other hand, unions are usually engaged in a drive for what may be termed satisfactory states of existence for their members— a morale-building relationship with supervisory foremen, the respect of others for good performance, a physical or a material situation which is comparable to that of their fellow workers or their neighbors. These are all satisfactory states of existence which they are seeking. They are not the pinpointed, well-focused objectives which management has before it.

And yet, both of these organizations must try to achieve these different objectives through the same medium; namely, the business, the firm, the corporation. Management is seeking to achieve its objectives, its pinpointed goals through the corporation. This involves change. It frequently involves a restructuring of the organization of the company in an effort to achieve what it is after. The union goals, on the other hand—the reaching and maintenance of satisfactory states of membership existence—very often require adherence to the status quo.

Even the vocabulary of the two organizations differs in ways that strikingly point up the values conflict. For example, management will regard efficiency as being a good word, a good objective, something which is conducive to the health of the organization. To the union, efficiency usually connotes some attempted means of chiseling the workers out of something which they have earned for themselves. Security becomes, in the union vocabulary, the desirable counterpart. But this very word, in reverse, usually chills management. It is not the kind of word to which management can respond.

Or take the word "ability." Again, to management this connotes a positive, affirmative quality, the kind of a criterion which should be used in the management of an organization. But to the union the term, ability, may represent the way in which management seeks to weasel some short-term employee into a position which is really due to the long-term employee. Seniority becomes, in their vocabulary, the preferable kind of attribute.

Or take the term "incentives." Again, for management this connotes something good, a driving force of which they are a necessary integral part; whereas, on the union side, incentives are usually tied up with rate busting, and undue pressures on the workers to achieve, or to produce. The responses are similar in connection with the term "scientific management," and the illustrations could be multiplied.

Hence, the vocabulary of these two groups reflects the inescapable conflict in values which is inherent in the very roles and the functions these two organizations perform.

Out of this background, and compounded by unremitting competitive pressure facing management (and size does not mean that companies can escape this competitive pressure; a General Electric or a General Motors cannot afford to rest on its oars simply because of its size) in the performance of its duties, one can understand management's view of unions as a force which interferes with management-espoused objectives. The union looms as an intruder which does not subscribe to management values and aspirations and which tends to frustrate the attainment of what management views as socially desirable ends.

In the light of this inescapable and continuous conflict between the parties, it is well to take brief note of the defense positions which each has prepared and the kind of rationale which each has mustered in defense of its attitudes.

Management and union positions

The issues have seldom been more sharply posed than in a discussion which took place some six years ago before the National Academy of Arbitrators between James Phelps of Bethlehem Steel and Arthur Goldberg, then of the Steelworkers' Union. Phelps rested his position almost exclusively on the doctrine of residual rights. The following quotation indicates the reliance which he placed on this argument.

The job of management is to manage. The operation of the enterprise at its maximum efficiency [one of the vocabulary words which is peculiar to management] is management's responsibility and obligation. If a management believes that, in order to discharge its obligations, it must retain in full measure the so-called prerogative of management, it has the right to refuse to agree in collective bargaining to restrict those rights. If the management should agree to limit its exclusive functions or even to delegate certain of its duties to a union, it can enter into an agreement that will clearly define how far it has agreed to go. To the extent the parties have not seen fit to limit management's sphere of action, management's rights are unimpaired by the contract.[5]

This is the doctrine of residual managerial rights which can only be given away by specific contract entered into in collective bargaining. Opposed to this is a philosophy which comes from a different set of values and which rests its argument primarily on the concept of consent of the worker, the basis for challenge of authority over history immemorial.

Arthur Goldberg said:

> A backlog of rights and practices and precedents does develop as the collective bargaining relationship continues, based not on pre-union history but based on the period of the collective bargaining relationship.
>
> . . . the practices which grow up during decades of a collective bargaining relationship cannot be swept aside . . . [they] inevitably represent the set of circumstances which formed the backdrop of the negotiation of the current agreement.
>
> . . . To the extent that present conditions and methods for change are not revised, they are accepted. Therefore, each party has the right to assume that changes in wages, hours, or working conditions not provided for by contract can be made only by mutual agreement or by following practices for making changes which have existed during the collective bargaining relationship or [and this is a phrase which has always puzzled me] by virtue of management's exercise of an exclusive right (such as the introduction of new products, new machines, new material, new methods of manufacture, etc.). [The rationale for the inclusion of these specific items was never very apparent.] To suggest that management can make changes at will unless the contract specifically bars it is unfair and can lead to placing so many bars in the contract as to make successful negotiation increasingly difficult and operations less and less flexible, with detailed consideration of the facts and merits of each case replaced by precise rules and regulations.[6]

---

[5] James C. Phelps, "Management's Reserved Rights: An Industry View," *Management Rights and the Arbitration Process*, Proceedings of the Ninth Annual Meeting, National Academy of Arbitrators (Washington, D.C.: Bureau of National Affairs, 1956), p. 117. The phrase in brackets is, of course, mine, not Phelps's.

[6] Arthur J. Goldberg, "Management's Reserved Rights: A Labor View," *Management Rights and the Arbitration Process*, Proceedings of the Ninth Annual Meeting, National Academy of Arbitrators (Washington, D. C.: Bureau of National Affairs, 1956), pp. 125-126. Again, the bracketed comment is mine and not Goldberg's.

My view is that both of these represent indefensible extremes. On the one hand, Mr. Phelps would seem to be relegating the union to the role of a simple supplier, a supplier of services akin to the supplier of materials and having no more stake in the continuing operation of the company. But, of course, collective bargaining itself imposes continuing obligations, including obligations to consultation. The element of mutuality applies to the relationship, and it is not simply a matter of legal contract that is involved.

On the other hand, Mr. Goldberg seems to limit management initiative, with a few exceptions that have been given no rationale, to situations in which the union has given its concurrence, which is not, in my lexicon, initiative at all but a method of converting the individual firm into a kind of legislative forum. This, it seems to me, is an indefensible attack upon that necessary functional aspect of management, the right of initiation. Somewhere there must be a middle ground between these two positions.

One of the problems confronting us is how to establish that middle ground. What kind of resolution can we bring to a conflict which is necessary, inescapable, and continuing? The conflict is one which cannot be easily or permanently resolved. But perhaps something can be done to lessen the conflict, to smooth the relationship between the parties, to reduce the areas of tension and to build up areas in which the parties can effect an adequate working relationship.

Some mitigation of this inescapable conflict has come over the years. We have made progress, in part by improved understanding on both sides, management and union. Whether this can be ascribed to the development of the human relations philosophy which has had such wide circulation, one does not know, but it probably has had something to do with it. But certainly both sides have become much more enlightened in their dealings with each other. There is growing appreciation of the idea that both the simple demands of a democratic relationship—namely, consent of those over whom authority is wielded—and the realistic pragmatic necessity of getting something done require this accommodation. Thus it is only good management to seek to secure consent of the governed who could otherwise make it impossible for management to achieve the very objective which it has set for itself. This, it seems to me, represents a forward advance, and I do not think there has been an increasing degree of enlightenment and understanding of the human relationships involved in the process.

One of the really great instruments for resolution of the difficulties which have been pointed out here is the grievance procedure. Where the parties are willing to experiment with an increasing use of this device (not more frequent use, but a wider scope for its operations, a more flexible approach to it) and where there is a willingness to experiment with ways in which grievance procedure can be used, we may have one device which can, in the future, to a greater extent even than in the past, be made an instrument for resolving on an ad hoc basis the kinds of disputes we encounter as we move along.

It should be added that in this process the terminal role of arbitration will continue to be a necessary one, even though the role of the grievance procedure may spread beyond the simple adjudication of terms of an agreement. The grievance procedure can operate at its most effective level when there is recognition on the part of all the parties to the process that what is necessary to observe is both the logic of the rule and the logic of the situation. These two are not always the same.

There is a need for somehow effecting an adequate compromise between the common rule, which applies in all situations, and the extraordinary solution which may represent deviation, a deviation which does not destroy the rule but only keeps the rule flexible enough to preserve it. This sort of experimentation involves developing a philosophy of the grievance procedure along lines which I think still lie largely ahead of us.

There is room for a more extended and deeper delving into the functioning of the grievance procedure in the union-management relationship than has been done. We need to explore, perhaps in a clinical fashion, some of the differences between grievance procedures which are on their face quite similar; the differences that exist between, for instance, the UAW-Ford relationship when Harry Shulman was umpire and that at GM when Ralph Seward was umpire. An intensive examination of the differences in these two relationships, what each was able to effect, and the difficulties that each encountered might help us in seeing more clearly in the future the ways in which this extremely important device, this invention which is one of our truly great social innovations, can be made even more fruitful in the future.

I have suggested that there are elements of similarity with the past in the conflict over managerial prerogatives as the union seeks to exercise them, and that there are also elements of dissimilarity. I have suggested that one of the important dissimilarities is that of giving legal sanction to the invasion by one group of the authority of another. I should like, finally, to focus on another dimension of this. It concerns the interplaying roles of productivity and efficiency in our economic processes and brings in several avenues of discussion and controversies ranging over a very wide economic area. Galbraith's concept of the "affluent society" is pertinent here, as is the current dispute between the railroads and the Railroad Brotherhoods over featherbedding. It is the question of the relative importance of efficiency and productivity in our economic life.

Efficiency and productivity

In recent years there has been a tendency to take the position that we are sufficiently wealthy in this country to allow us to be unconcerned about waste as it accumulates. Daniel Bell has put this into the thesis that one of the fruits of increasing productivity is the ability to be wasteful.

There is a measure of truth in this proposition. It is true that we can be less concerned about the need of exacting every last measure of human effort from our people and from ourselves because of the increasing efficiency of our productive machine. But I am somewhat fearful that the doctrine of the "affluent society" has reached the point where it is sapping some of our needed interest in efficiency and productivity.

This, for two reasons. On the domestic scene we are reaching a position where there will be an increasing confluence of views from all shades of political opinion—over the next five, ten, fifteen years, it is difficult to say just when—that the affluence about which we speak is in the private sector, but that in the public sector we are really facing a pretty shabby and run-down society. Our housing situation, our transportation situation, our educational establishment, our recreational facility are but portions of our public plant which in many respects is operating at a very low level. It is not getting any better but is, in fact, deteriorating.

I would expect as the years move by we will find, not that we feel we are living in such an affluent society, but that we must recognize and give up an increasing measure of private wealth to enable us to put back in working shape and improve our public plant. This will mean that we are going to need the fruits of a productive and efficient economy, so we cannot afford to be wasteful in this respect.

Second, moving from the domestic to the international scene, there is similarity no doubt in my mind that as the years go by we will have imposed on us as a society inescapable responsibilities to help improve the economic lot of underdeveloped countries abroad. In the same way that we now take it for granted that citizens of New York, by a progressive income tax, are helping to improve the lot, let us say, of residents of Oklahoma, or of Montana, or of other less wealthy states, the same kind of a demand will be imposed on us for overseas assistance, and we will in time learn to accept this. But it is also going to impose strains on our productive efficiency and we will find that we do not have quite the degree of affluence we once thought if we are to turn out this mountain of wealth which is going to satisfy our private wants, our public needs, and the international demands upon us. We will find that we have to produce and produce effectively to meet all these requirements. This may also mean that, to the extent our national objectives of increasing the productivity of other countries abroad is successful, we are rearing up more effective competitors for our own economy. What we are trying to do seems almost quixotic from one point of view—attempting to create a more rigorous competition for ourselves. Yet, over the long haul, this is surely the only way to accomplish our aims.

If change is the law of life in industry, and if one of the functions of unions is to try to insure that change does not do damage to the morale and material security positions of its members, then it becomes increasingly incumbent upon all of us to find more effective means of resolving the inescapable conflict. The means developed to eliminate wasteful practices from the industrial scene must be such that they do not damage those who are a necessary and integral part of that scene.

I do not think we can go on indefinitely assuming that the union position must be always accepted when it claims that practices which have been developed in the past should be left untouched in the present. There may well be instances where the extraction of a greater measure of productive efficiency will require an increasing acceleration of innovation, new processes, and new methods in the industrial scene. But this only underscores the necessity of our turning a much more critical eye to the question of how we can make such changes come about without exacting a price from those on whom the burden will rest. In this process we must try to establish ways, procedures, and new devices by which we can meet the legitimate demands, the necessary functional position, of the union when it seeks to conserve the security and the position of its membership.

Questions

1. What is the underlying basis for the conflict between the company and the union over the issue of management prerogatives? To what extent is it affected by the roles that each side must exercise?
2. What determines whether or not a particular decision is a management prerogative?
3. What effect, if any, may our frontier environment have had upon employer reaction in the last century to demands of unions for increased security and for the opportunity to exercise a greater role in decisions affecting employees?
4. What was the significance of the Phoenix Mutual Life Insurance Co. case?
5. In what ways is the conflict over management prerogatives a conflict of values and semantics?
6. To what extent do you agree or disagree with the statement by Mr. Goldberg that is quoted in this article?
7. Do you share the author's concern over the effect that the failure of our country to utilize our country's productive capacity may have upon society in the future?

39—STRATEGY AND TACTICS AT THE BARGAINING TABLE *

Thomas G. Downing

Though the overwhelming number of union contracts are settled without resort to a strike, conflict is an almost inescapable condition of the bargaining process. Every organization is committed to the pursuit of certain objectives—a statement that applies to unions no less than to the companies with which they bargain.

Sooner or later, these objectives are likely to clash. At first, the difference may not be serious enough to affect the traditional relationship between the parties; but as pressures build up, year after year, finally one side or the other decides to bring matters to a head. Instead of a routine negotiation, the company representatives are then faced with a situation in which, in order to preserve the company's favorable bargaining position, it may be necessary to go to the brink of war.

When, for whatever reason, negotiations deviate from the normal and the routine, skillful maneuvering is required of the company representatives. In fact, a high degree of bargaining skill is required of the management negotiator if the company is not to come off second best in the final settlement. Unfortunately, there are no standard texts the inexperienced negotiator can turn to for guidance when the going gets rough. Nevertheless, there are certain pitfalls he can learn to watch out for and shape his strategy accordingly. This article will endeavor to pinpoint some of the more common union tactics and suggest ways of countering them.

Logically, we might begin by considering the somewhat special case of bargaining on an initial contract. This, of course, differs somewhat from usual contract negotiations in that the parties are starting from scratch. The importance of the first contract cannot be underestimated—it is the chance to start off clean, without being weighed down by prior encumbrances. If the company is a multi-plant organization, the union will often copy many of the favorable

* From *Personnel,* Vol. 37, No. 1 (January-February, 1960), pp. 58-63. Reprinted with permission.

clauses contained in other plant contracts. Alternatively, it may put forward standard clauses taken from the contracts of competing companies. If the international union has an active and aggressive research department, this may help the local to draw up the whole contract, which will then be submitted as the union proposal.

The first session

The first bargaining meeting is a crucial one—it marks the beginning of the collective bargaining relationship and may well determine the whole trend of subsequent negotiations. Above all, it is a good opportunity to clear the air, especially if feelings have run high before the election. When, as so often happens, a fair amount of antagonism has been generated during the organization period, the conflict is likely to spill over into the initial bargaining sessions. Hence the company will be wise to indicate that, despite earlier differences, it fully accepts the fact that the union has successfully established that it represents a majority of the employees in the bargaining unit. The management negotiator should make it clear that the company genuinely wants to negotiate in good faith with the employees' duly authorized representatives. As a general rule, the employer is well advised to make every effort to create a favorable atmosphere during these first meetings. He is going to have to live with these people from now on.

Now let us turn to the more common situation where the contract is up for renewal and management has reason to believe that it is going to be confronted by various unacceptable demands. At the first meeting, the usual approach is for the company representatives to ask the union committee to read through and clarify the union proposals to make certain that there is no misunderstanding as to what the union is asking for. Some unions will submit their proposals before the first meeting, thus giving the company a chance to review and analyze the demands and compute the wage and fringe costs. Either way, in most cases, the union prefers to see some visible reaction to its demands when the parties meet.

In such circumstances, the company negotiator may decide to use the first meeting solely for the purpose of clarifying the union's proposals. Alternatively, he can start the ball rolling by asking the union to explain the reason for each specific proposal. In any event, the company representatives should make it clear early in the game that it is up to the union negotiating committee to justify its position. Merely stating that it wants, say, an improved layoff procedure, is not enough. The tactic here is not merely to put the union on the defensive, but to test the logic and sincerity of its position. Suppose, for example, that the union wants to revise the layoff procedure on a plantwide instead of a departmental seniority basis, as before. First, it can be asked, can they cite any actual instances where some injustice has occurred under the present system, or is their position a purely hypothetical one? Second, if they can point to some hardship case, is this merely an isolated example which does not warrant revising the entire layoff procedure? Third, has anybody really been injured, financially or otherwise?

It is surprising how often a union's bargaining committee will have failed to think a proposal through. Management can be sure that, if the union has taken pains to justify the soundness of its position, it will come up with most of the right answers to any questions that may be asked. Some proposals, however, originate in the fact that the union has had a membership meeting and opened the floor to any dues-paying member who wanted to put forth a demand. In such circumstances, unless the proposals are subsequently screened by the union committee, the company may be faced with "shotgun demands." It is always a problem, therefore, to distinguish what is real from what is unreal in what the union is asking for.

The general practice is to start by separating the noncost items from the cost items and to defer the latter until agreement has been reached on all or most of the former. This is good common sense—when it comes to the question of wages and fringe benefits, you do not want to have seniority problems hanging fire. Most conflict situations revolve around money in one form or another, so it is better to wash out, if possible, all the noncost items before bargaining on money begins in earnest. Of course, there are some unions that "die hard" on every single proposal and persist in wringing the sponge dry. They will never give up on any proposal until they have been convinced that it is not in the cards. The only way to counter this attitude is for the company representatives to be equally tenacious.

The noncost items

In bargaining on noncost items, ultimately the stage is reached where everything has dropped out but a few proposals on which disagreement still remains. Here, there are no hard-and-fast rules—each situation is different, and the employer must decide how to act in the light of his particular relations policy. One possibility is to trade—to concede one proposal against the union's withdrawal of another.

Though it is a truism to say that labor peace cannot be bought, it is also worth bearing in mind that negotiations are not unlike doing business in the market place—management need not be ashamed of assuming a position or attitude of flexibility. Nevertheless, while compromise or retreat is permissible, the company should avoid giving any impression of weakness. It is good strategy to put the union in the position of having to reciprocate after management has moved to its bargaining position. One must always be conscious of whose turn it is to act. It may not be fatal for management to act out of turn, but it may result in some undesirable complications.

The heart of the matter

Now we reach the nub of the problem—money. What to do when, say, the union asks for 40 cents an hour plus additional fringe benefits? To ask, as well you might, "What kind of a bargaining proposal is that?" is futile—the union expects a counterproposal from you. Suppose the company figures the settlement is worth 10 cents. Any counterproposal with a chance of ending up at 10 cents would have to start with a cut of 20 cents in present rates—but just try it! This is exactly what the union committee wants you to propose. Now they can really steam up the membership. Other companies are giving raises and this skinflint management wants to cut your wages, the rank and file will be told. So you don't want to make an offer until the union comes in with a realistic figure. You want them to drop down to a point where you can work up to your proposed figure of 10 cents. Meanwhile, the union accuses you of being unreasonable because you haven't made an offer. You are now on the horns of a dilemma, and this is where you learn that patience is indubitably a virtue.

In the early stages of negotiations, the union will probe for some indication as to whether management is likely to accept or reject the proposal under discussion. The tip-off may come in the form of summary dismissal of the demand or strenuous arguments against it. Alternatively, the management representatives may show no particular repugnance to the proposal, or simply table it. All these are signals to the union indicating where management stands without its having made any formal commitment on the issue.

As a rule, both parties will be prepared to retreat from their original stands and can be expected to move toward their final positions as the negotiations proceed. This is particularly true in the case of wage demands. The union, for example, may ask for a 14 cents an hour wage increase, while actually it would be willing to settle for 9 cents. Here, the union has a bargaining cushion of 5 cents— the difference between 14 cents and 9 cents. Management, on the other hand, while willing to agree if necessary, to 6 cents, will advise the union that no wage increase can be expected this time around; its bargaining cushion, therefore, is 6 cents, that is, the difference between zero and 6 cents. Hence, the difference between the union's real or minimum figure of 9 cents and management's real or maximum figure of 6 cents is likely to be the area of ultimate bargaining.

Industry or community wage surveys may reveal that other settlements have been in the neighborhood of 6 to 9 cents. Let us suppose then, that the union has reduced its demand to 9 cents and the company has offered 6 cents. Both parties have now reached their real positions. Where to go from here? Faced with the threat of a strike, most managements will reappraise their original position. They must ask themselves: "Should we take a strike for 3 cents?" Of course, it must be remembered that the union also must decide: "Is it worth striking for 3 cents?" The ensuing deadlock is likely to result in a compromise somewhere between 6 and 9 cents. Or the company may offer a counterproposal—another holiday, more generous vacations, or an additional severance allowance—in order to achieve a settlement. Of course, this situation is not confined to bargaining on wage items. The skill of the company negotiator may be equally put to the test on such issues as seniority, union security, pensions, work assignments, and a host of other intractable items.

If negotiations appear to have broken down, or if the company is anxious to impress the union with the finality of its position, an outside third party, either from the Federal Mediation and Conciliation Service or the State Mediation Service, can be called in. In considering such a course, the company should remember the old adage, "Always save something for the mediator." Since it is the mediator's job to prevent a strike, his assistance in ascertaining the ultimate position of both parties can be invaluable.

A device often used by unions, especially after feelings have been strained from a series of heated exchanges, is to put on an act designed to give the impression that further negotiation is fruitless. This may take the form of the union bargaining committee's dramatically exploding in an emotional outburst and walking out of the meeting. Or, if management has taken the initiative by suggesting that the meeting be broken up, with the aim of indicating the strength of its position and the futility of the union's, the union representatives may try to give the impression that the situation is more serious than management had supposed. The veiled threat of a strike may be forthcoming from the more vociferous and militant members of the union bargaining committee. To further impress management that the negotiations are headed for a breakdown, the union may even start making overt preparations for a strike. There may be visits to the local banks asking for extended credit for union members on mortgage payments in the event of a strike.

The false alarm

Within a matter of hours, word of this filters back, arousing precisely the excitement and alarm in management ranks that was intended. The company may, at this stage, reconsider its position and come back with some concession. If it does, it must at the same time make it clear that its retreat is conditional upon the union's retreating from its position also. In response to this tactic the union may move within its bargaining cushion, asserting, of course, that this really is its final stand, which in all probability it is not.

At this precarious stage, the company has to take good care that a strike does not take place as the result of a false break-off point. There should be avenues of retreat to the final bargaining position, otherwise the employer may find himself either having to take an unwanted strike or in an embarrassing position in the eyes of the union and the employees.

Eventually, the parties reach their real positions—often during the final days of negotiations, when the contract is about to expire. At this stage, all the excess proposals and counterproposals should be off the table and the real positions exposed. Any threat of a strike at this time constitutes, therefore, a serious situation, and must be regarded as such by management.

Management's choices

Here the company has three choices: (1) concede, (2) compromise, or (3) hold firm. If it decides to hold firm, it can back up its position by impressing upon the union what the strike would mean in lost wages for various periods of time and how long it will take the workers to make up the loss. Management can also appeal directly to the membership in order to swing the tide in favor of its final offer. Such an appeal usually takes the form of letters to the employees' homes, coupled with meetings by supervisors with their people, with the aim of pointing out the reasonableness of what the company is offering.

Unions are well aware of the fact that, in most companies, some limits are placed on the authority of management's representatives at the bargaining table. Naturally, they are interested in knowing just how far the company negotiators are empowered to go, and make all kinds of attempts to find out. Quite often the union will start a war of nerves aimed at breaking down the company's position and obtaining greater concessions than management had intended.

In a situation of this sort, a strike vote may be taken by the committee as a tactical weapon. The bargaining committee will request the membership to arm them with a strike vote in the event they are unable to work out a satisfactory settlement.

A number of managements have succumbed to this form of pressure. Actually, the strike vote has not been taken on the company's last offer—the union is merely using the vote to prove its economic strength. This, like many other union weapons, is in reality a union attempt to by-pass the company bargaining committee and appeal to top management. Gloomy articles in union newpapers have the same aim in view. An experienced appraisal of the situation is required here. If a company succumbs every time the union flexes its economic muscles it may find itself yielding more than its competitors. On the other hand, such tactics must be considered in the light of the actual bargaining situation.

Certainly they are not to be taken lightly—unions have learned from experience that these weapons often succeed where conversation and persuasion fail.

Questions

1. What may be the value and purpose of asking the union to explain the reason or justification for each proposal that it wants management to accept?
2. The author draws a distinction between the cost items and the noncost items in a bargaining agenda. Actually, is there such a thing as a "non-cost item" as far as management is concerned?
3. Under what handicap does management operate in making counter-proposals to union demands for wage increases?
4. What is a "false break-off point" and what problems may it involve?
5. What types of psychological pressures can a union use against management?

40—IS THE ARBITRATOR YOUR FRIEND? *

Lawrence Stessin

In the no-man's land of employee discipline, visibility is very poor. Rules and regulations are of some help—but who can design a set of rules that will provide for every contingency? Who would have dreamed, for example, of making a rule that "Any employee who shoots his wife will be subject to immediate discharge by the company?" Yet three companies that tried to dismiss employees on these grounds wished that they *had* made such a rule when the arbitrators considered these cases as matters of social impropriety rather than as violations of company rules.

Actually, it's not practical to run a company or a department by rules or formulas so rigid that they deny the supervisor his necessary elbowroom.

What about the union contract? Isn't that a useful guide to discipline? Unfortunately, it's not as useful as it might be. Both management and labor usually see fit *not* to pinpoint the discipline process in a collective-bargaining agreement. Contract references to discipline are typically sparse and vague, giving management the right to punish for "cause" or "just cause," or including the right to discipline within the framework of the "management's-rights" clause.

The manager is, then, often left without specific standards by which to gauge his actions in employee discipline. It may be worth while to see if some useful standards can be discovered from a study of arbitrators' awards in discipline cases that have come to arbitration. This article is based on such a study of arbitration awards in 900 cases involving discipline over a five-year period.

Can the arbitrator help?

In discipline cases, the role of the arbitrator is not usually limited by a tightly negotiated clause such as those covering seniority, pro-

* From *Supervisory Management*, Vol. 4, No. 8 (August, 1959), pp. 9-16. Reprinted with permission.

motions, and layoffs. Rather, he has an implied mandate to roam
freely, to indulge personal opinion and observation, and to take plenty
of "think time" (at $100 a thought—or so, at least, it seems when
the company gets the bill).

This lack of specific standards has disturbed many arbitrators.
One man said, "About all that an impartial arbitrator can do is to
decide the justice or injustice of the discharge in the light of common
sense, common knowledge of generally prevailing industry standards
for employee deportment, and common understanding." Another
noted that an arbitrator in discipline cases brings to a hearing "the
ethical teachings of his parents [and] religious advisers, the stereo-
types of his friends. His experiences and attitudes toward life, be
they hard or soft, may condition man in favor of or against tolerating
particular offenses, and may motivate him for or against mercy or
rigor." Still another commentator observed that the best he could
do was "to decide what a reasonable man would do under similar
circumstances and in that light decide whether the conduct of the disciplined employee was defensible or the disciplinary penalty just."

Is it reasonable, then, to look to the arbitrator for applicable
standards or guideposts for employee discipline? I think so. Despite
the personal nature of the arbitration award in discipline cases, the
arbitrators, sitting in collective judgment over the thousands of discipline cases that are appealed to them every year, have created a
pattern of standards, guideposts, and criteria. Although arbitrators
continue to maintain that there can never be a framework of policy
standards on discipline, a study of their awards reveals that one is,
in fact, being established. Let us consider some of these standards.

The boss is the boss

Management demands that the arbitrator acknowledge, in cases
involving refusal to obey an order, that *the boss is still the boss*. With
this principle arbitrators agree: In none of the cases analyzed in
this study has an arbitrator been "soft" on an employee who, when
told to do a task, balked or argued or questioned the employer's right
to give the order. As Harry Shulman, a pioneer arbitrator, said,
"An industrial plant is not a debating society; its object is production.
When a controversy arises, production cannot wait."

Arbitrators have, in some cases, supported employees who refused
to obey orders because they felt that their safety or health might be
endangered. But these decisions were based, not on the worker's
right to refuse an order, but on the grounds that management was

not behaving as it should. Concern for the health and safety of an employee is a management responsibility, and the manager who subjects his work force to hazardous or unhealthy conditions cannot expect immunity. However, the union view that an employee has the right to disobey an order because the boss is violating some contractual right has received short shrift from arbitrators. Thus, the right of management to issue an order and have it obeyed with dispatch is so universally accepted by arbitrators that it is, for all practical purposes, an undiluted standard of discipline.

Don't shove the foreman

The power and authority to direct the work force go hand in hand with another attribute of management: status. A worker who was fired for giving his foreman "a gentle shove," as the union called it, stayed fired after arbitration as surely as if he had hauled off and landed a haymaker. Managerial dignity and status must not be tampered with, say the arbitrators, and even employees charged with abusive language against a supervisor have received severe penalties. In 1941, Whitley McCoy laid down the principle that "no business can operate efficiently if the supervisory force is abused," and there has been no serious divergence from this view. Instances in which employees have been declared innocent in cases of assault or verbal abuse are so few that a common law may be said to exist for the support of management status by arbitrators.

The missing employee

A similar management orientation is evident in the area of absenteeism. Many hearings on employee absenteeism bring to light touching situations of sickness or family responsibilities. In the union's eyes, a worker who is forced to be away because of illness or family burdens should not be penalized. But arbitrators have consistently recognized the needs of the business as overriding, whatever the plight of the individual. As one arbitrator put it, "No matter how good the excuse for absence may be, the company is entitled to the attendance of workers. When an employee is absent so much, *even for the best of reasons*, that his services are of little or no value to the company, he cannot remain in the company's employ."

There are, of course, many reversals of management action in cases of absenteeism—but these do not indicate any shift away from the principle that management's job is, among other things, to protect the company's pocketbook. Management actions are reversed in absenteeism cases only when management has failed to practice what it preaches. Management decisions should not be based upon whim, fancy, or exasperation. Thus, when a supervisor suddenly invokes a rule against absenteeism after long neglect, such hasty action is viewed by arbitrators as behavior unbecoming to a manager. They insist that management cannot enjoy the prerogatives of authority and control without making use of the tools. Employers who have devised specific rules providing for a gradation of penalties, accompanied by appropriate warnings—and who have enforced these rules —have had no problems at arbitration.

Who's incompetent?

To judge from the record of defeats of employers in cases involving employee incompetence or negligence, it would seem that arbitrators are seriously curtailing a basic demand: the right to a fair day's work. Actually, however, arbitrators don't question the right of management to deal severely with an employee who is not carrying his weight in production or is incompetent or sloppy; what arbitrators *do* insist is that management come to a hearing on incompetence with clean hands. They have laid down some very specific standards:

(1) Before an employee can be disciplined for incompetence, the employer must show that he actually has standards of performance. Further, to sustain such a charge, the company must have adequate records which can be produced upon request at the hearing.

A case involving discharge for incompetence must be well documented because, in such cases, it's harder to convince the arbitrator.

(2) Before being fired for incompetence, the employee must have been told of his shortcomings and given an adequate opportunity to improve. He must have been warned that continued unwillingness or inability to meet the standard would result in disciplinary action.

Length of service is a mitigating force. The arbitrator asks, Why did he *suddenly* become incompetent? Why was there no earlier action?

(3) Management has the right to tighten production standards, but the employee must be given a reasonable opportunity to meet a new standard.

(4) Discipline for incompetence must follow some pattern of past practice; sudden crackdowns without warning are frowned upon as inconsistent with sound managerial practices.

(5) Management cannot demote an employee who is merely careless or negligent and expect this to be upheld at arbitration. Discipline is supposed to be a corrective measure, the arbitrator will hold, and the employee can be just as careless or negligent on the new job. If a man is careless or negligent over a period of time, he should be fired.

The high cost of walking out

Arbitrators most strongly show their managerial leanings when they render decisions involving strikes and walkouts. Arbitrators have allowed management every tool to curb and punish those who walk out in violation of their contracts, or who slow down rather than use the grievance machinery. The union usually argues that employees have walked out because management goaded them into it. "How much pressure can a man stand?" the union asks. To this plea, arbitrators have turned a deaf ear. As far as they are concerned, no matter what sins the manager commits, employees have no right to walk out during the term of the contract. They have their protective device in the grievance machinery. Whatever punishment management imposes on those who walk out, or on their leaders, has been approved in arbitration.

The union leader—shop steward or other official—has been particularly hard hit in the evolution of this standard. Arbitrators insist that these men have much more than a passive responsibility in a crisis. They must take active measures to keep their men from walking out—they must talk, threaten, cajole, and practically push the aggressive wildcatters back to their workbenches—if they want any sympathy from an arbitrator. Arbitrators do not take lightly the disruption of plant operations. They share with management the philosophy that time, properly used, is vital to the success of a business enterprise.

The long arm of management

In awards dealing with fights and altercations, arbitrators have carved out a set of criteria of considerable importance. What they have done is to extend the arm of management's control to areas outside the workplace. The old "sacred" rule that a man can do as he pleases outside the plant without fear of censure from his employer is no longer valid.

A worker who ran into his foreman at a race track and hauled off and belted him one—and shortly thereafter found himself fired—

discovered that the argument of outside privacy was of no avail. If the worker's action had been motivated by the fact that the foreman had given him a bad tip on a horse, he might have contended it was none of the company's business. But as it happened, the employee had vowed to "get" the foreman as a result of a hassle in the plant earlier that day. In that context, the employer's authority extended to the very shadow of the two-dollar window.

Arbitrators have become equally aware of the fact that a modern business enterprise is a glass house. The worker is no 8:00-to-4:00 automaton; he is a member of the community. A loose tongue used indiscriminately at a bar or other community gathering place can be punished by management if there is some evidence that such exercise of free speech might have harmed the company's reputation.

These important expansions of management rights show up with a high degree of consistency in arbitration awards.

The right to reconsider

One area, however, in which arbitrators have contributed significantly to the erosion of managerial authority is that of quits and resignations. The power of management to refuse re-employment to a worker who decided too hastily to quit his job has been considerably watered down in awards.

By managerial standards, a worker who has quit and then comes back to reclaim his job may often be denied employment because his action has disrupted the smooth flow of the enterprise. Must management rearrange its plans to take back an employee who stalked off angrily saying he would not return? Arbitrators say yes. They do not feel that the inconvenience to the company is more important than the employee's right to reconsider an action taken under emotional stress.

The greedy few

Discipline for stealing presents the arbitrator with special problems. Any attempt to discover criteria in this area is beset by special difficulties, for management will often discharge employees for violating various company rules rather than openly accusing them of theft —and arbitrators succumb to the same temptation. Thus, an employee with a record of missing funds may be let out for "carelessness." Furthermore, there are few arbitration awards on the subject because few of these situations reach the arbitration stage.

Punishment for gambling encounters some of the same difficulties. When an employee caught gambling is part of a professional ring, of course, there is little need to ponder. Pay-day poker or dice games, however, do not strike arbitrators as serious, and a minor disciplinary layoff for the first offense is about all that management is permitted. The difficulty arbitrators face is not in deciding on the severity of the penalty for gambling, but rather in reaching some satisfactory conclusion on whether the people so charged have really participated. Are workers who are standing around in the locker room allegedly watching a card game "participants" or "spectators"?

Consider the following case: Four employees were discharged after two warnings, for shooting dice. When their case came to arbitration, each man was placed on the stand. The first one claimed he had taken up a collection for coffee for the group and was on his way out to get the coffee. The second maintained that he had just arrived for the second shift and was getting ready to change his clothes. He said he never gambled—didn't even know how to shoot dice. The third vowed sanctimoniously that he never gambled, and looked upon the practice as a vice.

Finally the arbitrator came to the fourth man, who had been caught with the dice. "All these other men say they weren't gambling. But you—weren't you caught with a pair of dice in your hand?"

"Yes sir, I certainly was," was the amiable reply.

The arbitrator followed up quickly, "Then you *were* gambling, weren't you?"

The worker looked up, startled. "Gambling?" he exclaimed with indignation. "With *whom*, sir?"

What's the answer?

Is the arbitrator the manager's friend in the area of employee discipline? As long as he behaves in the image of good management, the answer appears to be yes. Arbitrators agree that the manager's basic jobs are to plan, organize, direct, and control, and this recognition is indicated in their awards in discipline cases.

Arbitrators have carved out a whole body of criteria, standards, and guideposts in employee discipline. It is now possible for the manager, through a little research, to predict closely the outcome of his disciplinary actions in the event that they are appealed.

Questions

1. What is the purpose of arbitration in the grievance procedure? What percentage of cases would you estimate reach an arbitrator?
2. It was noted that the labor-management contract usually does not cover the discipline process in detail. Are there advantages and disadvantages in this procedure to management? to the union? Discuss.
3. Do you feel that the support of management status by arbitrators is desirable? Why?
4. What should management do before discharging an employee for incompetence? Do you consider the requirements of arbitrators in this type of situation reasonable?
5. Would it be desirable and/or possible for a nonunionized company to have some type of arbitration process for grievance cases that could not be settled by the management and employees? Discuss.

41—CHANGING POLICIES IN PUBLIC EMPLOYEE LABOR RELATIONS *

Joseph P. Goldberg

Experience during the past decade has resulted in reexamination and revision of established policies in public labor-management relations and the establishment of new policies. The federal government, through its innovative Executive Order in 1962, further study of the issues, and a resultant revised Executive Order in 1969, has contributed much to this new spirit, as well as providing possible guides to policy. The agreement recently negotiated following the strike in the United States Post Office Department adds new facets to federal policy.

The huge growth in state and local government employment has made these equally important foci for public employee policies, as federal labor law specifically excludes these employees. The states have become important sources of experience as well, particularly in the variety of legislative policies and proposals among them. Although most recent state enactments have authorized collective negotiations (with attendant rights and machinery) and avoided explicit sanctions in the event of strikes, these are effective in only a minority of the states. A few have only "meet and confer" rather than negotiation statutes. Others have legislation only for specific occupational groups. The majority of states do not have statutes encouraging employee organization or providing machinery for regularizing public labor-management relationships.

The setting

The growth of public employee organizations, and increased negotiations and strikes in the public sector, have been subject to continuing and widening exploration of public employee policies at federal, state, and local levels. The spirit of such scrutiny has generally been one of accepting the rights of public employees, of providing them with a status consistent with that of private employees, and accommodating the special circumstances of public employment. The public sector's particular requirements, such as the

* From the *Monthly Labor Review*, Vol. 93, No. 7 (July, 1970), pp. 5-14.

need to continue public services, the absence of market factors permitting tests of strength through strikes and lockouts, and the traditional view of the sovereignty of the state, have served to restrain the full applicability of labor policies taken over from the private sector—but have not restrained the basic trend. Even the long-held view of government sovereignty vis-a-vis negotiations and agreements with government employees and their organizations is being reevaluated. Strikes and strike sanctions continue to be an integral subject of debate, but generally these are viewed as symptoms of conditions requiring for their resolution avenues to regularizing the rights of public employee organizations and systematizing the arrangements for making these effective in dealing with public employees. It is the widespread view that such arrangements will work toward the elimination of the instability which has produced wide strike activity.

There has been a significant trend in the past decade in the states toward accepting employee organizations, collective negotiations, representation machinery, and provisions for meeting strike impasses; but some observers view divergent and lagging developments as making for an intensification of strike activity. The different positions of the employee organizations is a recognizable factor in the diversity. However, all such organizations may be said to support the need for requiring collective negotiations and exclusive recognition, with civil service employee associations competing with labor unions for representation rights. The divergences among employee organizations are reflected in the evolution of union and some employee association support for national legislation establishing national machinery and national minimum standards, albeit authorizing state and local arrangements meeting or exceeding these.

Recent studies and membership trends

Additional ingredients in this stimulating mix of policy have been provided by a number of public commissions. Continuing exploration by commissions in various States has resulted in recommendations for statutory terms for public employee labor-management relations, most recently in Colorado, Tennessee, and Pennsylvania.[1] The National

---

[1] For analysis of earlier reports of state commissions, see J. P. Goldberg, "Labor-Management Relations Laws in Public Service," *Monthly Labor Review* (June, 1968), pp. 48-55; Russell A. Smith, "State and Local Advisory Reports on Public Employment Labor Legislation," *Michigan Law Review* (March, 1969), pp. 891-918.

Governor's Conference has issued annual supplements to its initial Report of the Task Force on State and Local Government Labor Relations, which endorsed statutes requiring collective negotiations.[2] The report of the Advisory Commission on Intergovernmental Relations (ACIR) is a more recent national expression of such recommendations, along with a substantial review of state and local labor-management policies. A majority of its 27 participants—including private citizens, United States Senators and Congressmen, federal government officials, governors, mayors, state legislators, and elected county officials—have stated that "it tends to view the meet and confer in good faith approach as being the most appropriate in a majority of situations in the light of present and evolving conditions in state and local employment." This view evoked a substantial and forceful dissent from a varied composition of its members, who support the requirement of collective negotiations.[3] Spokesmen for AFL-CIO unions in the public employee field have criticized the recommendation as a "backward" step.[4]

A new overview of the problem has been contributed through the privately endowed Twentieth Century Fund, a long-time contributor to policy development in the private sector, through its Task Force on Labor Disputes in Public Employment. The latter consisted of experts and practitioners in both the public and private labor-management sectors. Among other recommendations, the report endorses the statutory requirement that "the public employer has the duty to meet and negotiate with the union" and "that agreements be reduced to writing." There was a split on the breadth of the recommended ban on public employee strikes.[5]

---

[2] Supplement to *Report of Task Force on State and Local Government Labor Relations*, Committee on Executive Management and Fiscal Offices, National Governor's Conference (Chicago, Public Personnel Association, 1969).

[3] Advisory Commission on Intergovernmental Relations, *Labor-Management Policies for State and Local Government, 1969*, p. 99. The ACIR was established by Public Law 380, 86th Cong., 1st Session, 1959. The Commission includes 3 private citizens, 3 members of the U.S. Senate, 3 members of the U.S. House of Representatives, 3 officers of the Executive Branch, U.S. Government, 4 Governors, 4 Mayors, 3 State legislators, and 3 elected county officials.

[4] *AFL-CIO News*, April 4, 1970, p. 6.

[5] *Report and Recommendations of the Twentieth Century Fund Task Force on Labor Disputes in Public Employment, 1970*. Members participating as individuals were: Archibald Cox, Harvard University; Charles C. Killingsworth, Michigan State University; Joseph H. Loftus, U.S. Department of Labor; John W. Macy, Jr., Former Chairman, U.S. Civil Service Commission; Walter E. Oberer, Cornell University; William Simkin, Former Director, Federal Mediation and Conciliation Service; George W. Taylor, University of Pennsylvania; Saul Wallen (deceased); and Edwin E. Young, University of Wisconsin.

In the following summary discussion, varied practice and recommendations are summarized along with the considerations which are deemed characteristic of the public sector.

Public employee organization has grown at a rapid rate over the past decade, as total public employment increased by 45 percent (from 8.4 million in 1960 to 12.2 million in 1969) with a rise of 22 percent in federal employment (from 2.3 million to 2.8 million) and of about 56 percent in state and local employment (from 6.1 million to 9.5 million). The membership of government employees is divided among labor unions and employee associations. Union membership of government employees doubled between 1960 and 1968, from 1.1 to 2.2 million. Approximately 50 percent of federal employees are members, while about 8.5 percent of state and county employees are represented by the 804,000 union members at that level.

Substantial membership of state and county employees in employee associations, together with union membership, account for about 25 percent of all state and county employees. The National Education Association with its 1.1 million members supports affiliates which resort to strikes as a last resort and has acknowledged the possibility of a future closer relationship with the American Federation of Teachers.[6] The Assembly of Governmental Employees, a loosely confederated organization of mainly state associations of public employees, stresses philosophical differences with the unions over the merit system and strike prohibition, but acknowledges that it engages in substantially the same techniques as unions in competing with them for exclusive representation. It reported a membership of over 500,000 in 1969.[7] A recent BLS study reports a membership of about 265,000 members of local associations of public employees in 438 cities, competing with national unions for representation rights.[8]

Present policies

The issues involved in the growing number of public employee strikes reflect the changed state of public employee labor relations. Next to efforts to bring wages and fringe benefits into line with private sector earnings, strikes over union representation and union security issues were most prominent, reflecting both the frequent

---

[6] National Education Association, press release, January 25, 1970.

[7] ACIR report cited, pp. 123-124.

[8] BLS Summary Report, Municipal Public Employee Associations, January 1970.

absence in the public sector compared with the private sector of statutory machinery for representation arrangements and efforts to obtain initial agreements.[9]

Federal labor-management policies are currently governed by Executive Order 11491, Labor-Management Relations in the Federal Service, issued in October, 1969, revoking Executive Order 10988, Employee-Management Cooperation in the Federal Service. The revisions in the new Order are based on a review of experience and proposals made by labor organizations, agency officials, and non-governmental experts.[10]

Under the new order, the term "labor organization" replaces "employee organization." Employees continue to have a free and protected right to join or not join labor organizations. Organizations of supervisors and managers are excluded from the term "labor organization." Exclusive recognition is now the sole form of recognition, to be accorded to an organization receiving the majority of votes cast in a secret ballot election conducted in an appropriate unit.

Agencies and labor organizations are required to meet and confer in good faith on personnel policies and practices and working conditions, subject to applicable law and regulations, and execute written agreements or memoranda of understanding. Excluded from the requirement to meet and confer are the mission of the agency; its budget (including wages and fringe benefits), organizational setup, number of employees, and the grades and numbers of employees assigned; the technology of its work; and its internal security practices. The parties may, however, negotiate agreements on arrangements for employees adversely affected by the realignment of work forces or technological change. Management rights, in accordance with applicable laws and regulations, are specified and reserved. While no agreement may require an employee to join or remain a member of a labor organization, dues check-off is authorized on the basis of voluntary, written authorization. Grievance procedures may be negotiated which meet the requirements set by the Civil Service Commission and may include arbitration of employee grievances and of disputes over the interpretation of existing agreements. Agreements must be approved by the agency head if they conform to applicable laws and regulations.

---

[9] Sheila C. White, "Work Stoppages of Government Employees," *Monthly Labor Review* (December, 1969), pp. 29-34.

[10] Presidential Review Committee on Employee Management Relations in the Federal Service, 1968; Study Committee on Labor Management Relations in the Public Service, Report and Recommendations, 1969.

Consultation rights may be accorded by an agency on a national basis only to a labor organization that qualifies under criteria established by the Federal Labor Relations Council. The labor organization must be provided an opportunity to comment on proposed personnel changes, and its views will be carefully considered. Supervisors or associations of supervisors will be provided a system for intramanagement communication and consultation within an agency. However, provision is made for continued or initial recognition of units for management officials or supervisors represented by labor organizations which traditionally or historically have represented such groups in private industry and which already hold exclusive representation for such units in any government agency.

Standards of conduct for labor organizations and management are extended, making them comparable to those for private sector unions. Recognition may only be accorded to a labor organization free of corrupt influences and of influences opposed to basic democratic principles. They must file financial and other reports, provide for bonding of officials and employees of the organization, and meet trusteeship and election standards. Certain unfair labor practices by management and labor organizations are prohibited. Strike action or picketing in a labor dispute by a labor organization is an unfair labor practice. Strikes continue to be banned by federal statute.

Major innovations in the new Executive Order included the centralization of basic aspects of the administration of the federal labor-management relations policy. A Federal Labor Relations Council consisting of the Chairman of the Civil Service Commission, the Secretary of Labor, and other officials of the executive branch is to decide major policy questions, develop regulations, and handle appeals from actions of the Assistant Secretary of Labor for Labor-Management Relations. The latter will decide appropriate unit questions, supervise representation elections, prescribe regulations to effectuate the provisions on the conduct of labor organizations and management, and decide complaints of violations of these. In negotiations disputes, the Federal Mediation and Conciliation Service will provide assistance. In negotiation impasses, a Federal Service Impasses Panel is established as an agency within the Federal Labor Relations Council, with discretion to consider impasses on the request of either party, following failure of voluntary arrangements. The parties may only use arbitration or third party factfinding with recommendations to resolve an impasse on the authorization or direction of the Panel.

Postal agreement. New facets to federal employee policies have been provided by the recent agreement negotiated with the AFL-CIO, which includes joint sponsorship of a bill establishing the United States Postal Service as an independent government establishment, proposed pay raises, and collective bargaining over wages, hours, and working conditions generally subject to private sector collective bargaining. The coverage of wages and working conditions in bargaining in the Postal Service is a major change.

In addition, jurisdiction over unit determination, union recognition, and adjudication of unfair labor practice charges is assigned to the National Labor Relations Board under procedures comparable to those in the private sector. The strike impasse question, in recognition of the federal ban on government worker strikes, is met by the provision of mediation, a 90-day cooling off period with factfinding, with final and binding third party arbitration, if the impasse persists.

State and local developments

The ACIR report analyzed existing state statutes relating to public employees, and found 21 had comprehensive statutes, that is, statutes conferring organizational and representation rights on broad groups of state or local employees or both. Of these, 19 required public employers to deal with employee organizations but only 14 required mandatory collective bargaining. All required the execution of binding written agreements (one on the request of either party). "Meet and confer" provisions were effective in five States, with only one requiring written agreement. Exclusive recognition was accorded the majority representative in all of the 14 states requiring mandatory bargaining, but was required in only two of the "meet and confer" states. Detailed unfair labor practice provisions for both employer and employee organizations were set forth in the statutes of eight states providing mandatory bargaining. These states generally had provisions for mediation of unresolved negotiations, with 11 also providing factfinding procedures. Two "meet and confer" states had specific provisions for mediation only of representation and recognition disputes, and none provided for factfinding.

A number of the states dealt with above had special statutes covering such occupational groups as teachers, fire fighters, employees of publicly owned utilities, and nurses. Several of the 29 states lacking legislation covering state or local employees on a broad basis do have statutes relating to organization, representation rights, or impasse settlement for special occupational groups. Some authorized organization of employees either by statute, attorney-general opinions, or court decision.

This diversity, including complete or partial statutory voids in some states, and some persistent tendencies—substantially overshadowed nowadays—to stress strike prevention and sanctions, have produced a new orientation on the part of some employee organizations. Whether this orientation toward the enactment of national legislation establishing national minimum standards for representation and bargaining rights for public employees will be actively pressed remains to be seen. It is significant, however, that this is now one of the elements in the total evolutionary pattern of the law of public employment. As one union group expressed it recently:

> At the State and local level the cause of collective bargaining has met with despair and prejudice. It is this sense of hopelessness, coupled with the urgent need of a program to give every public employee the dignity and decency which derive from the justice and equity embodied in collective bargaining which leads to the call for a Federal minimum standard bargaining law—a Federal labor law for public employees.[11]

Legal proposal

The State, County, and Municipal Workers union has been in the process of developing a model federal statute proposal. Still in a developmental stage, provisions may include guarantees for state and public employee organization, representation, and collective bargaining like those for private industry employees under the Labor Management Relations Act. It would provide for a 5-member Public Employees Relation Commission. Election rules would be like those in the private sector. All state and local employees would be covered, except elected officials, with supervisors placed in separate units. Unfair labor practices would be specified, with procedures for complaints and hearings. Written agreements would be required, with the settlement going into effect automatically if the legislature takes no adverse action within 30 days. Dues check-off would be required on voluntary written authorization, limited to the exclusive representative where

---

[11] AFL-CIO Maritime Trades Department, *Final Report: Collective Bargaining in the Public Sector, 1969*, pp. 35-36.

one has been certified. The Federal Mediation and Conciliation Service would mediate contract negotiations at the request of either party, or on its own. If factfinding is necessary, the Service would provide the parties with a slate of factfinders, who would make recommendations for settlement, with public disclosure mandatory 15 days after the recommendations are submitted. The parties could agree to use other procedures and other agencies, or to agree to final and binding arbitration. As in the private sector, strikes would not be banned. Any state or political subdivision which enacts a law which substantially meets the provisions of the National Act could apply to the Commission for exemption from the National Act.[12]

A bill drafted by the National Education Association and introduced in the current Congress is entitled the "Professional Negotiations Act for Public Education 1969." It would cover the "professional employees of boards of education," excluding superintendents of schools. Professional negotiation, or "meeting, conferring, consulting, or discussing in good faith" terms and conditions of professional service would be required with execution of a written agreement if either party so requests. A Professional Education Employee Commission would be established in the Department of Health, Education, and Welfare to administer the Act. Organization rights, recognition rights, exclusive representation to majority representatives, and voluntary dues check-off are provided for. The National Commission would conduct hearings in contested recognition situations and order elections if necessary. Either party could call on the Commission for mediation in impasse situations, or the Commission could itself declare an impasse. If mediation were unsuccessful, either party could request submission of the issues to advisory arbitration, with the arbitrators's recommendations binding only if the parties had so agreed. Strikes would be specifically permitted, with temporary or permanent injunctions being issued only where findings of fact determine that the start or continuance of a strike would pose a clear and present danger to the public health and safety, or where the employee representative has failed to make a reasonable effort to utilize the mediation, factfinding, and voluntary arbitration machinery of the act. Unfair labor practices are set out, and the Commission is authorized to issue complaints, hold hearings, and issue orders. Here again, states which establish systems equivalent to the national system could apply for exemption.[13]

[12] *The Public Employee,* January 1970, p. 12.
[13] 91st Congress, 1st Session, S. 1951.

Other views

The reports of the Advisory Committee on Intergovernmental Relations (ACIR) and the Twentieth Century Task Force (TCTF) provide additional insights into the nature of policy views which are percolating in the development of law and practice in the public employee field. The ACIR may be said to reflect views by public managers and elected officials; the TCTF, the views of prominent impartial practitioners and legal experts. They do not necessarily encompass all of the views held by knowledgeable people.

The two reports diverge in one important respect. The TCTF report endorses collective negotiations, with one recommended principle stating that "the public employer has the duty to meet and negotiate with the union" in good faith, as is the statutory requirement in the private sector. To justify this stand, the report states: "In this matter, as in representative rights and in recognition, differences in the public and the private sectors are not such as to make inapplicable the rules of conduct legislated for private employment. As strike issues, these matters have been largely eliminated in industry. The extension of these rules to government labor relations can be a major contribution to stability."

The ACIR also recommended the enactment of state statutes "establishing the basic relationship between public employers and their organizations in arriving at the terms and conditions of employment; absence of such legislation tends to encourage chaotic labor-management relations, especially in local governments where the evolution of these relationships is left to chance and to the ebb and flow of political power and influence of employees and their organization and to widely varying administrative and judicial interpretations." The report stated that two routes were available for implementation, either collective negotiation or meet and confer provisions. The following are partial characterizations of these presented in this report: "While both systems involve continuing communication between the employer and employee representatives, under collective negotiations both parties meet more as equals. . . . Under a meet and confer system, the outcome of public employer-employee discussions depends more on management's determination than on bilateral decisions as 'equals.' "

"Given contemporary and evolving conditions in state and local employment," the majority ACIR view was to endorse the meet and confer in good faith approach. Stating that its recommendation was directed to those government seats which lack laws or formal policies on the subject—29 states, two-thirds of the municipalities with populations over 100,000, and half of the urban counties surveyed—the report stated: "These jurisdictions not only have failed to come to grips with a pressing intergovernmental issue, they have forfeited their basic responsibilities over to the courts, to the bureaucracy, and to the unpredictable play of political forces and the influence of employee groups." In the view of the majority, the obligation to "meet and confer *in good faith*" converts "the system into something broader and more balanced than the 'meet and confer' setup, but still something less than the glittering and often unfulfilled promises of a collective bargaining statute."

Express support for collective negotiations came from 7 of the 26 ACIR members.[14] Several of their views pointed to the prevailing trend in the state legislation enacted during the past decade toward requiring collective negotiations. All preferred collective negotiations, but some would have left "meet and confer" as at most a transitional alternative leading soon to negotiations.

The question of the right of public employees to strike continues to be a major issue in the consideration of appropriate legislation. Equally prominent in the deliberations are considerations of machinery to avoid strikes. The predominant view has been that statutory provisions assuring the right to organize, bargain collectively, together with the provision of machinery to deal with grievances, representation rights, and unfair labor practice charges would have as stabilizing an effect on public employee relations as they have had in the private sector. That this has not been so in some instances has resulted in emphasis also being placed on machinery to deal with bargaining impasses to avoid strike situations.

The ACIR report and a majority of the TCTF supported continuance of the prevailing ban on public employee strikes, under all circumstances. Within the task force, however, a minority went along with a universal strike ban only for firemen and policemen; for other public employees, only if the terms and machinery established by agreement had not been exhausted or when the public health and safety were truly imperiled as established by court findings. It

---

[14] Dissenting or excepting views were submitted by Robert P. Knowles, State Senator, Wisconsin; Edwin G. Michaelian, elected County official, Westchester County, New York; Raymond P. Shafer, Governor, Pennsylvania; Edmund S. Muskie, U. S. Senator, Maine; Robert P. Mayo, Director of the U. S. Bureau of the Budget; and Nelson A. Rockefeller, Governor, New York.

may also be noted that two state commissions, those of Colorado and Pennsylvania, recommended a limited right to strike for public employees, where these did not contravene contract terms and procedures, and where the public health and safety were not affected. These recommendations have not been incorporated in statutes, however.

Views on banning strikes give great emphasis to the provision of alternatives to strikes. The TCTF states that: "Threatening disputes should be subject to intense and continuing negotiations between the parties until all hope of agreement in that forum is exhausted. Then the techniques of mediation should be applied, and if that fails it should be followed by factfinding that will recommend the terms on which the disagreeing parties should end their disputes." The ACIR also stresses the need for avenues for eliminating impasses in two recommendations. States should "mandate the use of specific procedures (for example, factfinding, mediation, and advisory arbitration)" to resolve impasses under one recommendation. Under another recommendation, only mediation would be mandated, with the suggestion of state legislative authorization of additional steps.

Both the ACIR and the task force stress the need for the states to enact legislation to regularize labor-management relationships, including the establishment of independent agencies to administer the statutes. The ACIR recommendations are, of course, geared to the "meet and confer in good faith approach" and the task force to the more evident trend to collective negotiations.

Additional matters are covered in the reports, indicative of the efforts to meet significant issues which arise in employee relationships. The ACIR would require that state laws treat both state and local employees uniformly; the task force lays down general principles which are intended for uniform application. The ACIR would accord full "meet and confer" rights to the majority representative, but would not preclude informal recognition of minority group representatives. The TCTF stressed exclusive representation of the majority unions selected by employees as providing "the basis for a genuine bilateral union-management relationship." The ACIR does not deal directly with appropriate bargaining units in its recommendation, but would exclude supervisors from the grant of employee rights and privileges, while permitting them to join and be represented by organizations restricted to supervisors through which they could consult with employers on an informal basis. The TCTF stressed the practical need in public service for the largest possible unit for recognition, to avoid distortion resulting from fractionalized negotiations on cost items among agencies. The task force noted the provisions for separate units for employees and their supervisors in the federal law for private employees and recommended that the independent labor relations agency adjudicate representation questions among its functions.

In line with its "meet and confer in good faith" recommendations, the ACIR proposed "joint effort in drafting a nonbinding memorandum of understanding setting forth all the agreed upon recommendations for submission to the jurisdiction's governing officials." The TCTF stressed that: "when an agreement between the public employer and a union has been reached, it should be reduced to writing with both affixing their signatures to it," as involving more than a symbolic gesture, in providing a documentary reference if future questions arise over the agreement. On subjects which may be covered by memorandums of understanding, the ACIR would include "wages, hours, and other conditions of employment as fall within the statutorily defined scope of the discussions," with state statutes explicitly setting forth detailed management rights. The TCTF also recognized that some matters are covered by legislation and constitutional provisions in some states, thus limiting the authority of an administrator in an organized agency.

The TCTF further noted that labor agreements in the private sector and in state and local contracts contain management rights provisions, as well as in Federal Executive Order 11491. To cover the variety of discretionary authority possessed by public authorities, it stressed the need for "viable negotiations," which would not extend beyond the employer-agency's authority to make binding commitments. It emphasizes, however, that "no subject should be barred from consultations and discussion—in contrast to negotiations—however restricted the autonomous powers of the employer agency." Such limitations "may appear unduly restrictive to a healthy labor-management relationship," in the light of private experience. The task force goes on to state, "However, the government employee organization has a recourse not available to the union in private industry: it may take what it can get in limited negotiations, then lobby the legislature for nonnegotiable items."

Highlights of the mix of thinking now evident in the field of state and local employee-management relations indicate the complexities of the subject. To date, the recent trend in state legislation has been to comprehensive statutes providing for collective negotiations, with machinery comparable to that in the private sector. The absence of such action in the majority of states has produced the cross-currents already described: Employee organization proposals for national legislation establishing minimum standards; the ACIR majority recommendations for "meet and confer in good faith" state statutes as an acceptable approach for states which have otherwise failed to act; and the TCTF proposals for further extension by states of the collective negotiations legislation that has emerged as the prevailing approach in states which have acted. In the meantime, the pressures of employee unions and associations for representation rights and improved conditions are having their own impact on the developing trends.

Questions

1. What are some of the major changes that have been brought about in Federal Service labor-management relations as a result of Executive Order 11491 issued in 1969?
2. In general, what trend appears to be occurring with respect to labor relations with public service employees?
3. What principal differences still exist between labor relations in the public service and those in private enterprise?

42—UNION CONNECTS JOBS AND WORKERS *

The International Union of Electrical, Radio & Machine Workers (IUE) is making a richer life possible for thousands of men and women at the bottom of the job ladder. IUE in the past 3½ years has placed and arranged for training of more than 2,200 unemployed and underemployed men and women in good-paying jobs as electrical workers in factories in eight states. About two thirds of the trainees were new hires. The rest were upgraded to better jobs or retrained for different ones. Most of them were high school dropouts; one third were women; and a little more than half were Negroes or Spanish-speaking Americans.

Mrs. Juanita Dansby, for example, was earning less than $50 a week in a hospital before entering the program. IUE placed her in training as a regulator assembler at the Leland Airborne Products plant in Dayton, Ohio. Her earnings rose to $120 a week.

"I never thought I would know this much about electronics or have the opportunity to earn this high a wage," said Mrs. Dansby, mother of two children.

A plus to the union has been the added respect it has won from management. "It's been a real good project," said G. J. Chopp, industrial relations director of Stromberg-Carlson, Rochester, a subsidiary of General Dynamics. "We're high on it. Because it came to us under the auspices of the union, you can bet we took a real close look at it. They know that."

Cutting red tape

Taking care of the red tape for the companies where the trainees worked was one of the union's primary functions. Owen Hoey, the union's project director, and his staff of field coordinators established with the state employment services the need for training people in certain labor shortage occupations. They persuaded employers to sign a declaration of interest, negotiated the contracts, and worked

---

* From *Manpower*, Vol. 1, No. 11 (December, 1969), pp. 26-30.

with the employment service to recruit the disadvantaged. They also enlisted the advice and consent of IUE locals in the individual companies.

As a result, men and women who had never had decent jobs before went to work for such companies as Bendix and Emerson as chassis assemblers and system testers. And people already at work in such dead-end jobs as janitors, stockpushers, and laborers became television cabinet finishers, cable makers, and machine operators at wages of from $2.35 to $4.30 an hour.

Emerson found the program "particularly advantageous in training people from within to do higher jobs," according to P. R. Certo, industrial relations director. "We were at our wit's end to get people who could do finishing work on our cabinets. We were able to train and upgrade employees to handle this work through the program. We also used it to train final testers to do troubleshooting work on black and white television sets and then to train black and white troubleshooters to handle color sets."

In most cases, he added, this upgrading has meant "substantial improvement" in income for the workers.

Emerson, which has trained or upgraded nearly 250 men and women through the IUE project, wants to do more. "We're hoping to use the program in new job areas in the future," said Certo. "We'd like to use it in connection with a basic course in electronics, which will provide knowledge and skills the employee can build on."

IUE is qualified to help Emerson in this enterprise, judging by past history. It all began in the spring of 1966 when the Labor Department granted IUE a $156,000 promotion and development contract to arrange for on-the-job training for 1,300 disadvantaged men and women. The union, after passing the 1,400 mark, signed a second contract, this time a regular on-the-job training agreement for $657,000 in December, 1967. By September, 1969, more than 800 had been trained under the second contract, and the Manpower Administration had agreed to give the union $100,000 more to train an additional 1,000 persons.

The record to date has been good. The dropout rate under the first contract was only 4 percent, and thus far on the second it has been 10 percent.

The Labor Department and IUE recently signed a third contract, strictly for upgrading. About 7,000 IUE members now on the job in factories in nine cities will be given additional education and skill training. The $170,000 promotion and development contract will enable the union, with the aid of several major universities, to develop a practical program of improvement for its rank-and-file members.

Upgrading emphasized

The shift in emphasis to upgrading fits in with current Labor Department planning and with union needs. "At first, we felt that providing job opportunities for the hard core would help people and the economy in general, and we concentrated mostly on new hires," said William Gary, administrative assistant to IUE's president and project administrator. "The new contract, on the other hand, is for a different purpose. Because so much was being done for the hard core and the blacks, the guys who were employed in dead-end jobs complained that nothing was being done for them. So we came up with the education proposal for the 7,000."

IUE takes considerable pride in being one of the first unions tapped by the Department of Labor to embark on a national manpower development and training program. IUE International President Paul Jennings feels that unions often fail to get recognition for their efforts to fight unemployment and poverty.

"From the time of its founding 20 years ago, IUE has been concerned with opening up job opportunities for members of minority groups," Jennings said. "Long before present public and private efforts to help the disadvantaged, IUE locals were fighting for no-discrimination commitments and practices by employers."

When IUE signed its first training contract with the Labor Department in May, 1966, Jennings appointed Gary, then director of the union's social action department as overall coordinator of the program. The nuts-and-bolts work was delegated to Hoey, a former local president, who was named project coordinator.

Hoey carefully put together a staff of six district coordinators, selected from union members granted leaves of absence from their companies to work on the project. These men had an average of 15 years' union service, 7½ years in community relations, and almost 9 years of teaching and training experience. One man was assigned to cover New York and New Jersey, the other five each took one state—Pennsylvania, Massachusetts, Ohio, Illinois, and Missouri. A coordinator later was assigned to Indiana when a training project was launched there.

Training funds obtained

The coordinators were brought to Washington and trained with the aid of Department of Labor experts in contract work. Their first job when they returned to their districts was to establish with the state employment service the need for training people in certain labor-shortage occupations. Then they had to convince employers to provide the training.

The final step was tracking down training money. Promotion and development contracts cover only administrative costs; they do not include funds to carry out the actual training. Consequently, the union obtained the cooperation of such interested organizations as the Urban League and the National Association for the Advancement of Colored People, which had on hand training money from the Department of Labor and the Office of Economic Opportunity. The union brought available funds (about $194,000), the employers, and the trainees together.

"We were the catalysts," said Hoey.

The entire setup was streamlined for the second contract. The union requested and received training money from the Labor Department, so it did not have to approach interested companies with empty hands. The coordinators negotiated 26 agreements with 17 employers under the first contract, and 25 agreements with 19 companies under the second.

The first contract produced the "buddy" system, now widely used by employers training the disadvantaged under the Job Opportunities in the Business Sector (JOBS) Program. IUE originated the concept in 1966 and called it "Building Up Dignity Depends on You," from which the name buddy was derived.

"We based it on a one-to-one relationship," said Gary. "The man already on the job was persuaded to help the new man—or woman. We introduced the newcomer as an individual, not a hard-core case." It was the buddy's job to get the new man (or woman) to work if necessary, to counsel him, and to keep up his spirits.

IUE had no money for supportive services. That helps account for the comparatively low cost of the first two projects, a total of $1.1 million for an estimated 3,200 trainees (about $350 per trainee) to be placed by the close of the second contract, which is still operating.

Another factor in the low cost was the caliber of the recruits. Gary admits they were not the hardest of the hard core. "Many of them were perfectly capable people who had been held back out of sheer racial discrimination," he said. "They hadn't had a chance to work in a decent job."

To open up jobs for the trainees, the union attacked irrelevant educational requirements which had screened out the disadvantaged, particularly blacks and Spanish Americans. "In many cases, we persuaded employers to lower these requirements," said Gary. "A high school education is not necessary for most factory jobs."

Racial barriers also came tumbling down. One company in Memphis had only four nonwhite employees. After the first contract 76 blacks were on the payroll. A company in Ohio had never had a nonwhite worker in production operations. Within 6 months of signing up for the program, it had 59 blacks aboard, all in jobs paying a minimum of $2.75 an hour. A Massachusetts firm upgraded one Negro to foreman and another to assistant personnel director.

Training time varies, depending on the recruit's job readiness and the trade for which he is preparing. Eight chassis assemblers at Bendix were trained in 8 weeks. Stromberg-Carlson required 52 weeks (only 12 of them at government expense) to train 14 automatic screw machine operators. Some instructors were provided by the employers, some by the union.

One of the factors prompting the union's interest in training was the need to help IUE members displaced by advancing technology. As an example, Hoey cited a unit produced at a company where he once served as the local union president. The unit originally was about the size of a telephone booth and was produced by 15 persons working 8 weeks. Today the same product is about 15 inches square and a half inch thick, and a single worker can make it in 1 week.

Stromberg-Carlson added a warning note about this same problem early this year in a letter to Hoey which said: "The change from electro-mechanical to electronic switching is resulting in an obsolescence of skills now possessed by many of our production and inspection employees. Retraining and upgrade training programs will be necessary to effectively combat this situation."

So far about 17 percent of those trained under the second contract have been taught new skills. For some union members, the training came just in time. The Bendix plant in Franklin, Ind., for example, needed 38 workers for a new product line. Bendix was persuaded by the union not to hire help from the outside, but to retrain present employees in danger of being laid off because their jobs were marked for elimination.

The training has not been confined to urban areas. Stromberg-Carlson needed skilled workers to move from area to area building and installing central telephone exchange equipment for the independent telephone industry. When the firm had trouble recruiting men for these jobs at its Rochester home base, it decided to recruit and train in economically depressed rural areas around the Nation.

Working through the IUE program, field training operations were set up in Brookings, S. Dak., Everett, Wash., Tampa and Eustis, Fla., and Ardmore, Okla. Men were recruited—usually through the state employment service—not only from the vicinity of the training sites but also from poverty-stricken areas of West Virginia, Pennsylvania, Minnesota, and Ohio. Those who had to relocate were given allowances and all were paid $2 an hour while learning on the job from 10 to 15 weeks. After training they were moved into regular jobs that pay up to $4.30 an hour plus fringe benefits and travel allowances. Of 84 men recruited and trained in this manner, only five have dropped out.

Most of the new workers have made steady progress. One 40-year-old married man with a child, Earl Curry, of Racine, W. Va., was a $1.70-an-hour laborer when recruited. Today he earns $2.35 an hour, plus 15 percent in fringe benefits, and receives $70 a week living allowance. Robert Young, a 24-year-old married veteran with one child, formerly worked as a mail clerk for $1.50 an hour, in Tampa, Fla. He is now up to $2.52 an hour plus fringes and per diem.

Robert Flood, Stromberg-Carlson skills training director, said that although most of those recruited through the seven field locations were high school dropouts, they learned quickly. "It was intricate work but most of them were used to working with their hands," he said. "If you took an analytical, step-by-step approach, they responded rapidly. You can't just have them watch somebody else do it; you have to let them do it themselves. We did, and they learned it well."

IUE officials point out that the union's program does not relieve the employer of normal training expenses. Under the contracts, employers received $12 to $25 a week per trainee, which usually covers less than half the costs.

Setbacks acknowledged

The union acknowledges that the program has had failures as well as successes. A Rochester corporation trained 16 people with poor job histories as paper line assemblers but had to lay them off because of a contract cancellation. A Brooklyn firm trained 10 young women for coil winding jobs in television manufacturing. Only three of them are still with the company. The rest had had little or no experience with assembly work and could not adjust to it.

Overall, however, the dropout rate for the first two projects has been very low and the job performance of the trainees has been good. IUE now is pushing ahead with its new upgrading project. Gary feels that in some ways it will be even more effective than past programs for helping the poor.

"Moving our own people up will vacate jobs for new entries into the labor force," he said. "It's a cycle. Our original motivation was that we wanted to do something for the hard core. We thought jobs were the answer to racial unrest and poverty. We know better now. Low-level jobs alone won't do it. A guy has to know he can move ahead. A job becomes undesirable when it has no future. A man feels he can do just as well on welfare."

Questions

1. Are there any advantages to a union-sponsored program for upgrading workers such as the one described in this article as compared to one conducted solely by an employer?
2. What are some of the factors in this IUE program that may have contributed to its success?

CHAPTER 6

Remuneration and Security

A major concern of every organization is that of keeping costs under control. One of the largest, if not the largest, costs of operation in any organization is that of labor. Both companies and government organizations, therefore, are confronted continually with the problem of trying to relate the wages and fringe benefits that are paid to their employees to the contributions that each person is rendering. Since the nature of the job being performed and effort being exerted tends to differ from employee to employee, the problem of administering a remuneration and fringe benefit program is an exceedingly difficult and complicated one. The problem is complicated still further by the fact that remuneration should serve not only to reward an individual for his past performance but also to motivate him to improve his future performance. The fact that the motivational value to be derived by an individual from his remuneration is dependent upon the way in which it is administered and upon the particular needs of each individual does not make the process of remuneration any simpler. In recent years the motivational value of wages has been questioned by some writers. Recent research in the behavioral sciences, as well as the growth of fringe benefits, is cited as evidence to support the position that remuneration as it frequently is administered provides only minimum motivational value.

In this chapter the article by David W. Belcher defends the importance of money as a motivator and suggests why some contemporary wage and salary programs may be failing to achieve their intended objectives.

Burt K. Scanlan's article *Is Money Still the Motivator?* also is concerned with the use of wages to motivate employees. It emphasizes that the motivational value of wages is determined to a large extent by whether or not employees are able to perceive their wages as being equitable. Scanlan places considerable emphasis not only upon the development of an equitable wage system but also upon the presence of an effective communication program which enables employees to recognize it as such. In the article by Costello and Zalkind, the use of merit raises is discussed and suggestions are offered for improving the incentive value of them.

The article by Lesieur and Puckett provides a very detailed analysis of the Scanlon Plan including a description of the actual experiences of companies using it. The Scanlon Plan is one of the few incentive plans to be originated since the Scientific Management Era and to receive favorable acceptance. Both authors were associated with the late Joseph Scanlon, originator of the plan and, therefore, are exceptionally well qualified to discuss its operation and its merits.

The article titled *The Mythology of Management Compensation* by Edward E. Lawler, III, which continues the subject of financial incentives, is concerned with their use in management. Some of the concepts expressed in this article serve to complement those covered in the two preceding it.

In addition to seeking more money, employees are seeking more leisure time. Besides granting employees more holidays and longer vacations, some employers are introducing the 4-day week. The article titled *The Leisure Class* taken from *The Wall Street Journal*, which discusses some of the experiences, advantages, and disadvantages in connection with the 4-day week, is therefore a very timely one.

Payment for time not worked in the form of vacations, holidays, and shorter work weeks are only some of the fringe benefits that now exceed 27 percent of the labor costs in many organizations. The article by J. H. Foegen discusses some of the detrimental features of these fringe benefits and some of the growing problems they present to the employer and to society in general.

One fringe benefit that is becoming fairly universal is the financial retirement benefit of pensions. Even when the pension benefits satisfy the financial needs of retiring employees, as they usually do for executives, they do not necessarily solve the adjustment problems of retirement for those individuals who are involved. Harry W. Hepner in discussing *Corporate Executives Who Retire* describes some of the adjustment problems encountered by retirees and suggests ways in which they may help to resolve such problems.

43—OMINOUS TRENDS IN WAGE AND SALARY ADMINISTRATION *

David W. Belcher

Lately, the field of wage and salary administration has been attacked with increasing frequency. It has been variously charged with erroneous assumptions, stereotyped thinking, and misunderstanding of the nature of motivation.[1] This, therefore, would seem to be an appropriate time to try to assess where wage and salary administration now stands—and where it is going.

Actually, it has even been prophesied that the wage system itself will disappear; but this seems to be a question we need not concern ourselves with just yet. If advancing technology does lead to the demise of the wage system, this is a change that will undoubtedly take some time. Meanwhile, employees will continue to be paid for their work.

But though we may continue to believe in the viability of the wage system, this does not mean that we can view the future of the function of wage and salary administration in an equally positive light. It is not beyond the realm of possibility that this function could either disappear altogether, decrease greatly in importance, or become sufficiently routine to be taken over by one of the smaller computers. In fact, a number of trends, if not reversed in the near future, appear to point in this direction.

The first of these trends is the growing acceptance of Herzberg's satisfiers-dissatisfiers theory of motivation. This theory, which appears to destroy the concept of pay as a motivator, derives from a study of professional employees that found pay to be one of a group of factors that Herzberg classifies as dissatisfiers or maintenance factors. These are the factors that, if lacking or deficient, can reduce employee motivation; on the other hand, regardless of how much

* From *Personnel*, Vol. 41, No. 5 (September-October, 1964), pp. 42-50. Reprinted with permission.

[1] *See*, for example, F. Munson, "Four Fallacies for Wage and Salary Administrators," *Personnel*, July-August, 1963, pp. 57-64; R. T. Golembiewski, "A Behavioral Approach to Wage Administration: Work Flow and Structural Design," *Academy of Management Journal*, December, 1963, pp. 267-277; and A. B. Campbell, "Salary Administration: Fundamentals, Fallacies, Predictions," *Advanced Management-Office Executive*, February, 1963, pp. 11-14.

they are improved, they don't seem to improve job performance beyond the neutral point. Along with pay, such factors as supervision, interpersonal relations, working conditions, company policy, benefits, and job security were found to fall into this group.[2]

Among the employees Herzberg studied, the motivators were what he calls satisfiers or achievement factors. These are the factors related to success in work and individual growth—the nature of the work itself, responsibility, and advancement.

It is not difficult to understand the readiness of the average manager to accept this theory. Not only does it deal with factors he is familiar with and deals with every day; it also corresponds quite closely to his experience that employees often react somewhat tepidly to such inducements as better working conditions, greater job security, and higher benefits.

The behavioral scientists have also hailed Herzberg's findings as further substantiating Maslow's well-known theory that human needs ascend in a hierarchy, each level of which must be satisfied before the next level of needs appears.[3] Since satisfied needs no longer motivate, it is necessary, according to Maslow, to find out what level of needs an individual has reached in order to spur him to greater effort. In this country most people are no longer concerned about satisfying the basic needs for food, shelter, and safety, and are now at least at the third level in the hierarchy—the social needs. (Herzberg's theory seems to indicate, however, that present-day employees have progressed beyond this stage and are operating at the level of esteem and self-fulfillment.)

Pay still the most important

Though Maslow's theory has led some behavioral scientists to conclude that money has lost its power to motivate because people are now moved by needs that money can't satisfy,[4] it's still pretty generally assumed that money is what we primarily work for. If motivation is now recognized as being much more complex than we

---

[2] F. Herzberg *et al.*, *The Motivation to Work* (2d ed.; New York: John Wiley & Sons, Inc., 1959). Though the methodology of this study and overgeneralization of its findings have recently been criticized, acceptance of the theory has been encouraged by its agreement with Maslow's needs hierarchy and by managers' common-sense interpretation of employee reaction to Herzberg's maintenance factors.

[3] A. H. Maslow, *Motivation and Personality* (New York: Harper & Brothers, 1954).

[4] C. D. McDermid, "How Money Motivates Men," *Business Horizons*, Winter, 1960, pp. 93-100.

used to assume, pay still constitutes the most important single motivator used in our society.[5]

To regard Herzberg's theory as disproving pay as a motivator may be something of a misrepresentation of the theory itself. Rather, it can be argued that whether pay is an achievement or a maintenance factor depends on how pay is determined. If pay is geared to achievement and serves as recognition of achievement it would seem to be an achievement factor and thus a motivator. It is when pay is unrelated to performance that it serves purely as a maintenance factor.

The moribund merit philosophy

Unfortunately, it appears that the field of wage and salary administration is determined to make pay a maintenance factor— and thus to rob it of its motivation value. While almost every pay plan makes provision for what are called merit increases, in practice few increases granted fall into this category. Thus, a three-year study by the Brookings Institution of the effects of collective bargaining on management policy and practice in 150 U.S. companies found that while there was a great deal of management conviction about the merit philosophy, there was very little evidence that it was actually being followed.[6]

Corporate wage and salary administrators have been no less guilty than the unions in destroying the merit philosophy. Their insistence on "other bases for increases" and concern for consistency has led them to bury merit among such a myriad of other considerations that the recipient of a raise is fortunate if he can find where merit comes into the picture. Assuming that a man does get a raise for successful performance, if his previous raises have included "other bases for increases" he is likely to perceive his latest hike as being due to a tight labor market in his field, and any motivating value the increase might have had is lost.

Part of the difficulty, of course, is to convince management that money for economic adjustments serves a different purpose and must be separated from merit increases if the latter are to have any positive effect. Part is due also to the assumption that money in any form is an incentive. At the very least Herzberg's findings cast

---

[5] M. Haire *et al.*, "Psychological Research on Pay: An Overview," *Industrial Relations*, October, 1963, pp. 3-8.

[6] S. H. Slichter *et al.*, *The Impact of Collective Bargaining on Management* (Washington, D.C.: The Brookings Institution, 1960), p. 606.

serious doubt on the latter point. (A recent study found, though, that some overpaid people when placed on an hourly basis worked harder to redress the balance.[7])

Logically, at least, the wage and salary administrator who agrees to a program of increases on "an individual basis" instead of convincing management of the need to separate economic and merit adjustments is helping to destroy the motivating value of pay. The use of maturity curves in the administration of salaries for professional employees appears to be another sign of the death rattle of the merit philosophy. As with other systems, lip service is paid to merit but in practice the result is simply increases based upon seniority.

Thus, an apparent trend toward downgrading pay as a motivation tool is being reinforced by the people charged with seeing that payroll dollars accomplish the purposes of the organization. This seems to be the time for wage and salary administration to redesign pay plans to insure that pay operates as a motivator and to spend time educating managers in how pay can be designed to motivate.

The emphasis on techniques

Another trend in the field, which has lasted longer but shows no sign of changing course, is the emphasis on techniques rather than objectives. Wage and salary administrators seem to cling to methods of dealing with pay problems merely because things have been done this way for so long. Practices have grown into universal use simply on the basis of precedent, but few of the underlying assumptions of these practices have ever been tested or even questioned.

In fact, the basic assumptions of wage and salary administration have not been made explicit. They must be inferred from the policies and practices in common use. As a result, some of the recent criticism of the field has missed the point by attacking it as being based on certain assumptions that are not assumptions at all. Munson, for example, takes the position that wage and salary administration assumes that wages and salaries are determined by the market when, in fact, the failure of the market to answer most compensation questions is the basic reason for the existence of wage and salary administration.[8]

---

[7] J. S. Adams, "Wage Inequities, Productivity and Work Quality," *Industrial Relations*, October, 1963, pp. 9-16.

[8] Munson, *loc. cit.*

Another assumption, according to Munson, is that "the function of wage and salary administration is to relate (a) individual performance to (b) job worth to (c) market forces and, by juggling these three balls, arrive at a proper wage or salary." Actually, this is not an assumption of wage and salary administration but a description of attempts to measure contribution on three different scales. The basic assumptions are: (1) that contribution is a proper basis for wage and salary administration, (2) that contribution can be measured on these scales, and (3) a number of premises about motivation and employee satisfaction.

Typically, the practice of wage and salary administration appears to be based upon assumptions such as these:

1. Pay is an incentive to job performance.
2. Pay in the form of money has more incentive value than pay in the form of benefits.
3. Employee satisfaction with pay is evidence of its incentive value.
4. Consistent treatment of employees in the matter of pay is a prerequisite to obtaining incentive value from pay.
5. Incentive value is lost when employees are overpaid.
6. Employees react negatively to pay inequities.
7. Pay inequities are similarly defined by all types and levels of employees.
8. Employees regard internal pay inequities as more serious than external inequities.
9. Employees react only to gross external inequities.
10. Employee comparisons of pay are made first in terms of job, and second in terms of performance on jobs.
11. Employees compare their pay with that of people in similar jobs.
12. Employee comparisons of pay are uninfluenced by levels of aspiration and pay history.
13. Managers make pay comparisons that are essentially similar to those of rank-and-file employees.
14. Professional employees make external rather than internal comparisons.
15. Employees accept the concept of a hierarchy of jobs and pay.
16. Employees' determinants of the job hierarchy are similar to management's determinants.
17. Employees agree with management on what they are paid for and weigh the factors (performance, seniority, job knowledge and skill, labor market, and so on) the same.

In fact, little is known about the accuracy of these and other assumptions on which wage and salary administration is based. What is more serious, wage and salary administrators appear neither to question these assumptions nor to show any inclination to test them, despite the excellent position they are in to gather data and even to experiment. In fact, some even seem to be opposed to testing any assumptions at all.

Fortunately, a few studies are being made—chiefly by the psychologists.[9] The findings to date suggest that careful re-examination of current practice is overdue.

For example, as has already been pointed out, current motivation theory implies that, in the matter of the incentive value of pay, practice is pointing in precisely the wrong direction. The theory suggests that pay serves as an incentive only when it is designed to do so—when it is clearly seen as a form of recognition or evidence of achievement.

A recent study found that managers at the same level in different companies manifested a remarkable unanimity of opinion as to the relative pay they felt they should receive, whether they received it or not. At each level the managers also agreed that their pay differed from the level of compensation they deemed appropriate, and the lower the level, the greater was their perceived difference.[10]

This finding raises the question whether there is a positive or a negative relation between dissatisfaction and performance. Is there an incentive here that grows stronger with dissatisfaction with pay? If so, should not wage and salary administrators spend more time devising methods of channeling this incentive toward the achievement of organizational goals and less time trying merely to remove dissatisfaction? In fact, shouldn't wage and salary administrators see their job as *creating* dissatisfaction with present pay?

It would seem that the wage and salary administrator must decide whether pay is to be designed to satisfy employees or to motivate them. And, if motivation is the aim, he must then decide what kind—motivation to come and stay with the organization, motivation to produce, motivation to develop, and so on.

As for the problem of pay inequities, effective techniques for removing these depend upon the accuracy of the assumptions about how employees define inequities. Patchen, for example, found that an employee defines equity not only in terms of the absolute amount of his salary but also in terms of how his salary matches that of other people he compares himself with. If the difference between his salary and that received by these people seems to be appropriate in terms of the other differences between them (e.g., age, education,

[9] "A Symposium: Psychological Research on Pay," *Industrial Relations*, October, 1963, pp. 3-49.

[10] E. E. Lawler III and L. W. Porter, "Perceptions Regarding Management Compensation," *Industrial Relations*, October, 1963, pp. 41-49.

skill, and so on), then the comparison increases his satisfaction. If, however, the salary difference seems greater than these differences, his pay satisfaction is diminished.[11]

Another recent study found that first-line managers and higher middle managers (department heads, for example) tended to make intracompany comparisons, while middle managers closely compared themselves with groups outside the organization.[12] Further, those managers with more education were more likely to compare with groups outside the company.

These findings hold strong suggestions for both executive and professional compensation. With the growing professionalism in many positions, pay equity is more often defined by outside rather than by inside groups. The same study also found a strong relation between a manager's satisfaction with his pay and his belief that it was equitable in comparison with that of his subordinates—a finding that suggests a method of determining the points where internal or external comparison takes precedence.

Money vs. benefits

The typical assumption that money carries a higher value to employees than benefits has also been tested recently by Nealey. His study found that there are large differences in the value of a particular benefit from group to group, depending upon age, sex, marital status, number of children, type of job held, and yearly income.[13] That this should be so is not surprising, but it is at least possible that the common observation that benefit plans carry a low incentive value is merely the result of providing the same benefits to all employees.

A few companies are now permitting their executives to choose the components of their pay package with the aim of maximizing the motivation value of each pay and benefit dollar. While it might be troublesome administratively to extend the same practice to wage earners, the question whether wage earners should be permitted to choose among equal cost items in the light of their individual situations or be provided with an identical package whether they want it

[11] M. Patchen, *The Choice of Wage Comparisons* (Englewood Cliffs, N. J.: Prentice-Hall, Inc., 1961).

[12] I. R. Andrews and M. M. Henry, "Management Attitudes Toward Pay," *Industrial Relations*, October, 1963, pp. 29-39.

[13] S. M. Nealey, "Pay and Benefit Preference," *Industrial Relations*, October, 1963, pp. 17-28.

or not may well repay consideration. Actually, it may make more sense to allow rank-and-file employees to make such choices than to allow managers to do so. According to a recent study by Mahoney, managers want only a very small proportion of their compensation in the form of benefits.[14]

In the Nealey study, the pay and benefit choices of employees were compared with their attitudes toward company policy and practices on promotion, employment security, wages, and supervision. Dissatisfied employees preferred pay to benefits, Nealey found. He also found that preferences for pay increases over benefits declined as employee income increased. The Mahoney study, which was confined to managers, did not bear out this finding. It thus appears that managers and nonmanagers view compensation quite differently.

A more logical approach

The fact that it is possible to determine employee preferences on pay and benefits means that it is equally possible to ascertain their preferences as regards the weight to be attached to performance, seniority, job factors, and the labor market in determining pay. Wouldn't it make more sense to base wages and salaries on these actual preferences rather than unsupported assumptions about what they are?

The emphasis of wage and salary administration on techniques has obscured its objectives and made it possible to ignore the assumptions on which the techniques are based. When the field is defined as wage surveys, job evaluation, and merit rating, the internal logic is that equity and contribution are measured and the former is achieved by paying for the latter.

It is only when questions are raised about the ability of the techniques to measure and achieve equity and contribution that the underlying assumptions become apparent. Equity implies numerous assumptions concerning employee comparisons and perceived satisfactions or dissatisfactions with the results of these comparisons. Contribution implies assumptions concerning what measures of contribution are perceived as appropriate and, if more than one measure is to be employed, which should bear the heavier weight. Achieving motivation from wage and salary programs logically depends upon creating differentials that (1) are perceived as appropriate and

---

[14] T. A. Mahoney, "Compensation Preferences of Managers," *Industrial Relations*, May, 1964, pp. 135-144.

(2) motivate contribution to organizational goals. If the assumptions underlying programs designed to achieve equity or measure contribution are unrealistic, neither can be achieved.

"Specialist sclerosis"

Another trend worth noting is the fact that wage and salary administration is now in the advanced stages of "specialist sclerosis," or hardening of the administrative arteries. While the field is probably no more prone to this disease than other staff specialties, the adverse effects on the balance of the organization may be more severe.

The first symptom of specialist sclerosis is the forcing of old solutions on new problems instead of a search for new solutions. Thus, the past 50 years have been spent on improving the old techniques rather than on innovating. It has taken a little time, but the traditionalists have finally swallowed the maturity curve approach. (Not that the maturity curve represents any great improvement, but at any rate it is a new approach based upon at least one valid assumption—that professionals compare salaries with outsiders.)

The second symptom of specialist sclerosis is the tendency to make the job easier even at the cost of sacrificing organizational goals in the process. Thus the growing use of (1) global surveys, with their gross statistical instead of job comparisons, and maturity curves; (2) ready-made job evaluation plans; (3) other considerations (besides merit) in granting pay increases; and (4) methods that water down incentive plans instead of either eliminating them or designing new ones. The fact that the first tendency may turn out to be as good in terms of organizational objectives as the last two are bad does not alter the fact that all were probably adopted to make the job easier.

The third symptom is the tendency of the wage and salary administrator to become a policeman. Instead of perceiving his function as one of helping managers to accomplish the purposes of the organization, he sees himself as a man with his back to the wall of the corporate treasury with a single weapon to protect it—a baseball bat. Instead of perceiving himself as a trainer and innovator, he acquires police power and exercises control by approval. Apparently, he views his role as a bureaucrat in the worst sense of the word.

Last comes the reverence for techniques rather than ideas. Evidence of this symptom is the tendency to force programs upon managers instead of functioning as a source of ideas on how to get the most out of payroll dollars. Actually, the wage and salary administrator is in an excellent position to generate ideas for solutions to organizational problems.

From his knowledge of the labor market, the wage and salary man should be able to suggest: (1) job categories where it would be profitable to raise or lower hiring standards and pay, (2) job categories where further recruitment efforts should be broadened or curtailed, and (3) skills in long supply that could fill shortage areas with a minimum of retraining. From his knowledge of jobs in the organization, he should be able to offer suggestions for redesigning jobs, organization planning, and manpower budgeting. And from his knowledge of employees, he should be able to contribute to such problems as employee development and shifts in personnel beyond departmental lines.

In defense of the wage and salary administrator, it must be admitted that the ominous trends examined here did not entirely originate with him or even with his predecessors. The prevalent notion that pay has ceased to be a motivator is due at least in part to neglect of the motivation problem by economists, as well as to the emphasis by behavioral scientists on other factors in the work situation. But it must also be admitted that wage and salary administration policies and practices have reinforced rather than countered this viewpoint.

Of course, wage and salary administrators are not alone in failing to question or test the assumptions behind their practices, nor are they any more prone to specialist sclerosis than any other breed of specialists. But such excuses will not save the field from the destruction these trends portend. The only hope of reversing these trends lies in the encouragement of empirical research and a much greater willingness to innovate than wage and salary practitioners have manifested thus far.

Questions

1. What effect, if any, have the theories of Herzberg and Maslow had upon attitudes of some behavioral scientists toward the value of wages as an effective motivator?

2. What does the author consider to be the key factor in determining whether or not money will serve as an effective motivator?

3. In what ways have company wage and salary administration practices tended to reduce the motivational value of wages?

4. In this article the question "Shouldn't wage and salary administrators see their job as creating dissatisfaction with present pay?" is raised. What is this question getting at? What is your response to the question?

5. What major criticism does this article raise concerning the role of the wage and salary administrator? What suggestions does it offer regarding the improvement of this role?

44—IS MONEY STILL THE MOTIVATOR? *

Burt K. Scanlan

That wages play a paramount role in either detracting from or contributing to motivation cannot be debated. I would tend to disagree with anyone who would even remotely suggest that wages occupy only a minor role and are therefore deserving of nothing more than a passing reference. To the contrary, a wage system where problems or complaints (real or perceived) are present can offset and undo everything else that an organization or an individual manager may be attempting in the area of motivation. In short, the system for monetary reward of job performance is akin to the first stage of a rocket. If it fails, all else fails. Viewed another way there is nothing better than a good foundation. If the foundation is sound and a little care is taken in building the rest of the structure, it will stand for a long time.

So it is with wages. If the compensation system is well conceived and well administered, it can go a long way toward enhancing and augmenting motivational efforts based on other factors. Conversely, effort in other directions can be substantially weakened and in some cases made completely ineffective because of a poor wage payment system.

The Wage Level—A Critical Issue

The wage level refers to the amount of actual dollars a man receives for performing a given job. Historically it is this wage level that has received the most emphasis. In order to hire employees of all types, organizations have tried to keep abreast of what their competitors in a given industry or labor market are paying. In actually competing for certain types of labor, organizations have consistently raised the offering ante in hopes of being more successful in their staffing attempts. This practice has customarily led to competitors increasing their ante. Eventually everyone finds himself in the same

* From *The Personnel Administrator*, Vol. 33, No. 3 (July-August, 1970), pp. 8-12. Reprinted with permission.

position that he was in the first place. This type of bidding wars is an interesting one and also one which, I suppose, the organization must to a degree play if it wants to remain in the game.

It is interesting to note, however, that many of our more progressive companies are beginning to alter their strategy. Although they are not omitting reference to wages, they are placing increased emphasis on other job factors which hopefully will appeal to the candidate. These "other job factors" relate to the broader job climate which the employee will find. More specifically, emphasis is being placed on the opportunity to satisfy the social, psychological, and self-fulfillment needs. Accordingly, such things as challenge, achievement, JOB significance, freedom to work, etc., are being stressed. That employees respond to these types of motivators is confirmed by the numerous studies that have been carried out on labor turnover. Particularly among professional and semiprofessional people, it has been found that turnover is more frequently explained by the deficiencies in what have been previously labeled as motivational factors than dissatisfaction with wage.

For our purposes, however, the wage level issue has other significant aspects to it. If a man perceives that his wage level is too low in relation to the available market for his labor, he is likely to become dissatisfied. When this dissatisfaction appears, any number of things can happen. First, he may adjust his performance downward and put in only that amount of time and effort for which he thinks he is being compensated. Second, he may decide to reenter the labor market and thus seek an alternative source of employment which will not only pay more but, perhaps, also cure some of the other job deficiencies which bother him. The better qualified he is the more alternative sources of employment will present themselves and the more likely it is that eventually he will leave.

Finally, if for some reason he has decided he doesn't want to leave or that no interesting alternative sources of employment present themselves, he may adjust his performance downward as indicated earlier and also become one of those people who constantly find other things wrong in the environment. Enough of these people can have some serious long-range effects on the organization as well as the other employees.

The number of situations where wage levels are so far out of line as to cause real serious problems are probably not too many. When a situation like this does happen, the organization will usually make the necessary adjustments rather readily. There are, however, many cases where a single individual is out of line and there is a refusal to make any blanket adjustments. Then after a good man with a proven record of capability is lost, the organization ends up paying a new untried employee more than it would have taken to keep the older one. The above discussion thus supports the idea that an inadequate wage level can cause dissatisfaction.

The other side of the wage level coin is represented by the question—What happens if a man is very satisfied with his wage level? i.e., he feels that what he is paid is adequate or perhaps even more than adequate. The situation can further be amplified by assuming that over the years the organization has voluntarily (by its own initiative) continually raised the basic wage level whenever it felt the need, market, or job performance warranted it. Contrary to what has been published by some authors, it is my point of view that in a case like this wages can act as a satisfier and, therefore, also have a degree of motivational value attached to them. When a man feels he is being treated fairly, that he is being justly compensated, he will be more willing to voluntarily put in that little bit of extra effort and assume some personal responsibility for his performance.

Thus, the line between factors that cause dissatisfaction and those that result in motivation must be drawn with pencil not ink. There are shades of gray in between and the organization that wants maximum results will do well to recognize these. To perhaps overstate the point—show me a man who feels his wage level is what it should be, it is there because of voluntary action on the part of the organization, and it reflects the level of job performance, and I will show you a man for whom the wage acts as a motivator up to a point. The above observation is made with full recognition of the fact that to continually give something for nothing and not stress the responsibility and obligation which the employee has is to court trouble.

Equity in Wage Payment

More so than level, in many respects, the real critical issue with respect to wages today is that of equity. The question of equity in turn has two aspects to it. First, his perception of what he gets in relation to what he personally puts into the job, and second, his perception of what he gets in relation to other people performing the same or essentially the same job, but at a different level of efficiency. The issues involved in the first concern go back to the points discussed earlier and, therefore, will not be covered further. Rather, we will concentrate our discussion on the second point.

Employee perception is the key

Enough emphasis cannot be placed on the words "his perception of" for this is the critical issue. The organization and-or the individual manager may feel that there is a sound equitable relationship between performance and what might be called merit increases. If, however, the employee does not feel that his increases are equitable, problems will inevitably result. This situation of employee perception is illustrated by the following quotation:

> During a study of management development practice in some twenty-five blue chip companies a few years ago, I queried representatives of middle and lower management concerning the extent to which they perceived salary increases to be related to successful effort in developing subordinates. By far the most common response was a cynical smile! In only two or three companies did there seem to be a genuine perception that the relationships between these factors amounted to more than talk.[1]

It is clear then that when employees feel that there is little relationship between what they achieve and the wage they get that wages will have very little, if any, motivational value. When a situation like this exists, the organization must first undertake a critical analysis to determine whether what might be called "merit increases" are, in fact, being based on merit. If investigation reveals that, in a good number of cases, true merit is not being observed, it must then either straighten out the administration of the system or recognize in a practical sense that the system is only, in the loosest sense of the word, a merit one and not advertise it for something it isn't.

If analysis confirms that merit is being as reasonably well observed as is humanly possible, the key is better communication. It may be that employees don't understand, or perhaps lack appreciation for how the system works. Since employees have a vested interest in their wage, the organization and the individual manager have an

---

[1] Douglas McGregor, *The Professional Manager* (New York: McGraw Hill, 1967), p. 143.

obligation to thoroughly explain the intricate details of the evaluation process. Clarifying questions concerning it and reasonably justifying decisions which are made are also vital in this area. The final control must, of course, remain with the manager; but if he expects to prevent misunderstanding and dissatisfaction, he must assume the obligation to acquaint his people with the procedure.

A second area where proper communication can operate to prevent a "perception gap" concerns the process of post-informative discussions with subordinates. A great deal of the perception and resultant dissatisfaction problem can be alleviated if the manager takes the initiative to sit down with each of his subordinates and discuss his evaluation of their performance. Such a discussion, to be effective, presupposes that there has been prior *agreement* and *understanding* between the principles involved concerning all of the following:

1. What work or activities he is responsible for completing.
2. Major areas where he is accountable for achieving certain specific results.
3. What specific standards of performance he is expected to meet. Said another way, what specific set of conditions will exist when performance is as it should be.
4. Why the job and what it encompasses is important, where it fits, what are the consequences of inadequate performance, what is the contributory significance of good performance.

Assuming there is prior agreement and understanding in these areas, then there must be a meeting of the minds between the superior and subordinate concerning exactly where the latter stands in terms of his performance. The only way this meeting of the minds can be accomplished is through a face-to-face discussion where there is a genuine opportunity for the employee to participate through the free expression of his viewpoints. The superior is the key to a constructive discussion. The employee should not be put on the defense, and the superior must avoid falling back on isolated examples to justify his position. Although it is not always quite so easy, the objective is hopefully a mutual agreement on where he stands. Only after this type of communication has taken place should the matter of actual dollar adjustment be broached.

Amount of dollars committed

A second factor relating to the equity issue concerns the amount of dollars that are committed to wage increases. I have seen many cases where the potential of significant wage increase is held out in the form of a carrot. When the showdown comes, however, the increases given simply do not meet employee expectations. The very superior performers may receive 7 percent increases, those above average receive 5 percent, and those at average anywhere from 3 to 4 percent. To the man who has really produced in terms of effort and energy extended, the 2 or 3 percent differential is disillusioning, considering perhaps a 20 percent differential in level of performance. He thinks in terms of a 4 percent normal or standard increase for average performance and looks at what he gave and only ends up with 7. Since the cost of living has risen anywhere from 4 to 6 percent and a 10 percent surtax is in effect, it is no wonder that discouragement sets in. A few rounds of this and eventually he ceases to respond to the potential wage increase.

Thus, if the potential of a wage increase is to be used to induce or motivate high levels of performance, it must first of all be large enough to be perceived as being worth the extra effort. It is the individual employee via his own evaluation who determines whether or not the potential increase is significant enough to warrant the extra effort. Obviously, differences in perception can occur. In other words, the potential of receiving a given size increase may have greater influence on the performance of some than on others. As also indicated by the above comments, unless the difference in increases given adequately reflects differences in levels of performance, problems can occur. To assume that some type of policy on nondisclosure will prevent wage increase comparisons from being made neglects the fact of a real life situation.

The old versus the new employee

A third factor surrounding equity is the hiring of new people at the same, only slightly less, or in some cases, more than those who have been around for two or five years. No matter how much explaining and rationalizing is done it takes an exceptional man to keep "hanging in" and overlook this type of situation. The fact that there is the need to take this type of action in order to hire people is of small consolation. Also of small consolation are all the very reasonable and practical explanations and rationale which the organization gives. To the individual involved it is one of those issues that keeps gnawing away and ultimately takes a toll on his level of motivation.

Some Basic Guidelines for an Effective Wage Payment System

The issues which have been discussed on the preceding pages suggest many of the potential problems and difficulties which can arise concerning wage payment systems and wages in general. Using these as a base, the following guidelines for an effective system are suggested:

1. The general level of wage for any given type of labor must be kept consistent with what others are paying.
2. If dissatisfaction is to be prevented and harmony maintained, it should provide for periodic lump sum adjustment to prevent discrepencies between the newly hired and those who joined the organization at an earlier point in time. This is of particular importance in cases where the longer term employee is performing at a relatively high level. He is the one the organization can't afford to lose. If the longer term employee, on the other hand, is not at the efficiency level which might be expected, there is perhaps justification or some inequity. The general principle, however, is that such inequities usually cause problems.
3. If wages are to act as a motivator to any degree at all, then any increases which are given beyond some very minimum level must in fact, not just in theory, be based on merit.
4. Also, if the wage system is to have some motivational value, plus not cause dissatisfaction, the dollar differential between what the average versus the superior performance gets must be significant.
5. If wages are to be used to induce higher level performance, the amount offered in terms of increases must also be significant. What is significant depends, to a degree, on individual perception. As a generalization, it might be observed that the higher the wage level initially, the greater will have to be the premium offered. In any case, if 4 to 5 percent increases are rather standard anyway, it is doubtful that the potential of 7 will do much to motivate anyone.
6. Where the wage level is already relatively high, such as would typically be the case with professional employees, the real issue or crux to motivation may well be in the areas of job design or managerial leadership, not wages. In such cases, management cannot afford to be riding the wrong horse or, said another way, putting their eggs in the wrong basket. Thus, what factors motivate job performance—or cause dissatisfaction as the case may be—must be precisely pinpointed.
7. There is a need for a great deal more upward communication with respect to wages. This upward communication needs to take two forms. First, the individual manager must through close interaction get a better feel for how his people as individuals feel and perceive the issue. Second, higher administration must develop a greater sensitivity to what the real issues and problems are. It must be willing to attack these with a positive approach designed to achieve desired results.
8. As long as industry is concerned about motivating people to perform to the full level of their capability and to the extent that wages

can and do play a role in this process, perhaps a different approach than that used historically is needed. I would suggest that a wider application of the bonus process is needed. Recognizing the practical limitations of giving rather large permanent percentage increases in salary, it is maybe time that we reconsider the status of the annual permanent merit increase. In other words, don't send it to do a job it can't possibly succeed in doing. It is my belief that a *well-conceived* and *well-administered* bonus system, where at the end of a period a lump sum is distributed based on merit and performance in a true sense, may well be the new direction in which we move. As stated above, the use of this method should carry further down the line than historically it has. (Note: it may well be that the motivational value involved has little to do with the money itself but rather is a function of the recognition of getting it and the personal psychological value of having done a job well.)

In summary, the issue of wages as it relates to motivation and productivity is indeed a complicated one, having no magic or pat answers. What has been attempted here is to present some of the basic considerations and issues involved with the hope that they might stimulate some very objective analysis and discussion. Only in this way and with this approach can we hope to come up with a total system, a total plan which will in the long run prove effective and yield the desired results.

Questions

1. In what respects does an employee's perception of his wage payment affect the motivation he derives from it?
2. Do you agree or disagree that an employee will derive motivation from his wage if he is satisfied that its level is adequate?
3. In what respects may effective communication contribute to the motivational value to be derived from wages?
4. How do the views of the author on the subject of wage motivation compare with those of Belcher in the preceding article?

45—MERIT RAISE OR MERIT BONUS: A PSYCHOLOGICAL APPROACH *

Timothy W. Costello and Sheldon S. Zalkind

Despite widespread use, merit raises are currently being subjected to much criticism for failure to achieve their goals in the salary programs of many companies. An important reason for this failure may very well be that such plans do not allow for the operation of several basic psychological principles in the areas of motivation and learning.

Can the well-established principles of psychological reinforcement theory be blended with the practical requirements of a large organization, to produce an incentive pay system for white collar employees? We believe they can—if personnel administrators are willing to make innovations and then subject these to research validation. We describe both a suggested innovation in merit pay and a design for research on its effectiveness.

We first examine some problems of currently-used merit raise systems, then consider some relevant psychological principles, and go on to propose a new approach to merit pay. Some readers will find it a radically different approach and therefore unacceptable; others may complain of some practical difficulties. We would like to present the case for providing a more effective and motivating reward system than those currently in use.

Current systems

Merit raise systems, with minor variations, are standardized and rather well known. Usually a value is assigned to each job in the organization on the basis of a job evaluation program. This value is then converted to the dollars and cents that the company will pay for that job. This is almost always done in terms of a range or bracket, which may be about 30% of the minimum figure. Theoretically, movement through the range occurs on the basis of meritorious performance, which is frequently assessed through some formal program of performance appraisal or merit-rating. Merit raises are made on an

* From *Personnel Administration*, Vol. 25, No. 6 (November-December, 1962), pp. 10-17. Reprinted with permission.

annual basis at salary review time. Some companies, in addition, review salaries semi-annually for new employees; some consider senior employees only biennially.

Criticisms of present approaches

Although the usual system, on its face, seems to have much to recommend it, and is as a result widely used for salaried employees at middle management levels and below, personnel people who use a system of merit raises have many criticisms of it. The criticisms suggest that many companies feel they are saddled with a system that they know doesn't work.

A major criticism, and this must be considered basic in any wage and salary program, is that the program does not serve to motivate better performance. The principal difficulty is that an annual merit increase (or for young employees, even a semi-annual one) is too remote in time from the good performance the supervisor wants to reward.[1] As a result no connection is seen between the increased money and specific examples of good performance. The best attempts of supervisors to spell out such a connection by talking to the employees seem not to work. Even when the raise is tied in with merit rating, the end result is not better performance. Too often either a high merit rating is given to justify a raise awarded on some other basis or a low rating is given to justify inability to provide a salary increase.

A second criticism is that the "merit" raise has, as a matter of fact, become in many cases an automatic increment, rotated among the members of a department. This criticism is not directed against the intent of the system so much as it is against the framework in which department heads administer it. But, then, any system is only as good as those who use it allow it to be. So we must consider the system as it is used, not as it exists in policy manuals.

For both these reasons, its lack of perceived relation to particular performance and its confused relationship with automatic increments, the present system often leads to false expectations and inevitable

---

[1] For typical psychological principles and research bearing on this point *see* B. F. Skinner, "Reinforcement Today," *American Psychologist*, 1958, 13, pp. 94-99; C. B. Ferster and B. F. Skinner, *Schedules of Reinforcement* (New York: Appleton-Century-Crofts, Inc., 1957); R. B. Ammons, "Effects of Knowledge of Performance: A Survey and Tentative Theoretical Formulation," *Journal of General Psychology*, 1956, 54, pp. 279-299.

disappointment for many.[2] Failure to get a raise under these conditions may lead to reductions in levels of performance. In the absence of any clear cue system or gauges which an employee can use to assess his own performance in relation to a merit increase, and because the increase so often is used covertly to recognize another year of service, the average employee expectantly awaits salary review time with no realistic basis for his expectations of an increase or the amount of the increase. When he is rewarded with a salary increase, it often cannot match the amount of his expectations.

More subtle difficulties also develop with a merit raise system. Because the system as it now functions tends to pit one employee against another (a fixed budget to be divided in "your favor" this year and in "his favor" next year) rather than each person's own good or bad performance, it can undermine team spirit and prevent the development of cohesive work groups. Largely because of an absence of knowledge about the basis for a merit raise, particular merit raises given out covertly are described as unfair (the news almost always seems to get out). "Unfair," as is well known, is an even more condemnatory term for a salary system than "not enough."[3] Finally, the system tends to play into the need many employees have to complain about something. The particular pattern of merit raises is often griped about as a kind of scapegoat for other job factors that are either not so easily identified (e.g, factors in the nature of the work) or are too ego-deflating to be named (e.g., failure to develop on the job).[4] As a result the supervisor is confronted with gripes that are unrelated to the real cause of maladjustment. He can hardly handle the real problems effectively unless he knows what they are.

The end product of currently used merit raise programs would seem to be that not getting a raise is a major source of frustration; but getting one is not perceived as recognition for work well done. The merit increase neither motivates better performance in those who receive it, nor sets a motivating example for the others who do not. Both the money spent and the opportunity to meet the recognition needs of employees are lost.

---

[2] A study examining the effect of expectations on attitude and performance is A. J. Spector, "Expectations, Fulfillment, and Morale," *Journal of Abnormal and Social Psychology*, 1956, 52, pp. 51-56.

[3] For a full discussion of this point, *see* Paul Pigors and Charles A. Myers, *Personnel Administration* (New York: McGraw-Hill Book Company, 1956), p. 276 and pp. 284-285.

[4] F. Herzberg, B. Mausner and B. B. Snyderman, *The Motivation to Work* (2d ed.; New York: John Wiley & Sons, Inc., 1959), p. 82.

Some basic principles

Drawing from the abundant psychological research on learning and motivation we should like first to suggest some principles that must underlie any merit raise program. Then we describe a program which we believe uses these principles and, at the same time, meets the objections to merit raises that we have previously identified.

1. To effect a change in behavior—or in personnel language to motivate an employee to better performance—the desired response (higher productivity, learning a new job, a better attitude) must first be allowed (encouraged) to occur and then be reinforced by an appropriate satisfier *as soon as possible* after the behavior is displayed.[5]
2. The employee must be apprised of his performance (or, in psychological terms, given knowledge of results) as soon after performance and in as specific a fashion as possible. He must get to see the relationship between the goal set for him and what he is actually doing.[6]
3. The most lasting type of reinforcement (or the reward which is likely to keep an employee's performance at a high level for the longest time) is one that is given irregularly (but nevertheless in a fashion clearly related to specific performance) rather than after every example of good performance.[7] The latter condition is, as a matter of fact, impossible to maintain in the business organization.

It would seem that these principles, clearly established by a wide variety of research, are violated by present day merit systems. Such systems may be relatively easy to administer, but they don't seem to do what is intended.

What alternative might fit our knowledge of psychological principles and still be usable administratively?

For one thing, a *raise and a bonus need to be distinguished.* Obviously good performance, of the sort the administrator wishes to encourage, or reinforce, cannot be rewarded continually with raises, which then become part of the fixed salary of the individual. Raises cannot easily be given frequently, nor can they be easily linked to desired performance. But a flexible use of *bonuses* may help meet the criticisms of merit raises and still take advantage of the principles of reinforcement.

---

[5] Skinner, *op. cit.*
[6] Ammons, *op. cit.*
[7] In a recent article, Aldis has related schedules of reinforcement to varieties of wage and salary payments, with suggestions for some modifications. Owen Aldis, "Of Pigeons and Men," *Harvard Business Review*, July-August, 1961, pp. 59-63.

A merit bonus system

Suppose each department head were given a budget for labor costs, only *part* of which was to meet regular salaries, determined as now within the job evaluation framework, the other part to be used for merit bonus payments administered on a *monthly* basis. Such monthly bonus payments would be made to a number of employees after their supervisor had observed evidence of superior performance on their part. The possibilities for using such a device to meet the principles we have described can readily be seen. There are, of course, some hazards as well.

Let us first describe the specific procedures we believe must be followed if our suggested program is to work out practically and effectively from various points of view. Encouraging superior performance is only one, although an important one, of the many functions a salary program must serve. Meeting cost of living changes and providing additional salary for increased seniority are two other important functions. We take account of these, we believe, in the procedure outlined below.

1. Satisfactory lower salary levels have to be set for the various jobs through a job evaluation program, and, in relation to company policy and prevailing standards in the community.

2. The upper end of each bracket is also determined in the same fashion but with two other considerations in mind: (a) that progress in the bracket will be determined by years of service, providing certain minimum performance standards are met; and (b) that opportunity for earning additional income on the job will be provided through a monthly bonus system.

3. Over and above the salary budget needed for each department to meet its commitments described above, an allocation is made for merit bonuses to be administered by the first supervisory level in consultation with the next higher level. The specific sum can be determined as a percentage of the base salary budget and in relationship to particular company or departmental considerations. In any case, the bonus, if given, should be large enough to provide a noticable *month-end* increment for the rewarded employees. The question of how many employees receive bonuses any month is again a matter of company determination, depending on actual performance, general salary level, etc. What is most important is that the bonus not be "frozen" into the salary of the rewarded employees.

4. When the supervisor administers the program, certain conditions have to be met: (a) Standards of performance to be considered for bonus awards must be clearly spelled out and made known to all employees. In addition, of course, the new system must be discussed in staff meetings with employee groups; (b) As soon as the supervisor decides that a particular employee will receive an award, he

should inform the employee of that fact, the amount, and the reason for it. In doing so, the important point is to indicate that it is given as recognition of superior performance. The supervisor will also have to explain that the award is for this month only and will be awarded again as other improvements are observed. The system demands that not every improvement in performance be so awarded, from a practical company point of view, to keep labor costs within reasonable limits, and from a psychological point of view, to provide a periodic or irregular reinforcement. Bonuses should be awarded relatively frequently but neither consistently, nor whimsically unrelated to performance. Psychological research over the years (referred to above) demonstrates the superior effectiveness of irregularly given reinforcements for the maintenance of desired behavior over long periods of time. The point is a critical one in the plan we are proposing.

5. The initiative for helping non-rewarded employees to achieve a bonus award should come from the supervisor. An appraisal interview focused on coaching and counselling relationships to help the individual employee improve his performance might well meet this need. Appraisal interviews would in addition continue to be used to help all qualified employees to develop themselves for promotion opportunities.

Advantages and disadvantages

Let's first consider what such a program might hope to accomplish, then consider some of its hazards and limitations.

1. It meets the requirements of our three principles—good performance is rewarded soon after it occurs, specific knowledge of results is provided, reinforcement occurs on an irregular basis but clearly in relation to good performance, thus helping to maintain the desired performance over a longer period of time.

2. Merit awards are clearly separated from automatic increments. A good case can be made out for the position that an employee who has acquired another year's experience is worth more than one who has not. But particular meritorious service should also be rewarded apart from seniority. We believe our system meets both requirements of a salary program, but clearly distinguishes to the employee his salary potential and his merit bonus. Through automatic increments, and upgrading, basic salary can increase, while the added bonuses vary in relation to specific and recent performance.

3. The system provides opportunity for making use of recognition for work well done—a strong motive force in its own right.[8] In this way the money award serves two purposes: it is an economic reward and a psychologically satisfying symbol of a job well done.

4. The system provides specific focus for the appraisal interview for all employee levels. As a consequence it is more likely that such

---

[8] Herzberg, *op. cit.*, p. 60.

interviews will actually be undertaken and, when they are, they are more likely to do some good.

The system has some hazards and definite limitations, as all personnel administrators will quickly recognize.

Actually it is a modified type of incentive system for white collar workers, for whose work precise production measurements are not always possible. "Measurement" for the incentive award is the supervisor's judgment. If he is unfair, biased, or uninformed, the system will backfire—the present system, of course, now frequently backfires. Since he holds important sanctions over his employees, his own level of supervisory performance is crucial for the system. This, of course, is not necessarily all bad. Two things come to mind: evidence indicates that effective supervisors are seen as having more influence;[9] poor supervision is more likely to be made quickly apparent by ineffectiveness in administering the new bonus system and thus remedial measures can be adopted by those in higher echelons.

Payroll sections will surely complain about the additional work. But a little additional paper work should not be the basis for an administrative decision which should have major impact on employee performance. As a matter of fact payroll sections do effectively cope with comparable, more complicated piece-rate calculations.

Of a much more serious nature is the possible reaction of employees who are accustomed to fixed weekly, bi-weekly or monthly incomes, and who (perhaps we should add quickly) provide fixed, not always satisfactory, levels of performance.

In any case, our suggestion would be to try the system out under the controls and limits of the research design we describe in our concluding section. If employee attitudes are likely to be extreme and negative, the effect will be contained within a small section of the company and a change can quickly be made. If research suggests that the effects are good, a considerable bonus for both management and the employees is in the offing.

Research required

Obviously, we are not suggesting that all companies rush in and install this "New Plan" throughout their entire organization. The

---

[9] D. C. Pelz, "Influence: A Key to Effective Leadership in the First-Line Supervisor," *Personnel*, 1952, 29, pp. 209-217.

installation and implementation of any new plan usually is accompanied by much argument, debate and discussion, and we assume that the same would be the case here. What we are suggesting is that the potential effectiveness of this plan be tested carefully with adequate concern to obtain data, permitting it to be compared to present systems. The plan's potential utility should *not* be decided on the basis of mere impressions.

While a "let's try it out" approach would undoubtedly give some interesting results, the more fruitful test of the plan would come through a research approach. Let us sketch in some of the conditions for this research. Specific tailoring to particular organizational situations might be needed and could readily be provided.

The reader has possibly already anticipated the need to try the new system out with some units (as experimental groups) while *not* using it with other comparable units (or control groups) which continue with whatever present plan is operating. Administratively this would require that the organization be one with similar units, so located that communication between the groups would be quite unlikely to occur. Offices or plants in separate cities might meet this requirement. (The word "group" is used here to mean the experimental condition being used. In practice, many existing sections or work groups might be part of each "Group" discussed below).

The introduction of *any* plan or change can bring about two sorts of reaction which can affect the behavior of those involved, without the plan or change *itself* being responsible for the results. A more elaborate research attempt, beyond just an Experimental-Control Group comparison, might thus become necessary. The well-known Hawthorne studies dramatized the possible increments in attitude or performance that can occur by paying attention to people and by their awareness of being a part of an experiment. Thus our Control condition (of "no change" in plan) requires that one Control Group have no new plan, no change in emphasis on the present way of doing things, and no awareness of being part of a study. But another Control Group should be set up, *not* changing the present system, but making people conscious of merit-salary links. A "public relations" emphasis, with talks of a "new revitalized" program of merit raises, and of increased concern for evaluation (without actually changing—presumably—the merit or award system itself either in performance or in reward) would help control for the "Hawthorne effect." Obviously, while we would predict that the Experimental Groups would do better, in the long run, than this "Merit Conscious" Control Group, we can't be sure until the proper comparisons are made.

In addition to the "Hawthorne effect," the opposite effect—resistance to or suspicion of any change—could occur. Thus, our experimental conditions have to be subdivided. One Group would need to have the plan introduced with a minimum of fanfare, perhaps even with an arbitrary implication that there is reason to believe that it won't work but "we're trying it anyway." Another Experimental Group should have the plan introduced as the company "normally" might, with some publicity, explanation of the company's faith in it, etc., and indicating that it is being used experimentally with this Group. A third Experimental Group should take advantage of some of the concepts of "participation," with small discussion groups indicating their reactions to the plan, asking questions, etc., and seeking to minimize resistance. (They cannot "participate" in the fuller sense of helping to work out, or modify the plan or else, there go your controlled conditions for research).

We recognize that using two Control and three Experimental conditions poses additional administrative problems, beyond the simpler single Experimental—and single Control Group approach, but personnel administration is beginning to face up to the need for research validation of its techniques, even though the research, at times, might initially seem cumbersome.

What of the *measures* which would be used with various groups? Many of the standard criteria of organizational effectiveness should be obtained. Primary, of course, would be performance (or production) data. Absenteeism, turnover, costs, number of suggestions, grievances, dispensary visits, and similar objective data could be gathered. Performance ratings, both for those awarded and those not, could be compiled.

How people feel, both about the plan and other aspects of the job and the company, would be an important source of information on the plan. Surveys (before the experiment as well as later on) should cover the usual range of attitude and morale areas, and not just the pay question. Information should be gathered on the attitudes towards other members of their group, how they interact, feelings about those receiving bonuses, etc. The impact of the system on the entire group, the way in which it ties into a feeling of accomplishment and of recognition would be important to measure.

These measures, taken comparably for the Experimental and Control Groups, would provide the administrator with evidence as to whether the system has potential compared to the presently-used system. Whether or not the new system can be judged more effective depends, of course, on the over-all group performance, not merely on the performance of the rewarded individuals.[10]

We don't think the proposed Merit Bonus System (or any system) will solve all of management's incentive problems. But present systems of merit raises, though traditional, are not necessarily influencing people to perform well in their work. Separating bonuses from raises, providing much more frequent and irregularly spaced use of bonuses, and linking them closely to performance may be a way of taking advantage of the leads provided by research on motivation and learning.

Questions

1. What do the authors consider to be the principal limitations of most remuneration systems that they hope will be overcome by the system that they propose?
2. Upon what psychological principles is the system that they propose based?
3. What are some of the difficulties that are inherent in any bonus system which might be encountered in the one proposed by the authors?
4. Does the proposed plan resemble the Scanlon Plan?
5. What are some of the conditions that would have to be achieved in a company before it may be possible to embark upon the experiment suggested by the authors?

---

[10] There is evidence to suggest that, at times, awards given to some members of a unit help to improve the entire group's morale. S. A. Stouffer *et al.*, *The American Soldier* (Princeton: Princeton University Press, 1949), Vol. I, pp. 309-310.

46—THE SCANLON PLAN HAS PROVED ITSELF *

Fred G. Lesieur and Elbridge S. Puckett

This is an excellent time to take a good look at the general principles of employee participation in management—and probably the best time in history to examine the Scanlon Plan in particular. Recent technological advances involving the computer, numerically controlled machine tools, and many other forms of automated processes have brought the activities of blue- and white-collar workers closer together than ever before. The ability of these employees to work together and with management has an enormous impact on a company's success in utilizing the new technologies. Moreover, a recent Supreme Court decision may have a profound effect on some kinds of incentive systems, particularly those of the individual and small group types.[1] In affirming a union's right to discipline an employee who exceeds his piecework norm, the Court has, in the opinion of many observers, undermined a long-established sector of the incentive system.

In contrast to other, more limited forms of incentive schemes, the Scanlon Plan offers a flexible vehicle through which company, union, and employees can meet changes in conditions, in technology, and in corporate structure in a manner that is mutually rewarding for all.

In the first section of this article we will briefly outline the basic philosophy and structure generally employed in a Scanlon-type plan.

Next we will analyze the experiences of three companies that have employed the Scanlon Plan and Scanlon's philosophy successfully for a long period of time. It should be noted at the outset that in each of the cases the company was economically healthy and successful prior to its adoption of the Scanlon Plan. This is a reflection of the fact that the work of Scanlon and his successors since World War II has been largely with "normal, healthy cases," as opposed to the Depression cases with which he worked in the prewar era.

* From *Harvard Business Review*, Vol. 47, No. 5 (September-October, 1969), pp. 109-118. Reprinted with permission.
[1] See *Scofield et al. v. National Labor Relations Board et al.* (Wisconsin Motors), U.S. Supreme Court, No. 273, April 1, 1969.

In the third section we will draw some conclusions from these experiences and generalize as to their significance.

Operating Features

Although the Scanlon Plan is often thought of as comprising a structure of participation committees and a particular type of performance measurement, actually its most important feature is Scanlon's basic philosophy. Scanlon's first thoughts about employee participation in the workplace resulted from his experiences during the Depression, when citizens worked together in a common endeavor to solve the very austere problems facing the community. The first application of his philosophy, in a marginally profitable steel mill, contained no performance measurement or bonus provisions, but represented a successful attempt to harness the full efforts of management and the work force in order to save an organization that otherwise might very well have gone under.[2]

Scanlon deeply believed that the typical company organization did not elicit the full potential from employees, either as individuals or as a group. He did not feel that the commonly held concept that "the boss is the boss and a worker works" was a proper basis for stimulating the interest of employees in company problems; rather, he felt such a concept reinforced employees' belief that there was an "enemy" somewhere above them in the hierarchy and that a cautious suspicion should be maintained at all times. He felt that employee interest and contribution could best be stimulated by providing the employee with a maximum amount of information and data concerning company problems and successes, and by soliciting his contribution as to how he felt the problem might best be solved and the job best done.

Thus the Scanlon Plan is a common sharing between management and employees of problems, goals, and ideas. Scanlon felt that individual incentives worked against employee participation of this nature. He believed that individual incentives put the direct worker in business for himself, pitted him against the broader interests of the company, and produced inequities in the wage structure that in turn led to poor employee morale. His concept of a system of rewards that would stimulate employee interest and acceptance of technological

---

[2] For a full discussion of the work of Joseph N. Scanlon, see *The Scanlon Plan: A Frontier in Labor Management Cooperation,* edited by Fred G. Lesieur (Cambridge, The M.I.T. Press, 1958), Chapter I.

change involved an appropriate wage structure reflecting (1) individual skills and (2) additional rewards, based on the success of the enterprise, to be shared by all employees and management.

In almost all the cases with which we are familiar, companies implement this philosophy of participation with a committee system made up of departmental production committees and an overall screening or steering committee. However, in very small plants, one plantwide committee may be sufficient.

Production committees

Departmental production committees are made up of two or more employees, depending on the size of the department, and one or two management members. The management members are appointed by the company, and experience has shown that it is very important to have whoever is heading the department or area (such as a foreman, office manager, or chief engineer) take an active part as chairman of the committee. Employee members are usually elected by the employees in the department; in some cases they are appointed by the union leadership.

Committees meet regularly and discuss suggestions for improvements. The employee members must be allowed a certain amount of time to contact other employees to obtain new suggestions and to discuss the action taken on pending suggestions. In one very successful application of the plan which is reported later in this article, a company has broadened the duties of employee members to make them responsible for chasing down the results of pending suggestions. This job usually belongs to the foreman, but the company has found that putting the responsibility on the shoulders of employee members stimulates employee interest in general and facilitates getting rapid action on suggestions. This company has maintained a record for getting action on suggestions that is as good as any we have seen.

Is committee work time-consuming? Experience in all three of the companies to be reported shows that the amount of time employee members lose from their regular jobs, either in attending meetings or in contacting employees, is surprisingly low. The production committee gets together formally once a month. At this meeting its members:

1. Make sure that they have recorded each suggestion that has been submitted during the month and any action which has been taken. (Usually, one of the employee members has the responsibility for

seeing that all suggestions have been recorded and sent to the person or department in the company that types up the minutes of all production committees and returns a copy to each committee member.)

2. Process all suggestions, attend to previous suggestions on which action has not been completed, and then take up any other business considered important to the department's performance. (Such discussion may take many forms. Often a foreman or other member presents a departmental problem which he wants the committee to evaluate in the hope of achieving a solution. These problems range all the way from the layout of new equipment to cost factors on specific products.)

Although the majority of suggestions are approved by committees, the committees do not have the right to accept or reject ideas presented. That right is reserved by management. Moreover, there is one area of business that the production committee must *not* get into. This has to do with union business, grievances, wages, and so forth. The committee deals exclusively with operating improvements.

If the production committee has been functioning properly during the month and is doing its job thoroughly, the meetings described may take approximately one hour or slightly longer. If the production meeting is over in 15 minutes, it is clear that the committee is functioning strictly as a suggestion committee and probably is not getting sufficient management leadership and direction.

Screening function

The minutes of the production committee are forwarded as quickly as possible to the screening committee, which meets once each month—as soon as the accounting department can make available the figures reporting the performance of the previous month. The chairman of this committee is usually a top executive who serves along with other top executives from the various departments of the company. The president, steward, or other officer of the local union or unions involved usually serves, too, and employee members represent various areas. In some cases the employee member may represent two or more production committee areas; in other cases there may be an employee member from each production committee area. As at the production committee level, the employee members are usually elected by their constituents, but in some cases they may be appointed by the union. The screening committee members proceed as follows:

1. Their first order of business is to go over the performance of the previous month and analyze the reasons why it was favorable or not so favorable, as the case might be. One of the most important functions of each member is to understand fully the economic variables that affect the bonus result, so that he or she can impart such information to other employees. Employees must understand the results and have complete confidence in the method of measurement which is employed. In each of the three situations to be discussed, the company faced periods (sometimes of many months) when economic conditions offered little or no bonus opportunity. Yet, during such periods, participation and employee interest remained at a high level. The results attained during these periods of hardship, in our judgment, provide the real proof of how well Scanlon's philosophy was being implemented.

2. Their second function is to take up any company problems or matters of interest which management wants to communicate to all employees. For example, we have seen the sales department bring a competitor's product into the meeting, so that members could analyze the kind of competitive problems that they were facing. Again, samples of new products which the company has developed are often the topic of discussion, thus giving employees a chance to visualize the production problems they will eventually be facing. Usually an area of great interest at every screening meeting is the sales and economic outlook—the opportunities and possible problems that lie ahead.

3. They discuss and take care of any suggestions which have not been resolved at the production committee level. Hopefully, a vast majority of suggestions will have been handled at the lower level. However, there are certain areas (e.g., capital expenditures and new equipment) which involve the company as a whole, and problems in these areas must go to a higher level to be resolved. In a sense, the screening committee is also considered a kind of "court of higher appeal" for suggestions which have not met with approval at the production committee level but which the suggestor would like to have considered further.

In all cases there is no voting by the committee on suggestions, but there is thorough discussion of all points of view when there is disagreement. After careful consideration, management makes the final decision.

Measurement of rewards

From the standpoint of employees, the payoff of a Scanlon Plan is in dollars and cents. How is the amount of reward determined?

Companies employing the Scanlon Plan follow widely differing methods of measuring the amounts of bonus payments to employees. In some of Scanlon's early work, profit sharing was the basis of bonus rewards. In recent years the most commonly used type of measurement is what is loosely termed a sales value of production ratio, where the ratio of total payroll to sales value of production (net sales plus or minus the change in inventory) in a prior base period is compared with that ratio in the current period.[3] Any improvement in this ratio provides a bonus pool. Part of this pool is set aside in a reserve against deficit months (months when the ratio goes above that of the base period). The amount set aside is determined by analysis of past fluctuations in the ratio.

After removing the reserved amount from the bonus pool each month, the remainder is divided. Usually 25% is the company's share, and 75% is paid out to all employees as that month's performance bonus. Participation usually encompasses everyone in the company up to and including the president, or, in the case of a very large, multiplant company, everyone employed in the facility in which the plan is in effect. The bonus is distributed as a percentage of the employee's gross income during that accounting period, so that the bonus paid reflects differentials in wages or salaries paid for differences in job content. (Federal Wage and Hour Law provisions require that Scanlon bonuses be reflected in any overtime premiums which the employee earns. For this reason "gross income" must include overtime premiums.)

At the end of a "Scanlon Year" the reserve pool remaining after providing for any offsetting deficits is split up in the same manner as the monthly bonuses. The company retains its share, and the remainder is paid out as a year-end bonus (in the same proportions as the monthly bonuses).

Other types of measurements that have been used are for the most part similar to the one just described in that the total payroll of the participants comprises the numerator of the ratio. Variations in the denominator have entailed the use of:

1. Net sales without adjustments for changes in inventory.
2. Sales value added, where purchased materials are subtracted from sales value of production.
3. Physical production count, on which sales dollars are imputed (this is limited to the manufacture of a single product, and has some severe drawbacks).

Each of the three companies to be discussed employs a sales-value-of-production type of measurement. In one case, only finished-goods inventory is included in the calculations; it is priced at sales

[3] Ibid., pp. 65-79.

value. In a second case, work-in-process and finished-goods inventories are included, and they are factored to a conservative sales valuation. In the third case, all inventories are included, valued at cost in the same manner as on the company's financial statements.

Case Studies

Now let us look at the Scanlon Plan in practice. We shall take three cases, each representing problems and conditions different from the others, the one common characteristic being that the plan has been in effect ten or more years. The variety of these cases demonstrates how flexible the Scanlon Plan is; it can be tailored to fit a multitude of situations. For a summary of some of the company facts, see *Exhibit I*.

Atwood Vacuum Machine Co.

This family-owned company, with its corporate headquarters located in Rockford, Illinois, has had the Scanlon Plan for 14 years. Six plants are covered. Total employment is in excess of 2,000 people. Everyone participates in the program, including the president of the company. At the time the Scanlon Plan was implemented, an individual incentive system was dropped.

Atwood is a supplier of automotive parts hardware to all of the major automobile manufacturers. It also has a general product division which manufactures proprietary products, such as trailer hitches, brake actuating systems, and trailer hot-water heaters. Each of the plants bargains individually with an independent union.

With a major share of its volume going to the automotive industry, the company is faced with the possibility of going out of business each model year. The fact that the company is making a certain component for the auto industry in 1969, for instance, certainly does not guarantee that it will be making it in 1970.

Each plant has its own Scanlon production committees. These committees are composed of employee, union, and management representatives. However, there are only two plants holding monthly screening committee meetings; the plants located within a 55-mile radius of Rockford attend the screening committee meeting held there, while at the same time the other two plants, located over 200 miles

EXHIBIT I. THREE COMPANIES USING SCANLON PLANS

	Atwood	Parker	Pfaudler
Number of employees	2,000	1,000	750
Number of plants	6	1	1
Union affiliations	3 (independent)	2 (AFL-CIO)	2 (AFL-CIO)
Product	Automotive hardware	Writing instruments	Project engineering, Glassteel equipment, stainless steel equipment, food-filling equipment
Type of production	High volume; competitive	High-volume consumer item	Custom as well as standard fabricating
Type of bonus measurement	Payroll/sales value of production	Payroll/sales value of production	Payroll/sales value of production
Frequency of reviewing measurement	Annually	Periodically	Periodically
Prior incentive plans	Individual incentive	Individual incentive	No incentives

away, join in holding a screening committee meeting. The company sends at least one executive from the main plant to attend the latter meeting.

Top management feels it is imperative that all of these plants operate under one plan. Depending on how severe the model changeover may be in a given year, one plant may very well be affected more than another is. Having them all together provides much-needed stability. It also facilitates the transfer of jobs from one plant to another.

Turning now to the record of incentive payments under the plan, the most important facts are these:

1. During the 14 years of the Scanlon Plan at Atwood, annual bonuses have ranged from a high of approximately 20% of the payroll to a low of approximately 5%.
2. In the 187 periods of operation (the company's accounting year consists of 13 four-week periods), bonuses have been earned in 163 periods.
3. The highest monthly bonus was approximately 26%.
4. There has been a close correlation between annual profits and bonuses paid.

In terms of suggestions received under the Scanlon Plan, Atwood has no peer. Over 25,000 suggestions have been turned in by employees.

A significant indicator of the efficacy of an incentive plan is whether sales or production grows in proportion to payroll. If payroll grows proportionately larger over the years, that is a *sign* (not necessarily an absolutely correct one) that incentives are not as effective as they should be. What is Atwood's experience in this connection? The measurement of performance used is total payroll to sales value of production; this ratio today is within 0.5% of the ratio at the time the plan was started 14 years ago. This is evidence of increased worker efficiency combined with willing acceptance of the technological changes introduced by management. Because of the volatility of the Atwood business, the method of measurement is evaluated every year.

Parker Pen Co.

In this company the Scanlon Plan is used solely in the Manufacturing Division, located in Janesville, Wisconsin. There are approximately 1,000 employees covered by the plan; it has been in operation for 14 years. There are two international unions involved; one is the United Rubber Workers of America, AFL-CIO, Local No. 663, covering the production workers, and the other is the International Association of Machinists, AFL-CIO, Lodge No. 1266, covering the tool room group. The company manufactures superior-quality writing instruments which are sold domestically and exported throughout the world. The Janesville plant also supplies component parts to Parker subsidiaries located throughout the world.

Management installed the plan after disposing of an individual incentive system. That system had been in effect for many years, and both management and the union felt it had outlived its usefulness.

Under the system, the company had had trouble introducing automated or mechanical changes. Moreover, by 1954, costs had risen so that approximately 50% of the company product was being made outside of Janesville, and the Janesville plant was gradually becoming an assembly operation.

Probably one of the greatest benefits the company has received from the plan has been the acceptance of automation by the people involved. Partly as a result, the company now manufactures better than 80% of the product in the Janesville operation.

Unlike the other two companies described in this section, Parker makes a consumer product and hence gets locked in to certain price categories. For instance, the current Jotter ball pen, an important part of the company line, had a price of $1.98 established in 1955. The same price is in effect today. (How many other things can you buy today that have the same sales price as they had 14 years ago?)

As for bonuses paid, some of the salient facts are these:

1. The highest yearly average has been approximately 20%, and the lowest, 5½%.
2. During the 168 months of operation, bonuses have been paid in 142 months. The highest monthly bonus was approximately 30%.
3. The correlation between bonuses paid and division profits has been excellent.

If one were to ask management what it feels is the most important asset that the Scanlon Plan has brought to the company, the answer probably would be willingness to accept change. Out of this cooperative spirit have developed more jobs, whereas the trend was to fewer jobs prior to installation of the plan. As for the ratio of payroll to sales which is used for measuring bonuses, it is slightly in excess of one percentage point of what it was back in 1954. This fact is evidence of increased worker efficiency along with willing acceptance of technological changes introduced by management.

Pfaudler Co.

This company, a division of Sybron Corporation, is located in Rochester, New York. It produces chemical, pharmaceutical, food-manufacturing, and brewery equipment. The Scanlon Plan has been in existence at Pfaudler's for 17 years; the number of employees covered by the plan is approximately 750, and they work in the Manufacturing Division. There are two unions involved, the United

Steelworkers of America, AFL-CIO, Local No. 1495, and the Coppersmithing Branch of Sheet Metal Trades, Local No. 356.

On many occasions we have heard executives at Pfaudler describe it as a "large job shop." By that they mean that much of its product is scientifically engineered and tailored to fit a specific application of a customer company in the chemical industry. Sales are highly volatile. For instance, because Pfaudler supplies in excess of 70% of the world's needs for glass-lined chemical equipment, it is faced from time to time with either a substantial backlog of orders or a pronounced lack of orders. The company's manufacturing cycle—the period from the time when an order is booked to the first delivery on the order—is generally 12 weeks.

The plan has been most effective in dealing with either an overabundance of orders or a lack of them. As a result of the work of the various production committees and the screening committee, these ups and downs the company faces have been shortened on the downward cycle; the cooperation of the people involved has very often brought in work that otherwise would have gone to someone else.

The type of activity that the screening and production committees have engaged in has been very broad in range. For example:

> Several years ago a major chemical company had a disastrous explosion at one of its operations. The company was desirous of placing the entire order of approximately 20 large units with Pfaudler, but was hesitant to do so because of the length of time before delivery could be expected. The Pfaudler management got the screening and production committees together for a series of meetings and discussed the order with them. It meant producing the equipment in a 7-week cycle rather than the normal 12-week cycle for this type of equipment. In these discussions, ways for doing the work were considered which demanded extreme flexibility in the plant. The discussions were fruitful, and the production time was shortened. Pfaudler was awarded the entire order and went on to meet the delivery deadline. Significantly, other work scheduled to be completed during this time was also kept on schedule.

During each rebuilding and expansion program that the company has undertaken, production committees in the areas affected have had an opportunity, prior to the program getting under way, to pore over the blueprints of the work to be done. Committee members have raised questions concerning the layout of the equipment and recommended changes to ensure the best possible utilization of the new facilities.

Thousands of suggestions for change and improvement have been studied. Many of the ideas have produced substantial savings in cost or have brought improved quality.

As for the bonuses paid to employees participating in the plan, the highlights of the past 17 years are as follows:

1. The highest annual bonus year was 17½% of wages for the year, and the lowest was approximately 3% of wages.
2. Over the 204 months of operation, bonuses have been paid in 179 months.
3. The highest bonus earned during a given month was approximately 22%.

Major Findings

It is interesting to note that two of the three situations discussed had individual incentive systems in effect prior to installation of the Scanlon Plan. Both companies were (as they are today) high-volume producers of standard products—situations which would be expected to lend themselves very well to the use of standards and individual incentive arrangements. However, in both cases it was found that a Scanlon-type plan achieved better results than individual incentives did. In this respect, the cases are typical of many others in corporate experience. Why does the Scanlon approach lead to better results? Reasons like the following are important:

1. Working under the Scanlon Plan, an employee finds it more natural to take a broader view of the company's problems.
2. Management finds it easier to stress quality production, if that is important, in a Scanlon Plan environment than where the direct worker is paid according to his specific operation.
3. Getting the cooperation and support of the indirect servicing groups—i.e., tool room, maintenance, and materials handling—is much easier when these groups receive incentive earnings.
4. Through their committee activity, managers are able to discuss company objectives with employees and attain a response that is not possible under an individual incentive system. It is very important that the participants look on the success of the enterprise as being the basis for their own individual success. When this attitude is present, the entire organization responds to problems—such as quality problems, stepped up schedules, and customer delays—in a way calculated to get them solved as quickly as possible.

The third company—Pfaudler—did not have individual incentives prior to adopting Scanlon. It had never felt that its type of production lent itself to incentive systems other than the plant-wide type. Its experience under the Scanlon Plan has been much the same as at Atwood and Parker in terms of employee interest in better job methods, better quality, and better productivity generally.

Acceptance of change

One of the most interesting aspects of the experience of these companies (and of numerous others) concerns employee attitudes toward technological change and new equipment. While there is a natural human reluctance to change, employees in Atwood, Parker, and Pfaudler are now pushing management to bring in new equipment and to get it operating properly for the benefit of all. In one case, the company had introduced a substantial amount of equipment which was not functioning up to expectations. At production and screening meetings, employee members pointedly and vociferously kept suggesting how the equipment could be utilized to better advantage.

In the three companies, managers devote a portion of the time at production and screening meetings to discussion of future plans with respect to plant expansion and new equipment. Pfaudler has had excellent results in the plant expansion programs it has undertaken in Rochester by submitting the detailed blueprints of equipment layout and other matters to the production committees that would eventually be located in the areas of expansion. Suggestions made by employees have sometimes led to modifying or changing the layout, which has resulted in a smoother flow of work through the department.

Management finds that discussing plans well in advance creates an interest in the organization and minimizes fears that might otherwise develop. Its experience has shown that thorough discussion of planned changes enables members of the organization (management as well as employees) to realize that the new technology is not going to bring with it all sorts of ills that cannot be solved satisfactorily.

Measuring performance

The three companies in the case studies take different approaches to the question of how best to measure performance and review the measurements used:

1. At Atwood, management feels it must review performance measurements at the end of each automotive model year. The new product mix and its effect on normal labor content in the sales dollar becomes a fundamental part of this review, along with the other

economic variables which might affect the equities of the parties in the plan.

An interesting aspect of this review is that the accounting services have been set up so that a computer can execute the very voluminous computations needed to determine whether a very complicated new product mix has a different average direct labor content than did the previous one (differences are based on the volume projections which have been supplied by the automotive companies). Although the ratio of labor to sales may change from year to year, it has never changed much more than one percentage point at a time, and it is currently within one half of a percentage point`from where it started 15 years ago.

2. At Parker, management began by changing the basic labor-sales ratio every time a measurable change occurred which might affect the norm. During the first year the ratio was changed twice. Then it was determined that a complete review would be made once each year and the ratio changed only at that time, if need be. After several years of such studies, it was decided that the situation had shown such stability that an annual review was not needed. Since then, the norm has been reviewed only when major changes in conditions have occurred.

As has been mentioned, prices for the company's products have been extremely "sticky" during the recent years of general price inflation. At the same time, the company has negotiated regularly with its two unions and has increased wages in line with area and national patterns. Hence, with little price relief available, the company has had to work very hard in the area of technological change in order to maintain the ratio of payroll to sales prices within one and one-half percentage points of where it was 15 years ago. The cooperation and interest of employees has been a key ingredient in the success of this effort.

3. The approach at Pfaudler has been to leave the measurement ratio alone unless changing conditions require a new norm. Management feels that prices of company products can follow wage increases, thus allowing a good degree of stability in the ratio. However, management does maintain a constant watch on the labor content in the product mix, as it bids repeatedly on large contracts.

Over the years, the corporation has experienced a great degree of growth as a result of mergers and acquisitions. Corporate personnel have been moved from the plant to a new corporate headquarters and are no longer part of the Scanlon Plan. Consequently, the labor-sales ratio at Pfaudler is substantially lower today than it was 17 years ago.

Impact on efficiency

One highly significant conclusion that emerges from corporate experience with the Scanlon Plan concerns the relationship between the kind of production process involved and the quality of employee participation. The nature of the production process may influence the *direction* that participation and suggestions take, but the general quality of participation can be equally high *regardless* of the type of operation. The three cases described are one demonstration of this finding.

At Atwood the volatility of the product mix and the rigorous demands of the auto industry exert a great deal of pressure on management to evaluate suggestions immediately and apply them (if they are useful) as soon as possible. A vast majority of the suggestions are processed within one month of the time of submission. Because of high production runs, a small saving per unit of product cost can add up to a substantial saving in total if the timing is right. For instance, at the beginning of production of a new model, an improvement in tooling may be very profitable. Toward the end of the model run, however, improved tooling may not be feasible because the costs cannot be amortized over a large enough volume of production.

At Parker Pen, as at Atwood, a suggestion affecting a high-volume product can produce a substantial saving. However, the relationship of the company to its market makes the situation quite different. Whereas Atwood may be concerned with the approval of only one customer, Parker's customers number in the thousands. Where a suggestion involves changing the aesthetic appeal of a particular writing instrument, a very difficult judgment must be made concerning the impact on sales. Suggestions may take longer to be resolved in this kind of operation, and the technical evaluation may be further removed from the eyes of the employee.

Management has found that where a marketing decision is involved, it is very important to get a complete answer back to the employee so that he maintains his interest in further participation. If the employee feels that his suggestion got short shrift from someone "on the hill," it is difficult to get another idea from him.

At Pfaudler the value of one unit of product is so high that one failure can be costly. Also, the technology of glassteel makes the production problem an interesting challenge. While there is great emphasis on implementing new ideas so that they can be utilized on the current equipment in the plant, suggestions may run into technical ramifications that require a year or longer to resolve.

In short, the success of the Scanlon Plan is measured by the ability of the organization to tackle and solve the problems posed by production. In spite of the wide differences in operations in the three companies described here, they all have experienced a high degree of participation which has contributed to production efficiency.

Union reactions

How do unions react to the Scanlon Plan? Do they benefit as employees do? In each of the three situations described, the unions have negotiated regularly and have attained increases in wages and fringe benefits in line with patterns established in the labor market, the industry, or the nation generally. In none of these companies, nor in others we know that are using the Scanlon Plan, has there been less employee interest in the results of negotiation or in the union generally. Moreover, having been involved daily with the company's situation as a result of Scanlon Plan participation, union officials find themselves approaching the bargaining table with much more knowledge of the company's situation; thus they are better able to tell fact from fiction in management's statements. By the same token, the company has a better understanding of the union's problems and needs.

In many union-management relationships the most difficult problem for the union leader is to get top management to sit down and discuss the various problems that are plaguing the union and its membership. A basic prerequisite for success with the Scanlon approach is that management be "willing to listen." Where the plan is in operation, therefore, it should not be surprising that the number of written grievances has dropped markedly. This does not imply that there are no longer any problems or that the unions play a lesser role in solving problems. The significance is that mutually satisfactory solutions were developed without going through four stages of grievance procedure and on to arbitration.

As every international union representative knows, the local which is most difficult to satisfy is the one which deals with a company that says *no* to everything. If the Scanlon approach eases such a relationship, it will surely result in a membership that is better satisfied with the efforts of the international union.

Conclusion

The three situations described in this article pose just about all of the kinds of *problems* that most industrial plants are facing today.

What may distinguish the three companies more is that they all have good management. If you talk to the president or other managers in the companies, you find one common characteristic: they all know there is no substitute for good management. It is also important to note that in each of the companies the union is ably directed. In other words, the Scanlon Plan is not used as a crutch for good leadership.

Each of the companies described has gone through business cycles, through good times as well as bad. Executives in the plants will tell you that the value and strength of a Scanlon Plan is just as good when the going is rough as when business is good.

Probably most important to the success of a Scanlon Plan is that everyone in the organization knows management wants to work with employees to improve operations. This should be made very clear to all personnel from top to bottom. The message of the Scanlon Plan is simple: operations improvement is an area where management, the union, and employees can get together without strife. Collaboration is part of the job. In applying a Scanlon Plan, a company in essence says to its employees, "Look, we can run the company—we have run it for a number of years—we can run it well. But we think we can run it much better if you will help us. We're willing to listen."

Questions

1. What do the authors consider to be the features of the Scanlon Plan that contribute the most to its success?
2. What role do committees play in the operation of the Scanlon Plan?
3. Do you believe that the Scanlon Plan would tend to encourage or to discourage the introduction of automation?
4. What may the Scanlon Plan help to motivate besides the output of the workers?

47—THE MYTHOLOGY OF MANAGEMENT COMPENSATION *

Edward E. Lawler III

A host of decisions have to be made every day concerning compensation practices, decisions that are of critical importance in determining the success of any business organization. Unfortunately, relatively little is known about the psychological meaning of money and how it motivates people. Unanswered are such critical questions as:

- How often should a raise be given?
- What are the effects of secrecy about pay?
- How should benefit programs be packaged?

In the absence of systematic knowledge, executives have had to answer these kinds of questions for themselves. Many have drawn primarily from their own and others' experience in arriving at their answers. Unfortunately, common sense derived from experience can be loaded with implicit assumptions which may not be as valid as they seem. It is my purpose here to examine a number of commonly accepted assumptions about pay and to attempt to determine if they are valid.

What are the currently accepted principles and assumptions about how pay should be administered? In order to answer this question, a study was conducted among 500 managers from all levels of management and from a wide variety of organizations. The managers were asked to indicate whether they agreed or disagreed with five statements that contained assumptions about the psychological aspects of management compensation—assumptions which have important implications for the administration of pay. The following are the five assumptions and the percentage of managers agreeing with each:

1. At the higher-paid levels of management, pay is not one of the two or three most important job factors (61 percent).
2. Money is an ineffective motivator of outstanding job performance at the management level (55 percent).
3. Managers are likely to be dissatisfied with their pay even if they are highly paid (54 percent).

---

* From *California Management Review*, Vol. 9, No. 1 (Fall, 1966), pp. 11-22. Reprinted with permission.

4. Information about management pay rates is best kept secret (77 percent).
5. Managers are not concerned with how their salary is divided between cash and fringe benefits; the important thing is the amount of salary they receive (45 percent).

As can be seen, better than 50 percent of managers participating in the study agreed with the first four assumptions and 45 percent agreed with the last assumption.

Recently, research results have begun to accumulate which suggest that some of the assumptions may be partially invalid and some completely invalid. Let us, therefore, look at each of these assumptions and examine the evidence relevant to it.

What is the role of pay?

The history of the study of pay shows that we have progressed from a model of man that viewed him as being primarily economically motivated to a view that stresses social needs and the need for self-actualization. Unfortunately, in trying to establish the legitimacy of social and self-actualization needs, the proponents of this view of motivation tended to overlook the importance of pay. In some cases, they failed to mention the role of pay in their systems at all, and in other cases they implied that, because workers and managers are better off financially than they used to be, pay is less important than it was previously.

Because of this failure to deal with the role of pay, many managers have come to the erroneous conclusion that the experts in "human relations" have shown that pay is a relatively unimportant incentive and, as a result, have accepted the view that pay is a relatively unimportant job factor.[1] This is illustrated in the results of my study mentioned above. When the managers were asked to indicate how they thought the typical expert in human relations would respond to the statement that for higher-paid managers pay is not one of the most important job factors, 71 percent of the managers thought that the majority of the experts would agree with it, while 61 percent said they agreed with it themselves.

---

[1] This is not to imply that the leading figures in the "human relations" movement do not understand the importance of pay. But, by emphasizing other rewards and by not dealing explicitly with the role of pay, they have opened the door for others to interpret their writings as implying that pay is unimportant.

Undeniably, those writers who have stressed social and self-actualization needs have performed an important service by emphasizing the significance of nonfinancial incentives. It is now clear that people are motivated by needs for recognition and self-actualization as well as by security and physiological needs. But does this mean that pay must be dismissed as unimportant? I do not think the evidence justifies such a conclusion.

The belief that pay becomes unimportant as an individual accumulates more money has its roots in an inadequate interpretation of Maslow's theory of a hierarchy of needs. Briefly, Maslow's theory says that the needs which individuals seek to satisfy are arranged in a hierarchy. At the bottom of the hierarchy are needs for physical comfort. These lower-order needs are followed by such higher-order needs as social needs, esteem needs, and, finally, needs for autonomy and self-actualization.

According to Maslow's theory, once the lower-order needs are relatively well satisfied, they become unimportant as motivators, and an individual tries to satisfy the higher-order needs. If it is then assumed, as it is by many, that pay satisfies only lower-level needs, then it becomes obvious that once a person's physical comforts are taken care of, his pay will be unimportant to him.[2] But this view is based upon the assumption that pay satisfies primarily lower-level needs, an assumption which I question.

Pay as recognition

I would like to emphasize the neglected viewpoint that pay is a unique incentive—unique because it is able to satisfy both the lower-order physiological and security needs and the higher-order needs, such as esteem and recognition. Recent studies show that managers frequently think of their pay as a form of recognition for a job well done and as a mark of achievement.[3] The president of a large corporation has clearly pointed out why pay has become an important mark of achievement and recognition for managers.

---

[2] It should be pointed out that neither Maslow nor any of the leading figures in the "human relations" movement has stated that pay satisfies only lower-order needs. Others make the interpretation that it satisfies only lower-order needs (e.g., Robert B. McKersie, "Wage Payment Methods of the Future," *British Journal of Industrial Relations*, I [March, 1963], 191-212).

[3] Edward E. Lawler and Lyman W. Porter, "Perceptions Regarding Management Compensation," *Industrial Relations*, III (October, 1963), 41-49; and M. Scott Myers, "Who Are Your Motivated Workers?" *Harvard Business Review*, XLII (January-February, 1964), 72-88.

Achievement in the managerial field is much less spectacular than comparable success in many of the professions . . . the scientist, for example, who wins the Nobel prize. . . . In fact, the more effective an executive, the more his own identity and personality blend into the background of his organization, and the greater is his relative anonymity outside his immediate circle.

There is, however, one form of recognition that managers do receive that is visible outside their immediate circle, and that is their pay. Pay has become an indicator of the value of a person to an organization and as such is an important form of recognition. Thus, it is not surprising to find that one newly elected company president whose "other" income from securities approximated $125,000 demanded a salary of $100,000 from his company. When asked why he did not take a $50,000 salary and defer the other half of his salary until after retirement at a sizable tax saving, he replied, "I want my salary to be six figures when it appears in the proxy statement." [4]

It is precisely because pay satisfies higher-order needs as well as lower-order needs that it may remain important to managers, regardless of the amount of compensation they receive. For example, one recent study clearly showed (Exhibit 1) that although pay is slightly less important to upper-level managers (president and vice president) than it is to lower-level managers, it is still more important than security, social, and esteem needs for upper-level managers.[5] At the lower management level, pay was rated as more important than all but self-actualization needs.

We can turn to motivation theory to help explain further why pay is important to many managers. Goals that are initially desired only as a means to an end can in time become goals in themselves. Because of this process, money may cease to be only a path to the satisfaction of needs and may become a goal in itself. Thus, for many managers, money and money making have become ends that are powerful incentives. As one manager put it when asked why his salary was important to him, "It is just like bridge—it isn't any fun unless you keep score." In summary, the evidence shows that, although pay may be important to managers for different reasons as the amount of pay they receive increases, pay remains important to all levels of management.

---

[4] Arch Patton, *Men, Money, and Motivation* (New York: McGraw-Hill Book Co., Inc., 1961), p. 34.

[5] Lyman W. Porter, "A Study of Perceived Need Satisfaction in Bottom and Middle Management Jobs," *Journal of Applied Psychology*, XLV (February, 1961), 1-10.

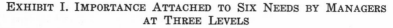

EXHIBIT I. IMPORTANCE ATTACHED TO SIX NEEDS BY MANAGERS
AT THREE LEVELS

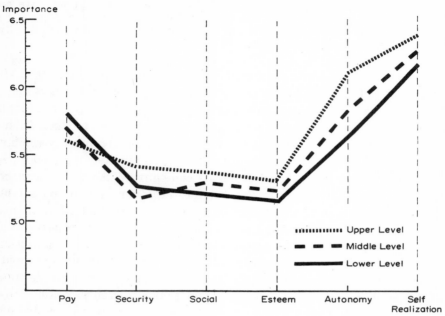

The evidence that is usually given to support the belief that pay is ineffective as an incentive is the finding that a number of incentive plans have failed to produce expected increases in productivity. This view is expressed well by the following statement of a company president: "Wage systems are not, in themselves, an important determinant of pace of work, application to work, or output." [6] That this view is being more widely accepted by managers in industry is reflected in the decline of the use of incentive systems at the worker level. In 1935, 75 percent of a sample of companies replied that they used wage incentive programs. By 1939 the number had fallen to 52 percent and by 1958 to 27 percent. The fact that managers have tended to stop using incentive plans for their workers points up the general disillusionment with the effectiveness of pay as an incentive among managers. This disillusionment is also reflected in my study which showed that 55 percent of the managers sampled felt that pay is not a very effective incentive at the management level.

---

[6] Wilfred Brown, *Piecework Abandoned* (London: Heineman and Co. Ltd., 1962), p. 15.

Managers' pay

What experiences have these managers had that might cause them to be disillusioned? I believe that one cause of the disillusionment is in the misunderstanding of how pay functions as a motivator. In current practice, the logic is that if pay is tied to productivity, then productivity should increase. This logic seems to be supported by the law of effect which states that behavior (productivity in our case) which is seen as leading to a reward (pay) will tend to be repeated.[7] However, recent research shows that one problem is that, although incentive schemes are designed to relate pay to productivity, many managers do not see them as doing this. I have considerable evidence that many managers who work under systems which, as far as their organizations are concerned, tie productivity to pay simply do not feel that better job performance will lead to higher pay.

I recently distributed a questionnaire to over 600 middle- and lower-level managers in a variety of organizations. These managers were asked what factors determined their pay. The consensus of these managers was that the most important factor in determining their pay was their training and experience, and not how well they performed their jobs. A look at the relationship between how well they were performing their jobs as rated by their superiors and their pay showed that they were correct. There was virtually no relationship between their pay and their rated job performance. Under these conditions, there is no reason to believe that pay will function as an incentive for higher job performance, even though these organizations claimed to have incentive pay systems.

Some other data that I collected from the same managers show one condition under which pay can be an effective incentive for high job performance. Of the managers studied, those who were most highly motivated to perform their jobs effectively were characterized by two attitudes:

- They said that their pay was important to them.
- They felt that good job performance would lead to higher pay for them.

---

[7] There is evidence that the law of effect can work where a clearly perceived relationship between the behavior and the reward does not exist. However, the important point is that rewards are maximally effective when they are seen as being clearly tied to the behavior that they are intended to reward. (See, e.g., John A. McGeoch and Arthur L. Irion, *The Psychology of Human Learning* [New York: Longmans, Green and Co., 1952].)

To return to the law of effect, for these highly motivated managers, pay was a significant reward and they saw this reward as contingent upon their job performance. Thus, it would seem that one of the major limits on the effectiveness of pay as an incentive is the ability of management to design compensation programs that create the perception that pay is based upon performance.

It is not enough to have a pay plan that is called an incentive system. Not only the people who design the plan but the people who are subject to the plan must feel that it is an incentive plan. At the management level, one step in the direction of tying pay more closely to performance might be the elimination of some of the stock option and other deferred payment plans that exist now. Many of these pay plans are so designed that they destroy rather than encourage the perception that pay is based upon performance. They pay off years after the behavior that is supposed to be rewarded has taken place, and in many cases the size of the reward that is given is independent of the quality of the manager's job performance.

There are two other factors which suggest that cash payments may be particularly appropriate at this time. A recent study found that managers preferred cash payments to other forms of compensation.[8] Further, the new tax laws now make it possible to get almost as much money into the hands of the manager through salary as through stock option plans and other forms of deferred compensation.

In addition to failing to create the perception that pay is based upon performance, there are two other reasons why incentive plans may fail. Many pay plans fail to recognize the importance of other needs to individuals, and, as a result, plans are set up in such a way that earning more money must necessarily be done at the cost of satisfying other needs. This situation frequently occurs when managers are paid solely on the basis of the performance of their subordinate groups. Conflicts appear between their desire for more production in their own groups, no matter what the organizational costs, and their desire to cooperate with other managers in order to make the total organization more successful.

A second reason why incentive plans fail is that they are frequently introduced as a substitute for good leadership practices and trust between employees and the organization. As one manager so aptly put this fallacious view: "If you have poor managers you have to use

---

[8] Thomas A. Mahoney, "Compensation Preferences of Managers," *Industrial Relations*, III (May, 1964), 135-144.

wage incentives." Wage incentives must be a supplement to, and not a substitute for, good management practices.

The results of Herzberg's study of motivation have been frequently cited as evidence that pay cannot be an effective motivator of good job performance.[9] According to this view, pay operates only as a maintenance factor and, as such, has no power to motivate job performance beyond some neutral point. However, this interpretation is not in accord with the results of the study. The study, in fact, found that pay may or may not be a motivator, depending upon how it is administered. A careful reading of Herzberg shows that where pay was geared to achievement and seen as a form of recognition by the managers, it was a potent motivator of good job performance. It was only where organizations had abandoned pay as an incentive and where organizations were unsuccessful in fairly relating pay and performance that pay ceased to be a motivator and became a maintenance factor.

Incentive for performance

In summary, I think the significant question about pay as an incentive is not whether it is effective or ineffective, but under what conditions is it an effective incentive. It appears that pay can be an effective incentive for good job performance under certain conditions:

1. When pay is seen by individuals as being tied to effective job performance in such a way that it becomes a reward or form of recognition for effective job performance.
2. When other needs are also satisfied by effective job performance.

The statement is frequently made that, no matter how much money an individual earns, he will want more. And indeed, as was pointed out earlier, the evidence does indicate that pay remains important, regardless of how much money an individual earns. But the assumption, accepted by 54 percent of the managers in my study, that managers are likely to be dissatisfied with their pay even if they are highly paid does not follow from this point. There is an important difference between how much pay an individual wants to earn and the amount he feels represents a fair salary for the job he is

---

[9] Frederick Herzberg, Bernard Mausner, and Barbara Bloch Snyderman, *The Motivation to Work* (New York: John Wiley and Sons, 1959).

doing. Individuals evaluate their pay in terms of the balance between what they put into their jobs (effort, skill, education, etc.) and what they receive in return (money, status, etc.).[10]

Dissatisfaction with pay occurs when an individual feels that what he puts into his job exceeds what he receives in the form of pay for doing his job. Individuals evaluate the fairness of their inputs relative to their outcomes on the basis of the inputs and outcomes of other employees, usually their coworkers. Managers tend to compare their pay with that of managers who are at the same management level in their own and in other organizations. Thus, dissatisfaction with pay is likely to occur when an individual's pay is lower than the pay of someone whom he considers similar to himself in ability, job level, and job performance. But when an individual receives an amount of pay that compares favorably with the pay received by others who, he feels, have comparable inputs, he will be satisfied with his pay.

However, because an individual feels his pay is fair, it does not mean that an opportunity to make more money through a promotion or other change in inputs would be turned down, nor does it mean that more money is not desired. It simply means that at the moment the balance between inputs and outcomes is seen as equitable.

The results of a recent study of over 1,900 managers illustrates the point that managers can be, and in fact frequently are, satisfied with their pay.[11] The managers were first asked to rate on a 1 (low) to 7 (high) scale how much pay they received for their jobs. They were next asked to rate, on the same scale, how much pay should be associated with their jobs. As can be seen from Exhibit 2, which presents the results for the presidents who participated in the study, those executives who were paid highly, relative to other presidents, were satisfied with their pay. For this group [12] (earning $50,000 and over), there was no difference between how much pay they said they received and how much pay they thought they should receive. However, those presidents whose pay compared unfavorably with the pay of other presidents said there was a substantial difference between what their pay should be and what it was.

---

[10] J. Stacy Adams, "Wage Inequities, Productivity and Work Quality," *Industrial Relations*, III (October, 1963), 9-16.
[11] Edward E. Lawler and Lyman W. Porter, *op. cit.*
[12] The presidents in this sample tended to come from smaller companies and, hence, the relatively low-level of their compensation.

EXHIBIT II. ATTITUDES OF CORPORATION PRESIDENTS TOWARD THEIR PAY

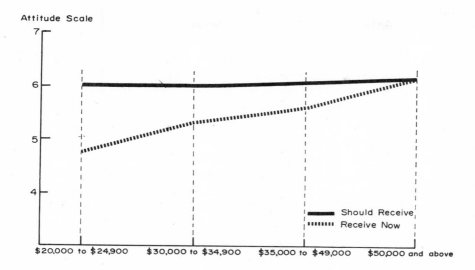

The same results were obtained at each level of management down to and including the foreman level. The highly paid managers at each level were quite satisfied with their pay; it was the low-paid managers at each level who were dissatisfied. In fact, highly paid foremen ($12,000 and above) were better satisfied with their pay than were company presidents who earned less than $50,000.

There is some evidence that managers can, and do, feel that they receive too much pay for their management positions. Of the 1,900 managers studied, about 5 percent reported that they received too much pay for their management positions. These managers apparently felt that their outcomes were too great in proportion to their inputs when compared with those of other managers. Although the number of managers who feel that their pay is too high is undoubtedly small, as indicated by the 5 percent figure obtained in this study, the fact that this feeling exists at all is evidence that individuals do not always feel they deserve more and more pay.

The feeling of overcompensation by some managers is also evidence that some organizations are not doing the best possible job of distributing their compensation dollars. It may be wise for organizations to give more weight to the value that subordinates and peers place on a manager's job performance when they are considering pay raises for a manager. Giving a high salary to a manager who is considered to be a poor performer by other employees can have several negative effects.

First, it can cause dissatisfaction with pay among other managers: dissatisfaction that comes about because managers who are good performers may come to see their own pay as suddenly inadequate relative to the pay of someone whom they regard as a poor performer, but who has received a raise. If such practices are followed, it is undoubtedly true that good performers will never be satisfied with their pay.

Second, and more important, giving a raise to a poor performer is a signal to other managers that pay is not necessarily based upon merit: an attitude that can destroy any motivational impetus that might be created by an otherwise well-administered compensation program. As can be seen from the results of my study of manager's assumptions about pay administration, perhaps the most commonly accepted axiom of good personnel practice is that information about management compensation rates should be kept secret. Many organizations go to great lengths to maintain this secrecy. Information about management pay rates is frequently kept locked in the company safe and the pay checks of top management receive special handling so that the size of the check is not known even by the personnel manager.

The reason typically given to defend the policy of keeping pay information secret is that secrecy helps to reduce dissatisfaction with regard to pay. According to this view, managers who do not know how much others earn are not likely to feel their pay compares unfavorably with that of other managers. Thus, personnel managers are never faced with a situation where Joe thinks he is better than Jack but knows that Jack is making more than he.

Pay rates secret

However, such reasoning fallaciously assumes that secrecy policies eliminate pay comparisons. As was pointed out earlier, the evidence indicates that managers do evaluate their own pay in terms of what other managers earn. What is not clear is what effect the secrecy policies have on the accuracy with which managers estimate the pay of other managers and the effects of the secrecy on how satisfying and motivating these comparisons are.

In order to gather some evidence that might serve as a basis for evaluating the effects of secrecy, I recently conducted an attitude survey. Questionnaires were completed by 563 (response rate 88.7

percent) middle- and lower-level managers in seven organizations. Four of the organizations were private companies engaged in a wide variety of activities ranging from rocket manufacturing to supplying gas and electricity. The other three organizations were government agencies also engaged in a variety of activities. The four private companies all had strict secrecy policies with regard to management compensation rates, while the three government agencies did make some information public about their pay rates.

A two-part questionnaire was used. The managers were first asked to estimate the average yearly salary of managers in their organizations who were at their own level, one level above them, and one level below them. The organization provided actual average salaries in order that comparisons could be made. The managers were also asked to indicate how well satisfied they were with several aspects of their organizations' compensation systems. In addition to being asked to express their satisfaction with their own pay, they were asked to indicate whether there was too much or too little difference between their own pay and that of their superiors, and between their own pay and that of their subordinates.

The results of the study clearly showed that the managers did not have an accurate picture of what other managers in their organizations earned. Apparently, the secrecy policies were effective in keeping these managers from knowing what other managers earned. However, rather than committing random errors in estimating other managers' salaries, these managers consistently tended to overestimate and to underestimate. When the managers were asked to estimate the pay of their superiors, they consistently underestimated. When they viewed the pay of their subordinates, they consistently overestimated. One-third of the managers overestimated the pay of their subordinates by more than one thousand dollars. Similarly, they also tended to overestimate the pay of managers at their own level.

Interestingly, the managers in the government organizations were consistently more accurate in estimating the pay of other managers than were the managers in the private organizations. Because the government managers had more information about the compensation programs of their organizations, it was expected that they would be more accurate. However, this finding does serve to emphasize the point that the cause of the managers' misperceptions of other managers' pay was the secrecy policies of their organizations.

The question that now remains to be answered is what effects did these distorted pictures of what other managers earn have on the managers' job satisfaction and job performance. The effects on satisfaction with pay can be seen in the managers' answers to the three questions concerned with satisfaction with pay. They stated that there was too small a difference between their own pay and that of their superiors and also too small a difference between their own pay and that of their subordinates. These attitudes are not surprising since the managers tended to see these differences as smaller than they actually are.

Effects of secrecy

Secrecy policies are causing some of this dissatisfaction by giving the managers inaccurate pictures of what others earn. Since managers evaluate their own pay in terms of what others earn, it is not surprising that the data show that those managers who feel their own pay is too close to that of their superiors and subordinates also feel that their own pay is too low. Undoubtedly, part of the managers' dissatisfaction with their own pay has its basis in unfavorable pay comparisons between what these managers know they make and what they think other managers make. On the basis of this evidence, it appears that one effect of secrecy policies is to increase dissatisfaction with pay.[13]

There is another way in which secrecy may contribute indirectly to both increased dissatisfaction with pay and lower motivation to perform a management job effectively. Secrecy allows a manager to avoid the responsibility of communicating to his subordinates his evaluation of their performance.

An example of what can and frequently does happen is that a manager who has to distribute raises capitalizes upon secrecy to avoid what he considers to be an unpleasant task. The manager does differentially distribute raises among his subordinates on the basis of their performance. So far, so good! However, when he explains the raises to his subordinates, if he does this at all, he tells all of them that he has given them as large a raise as he could and that he is satisfied with their performance. The manager may reason that he

---

[13] Further support for this interpretation comes from the finding that there was a significant tendency for those managers who had an accurate picture of their subordinates' pay to be more satisfied with their own pay than were those managers who had an inaccurate picture of their subordinates' pay ($r = .35$, $p = .01$).

has done the right thing. "After all," he thinks, "I did reward good performance with higher pay and I didn't cause any unhappiness as I would have if I had told the poor performers how dissatisfied I was with them."

However, the differential raises have no positive effect since they do nothing to encourage the perception that pay is based upon performance. The good performer is not sure he is getting a larger raise than the poor performer, and the poor performer may feel he is being rewarded for the type of performance he has been demonstrating. Eventually, of course, the word begins to get around about how much other people got in raises (undoubtedly slightly inflated), and this information is bound to make a number of managers unhappy with their pay, as well as distrustful of their superiors.

The secrecy policies of organizations and the consequent tendency for managers to estimate incorrectly the pay of other managers may also affect the managers' motivation to perform their jobs effectively in other ways. Several studies have shown that accurate feedback about task performance is a strong stimulus to good job performance.[14] People perform better when they receive accurate information about how well they are performing relative to some meaningful standard. For managers, pay is one of the most significant and meaningful pieces of feedback information they receive. High pay is considered a sign that the manager's job performance is good. Low pay is a signal that the manager is not performing his job well and that new behavior is needed.

The results of this study indicate that, because managers have misperceptions about what other managers earn, they are unable to evaluate correctly their own pay. Because of the tendency managers have to overestimate the pay of their subordinates and peers, the majority of the managers see their pay as low and in effect are receiving negative feedback. Moreover, although this feedback suggests that they should change their job behavior, it does not tell them what type of change they should make in their behavior. In cases where managers are not doing their jobs well, this negative feedback is undoubtedly the type of information that should be communicated; in other instances, it gives a false signal to change to those managers who are performing their jobs effectively.

---

[14] Victor H. Vroom, *Work and Motivation* (New York: John Wiley and Sons, 1964).

Reduced motivation?

Increased pay is one of the most significant rewards that an individual receives in return for taking on the responsibilities and work associated with higher-level management jobs and, therefore, is one of the important incentives in motivating managers to work toward obtaining higher-level jobs. However, as pointed out earlier, our data indicate that managers tend to underestimate the pay of managers at higher levels. This has the effect of making the attainment of higher-level jobs less desirable because it causes managers to underestimate the rewards that are attached to the positions. Thus, the secrecy policies of organizations may be indirectly reducing the motivation of managers to gain higher-level jobs.

If, as the evidence indicates, secrecy policies have significant costs in terms of job satisfaction, motivation for effective job performance, and motivation for promotion, does it not seem logical that organizations should alter these policies? Perhaps organizations that now have secrecy policies could give out information on pay ranges and average salaries for all management levels. If they started by giving out only partial salary information, they could better prepare their employees for full disclosure, and eventually the salaries of all members of an organization could be made available to all other members of that organization. It may well be better to provide an individual with accurate information upon which to make pay comparisons than to have him make unfavorable comparisons based upon misinformation.

Role of fringe benefits

When any organization is asked to determine how much money it spends on compensation, it usually adds the money spent for salaries and fringe benefits. Similarly, an organization determines how much money an individual earns by adding his salary and the costs to them of his benefit package. Union contracts are typically spoken of as settlements involving an x cents per hour compensation package. Implicit in these measures of compensation cost is the assumption that a dollar spent on cash salary is equal to a dollar spent on life insurance or other fringe benefits. From an economic standpoint and in terms of costs to the organization, it seems reasonable that the value of a compensation package is equal to the simple sum of all its parts. It is probably the reason why 45 percent of the managers sampled endorse the view that managers are not greatly concerned with how their pay is divided among various fringe benefits.

However, I would like to suggest that dollars spent on the different parts of the compensation package may not be equal in terms of what they earn in the recipient's perception of the value of his compensation package. Several studies have shown that individuals value some compensation benefits more than others, even though the cost to the company is the same.[15] For example, one study found that employees strongly preferred receiving hospital insurance to receiving additional pension money, even though the insurance and the pension plan cost the organization the same amount. In effect, a dollar spent on compensation can have a different value to the recipient, depending upon the type of benefit the organization chooses to buy with it.

The studies on compensation preferences among both workers and managers show that the preferences of individuals for different benefits vary greatly, depending upon such factors as their age, sex, number of children, and marital status. For example, older workers value pension plans much more highly than do younger workers, and unmarried men value a shorter work week more highly than do married men. These studies suggest that, at the very least, organizations may need different benefit packages in different locations, depending upon the personal characteristics of the workers in each installation.

A further step that organizations could take would be to design different packages for groups of individuals who have similar characteristics. Indeed, it may be that the optimum solution to this problem of different compensation preferences is for organizations to adopt a "cafeteria" compensation program. A "cafeteria" compensation plan would allow every employee to divide his compensation dollars among the benefits offered by his company. This would allow each employee to select the compensation options that he values most without adding to the compensation costs of the company. Previously, such a program would have been impractical because of the high administrative costs that would be involved. However, with the advent of the computer, it is possible.

"Buffet" benefits?

"Cafeteria" wage plans would appear to have a particularly bright future among managers where union negotiations and contracts are not likely to be a hindrance. "Cafeteria" wage plans have two additional benefits that strongly argue for their use.

---

[15] Stanley M. Nealey, "Pay and Benefit Preference," *Industrial Relations*, III (October, 1963), 17-28; Thomas A. Mahoney, *op. cit.*; and I. R. Andrews and Mildred M. Henry, "Management Attitudes Toward Pay," *Industrial Relations*, III (October, 1963), 29-39.

First, they allow employees to participate in an important decision about their jobs. Even among managers, opportunities for actual participation as contrasted with pseudo-participation are rare enough so that in every situation where participation can be legitimately and reasonably employed, it should be.

Second, "cafeteria" wage plans help to make clear to the employees just how much money is involved in their total compensation package. There are many reports of situations where employees do not even know of the fringe benefits for which their organizations are paying. With "cafeteria" wage plans, this situation would be virtually eliminated.

Research conclusions

What are the lessons to be learned from the recent research on the psychological aspects of compensation practices? I believe that the following conclusions are warranted.

- Even at the higher paid levels of management, pay is important enough to be a significant motivator of good job performance. However, it will be a motivator only when it is seen by the managers themselves to be tied to their job performance.
- Managers can be, and in fact frequently are, satsified with their pay when it compares favorably with the pay of other managers holding similar positions.
- Secrecy policies have significant hidden costs attached to them. The evidence indicates that secrecy may lead to lower satisfaction with pay and to a decreased motivation for promotion.
- In order to get the maximum value for money spent on compensation, organizations may have to institute "cafeteria" wage payment systems. Such a system would allow each manager to select the benefits that have the greatest value to him.

What the future holds

Will organizations be willing to innovate in the area of salary administration and to implement such programs as "cafeteria" wage plans and openness about salary levels? This question can finally be answered only five or ten years from now when we will know what the wage program of the future looks like. However, there are at least two reasons for believing that organizations will be slow to consider these new programs.

First, as one critic has put it, most organizations seem intent on keeping their compensation programs up with, but never ahead of, the Joneses in a sort of "me too" behavior.[16] It is unfortunate that many organizations got so badly "burned" when they tried to install incentive wage schemes that ignored needs other than that of money. Undoubtedly, this experience has led to the current air of conservatism that exists where innovation with regard to salary administration is concerned.

Second, since none of the implications for practice that have been drawn from the results of this group of studies offers a miraculous cure for the present ills of any organizations' compensation program, slow movement may be desirable. These studies imply that there may be better ways to do things, but they also imply that there may be costs and risks involved in trying these new policies.

For example, the idea of eliminating secrecy, no matter how well handled, will probably cause problems for some employees. In particular, openness will be difficult for the relatively low-paid managers to handle. But I believe that the gains would outweigh the costs and that there would be an overall gain in motivation as a result of openness with regard to pay. I am led to this belief because, by making pay information public, pay can become an effective satisfier of such needs as esteem and recognition and thereby become optimally effective as a stimulant of effective performance. The same general point is true about "cafeteria" wage plans or tying pay more clearly to performance. There are certain costs that are associated with this type of innovative behavior, but there are also large potential gains possible where the practices are successfully installed.

I have found that the top management of organizations is always questioning and testing the value of their present compensation systems, and I hope that the ideas and research results presented here will be of aid in this process of inquiry and self-correction.

Questions

1. What position does the author take with respect to the motivational value of compensation?
2. Why have some managers tended to become disillusioned over the value of pay as a motivator?
3. What are some of the reasons why many financial incentives have failed to achieve their intended objectives?
4. How does the position taken by this author compare with those of Burt K. Scanlan and of David Belcher in the preceding articles?

---

[16] Marvin D. Dunnette and Bernard M. Bass, "Behavioral Scientists and Personnel Management," *Industrial Relations*, III (May, 1963), 115-130.

William M. Carley and Tim Metz

Thank God it's Thursday.

That's what L. C. Clayton of Braintree, Mass., is thinking this morning. Today is the last day of the work week for him, and the 24-year-old bachelor is happily looking forward to his regular three-day weekend. For the four-day week, a dream of the future for most workers, is a fact of the present for Mr. Clayton and some 7,000 other Americans at nearly two score corporations.

The workers love it, which is less than surprising. After all, who wouldn't like to work fewer days for no cut in pay? What is surprising, though, is that the employers love it, too. The four-day week, many employers say, increases productivity, decreases absenteeism, boosts worker morale, and cuts worker turnover.

"We started the four-day week here last year to attract employees," says Jerry Silverman, general manager of Interstate Inc., a maker of paint rollers and the employer of Mr. Clayton. "We used to run ad after ad and get nowhere, but now we run an ad saying 'Work Four Days, Get Paid for Five,' and we get an overwhelming response." And the happy employees work so hard that Interstate has cut labor costs to 14 percent of sales from 16 percent, Mr. Silverman says.

John Hancock mulls move

As this pleasant word gets around, more and more companies are considering switching to the four-day week. Kenneth Wheeler, a Lowell, Mass., management consultant who wrote a piece on the four-day week for the *Harvard Business Review* a few months back, says 75 companies have contacted him for additional information. At least one corporate giant is considering making the switch; John Hancock Mutual Insurance Co. says it is "seriously studying" the four-day week for its 7,000 employees in the home office in Boston.

---

* From *The Wall Street Journal*, October 15, 1970. Reprinted with permission.

Some authorities say the four-day week will become widespread before too long. Riva Poor, a Massachusetts Institute of Technology graduate student, has studied the phenomenon extensively. She predicts the four-day week "will sweep the country—and much faster than the five-day week replaced the six-day week," a move that spanned some four decades between 1908 and the end of World War II. The nation's third-largest union, the million-member United Steelworkers of America, has recently added the four-day week to its list of goals in next year's bargaining, though how hard it will press this request isn't known.

Some deplore the trend. Leonard Woodcock, president of the United Auto Workers Union, vows to fight the four-day week because he believes it would lead to more moonlighting and thus help some workers get two jobs while others have none. And a suburban Boston housewife doesn't like the plan because her husband is now underfoot on Fridays.

"When he's here I can't get anything done—it's fixing breakfast, lunch, and dinner, breakfast, lunch, and dinner, and he's always bothering me in between," she says.

Most people like plan

Most companies that have gone to the four-day week require their workers to put in nine, or sometimes ten, hours a day, and some workers don't like that. At Interstate, the paint roller company, 10 women—20 percent of the work force at the time—quit when the four-day week was instituted last year. They cited fatigue and interference with getting youngsters off to school. The Interstate work day was increased to nine from eight hours at the time. Most companies on the four-day week give Friday, Saturday and Sunday off, though some give three other days, a practice some employees don't like.

But the vast majority of affected employers and employees hail the trend. "It's the coming thing," says Albert Lewis, director of industrial relations at C. A. Norgren Co., a Littleton, Colo., maker of valves, filters, and other products. "People just have to do certain things like take the car to the mechanic or the youngster to the doctor, and if they don't have enough time they'll just exploit your sick-leave system."

Norgren's 450 employees at Littleton started on the four-day week last month, and it's too early to say if absenteeism has been cut, but the evidence is clear at Geo. H. Bullard Co. in Westborough Mass. This producer of abrasive products went to the four-day week last year. Before then, absenteeism was averaging about 10 percent on Mondays; now it has "virtually disappeared," says Kenneth Ferguson, general manager. He also says the workers are working harder than before and productivity has risen 10.2 percent.

Ed Walsh, president of Rex Paper Box Co. in Braintree, Mass., cites still another advantage of the four-day week. "We had a tremendous turnover problem," he says. "Inexperienced people, instead of neatly cutting the excess from cardboard to be used for boxes, would cut all over the place and ruin material." Also, inexperienced workers couldn't efficiently run the machine that glues the boxes together.

Since Rex moved to a four-day week last year, however, the 65-man work force has become very stable, Mr. Walsh says. The company is saving $25,000 a year because fewer materials are being spoiled, and the gluing machine is operating 20 percent faster than before. These are factors in a sharp improvement in Rex's sales and profit, Mr. Walsh says.

The employees are even happier than the employers. Though putting in four nine-hour days means the employees work as much as most American workers—the average work week now is 37.3 hours, according to the Labor Department—the four-day workers say it's like having a holiday every week.

"It gives me more time with the kids," says Lori Coffelt, a personnel technician at C. A. Norgren. Lillian Russell, a worker at Interstate's paint roller plant, says the extra day off "gives me a chance to do things I can't or don't want to do when my husband is home, like the ironing and washing." Bob Willet, a young worker at Lawrence Manufacturing Co., a Lowell, Mass., textile firm, spent his extra day off this summer at the beach with his girlfriend, but now "I've enrolled in college because I think that Friday off will just about give me enough time to keep up with my studies."

Louis Saulnier, a foreman at Rex Paper Box, spends some free days helping his youngsters with Boy Scout projects. "Other days, the family will just pile in the car and we'll drive up to New Hampshire, pay a farmer a dollar and pick some apples. We never realized how nice that one extra day can be."

Dick Travers, general manager of Milton Machine Corp. in East Weymouth, Mass., says his workers have taken a variety of moonlighting jobs—"cabdriving, running a landscape business, working in a pizza parlor, you name it." The moonlighters "are mostly younger men with a lot of young children and they really need the money."

Workers on the four-day week cite advantages other than the extra time. Commuting costs are cut 20 percent, for instance. "Some of our people drive as far as 80 miles each day, so saving that trip once a week can be helpful," says Mr. Lewis of C. A. Norgren. Mrs. Coffelt, the personnel technician there, says the extra day off saves her $4 a week in baby-sitting fees.

And L. C. Clayton, the young bachelor at Interstate, says the four-day week aids in another way. "I've got three nights a week to chase girls, instead of two," he says. "I think it helps."

Questions

1. What are some of the possible advantages favoring the four-day week?
2. What are some of the conditions that may limit the adoption of the four-day week by some employers?
3. Can you anticipate any problems that a four-day week may create for the individual? For society as a whole?

49—FRINGE DETRIMENTS *

J. H. Foegen

As fringe benefits—non-wage, supplementary payments made to employees—continue to increase from year to year, it becomes increasingly important to recognize the existence of, and to take a good look at, the bad as well as the good side of those benefits. For purposes of this discussion, the negative side will be called "detriments." After a brief look at some of the reasons why the present fringe situation developed, attention will be given first to the prospect of the possible detrimental aspects of fringe as it presently exists, and then to the possibility that present benefits may well turn into detriments at some time in the future.

Perhaps the most important thing to note in talking about the background of fringe benefits is that fringe was never designed or intended to become what it has in fact become. As the term "fringe" itself implies, these benefits were to be clearly marginal items, incidentals intended to supplement the money wage payment, but no more than that. Obviously, as a result of continuous growth both in scope and in depth, fringe is much more important than this today.

The big reason for this is that growth was seldom consciously planned.[1] From time to time, different benefits were added, more or less opportunistically, until the present-day hodgepodge resulted. Since few if any controls were developed, it was only natural that such would be the case, given a number of important operating factors.

Causes of fringe

One of these factors was simply the conscientiousness of some individual employers. Some company managements, from the early days of industrialization to the present, have been firmly convinced that workers should be considered human beings, not just inanimate factors of production, and should therefore be treated as well as possible.

---

* From *Personnel Administration*, Vol. 25, No. 3 (May-June, 1962), pp. 13-18. Reprinted with permission.

[1] This idea is discussed more fully in the author's article, "Product Mix for Fringe Benefits," *Harvard Business Review*, July-August, 1961, p. 64.

Not only should the wage paid be a "just" wage, in the sense of adequacy and equity, but working conditions and job security should be the best that management could provide while still looking out for the legitimate, reasonable interests of capital and customers. Under the pressure of competition and the profit motive, unfortunately, these circumstances occurred in fairly isolated cases. Nevertheless, *some* employers did have a sense of responsibility toward their workers, as evidenced by a few unilaterally-initiated pension plans that antedate the turn of the century.[2]

Another of the causes of the birth of fringe, one that the previously-discussed employer conscientiousness often shaded into, was paternalism. Although remnants of both of these factors still remain today, the former usually evokes the picture of the pre-World War I period in industrial history, while the heyday of paternalism is considered by most to have been in the 1920's. The basis of this philosophy of course was the idea that the worker had to be looked after, and taken care of as well as possible, usually for one of two reasons, and possibly for both.

On the one hand, paternalism bolstered the ego-satisfaction of the employer. Employees were seen as essentially inferior, and unequal to management in ability and status. This was no fault of their own, however, and so, being utterly dependent upon the employer for their livelihood, it was the duty of that employer to watch out for them, much as a father looks out for his minor children. Psychologically, it made the employer feel superior if he could voluntarily provide certain benefits for his workers.

It is entirely possible, of course, that the resentment in the ranks caused by this management attitude contributed to the rise of unionism. It is also interesting to compare this situation with that of the present, when gains for the workers are claimed by the union in many cases, and when the union likes to give the impression that the worker would get absolutely nothing were it not for that union's efforts; this certainly does little for the employer's ego-satisfaction.

In addition to the bolstering of the employer's ego, paternalistic handouts of benefits or fringe also occurred in an attempt to keep unionism from getting a foothold in the plant. The theory was that if the employees got enough wages and benefits from the employers, they would see no need for a union. It is somewhat ironic that in

---

[2] Credit for the first U. S. private pension plan is usually given to the American Express Co., 1875. For additional discussion, *see* Robert Tilove, "Pension Funds and Economic Freedom" (New York: The Fund for the Republic, 1959).

paternalistically passing out favors to the workers in order to forestall the rise of unionism, management actually was bringing about more rapidly the very situation it was trying to prevent. Such was the case, however, and paternalism gave impetus to the rise of fringe both directly, in the case of employer handouts, and also indirectly, to the extent that it fostered the growth of unions, which in turn put on pressure for still more benefits.

This union pressure was and is a third major cause of fringe growth. It began to make itself felt in the 1930's and 1940's, as unions, coming into a more favorable political climate first, followed by a more favorable economic one as well, became progressively stronger. It continues today in unrelenting fashion. As unions became stronger economically, they naturally demanded increasingly better wages and working conditions, and, by threatening strikes or by actually carrying them out, they often got what they asked for.

A final cause of fringe growth, one that many feel is the most important one, was the imposition of wage controls by the government during World War II. Wages were frozen during much of this period as an anti-inflationary measure. Fringe benefits, however, since they were of a non-monetary nature or would not require immediate money payments, were allowed to increase. Unions, taking their cue from Washington, used them as a way to get around the static wage situation. In 4 wartime years, the habit of asking for and getting fringe benefits became ingrained enough so that later, when wage controls were lifted, unions continued to ask for increases in fringe as well as in wages and other working conditions.

In all times except the very recent past, however, regardless of whether it resulted from employer conscientiousness, paternalism, union pressure or wartime wage controls, fringe was still a marginal, supplementary payment. Today, however, with fringe running between 20% and 25% of a company's payroll,[3] and with no letup in sight, a second look is being taken at the whole concept to see whether perhaps the benefits are not all that they seem to be. In the present discussion, consideration will be given first to some detriments already present in the fringe situation, and then to some possible future problems.

---

[3] According to "Fringe Benefits—1959," in which the U. S. Chamber of Commerce reports on a survey of 1064 reporting companies, "The average payment in 1959 was 22.8% of payroll, 54.8¢ per payroll hour, or $1132 per year per employee" (p. 5).

Before proceeding further, however, it should be admitted that fringe benefits do not constitute a detriment directly either to the individual or the economy in the short run. The individual worker will not refuse more paid vacations, sick leave, group insurance and the like. But from the standpoint of the economy as a whole, and even from that of the individual in the long run, there is ample reason for serious reflection.

With that important qualification out of the way, let us consider a few of the bad points or detriments in the present fringe situation.

Fringe detriments

Perhaps most obvious of the three to be considered here is that most fringe contributes to inflation, if inflation is currently a problem, and puts an immediate additional squeeze on profit margins regardless. The reason, of course, is that most benefits cost the employer money, and this money has to come from somewhere. It will not come from sacrificed profits if management can at all avoid it. It might come from increased productivity, although conditions are not always favorable. It might even come from intended or possible wage increases that have gone by the board in order to provide for added fringe, although this is difficult to prove. The most likely source will be in prices, and, if prices are raised to cover the increased cost of added fringe, inflation receives that much more impetus.

Somewhat less obvious is the fact that fringe has a tendency to freeze labor mobility. Most benefits are as yet not vested, that is, their receipt is contingent upon continued employment by the granting company. To the extent that this is so, a considerable number of employees can be expected to remain with the firm even if they might otherwise like to leave, and even if it might be a good thing for the economy as a whole, if they *did* leave. If a family man has built up considerable seniority rights with a company that is also contributing every month to a fund that will provide him with a pension when he retires, but only if he continues to work for the company, it is very unlikely that the employee will leave that employer for any but the most drastic of reasons.

As another example, the "fringe benefits" of having lived in a community for a long time are not vested, i.e., if you leave the community, friends, relatives, and a familiar situation will of necessity be left behind. This keeps many people today from moving out of chronically depressed areas. While this is an understandable human reaction, it nevertheless inhibits the mobility of the work force. The hold that company-granted fringe benefits have on workers in a sense artificially reinforces this natural tendency.

This is not to say of course that mobility is all bad. Employee turnover remains a costly problem to most employers. A stable group of workers with the security of various fringe benefits may have high morale and be an advantage in many ways to the employer. But again from the standpoint of the whole economy, efficiency and prosperity demand at least a reasonable minimum of labor force mobility, and non-vested fringe is here an inhibiting factor.

Perhaps least obvious of present day fringe detriments is that fringe inhibits the worker's freedom of choice in spending his money. In other words, the worker might not want what he is getting; he might well want something else in the way of benefits, or even cash, instead.[4] He might well prefer more pay instead of more holidays or insurance; he could then spend that pay for the goods and services that he individually chooses. To the extent that the union bargains or the employer gives a certain fringe benefit, however, his freedom of choice in spending his money is to that extent effectively curtailed.

In this way, fringe bears some similarity to taxes. Under the present Federal income tax laws, the government takes part of an employee's wages in taxes, and theoretically at least pays him back in the form of various "fringe benefits" i.e., roads, defense, aids to education and so forth, whether the individual wants these things or not. In similar fashion, under a regular fringe benefit setup, the employer withholds part of what the employee at least *might* otherwise get in wages, and pays it to him as fringe that the collective body, the union, has bargained for him, whether he as an individual wants it or not. In both cases, either the government or the employer is spending the employee's money for him, and his freedom of choice in spending it is decreased.

Regardless of the benefits to be found in fringe, detriments in the present situation can also be seen in the areas of inflation, labor mobility, and individual free choice in the spending of income.

---

[4] The assumption is that if the fringe benefit were not received, then its equivalent value in cash would be added to the worker's pay check. This is not necessarily true.

Future problems

The biggest problem, however, is not to be found in the present, but in the future. If fringe as it exists today is still on balance good—and this, it seems, can at least be effectively argued—then given the continued increase in its depth and scope, will fringe turn into a detriment at some point in the future? Or can it continue to increase as at present with no untoward consequences, as some say wages can? Is "creeping fringe" of no danger, as some say "creeping inflation" is no danger? Nobody really knows, of course, but the problem gives rise to a number of questions that are worth considering.

For example, what happens when fringe approaches, reaches, or even passes 100% of payroll? Obviously, it started out at zero per cent. It is now in the range 20-25% and continues to increase. What happens when money wages becomes less important than fringe, or even equally so?

This is somewhat similar to a problem found in the area of unemployment compensation. A perennial argument here is what would happen if unemployment compensation benefits were to approach 100% of regular earnings. Unemployment compensation as originally intended was supposed to be "fringe" or marginal, or subsistence-type income. But with supplementary unemployment benefits, some workers can already collect 65% of their previous take-home pay, and the auto workers' union wants to raise this to 80%.[5] If and when the union is successful, this will begin to approach 100%. If unemployment compensation becomes as great as normal wages, will people prefer not to work? In similar fashion, if fringe becomes increasingly more important, will money wages lose all significance and/or disappear, and will workers' pay be entirely in fringe, with all the ghosts of "welfare statism" that possibility conjures up?

Another question: What will happen to the wage structure as more and more fringe is added? This structure, the result of job evaluation and subsequent pricing, has in the past been based on skill, responsibility, working conditions, and training as well as on experience. But much fringe is granted either across the board, or is related only to seniority, for example such things as holidays and vacations. As fringe grows absolutely and relative to wages, will this tend to make the wage structure obsolete? If so, perhaps a "fringe

---

[5] *Wall Street Journal*, June 28, 1961.

structure" might be a helpful or necessary supplement, to show who gets how much fringe and why.

Along another line of thought, can a company grant too much in the way of fringe benefits, the emphasis here being on the word "benefit" rather than on the word "fringe"? There is some criticism already heard of a growing "private welfare state" that supplements whatever similar trend exists in the public area. In other words, can employees absorb an unlimited amount of benefits without danger to their own self-reliance? The idea of being taken care of either by the social programs of the state or by the fringe programs of large corporations or both seems to be not unpopular even today. The joke about the new employee asking an employment interviewer what kind of pension plan the company has is all too familiar. But is this really a joke?

Finally, since large firms can usually pay the most benefits, as fringe levels increase and as prospective entrants into the labor force become increasingly fringe-conscious, what effect might this have on the ability of small firms, of necessity relatively poor in fringe, to compete in the market and to continue to exist? Business and government continue to pay lip service to the need for small firms and for competition, but if large concerns are able to offer not only lower prices to the customer but also more and better fringe benefits to employees increasingly sensitive to such things, what chance will small-firm competition have?

Conclusions

In conclusion then, the following points can be made: (1) The concept of fringe is undeniably well established. Employers, unions and workers have all become accustomed to it and it is not likely to fade from the scene in the foreseeable future. Whether viewed as non-money wages, or as something entirely separate from wages, it has at any rate been accepted as a part of working conditions, and union philosophy is pledged to continued improvement in this area. (2) Fringe continues to look good to the individual and in the short run, regardless of its real or imagined long-run consequences for the economy. (3) Serious misgivings do arise, however, in the areas of inflation, labor mobility, spending choices, wage structures, self-reliance, competition, and the relative importance of fringe as against payroll.

Questions

1. In what ways have fringe benefits departed from the purpose for which they were established originally? What are the reasons for this departure?

2. What reasons did employers have originally for establishing fringe benefits? How do these reasons differ from those upon which fringe benefits are being installed today?

3. In what respects does the author feel that some fringe benefits possibly have worked to the detriment of both the employer and employee?

4. Do you agree or disagree with the criticism that fringe benefit programs are creating a "private welfare state"?

5. How serious do you feel is the effect that fringe benefits have upon an employee's freedom of choice?

6. To what extent, if any, should a company be expected to provide for the welfare of its employees beyond providing good wages and working conditions?

50—CORPORATE EXECUTIVES WHO RETIRE *

Harry W. Hepner

If you were to ask yourself "What percentage of executives who retire are happy in their retirement?" you would not get very reliable answers by asking them the question. The percentages of favorable answers would probably be too high. Besides, answers to yes-no types of questions would not give you very much insight into the nature of their true feelings about retirement.

The difficulties involved in getting dependable answers became clearer to me when I asked a banker of a popular retirement area to describe the psychological state of most of the businessmen with whom he deals after they have retired from responsible positions in business. He thought several moments and gave his answer, carefully phrased: "When I first ask the question as to how they like retirement, the answer is usually along this line: 'Just great! I wouldn't go back to work again if I could!' However, when I get better acquainted with them or talk with some of these same individuals after they have had a few drinks, I am likely to get an entirely different slant such as: 'Retirement to me is a disappointment. I feel useless, unasked to do the things I worked so hard to learn to do in my work years. I've lost a lot of the old zest I had for living when I went to work every day.'" And then he added: "Most are best described as in a state of *quiet frustration.*"

Incidentally, this kind of description differs markedly from the answers you would be likely to get if you were to interview retirees from the lower occupational levels and those from positions of little responsibility. They do not usually react to retirement in the way that executives are affected.

How recently retired executives are affected

The kinds of problems you are likely to hear mentioned by recently retired executives vary with the individual. However, the thumbnail sketches that follow may enable the interested reader to note

---

* From *Michigan Business Review*, Vol. 22, No. 3 (May, 1970), pp. 13-18. Reprinted with permission.

whether he is likely to have certain frequently mentioned problems when he retires.

A. "I miss the corporate context in which I worked."

The man who is still working is not likely to appreciate this problem until some time after he has been retired. Mr. A, as an example, had a work environment like that of the typical corporate employee. Each day, when a corporate employee comes to work, he usually comes to a specific building at a definite time of the day to go to his office or his work area. He answers numerous telephone calls. Other employees and schedules remind him of things to do. He is pressed for time. His tasks are directly or indirectly important to other members of the whole scheme of operation around him. He is a member of a work group that emphasizes objectives: higher productivity, lower costs, higher sales, or improved profits. He is conscious of his place in the company's objectives. He feels needed and worthwhile as a person. But when he retires, he has no specific place to go. He has no associates whose work is closely related to what he does. He is not pressed for time. Profits are not even considered if he, for example, works in a local volunteer organization. As a result, the world of retirement is unsatisfying, sterile, dull.

B. "I have no important decisions to make any more."

Decisions made by an executive before he retires from business are likely to have some influences on money, productivity, or other relationships that contribute to the success or failure of a going enterprise. Many an executive takes considerable pride in his ability to come to a decision among several courses of action. He can reach a decision quickly on the spot or after detailed consideration—whichever procedure is appropriate to the problem. He will tackle any problem in his functional field and act with conviction and certainty in his mind.

When he retires, he will not have this kind of responsibility. He probably knows of no one who is likely to give him daily opportunities to make crucial decisions.

C. "I took considerable pride in my ability to develop team spirit."

Mr. C achieved a high level of ability to develop team spirit among his subordinates and associates. When he noted that certain members of his group disliked each other, he had the knack of getting them to work together. He reduced frictions. He overcame resentments and pettiness by getting everyone involved in achieving something of importance. He made men feel responsible for getting their work done. When errors occurred he did not pin the blame on any one person but let all the members of the group know that he expected the men to help each other to overcome errors, to prevent them before they occurred whenever possible. He gave credit when credit was due. As an effective leader of work groups, his constructive spirit even permeated other groups for whose work he was not directly responsible.

Now that he has retired, he realizes that he will have difficulty in finding a place that will require his type of leadership and supervisory skill, particularly a place where he will be responsible for the spirit of members of groups comparable to those he has left. He has discovered that the local service organizations of the volunteer type do not seem to be especially interested in utilizing his special abilities.

D. "How can I use the vast fund of information that I developed over the years?"

No wonder this is a common feeling on the part of retirees. Think of the many facts which an alert man such as an executive learns over the years in his occupation: the histories of people in the company, records of products produced, and know-how of procedures involved in the numerous operations of a business. The failures and successes that accompanied events of great and small significance are stored in his memory. These facts could, at times, be valuable aids in reducing failures and increasing successes of new products being developed. Who wants them from a retiree? He has had his day.

E. "I devoted most of my working life to the interests of the company."

Many an executive was wholeheartedly devoted to his work and the company. He often worked long hours without expectation of extra pay or recognition. To a large extent, he not only worked for but also lived for the company. His social life was centered around employees or customers. Typically, he had few or no special hobbies or recreational interests. Telling him to get interested in a hobby is not likely to be of any help to him now—he knows that hobbies are not acquired by command but by a long-term interest that has motivated the individual for years—years before he suddenly recognized a need for a hobby. When he retires, he feels lost, unwanted, unless he finds a new focal center of attention.

Trying times for certain executives

The last few years before retirement are terribly trying to many executives. Perhaps the strongest emotions take place in the mind of a type of ambitious individual executive who, when he approaches or has lived in the early years of retirement, is disappointed in himself and the way things worked out for him. Most of these men did very good work, had strong drives to get ahead, and pictured themselves as attaining a certain level of responsibility, a high status title, or a salary in a better income bracket. In the mind of the individual, he had earned the sought-for objective. But somehow, things just did not work out the way he had hoped. Still, he nurtured the hope that the reward would come to him before he actually retired.

Men who have this kind of self-image and never attain their hoped-for reward are apt to welcome retirement in a sad sort of way. They give up. Some enter retirement with a burden of bitterness that causes them to avoid talking about their history and the company. They do not correspond with any of their old colleagues. Nor do they attend many annual parties given by the company to their old retirees. Far too many executives and other able men of American corporations have retired with deep-seated "grudges" against the company to whom they had given years of selfless devotion. Instead of being rabid critics of their company, they ought to be enjoying exciting challenges, new satisfactions, and living anew—more richly than they could when they were working full time.

"Work arrangements" in terms of the retiree's old patterns

Prospective retirees who would like to continue to utilize the benefits of their years of experience with a company may request management to arrange an opportunity to continue to work on a full- or part-time basis.

Many an executive realizes that once he leaves his organization, the perspective and judgments which he developed in his years of experience are not likely to be sought by some other organization. Small wonder that when Harold R. Hall, Graduate School of Business Administration, Harvard University, made his famous study of 125 retired executives and 325 active executives of companies, he found that when the wishes of executives were considered at or near the normal age of their retirement, about 90 percent would have liked to continue active and productive assignments with their companies, with a new business firm, or with some public service activity. *Approximately three-fourths of the executives wanted to continue with their old organizations, full-time or part-time.*

The most common form of continuation is a consulting arrangement. In some cases, men in this category do provide helpful counsel or enable the company to maintain profitable relations with valued customers. No statistics regarding the benefits to the company nor the satisfactions that accrue to the retirees are available to me; but my impressionistic findings are that a very high percentage of these consultants think of themselves as part of the company's nonessential overhead.

Perhaps one of the most annoying privileges of all that a few executive retirees manage to arrange for themselves is the kind where the executive continues on a part-time basis which allows him to work when he wishes and to enjoy retirement whenever he prefers! This kind of in-again-out-again privilege usually means that the executive's successor must defer to the old man who comes around to find fault occasionally but does not actually assume responsibility for his own decisions or recommendations. The few younger men who endure this frustrating arrangement are under terrific stress and in conflict within themselves to the extent that some suffer from stomach ulcers or other psychosomatic ailments. Most smart executives, when the time comes for their retirement, get out and let the new generation take over. They have definite projects in mind, projects and programs which offer the executive self-fulfillment and utilize some of his best potentials.

New projects that utilize the retiree's old patterns

The executive who wishes to remain mentally active by working with the people of his industry or profession (but not with his old company) can achieve a sense of usefulness and a happy retirement by developing a special project of his own.

This kind of project does not call for retaining a working relationship with his old company nor does it require working a normal work week. The project usually involves a new relationship with people and problems that the retiree dealt with on his old job.

Most important of all, it should develop new purposes in life and bring about a forward orientation through the pursuit of the project. It should result in the occasional contact with and the enjoyment of old friendships as well as lead to new friendships. It should enable the retiree to feel that he is still active in the mainstream of usefulness to others.

The starting point in the pursuit of a project of this type is to think of some of the problems of an industry which the retiree knows. The problem he decides to pursue need not be a new one—lots of old unsolved problems can be found in any industry.

Examples of industry projects to consider

You will be able to think of several possible projects if you will recall some of the occasions when you said to yourself: "I believe that a company of this industry could make more money, reduce their costs, increase their sales, or improve their profits in regard to problems mentioned by responsible men in business:

1. A *credit man* of an industrial firm wonders why managements do not utilize their credit services more often to increase sales by helping customers through special financing methods that would reduce losses and at the same time increase sales. When he makes it a retirement project, he finds that he is welcomed by other credit men, company treasurers, and marketing executives.
2. An *accountant* says: "Why don't more people in the company utilize what we could do for them?" This question has probably been applied most often to marketing. "Why don't the people in marketing ask for the accounting department's records of sales of specific products by areas?" For many marketers, distribution costs exceed production costs. Effective cost accounting procedures help assure the most efficient distribution expenditures.
3. A man from *Research & Development* says: "What *developments,* particularly recent inventions and new product designs used in other industries, are likely to affect sales or methods of our industry, the industry where I worked?"
4. A *production* man in a manufacturing plant has selected for purchase millions of dollars worth of production equipment. He has tested the equipment and developed techniques for reducing a wide variety of manufacturing costs. When he retires, hundreds of manufacturing executives would be glad to buy an industry report on the significant findings gleaned in his own plants and from other plants that he could visit in his retirement. (He might need a coauthor to help do the writing of the report but that could easily be arranged.)
5. *Trend studies* offer opportunities for projects by retirees of every industry. If you will think of bothersome problems in relation to trends and dig in the trade journals of your field, you will probably come up with a challenging problem or two that excites you as suitable for you in your retirement. Discussions with several knowledgeable colleagues should lead to a better definition of the problem and suggest appropriate procedures for getting answers. After that, you may want to correspond with or interview members of the industry's trade association headquarters.

The real enjoyment in doing a project

Each of us has his inner psychological needs at different times in life. Right now as a retiree, you probably have a need to feel that you are useful by doing something for someone else, to be making a constructive contribution in this world of ours, and to give yourself some meaningful excitement instead of empty hours of idleness. Retirement activity should, at times, be as exciting as mountain climbing or playing in a golf tournament.

If you do a purposeful project, you will discover that you gain certain benefits which only you as a retiree can appreciate. You will feel that you are not throwing overboard all that you learned in the past, but that you are a worthy, though an unofficial, member of an active group; that you are exchanging ideas with people whom you respect; and that there is added purpose in your life, a kind of purpose which you are uniquely qualified to give.

You gain prophylactic benefits. As you know, aging people who are busy performing interesting activities have less tendency to relive the past by the usual boresome talkativeness. Busy people with important purposes in mind do not need to glorify their past when the present is exciting.

As a prospective or actual retiree, you need recognition for the person you are now in your present years of retirement, not for the person you were years ago.

Project: keeping in touch with ambitious young men

As one retired executive stated: "Every man who has advanced to a responsible position will, if he is worth his salt as a leader, take an interest in and keep in touch with several bright young men after he retires."

The retiree who identifies with both his industry and the younger generation wants to see able young men come into business and have successful, happy careers. He knows that business as well as every other honorable field of work must grow and fulfill its socio-economic responsibilities by selecting, training, and inspiring men who have good potentials for growth. He can keep in touch with and contribute his friendly influence to a few young men who he knows and admires. If this idea appeals to you, *choose the kind of young people with whom you would like to communicate and then prepare yourself to have them think of you as a friend.*

Most young people have good potentials, even though many are trying hard to find themselves, and some are failing miserably. A small percentage will become drug addicts, criminals, or other deviants, but that has been true throughout human history. And it will continue indefinitely. That simply means that if you want to make a contribution to several members of the younger generation, you will have to decide which kind of young people you wish to reach. Well, why not decide to understand a few of the ambitious young people who are working in companies of the industry in which you had your career? You probably know more about that category of young men than any other one classification.

Obviously, you cannot be helpful by simply going to a young employee and implying: "Young man, talk over your problems with me and I'll give you the answers." Most of your preliminary preparation for effectiveness will be in making certain mental shifts from some out-of-date rigidities you may have developed years ago.

Measure your ability to counsel young men by the extent that you have acquired the knack of asking questions that enable the confused employee to answer his own questions. If you are successful in establishing rapport to the extent that he wants to ask you questions about his work situation, you may be able to counsel him indirectly without his thinking of you as a counselor. Bear in mind that your objective is not that of becoming a counselor but a trusted friend with whom certain young men discuss their problems. As an example, you should not give him the usual advice or pep talk that he lacks initiative nor that his education must be unlearned. Also, recognize that a young man does not want sympathy—he needs a colleague who can offer useful suggestions and a friend who likes him and believes in him in spite of his claim that others have thus far ignored his potentials. This means that the more you can get him to talk about himself and express his feelings, the clearer your picture will become of how he sees himself and his relationship to you.

The retiree can strike out in wholly new directions

As you may have observed, it is necessary for many able retirees to direct a large share of their time toward a new activity, preferably one of a creative nature. It may be an old hobby or a new interest. The reason for recommending a creative interest is that the mentally alert retiree wants to continue to increase his growth as a person after he retires. And growth as a person can come about only when a man adds to what he already knows and can do. New ways of perceiving and thinking, practiced every day, are just as essential to psychological expansion in retirement as in the work years.

This does not imply that every retiree should take formal educational courses or read a lot of books in the hope of becoming a so-called creative thinker. Rather, it should be recognized that many growth-minded men devote some of the thinking in their later years to their interpretation of what life is all about. Each man wants to decide for himself life's significant meanings for him. In retirement, some of his available time can be productively invested in the quest for a personal philosophy.

Now that your retirement has given you extra time to observe objects and events and to think about them, you realize more fully that objects and events of today can have meanings which they did not have for you in your earlier years. The important recognition in your maturity is that objects and activities can have meanings more important than or in addition to those of self-satisfaction, recreation, or usefulness. They can be perceived in terms of greater values as indicated by their agelessness, their reappearance in generation after generation. You can learn to perceive ordinary objects and events in the same ways that great artists, religionists, and philosophers perceive them.

In the practice of this pursuit, you will sense that you are attaining a satisfying inner growth that leads to the serenity and wisdom that men have had to earn for themselves throughout the history of civilized man.

As a man grows older, his concern with the inner life is likely to increase. You can often note this in the kinds of books that many older men read and the questions they ask themselves. David L. Gutmann, a research psychologist, has made several studies in this field and found, for example, in a study of 145 men aged forty to seventy-one that: ". . . older men fall off markedly in active participation with the outer world, shifting their attention to intrapsychic events. Whereas the forty-year-old man tends to ignore the inner life and strives to dominate the outer world, older respondents seem to deploy their energy inward in the attempt to master the psychic life."

The basic hopes and fears, the delights and despairs, and the problems and frustrations that are the lot of mankind today have been described by great minds for the past thirty centuries. And yet to each of us in our time, the experience of recognizing age-old truths appears to be as new as though we were their first discoverers. We as individuals need this experience of discovery, for that is the way we learn to live anew through the opportunities available to us in our later years.

Questions

1. The author cites a number of satisfactions from their jobs that executives miss upon retirement. What is the most significant loss that many executives experience upon retirement?
2. What are some of the problems that the retention of retired executives on a part-time basis may create for the organization?
3. Many people look forward to retirement because they believe it will give them time to do those things they have been wanting to do such as travel, read, pursuing hobbies, and recreational activities. To what extent are such individuals likely or unlikely to realize these anticipations when they retire?
4. What particular advantages do projects have to offer retired executives over other types of retirement activities?

INDEX

Subject